THE BEST OF RESURGENCE

The Best of
RESURGENCE

A SELECTION FROM THE FIRST TWENTY-FIVE YEARS

Edited & introduced by John Button

With illustrations by Truda Lane

GREEN BOOKS

First published in 1991 by
Green Books
Ford House, Hartland
Bideford, Devon EX39 6EE

Cover illustration
by Jackie Morris

Typographic design and photosetting
in 10 on 12.5 pt Galliard
by Five Seasons Press, Hereford

Printed by Biddles Ltd
Guildford, Surrey

Printed on recycled paper

British Library Cataloguing in Publication Data
The Best of Resurgence: a selection from the first 25 years
1. Society
I. Button, John *1949–*   II. Resurgence
301

ISBN 1 870098 27 7

Contents

Contents *(continued)*

Introduction

EARLY IN 1966, the era of The Rolling Stones and the Committee of 100, John Papworth decided that what was missing from the burgeoning alternative scene was an independent voice for peace and decentralist ideas. He called his concept The Fourth World and the magazine which was to be its mouthpiece, *Resurgence*.

In those pre-feminist days he wrote in the 'Statement of Intent' which prefaced the first issue of the magazine, 'Men will not come to reject our war societies until they have some coherent alternative to which they can turn. We think this alternative, based on love, non-violence, personal dedication and the power of the individual to make his own decisions, is today the only alternative to the monstrous biological anticlimax towards which human society is clearly moving.

'It is evident that such an alternative will embrace a multi-cellular, power-dispersed world civilization, rather than the totalitarian, state-power giants that dominate it today, and we propose to concern ourselves no less with the enormous task of making explicit the new theoretical approach to politics it requires.'

It was a big, bold statement, in many ways years before its time, and in the intervening quarter century there have been several times when few thought that John Papworth's visionary publication had much of a future. Yet, of all those brave little magazines like *Vole* and *Undercurrents*, *Resurgence* alone continues to appear every other month, pushing forward the frontiers of what has become known as the green world view, probing, questioning, celebrating, envisioning and re-visioning.

For the first four years, with John Papworth at the helm, *Resurgence* set the course which it still maintains, stressing the importance of decentralist politics, appropriate scale, holistic thinking and nonviolence. Since the only illustration was on the front cover and the inside text was set small to use the space efficiently, those early issues tend towards the indigestible. The fact that it was almost without exception a male—and a very serious male—preserve didn't help matters.

By mid-1970 *Resurgence* hit a low financial ebb; costs were escalating and circulation—then at around 1,500—was stagnant. The 'Economy Issue' of late 1970 consisted of little more than an urgent appeal for funds. It was at this time that John Papworth left Britain to take up an advisory post with the Zambian government, leaving *Resurgence* to the whims of a keen but transient string of temporary editors.

In 1973, however, Hugh Sharman took over the magazine and Satish Kumar —recently arrived from India after a two-year peace pilgrimage—started to edit the magazine. *Resurgence* rapidly became more attractive and more approachable, and a change to offset printing allowed the creative use of illustrations and varied layouts. Many of the regular contributors, notably E. F. Schumacher and Leopold Kohr, continued to write regularly for the magazine, though there was a noticeable shift from the polemic to the practical.

At the end of 1976 the magazine's subtitle changed from 'Journal of the Fourth World' to 'Small Nations, Small Communities and the Human Spirit'. The text was still on the solid side though now interspersed with drawings, and many of the contributors still to be found in the pages of *Resurgence* were well-established.

The January-February issue of 1981 saw the magazine's masthead reach its current maturity and the inside design the degree of user-friendliness its readers have now come to expect. John Moat's 'Didymus' column had arrived with a vengeance, as had Kirkpatrick Sale's 'Letter from America'. The small ads, an essential and much-loved ingredient, now filled a whole page, helping the magazine to raise some much-needed income.

At the end of 1984, the November-December issue welcomed *Undercurrents* readers into the *Resurgence* fold following an insuperable financial crisis at the former magazine; this helped to boost circulation to nearly 8,000 and for the first time allowed the use of full colour on the magazine's cover. Mid-1986 saw the regular introduction of themed articles—'The Hidden Costs of Food Production', 'The Multicultural World', 'Education on a Human Scale' —as *Resurgence* continued to push forward the leading edge of what was increasingly becoming referred to as 'the green world view'. The magazine had never been slow to respond to ecological issues; indeed, to a large extent it was *Resurgence* that foresaw the burst of interest in 'ecology' which filled the fledgeling colour supplements in 1970. In 1980—yes, ten whole years ago—it dedicated an issue to the nascent concept of 'green politics'.

With the January-February issue of 1988, *Resurgence* reached the stylish open design it has today, continuing to display a standard of writing which—considering that all its contributors offer their material without expectation of financial reward—stands comparison with any contemporary journalism. With a circulation hovering around the ten thousand mark, eight or nine pages of adverts which any green-tinted publication would be proud of, and an unrivalled place in the annals of twentieth century alternative magazine publishing, *Resurgence* and its loyal band of frontline thinkers and activists deserves to feel proud of its achievement. Its relentless concern with the vital issues of our times—world peace, human rights, land reform, the international food trade, east-west relations, the arts, the links between spirituality and politics and much more—has provided a platform and resource to inspire and inform the magazine's ever-growing number of readers.

The first 150 issues of *Resurgence* contain well over three thousand articles; nearly five million words. Looking back through that boxful of collected wisdom is a daunting and humbling task. The distinct impression you are left with is that there is absolutely nothing new left to say—whatever exciting insights you might be blessed with have all been thought by someone before you, written about eloquently, and ensconced within the pages of *Resurgence*!

The sixty or so articles in this anthology demonstrate the breadth and depth of this remarkable insight, showing very clearly how the many strands of decentralist, ecological, appropriate-scale theory and practice intertwine and interact. Here are some of the classics of green thinking, like Schumacher's 'Buddhist Economics' and Barbara Ward's 'Save the Planet', together with the uplifting and heartfelt stories of those many pioneers who have put their philosophy into action—Helena Norberg-Hodge in Ladakh, Wendell Berry in the USA and, to round off the volume, Jean Giono's almost incredible tale of the French farmer who planted a forest single-handed.

In editing this important volume I have done my best to keep faith with the original, at the same time pruning a little here and there to allow as many people as possible to have their say. The language of 'man' and 'mankind', an unaware and often oppressive usage so prevalent in the early years of *Resurgence* and only now being questioned, has been ameliorated except where this would in my opinion have upset the poetry of the piece (see Elsa Morante's 'The Poet and The Bomb', for example).

The compilation of *The Best of Resurgence* has been both fascinating and immensely rewarding, rather like exploring the attic of a jackdaw-like collector of alternative memorabilia (I wonder how many ageing hippies' attics contain bundles of *Resurgence* back issues?). I would like to think of this collection providing as much pleasure and inspiration for you as it has for me.

John Button
Stroud
Gloucestershire
February 1991

Healing & Caring

Let the Good Times Last

ANNE HERBERT

START WITH WHEN IT FEELS GOOD. Then stay there longer. It works. Sometimes when I think about the suffering in the world, I think that the best thing I can do is join right in. I can't quite kid myself that it helps anyone, but sometimes it feels like it relieves the pressure on me. I don't have to deal with feeling good on a planet where children and rain forests are killed for no reason. Being miserable keeps me preoccupied with myself, so I don't have to think about children and trees and poisoned water so much.

Feeling good works, I know that too. I know that when I feel great, when whatever work I'm doing comes easily and naturally, when I feel like I'm on a roll and everything I try to do happens smoothly, at those times I do great work, work that might be of help to other people. When I'm miserable I mostly produce glum, trite thoughts that I don't have the energy to write down.

Feeling good works. Producing good work and feeling good are connected. Here's a theory: everyone experiences time in working when work is a joy, when they have intuitive flashes they haven't had before, when their energy just seems to keep on flowing and they produce more and better work than they have before. The next part of the theory is that once you recognize and value those times, you can learn to be there more, produce better work, feel great and do great at the same time.

That's the theory. The question is, can environmentalists, peace workers, aspiring social-change agents of all kinds seek out the kind of work high that makes work fun, self-rewarding and nourishing? Do we even want to feel good as we do good work? Do other do-gooders, like myself, have a secret commitment to feeling lousy in a lousy world?

The theory I've just outlined about terrific feelings and terrific work going together comes from *The C Zone: Peak Performance Under Pressure*, a book by psychologists Robert Kriegel and Marilyn Harris Kriegel. The question about how this theory applies to doing Earth healing work is mine, and occurred to me as soon as I read the book.

My reaction in reading *The C Zone* was 'This is true. This is important but why have you slanted all the examples towards business?' I was concerned about the business slant because I wanted my friends to read the book and get the ideas, and I was afraid they wouldn't get past all the stories about getting a sales presentation ready or going to a marketing meeting. True, the business community offers a clear and well-defined market for ideas about how to succeed and feel good at the same time, but environmentalists and peace people want to succeed too.

Don't we?

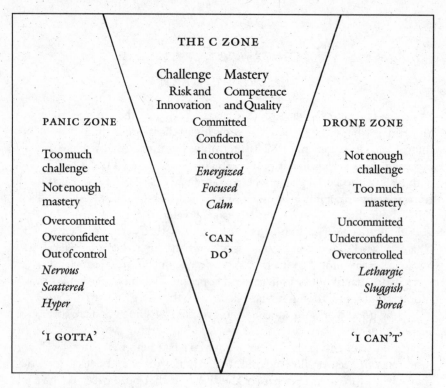

THE C ZONE

Challenge Mastery
Risk and Competence
Innovation and Quality

PANIC ZONE Committed
Confident

Too much In control Not enough
challenge *Energized* challenge

Not enough *Focused* Too much
mastery *Calm* mastery

Overcommitted Uncommitted
Overconfident 'CAN Underconfident
Out of control DO' Overcontrolled
Nervous *Lethargic*
Scattered *Sluggish*
Hyper *Bored*

'I GOTTA' 'I CAN'T'

DRONE ZONE

But do do-gooders buy books about how to be effective? Don't we just go on thinking good intentions are enough until the lack of results in our work wears us down and we stop trying? That's not completely fair, of course, but there's something there. Can healing the Earth be a delight? Will it ever happen if it isn't?

Contrasting the expectations of business people and people in change groups proved sobering. I felt the Kriegels should do workshops in social change groups, but do social change groups have any interest in workshops to help people feel better about their work? Businesses pay for stuff like that all the time. The only time I have known social change groups do attitude help for workers is when the group is in deep trouble, about to fall apart; then the group brings in a few trainers to try to help people talk to each other about their anger. What fun.

I don't know if training workshops work, even for business, but they do show an interest in helping people get into their work that seems uncommon in social change groups. It often seems to me that people are supposed to bring their interest and enthusiasm into the job with them and then hope it lasts them through low pay, office politics, and the unpredictable activities of the strong figure, usually male, who founded the organization and still dominates it at will.

Are we having fun yet?

The C Zone is about what it's like to be in the place where work is fun, how we wander out of that place, and how we can get back. Do you remember a time when work was smooth and easy and felt great and you were producing wonderful results with what felt like little effort? Can you think of any words that described what that felt like to you?

I saw Marilyn Kriegel ask that question to a group of people who worked in a hospital, and she instantly got back words like, 'terrific, exhilarated, expanded, flowing, energetic, calm, serene, full, peaceful'. She says she and Bob can get words like that from any group of people. People know the experience. How come we don't have the experience more?

The Kriegels call this 'operating in the C zone' a time when you can do no wrong, named after the 'C' words that apply to being there—centred, committed, calm, in control.

The way we get uncentred happens like this. People tend to prefer either challenge or mastery—some people like learning new things more, some people like doing things they already know how to do. People can fall into doing too much of what they naturally like, and not enough of the other thing. People like me, who like the challenge of doing new things, can take on too much new stuff without enough in their lives that they've mastered. They freak out and move into the panic zone. Being in the panic zone is a lot like having a type A personality— the kind that is likely to have heart attacks. People in the panic zone feel like they don't have enough time, are irritable with other people, are tense all the time, and say, feel, think and live 'I gotta.' If anyone tells them to slow down, lighten up, look at the big picture, they say, 'Oh no, I gotta blah dee blah blah blah or else . . .' Or else unspecified bad things will happen.

I feel that many environmentalists and peace workers live in the panic zone, and think that putting other people in the panic zone is the best, maybe the only, strategy.

But clear thinking and wisdom are not characteristics of the panic zone. Thinking 'I gotta' do something fast *or else* doesn't produce quality actions. Now I'll tell you about the other end, the drone zone.

When people who like mastery, doing things they know how to do, honing things to perfection, do that to the exclusion of taking on new challenges, they go into the drone zone. They're afraid to make any move—it's too scary. Any idea of change or expansion in their lives produces the words 'I can't'. They feel bored and stuck and can easily get depressed.

The 'I gotta/I can't' contrast is amazingly observable. I hear it in myself. In writing and work, I'm a challenge/panic type and often say to myself, 'I gotta do something in a certain way by a certain time.' This is often inaccurate, and only serves to make me tense. In my personal life I can easily enter the drone zone, and when I think of, for example, moving to a nicer place or meeting new people, 'I can't' followed by dozens of excuses follows.

The C Zone has lots of practical exercises about how to move out of whatever your habitual dead centre is. The simplest, and one of the hardest for me, is the one for panic zone people which consists of stopping and taking three deep breaths. Amazing. When I notice I'm freaking out I sometimes remember that and say to myself, 'I don't have time to take three deep breaths. I gotta . . .'

Don't have time to take three deep breaths? That's nuts. It's also exactly precisely where a lot of peace people, environmentalists, and social change people put themselves. We can't stop to think about what we're doing because we gotta do what we gotta do.

What do we like about life in the panic zone? I like operating in the panic zone because it makes me feel important. I used to be an editor at *Whole Earth*, acting the way that editors at *Whole Earth* and other publications often act. I put off decisions till the last minute, got copy in late, had production people breathing down my neck. That made me tense. It also made me feel important. There were lots of really urgent things waiting for me. People wanted me to do stuff now. They might have been angry at me, but they were certainly paying attention to me.

It's possible to construct organizations, campaigns, whole movements that way—everybody feeling behind, feeling there isn't enough time, feeling important because every little thing is urgent. Desperation in the place of good design.

Life in the panic zone is tiring. Never catch up. One crisis after another. And if I'm living in crisis it's hard to take time to think about how to avoid future crises. It just goes on, in a way described by Peter Berg in the Fall 1983 issue of *Raise the Stakes*, a magazine of bioregionalism. Peter writes, 'Classic environmentalism has bred a peculiar negative political malaise among its adherents. Alerted to fresh horrors almost daily, they research the extent of each new life-threatening situation, rush to protest it, and campaign exhaustively to prevent a future occurrence. It's a valuable service, of course, but imagine a hospital that consists only of an emergency room. No maternity care, no paediatric clinic, no promising therapy: just mangled trauma cases. Many of them are lost or drag on in wilting protraction, and if a few are saved, there are always more than can be handled jamming through the door. Rescuing the environment has become like running a battlefield aid station against a killing machine that operates just beyond reach, and that shifts its ground after each seeming defeat.'

It's scary working in an emergency room, important-feeling, and for many people, exhausting,

What would it be like if we stopped our chain of reaction to other people's actions and listened to ourselves and to each other about the best thing to do, what we would each enjoy doing for the healing of the Earth and the Earth's people? I think we'd get more done in the long run, although stopping would feel very, very strange.

Not only do we often work in panic, we often act as if panic is the life we want to convert people to. We send mailers that say, '*This* is what you should be scared about.'

That isn't the revolution. That isn't a real change. We live in a panic-driven culture, and if we are panicked we aren't changing the process; we *are* the process.

Operating our social change efforts in the panic zone often ends up putting us in the drone zone at other times. Because we don't feel we have time to think and dream about work to do, we end up doing the same kinds of things again and again. 'Another boring demonstration for peace.' It feels that way sometimes. Doing stuff again and again that we've done before and not getting much out of it.

What would it be like for the whole environmental movement to operate in the C zone. Or the peace movement? How would it feel? What would we do?

I saw a saying someplace: 'If you want to make the world better for a year, plant a garden. If you want to make the world better for forty years, plant a tree. If you want to make the world better for a century, educate the people.' To which I would add, 'and let the people educate you.' Neither Gandhi nor Mao really found their message until they lived in the villages and let the villagers teach them. Large change doesn't come from clever quick fixes from smart tense people, but from long conversations and silences among people who know different things and need to learn different things.

We may not have enough time to do that, but we don't know what time it is, so we might as well choose to live in the kind of time that helps us do the best work. It's about time for a frolicsome, fun-filled Six Minutes Till Midnight Thanksgiving and an Ain't It Great to Be Wrong Party.

We need to take the time to think and dream about our visions and talk them over with others. Let's take the time we need and start to create the future we want. Start to create our own good things instead of being trapped in scared reaction to other people's threats. It'll be fun.

When life feels good and is productive, time isn't long or short—it's right. In the C zone, between mastery and challenge, it always feels like there is enough time for both. Enough time to learn what I need to learn, enough time to do what I'm doing really well. That time isn't measured on a clock but exists when we find work we really want to do, and are able to do it as well as we can. If we're in a movement where that happens a lot, recruitment won't be a problem. People will want to join in, support us in our work and get our support for theirs. And when we're operating that way we aren't just eternally criticizing the old games. We're playing the new game. We are what we hope for.

What can we do about the drone zone where most things we use in our lives are made? Factory work was designed to put people in the drone zone. The way to much mastery: give people a job they can master in a day and keep them at it for forty years. I don't like getting my goodies from that. I don't like that the bad things about factory work are getting worse with computers. Making computers and other electronic equipment involves dangerous chemicals, is usually done by non-unionized people, predominantly women, and is now often done overseas by very poor women who don't have many choices in their lives.

Could we make all these things without devastating boredom? In the drone zone, time is eternal and oppressive. It's not fun and it just goes on. It takes the clock years to go from four-thirty to a quarter to five. Millions of jobs are designed to be like that. How can we make that different?

If the environment is to be healed there will be many many kinds of jobs for people to do. Outdoor persistence and mastery jobs. Indoor challenge and talking jobs. Jobs we haven't yet imagined.

When we're thinking of changing things for the better we unconsciously exclude many people from our efforts, or unconsciously assume they are a burden we have to somehow bear and drag along.

Let's include everybody in. Everybody should be able to live out their unique good times. Making a place where that can happen is what all our movements are about.

A peace/green/justice movement that works will look unlike anything we've imagined. It will feel like the most alive times in our lives. It will have in it many people we didn't think we were going to talk to. They won't join us. We won't join them. We'll meet in the unsuspected new place where we can all play our best game together.

We're going to need a lot more mastery if we're going to nurture and heal the Earth we have harmed. I read recently about a couple who are looking for fifty badly eroded acres to spend twenty years restoring. Yes. We need to do a lot of work like that. You can be sure when they find their fifty acres a hyped-up, urgent, gotta-fix-it-now approach will do them no good. And they'll have really mastered that piece of land in twenty years.

Some people truly like to work in emergency rooms. It's the right level of challenge for them. Any community needs firefighters and has people who want to fight fires. In environmental work we need to make places for people who don't like responding fast to an immediate crisis. We need to start doing the slow healing of damage that has already been done, start the slow growing of farms and parks of the future. Nature works slowly. To work with nature we need to learn to slow down.

Of course, if we all got as hung up on mastery as we now are on challenge we'd be a stagnant group. However, currently that doesn't seem like a real danger. We're surrounded by and participating in endless thrilling tales of trying to do way too much in way too short a time and getting away with it.

We lose track of the kind of quality that mastery can bring—a kind of quality that our environment and our souls greatly need. Working frantically on deadline creates brilliant compromises, intense group emotions, efforts that are amazingly good considering how little time and thought we let ourselves take. We don't even know what we're missing. Building the good future needs better than creating one brilliant last-minute solution after another.

Whatever the project, if you stay up all night working to complete it as well as you can under the circumstances, the project will seem very important and you will feel important, and exhausted.

In the C zone, however, things don't have to feel that important because working feels so good. It feels like it fits right in with the joyful parts of the world. The work doesn't have to be the messiah and neither do I—we're just being what we are very well and having fun.

'Having fun' might be a better way of saying 'peace'. 'Peace' is often a loaded empty word. I say I write about peace; people react like I'm dreaming of a boring world without conflict, or that I'm ignoring the many pains that exist in this world we know. What do I mean by peace?

Can you remember a time when you were working or playing with a group of people and everything seemed to come very smoothly? You could all decide what to do intuitively; anything one person couldn't bring off another person did with ease.

What are some words you'd use to describe how that felt to you?

When Marilyn Kriegel asks her version of that question—when did you as an individual have a work high?—she says the most common word of description she gets from people is 'natural'. Right. Having things be smooth, productive, fun, and great-feeling feels natural. Feels natural when it happens to one person, feels natural when it happens to a group.

That happens in change groups as in other groups, but I think we don't value it enough. It's the way to do good work and keep doing it. It's the way to live in the world we dream of now. After all, peace among ourselves and the environment doesn't mean we'll be spending all our time scraping for funds and infighting. We need to start running the experiment now.

Peace. It happens all the time. If it didn't we'd be either dead or utterly miserable. What's wrong now is that a lot of people don't get to have that smooth, great feeling themselves or in a group because they're so busy struggling to survive, or struggling to overcome barriers other people have put in their way, or struggling to live in a natural environment that is too injured to support them. We want to make it so all people and other living creatures have a chance to find their own great-feeling zone to play in, to work in, so people can be their own unique selves in a world that isn't out to smash them before they start.

July/August 1985

Serving the Handicapped

JEAN VANIER

IN 1963, WHILE I WAS TEACHING PHILOSOPHY at the University of Toronto, I visited France, where I went to see Father Thomas Philippe, a Dominican priest whom I had met some years earlier. At that time, Father Thomas was chaplain to a Residence for thirty men with a mental handicap in Trosly-Breuil. It was the first time in my life (I was thirty-five) that I had met people with a mental handicap. I was amazed and bewildered, and somehow a little overwhelmed. The cry of anger in those men, their deep sadness and at the same time their incredible cry for relationship, moved me.

These men seemed so different from my students at the University who seemed only interested in my head and in what they could get out of it in order to pass their exams, but were not at all concerned by my person. These people I met in Trosly could not care less about what was in my head; they were interested in my person. It was obvious that they craved friendship, a relationship where they would be seen as unique. Somehow their cry evoked something deep within me. But at the same time I was overwhelmed by their needs.

That is how I became interested in the plight of these people, and I began visiting asylums and hospitals. I saw many men and women living in crowded and most unbearable situations.

And so it was that a few months later I bought a house in Trosly, and invited two men to come and live with me. Both had mental handicaps; neither had any family as their parents had died. They had been put into a rather dismal institution. We started living together in a small rather dilapidated house. We began to discover each other. They had their anger and fears, but also their hopes. I too had my anger and fears, but also my hopes. Little by little I discovered the immense pain hidden inside the loneliness they felt, their broken self-image, because they had been pushed around so much in life and had received so little respect. I also came to know their incredible goodness.

Other people came to help, and so we were able to welcome more handicapped people. My idea was to create a little 'home', a little family, for those who had no 'home', no family. I did not want l'Arche (the name given to that first home) to be an institution, but a community where each person had his or her place, where we could work, grow, celebrate and pray together.

The French government recognized us quite quickly. It was in need of places to welcome people with mental handicaps. We were thus able to buy another home in the village, and little by little we grew. There are now some four hundred people in our community, in many small homes scattered throughout Trosly and the neighbouring villages. Each home is as independent as possible.

Other people from other countries come to visit or to live with us for a while. Some were deeply touched by their experience here and in union with us they began to found similar communities in their own country. Now in 1985, there are seventy communities in sixteen different countries. We have a little community near Ouagadougou in Burkina Faso where we have welcomed four children who had been abandoned. We have started a school for them and for some of the handicapped children in the area. There is a community in one of the slum areas of Tegucigalpa in Honduras, where we are trying to serve the needs of handicapped people there. In the centre of Calcutta we were given a house and the basement of a church for a workshop. We have communities in Scotland and Ireland. In England there are four communities, in London, Bognor Regis, Liverpool and near Canterbury. Each one is inspired by the same spirit and lives off the same principle: to create community with people who have a mental handicap. All these communities are grouped together in a rather loose-knit federation, and all the communities are part of the larger family of l'Arche.

The inspiration at the basis of each community is religious, but the ways of expressing the love of God may be different. I myself am Roman Catholic and the first community of l'Arche in Trosly was inspired by my faith and by the faith of Father Thomas Philippe. We wanted the community to be a place of love and hope, a place of sharing, a place where people could find peace of heart and forgiveness. We wanted l'Arche to be a place where the poorer person was at the centre rather than the 'helpers'. In England our communities welcome predominantly Christians from the Anglican tradition. Very quickly our homes there became ecumenical. In India our communities are essentially made up of Hindus, Moslems and Christians. Yes, our differences are sometimes painful, but we are learning that the poor can call us to unity.

Many things happen in our communities. There are crises of all sorts. Some people need good psychological help; some take a long time to find any peace of heart or healing. Some like to work, others hate it. There is joy, there is pain; it is the joy and the pain of living together.

Most of the people we welcome are called to be with us all their lives but this depends, of course, on the gravity of their handicap. A few leave and get married. But the majority are much too severely wounded. Assistants come for periods of one or two years, and more and more are putting their roots down in community, making a life commitment to the family. This, of course, is essential. There are so many people in institutions or living more independently in apartments, but who are yearning for a network of friendship, a community life. They have contact with professionals who are prepared to work with them and who do a magnificent job. But there are few people in society willing to climb down the ladder of success and to become a brother or a sister to a person with a mental handicap.

It is true that sometimes it is very taxing to live with people in deep anguish and stress. Experience at l'Arche has shown us that it is also important to care for the carers. Assistants too need to be supported and helped in many ways, particularly if they are called to put their roots down and to stay the rest of their life in a community. With twenty years' experience we now see clearly that they can only do this if they discover that the person with a handicap is a source of life and strength for them; if they themselves are not there just to 'do good' to another but also to receive something from her or him; that they too are called to live in community and to be nourished by those who are at the heart of the community.

Our society frequently sees the world in the form of a ladder: there is a bottom and a top. Everything and everyone encourages us to climb up that ladder, to seek success, promotion, wealth and power. At l'Arche, in living with our wounded brothers and sisters, we are discovering that if we are to live humanely, it is not the ladder that we should take as a model, but rather a living body. In a body there are many different parts: each one is important, even the smallest and the weakest. No one part can say it is the best and that it does not need the others. Each part is made so that the whole body can function well. In the body, even the weakest members know they are needed and important.

People with a mental handicap who come to our communities are called to rise up in hope and to discover the beauty of their beings and their capacities, no matter how limited these may be. Those who come to help are called to what is most beautiful in their own hearts: the capacity to be present to give life, through their love, to those in distress. And thus the body is formed. We discover we are linked together.

Because we are linked together we learn to forgive each other, for we can so easily hurt one another when we live together. We learn to celebrate the fact that we have been called together. Little by little we become people of joy because we are people of prayer, people within a covenanted relationship.

May/June 1985

A Barefoot Doctor

CAROLINE WALKER

IN DECEMBER 1988 A REMARKABLE COMMUNITY IN INDIA celebrated its twenty-fifth birthday. Since its founding by Dora Scarlett, Seva Nilayam (House of Service) has been giving free medical care to village people in a rural area of Tamil Nadu.

Dora Scarlett, now in her eighties, is one of those people who seldom speak about themselves. After the Second World War she lived in Hungary, working for Radio Budapest until 1956; then in 1960 she began working with the YWCA in a village clinic eighteen miles from Madras.

In time, however, as roads were built and bus routes opened up into the countryside, the need for basic health care in that area lessened. Dora and a local farmer decided to look for somewhere more remote and found a village sixty miles west of the great temple city of Madurai. The farmer, Mr Reddy, and his wife were severely criticized by their families for setting off with this unknown foreign woman. Talking of their departure, Dora said: 'When we came out of the clinic building and locked the door for the last time I had no idea what lay ahead. I had learned a lot about one village, but I was to see far different scenes and far different villages.'

One day when she visited me she remarked, looking round the large court-yard we shared with a local farmer, 'Well! This is much better than when *we* started: we only had one tiny window-less room in a narrow courtyard full of goats and boys!' From Dora's writings, a vivid picture of the early stages of their work emerges: 'To begin our work we had to learn the geography of this region, and for this purpose we walked through all the villages, barked at by village dogs, stared at by village children, but very hospitably received by many house owners. We had a small bag of very simple medicines. Sometimes we sat in the yard of one of the bigger houses, and the local people gathered there to tell us of their needs and difficulties. We found seriously ill people lying in dark and smoky huts without any comforts. The whole of the village was around us. We heard the children droning the alphabets in the schools. We saw the labourers returning from the fields and heard the tinkling of cow bells as the herds came home in the evening.'

These early experiences formed the bedrock on which the philosophy of Seva Nilayam was built: real knowledge of, and respect for, the village way of life, humility in the face of its harshness and beauty.

I sometimes used to sit beside Dora as she dealt with the long line of patients waiting under the shady trellis at the front of the clinic. Some were to be referred inside for dressings; some needed a slip for medicines; some serious cases would have to go on to hospital. But Dora really looked carefully at each one; taking hold of their hands, she would slowly question them about their problems: 'The hands always tell their story. As we live among working people we see many work-worn hands, especially those of people over middle age. Looking at them we see days of toil, of grasping tools, hauling on ropes, binding sheaves, pulling weeds, cutting firewood.'

This respect and care for the individual has often been romanticized, idealized; Seva Nilayam's approach is never sentimental: 'Of course, we are not always radiating smiles. We can get irritated with the patients. Sometimes they start a quarrel amongst themselves, pushing each other and arguing in shrill voices. Some are garrulous, and it is hard to sympathize with people who will not stop talking about trifling or imaginary ailments.'

In a letter entitled 'Compassion', Dora describes the kind of encounter that I, too, learned to dread: 'Parents came more than eighty miles, bringing a child who was obviously suffering from brain damage, perhaps due to previous meningitis. The face was vacant, the eyes unresponsive, and the legs dangled helplessly. "What made you think of coming here?" we ask. "We heard of someone who was cured by you, and people tell us you take care of patients." The parents stand with hopeful, questioning eyes. This is a moment we would gladly escape from.'

Those who know about this kind of work will know how rare this humility is. We prefer to talk about what we can do, not about our powerlessness in the face of suffering and death. But true compassion says Dora 'is a very tough discipline. Compassion means feeling *with* others, not feeling *for* them, as though we were standing on a higher level, and had just so much pity to dole out. It makes us one with all living beings.'

Seva Nilayam's daily life reaffirms this oneness. Early in the morning the milk is brought in, foaming in its brass pail, from the cowshed, where there is nearly always a calf to admire. Eggs may be found in the hen house, bananas brought in from the garden. On each of our visits there was always something special: bright green wing beans, full of protein; new baby carrots, carefully nurtured by Dora; lemon cheese made with their own lemons; home-made yoghurt and ghee. I would be taken to the farm or garden to see the brilliant green of the young paddy, the rare flower on the jack-fruit tree, a new vine. There are always dishes of precious seeds drying on Dora's table, and a nursery of young plants outside her room. Working with the land to make it productive, they share in the daily labour of most of their neighbours. 'He is a very good farmer,' is one of Dora's highest forms of praise.

Seva Nilayam's land, with Mr Reddy's farm adjoining, is not only used economically and productively; all spare corners have been planted with flowering plants and trees, of which India has some of the most beautiful species. Twenty-five years ago these few acres were red, rocky, bare earth, featureless and unwatered. Now, after countless hours of labour, and thanks to a miraculous well which never goes dry, there has grown 'an oasis of colour and beauty. There is the glorious gul mohur or flame tree, entirely covered with scarlet blossoms in May; the Indian laburnum, with drooping gold chains; the frangipani, or temple tree, which strews the ground with waxy-white, gold-centred blossoms and the bougainvillaea with rose, red or purple flowers. In every odd corner we have planted hibiscus in shades of yellow, orange and red for contrast, the brilliant blue morning glory ramps over the roof.' It is not surprising that Seva Nilayam chooses a tree for its symbol.

First-time visitors, especially if they have been to other projects, sometimes express surprise at the somewhat austere simplicity deliberately chosen at Seva Nilayam. 'Why no fans, no comfortable armchairs?' they may ask, and, in the rainy season, 'why no roof on the bathrooms?' But most come to admire the strict economy and delight in the beauty of the place. A bucket of cold water ladled over yourself as you peep over the bathroom wall to see the sun's last rays catch the glowing black granite hills nearby, whilst the far hills in shades of blue and grey march off under the clouds to the Kerala border, might convert the harshest critic.

Simplicity also shows in their refusal of many offers of a vehicle. To all the arguments which insist 'You can reach more people' Dora replies that you will not be able to reach them in depth; relationships will suffer. Preferring the enforced conviviality of the lurching, crowded and dusty country bus has some advantages. 'Bus manners,' Dora remarks drily, 'allow you to mind other people's business as well as your own.'

In her letters Dora celebrates the life of the people she has now served without a break for twenty-five years: the mysterious life of the local forest tribes, the value of working animals, the elegant simplicity of the 'banana leaf economy', the quiet dignity of a poor girl's funeral, the resilience of the poor in the face of devastation, and the ephemeral art of the kholam, the ritual patterns drawn in powder every morning outside even the poorest of huts, trodden away by feet in the course of the day, reminders of the passing away and renewing of life. Most of all she writes about the joy of the village festivals: Ayudha Puja, where working people pay respect to the tools of their trade; Deepavalli, when the village is ablaze with tiny lights; and Pongal, the celebration of the harvest and homage to working animals.

'You would have to be at Seva Nilayam,' she writes, 'to see what joy can be given by glass marbles costing about twelve English pence a hundred. Or a breakfast of rice cakes. Or a sari of printed cotton. Or a shirt made out of dressmaker's pieces. It is one of the paradoxes of life that only those who know sorrow can truly know joy, and only those who are poor, can know what it is to feel rich.'

May/June 1989

Acupuncture: China Shows the Way

ROGER HILL

A GROUP OF NINETEEN OF US, practising acupuncturists and orthodox doctors with an interest in Chinese medicine from Britain, Canada and the United States, have recently returned from an extensive tour of eastern China. A prime reason for our visit was to discuss training standards for traditional Chinese medicine. Twenty-four colleges offer university level five-year courses, and we are able to visit the principle ones at Shanghai, Nanjing and Peking. Entry to the colleges is very competitive; last year there were 10,000 applicants for the fifty places available in Peking. For all students there is a common training in regular anatomy, physiology, pathology and the other essential grounding for medical care, then the course separates those who are to specialize in acupuncture from those who intend to specialize in traditional internal medicines. Some knowledge of both is taught to both groups for they are essentially interdependent skills sharing common theoretical procedures. Thus there are three streams of medical education, each lasting five years—orthodox western medicine, acupuncture and traditional medicine.

There are also two large colleges of traditional pharmacy, one in Peking serving the north, and the other for the south in Nanjing. There are literally thousands of herbal, marine, animal and mineral elements in traditional medicines. Until the 1949 Liberation their effective combinations were known often only to families of doctors or to particular local districts, but the Revolution—that great leveller—wrested out the secret formulae and made the knowledge available nationwide. Those medicines that are known to be susceptible to manufacture and storage are being produced in some 800 factories. More than 3,000 traditional medical products are now available for domestic and foreign use.

As an example the Hanghzhou Second Traditional Chinese Pharmaceutical Works is particularly proud of its 'Recovery of Youth Tablets' based on the secret Ming dynasty (C13-16 AD) formulae, which contemporary research shows to prevent the ageing process at cell level. It has been extensively retested on some victims of debilitating strain and found to restore resilience to body and mind. Naturally it is contraindicated in pregnancy and for those aged under thirty who are still growing.

The relationship between western orthodox medicine and traditional medicine is subject, in practice, to all the variables that might be anticipated. Some hospitals and clinics are almost wholly devoted to only one approach, but most work with a healthy mixture—'It is better to walk on two legs than one,' said Chairman Mao.

The choice of treatment depends on the combination of patients' preferences, doctors' judgements and the politics and orientation within a particular clinic.

There is a large degree of overlap between the categories of illness helped by both. If a treatment by one scheme is found to be not effective, there is no hesitation in calling in the assistance of the other.

The traditional medicine departments of all the hospitals we visited were very well patronized. Most work on an out-patient basis with patients either walking in or being carried in on stretchers by their friends. The wards are simple, clean enough, and full of people. The notion of privacy is not widespread in China and certainly has no place in hospital life. Illnesses are common property between those in a ward (though infectious diseases are given their proper respect). One healthy aspect of this is the mixture of physical problems with psychological ones; the hemiplegic will be treated alongside the depressed. We saw one overt psychotic being treated in a room otherwise full of patients suffering from various physical disorders. Family and friends often play a significant part in patient care in hospital.

We saw treatments at every rung in the hierarchical scale of medical organization. For example, we spent time in the clinic of the Plom Valley Tea Production Brigade where Dragon Lake Green Tea has been grown for more than a thousand years.

It is run by two 'barefoot doctors' trained to cope with first-aid and preventive medicine for the whole large village. Their work includes dealing with cuts and colds, pre-and post-natal services, contraception, midwifery for normal births, health education, ensuring clean water supplies and proper sewage disposal, and arranging for the seriously ill to be sent to the local hospital twenty miles away or visited by a travelling specialist.

This close liaison between health worker and people seems to be the fundamental reason for the dramatic improvement in health for every Chinese person over the last twenty-five years. It is such a wise expenditure of resources, especially for a country which is not rich in material assets. Treatments are simple and will include common western synthesized drugs, acupuncture, and simple traditional medicines, many of which are grown on the commune. The preference will be for the latter because they are cheaper and more familiar. All health care in China must be paid for either by the individual or by the commune on his behalf. Only those working directly for central government receive free treatment.

When the barefoot doctor service was started the emphasis was on providing workers who did their ordinary work in factory or fields but who also served health-care part-time. The new emphasis is to upgrade the barefoot doctor and to make him or her a full time professional.

Acupuncture analgesia's development was largely sponsored by Chairman Mao, and in the general process of his dethronement that is currently underway there are some murmurs from within China against it. However our experience, backed by that of my previous visit to China three years ago and that of many other visitors, is that it is extensively and exclusively used in about fifty per cent of cases needing pain relief whether they be in surgery, dentistry or childbirth.

Sometimes muscle relaxants are also used and morphine-based drugs are always available on standby. We saw heart surgery where both these extra aids were used though calling them in was exceptional, most cases even as critical as this rely on acupuncture alone.

Treatment is effected by very fine stainless-steel needles inserted at one or more of the thousand or so acupuncture points on the body. The length of time that the needles remain in the body and the sort of manipulation that is required, if any, are matters of fine judgement by the practitioner. Sometimes a herb or moxa (*Artemisia latiflora*) is also burnt on the needle or near the skin to provide warmth and stimulation. There is negligible discomfort with either method.

In a small-town hospital totally unprepared to receive foreign visitors—we were their first—we saw the removal of a substantial tumour of the thyroid. The patient, a man in his thirties walked to the operating table, two simple acupuncture points were selected on the forearm, the needles were inserted and connected to the electro-stimulator. During the twenty minutes' induction period, the patient was prepared for surgery. The operation proceeded with incredible deftness and speed. Throughout the operation the patient was smiling and was obviously painfree. Thirty-five minutes later it was all over, he was stitched up, the two acupuncture needles were removed from his arm, he got up from the operating table and walked back to his ward, giving us a cheerful wave as he went.

Although traditional Chinese medicine provides part of mainstream health-care for about one third of the world's population, mainly in the Far East, it has only recently been introduced effectively to the West. Acupuncture is more widely available than traditional medicines for which the Euro-American herbal tradition provides a good substitute. There are some difficulties, both on conceptual and formal levels in the introduction of acupuncture. In the West, 'scientific' medicine (that which can be expressed in terms of contemporary anatomy, physiology and biochemistry, and for which specific disease categories can be treated by specific treatments to give statistically measurable results) is firmly in command.

Although acupuncture offers no contradiction to this, it is certainly true that few of its attributes can be explained yet in these terms, except perhaps pain relief. Moreover, most serious students of the subject believe that if acupuncture is to be fully taught it can only be done so in its own poetic and symbolic language which in some superficial ways is closer to ancient Greek medicine or homoeopathy than to modern medicine. Though little contradiction is inherent, a definite shift in attitude is necessary to tune into the benefits of this long-established tradition. There is a very small hardline minority which argues that the language of acupuncture and traditional Chinese medicine is bunk and should be totally abandoned in favour of neurological explanations. I believe that this limited view annuls the wide range of benefits of acupuncture and emasculates a long and proven tradition.

On the formal, legal level, the medical professions of one or two Western countries, notably France, have closed ranks tightly with a view to excluding any but registered doctors from practising acupuncture. The majority, however, view acupuncture as a specialized skill that requires a training along Chinese lines rather than that of a normal passage through an orthodox medical school topped-off by a weekend's course in acupuncture. Already several American States are establishing Registers of Acupuncturists similar to those for the other professions—dentists, vets or doctors. It is likely that European countries will follow in due course.

Because the established medical systems in the West offer a generally excellent service, and in Britain an apparently almost free one, the needs and emphasis of acupuncture here are different from those in the East. Thus we rarely see the self-limiting, short-term illnesses which are the main staple of the general practitioner's surgery. Many patients come to us as a last resort; they have tried every other avenue but still remain with their chronic illness. Other patients will come because, although orthodox medicine's diagnostic procedures can confirm that they do not have a life-endangering illness, the constellation of major or minor symptoms defies confident diagnosis or treatment.

One major advantage of traditional Chinese medicine is that it views health from a different point of view, through a different pair of spectacles, and thus what may seem to be an insoluble problem to Western medicine may fit very clearly and naturally into the diagnostic and treatment procedures of Chinese medicine. This is particularly true of those illnesses which are categorized in the West as psychosomatic or functional disorders. In properly conducted Chinese medicine body and mind are given equal attention. Some people also come for preventive treatment, to maintain good health, to ensure a balanced flow of energy that is in step with the natural cycles. This approach is deeply enshrined in the classical Chinese tradition of medicine, which is not merely a safety net for acute illness but is sensitive enough to make a useful contribution throughout life.

Chinese medicine springs from a Taoist view of human beings as microcosms of nature. Balance is the key concept. Illness is an indication of, and indicated by disturbed energy (Ch'i) on physical, mental and spiritual levels as reflected in the twelve main meridians or pathways of energy. The aims of treatment are to strengthen the overall homoeostasis of the body/mind to encourage the natural self-healing mechanism inherent in us all, to relieve the presenting symptoms and to restore the patient to harmony.

The following extract is taken from the Judges' ruling at the Texas Federal Court in July 1980, in which the right to practise acupuncture in that State was established: 'The traditional Chinese explanation of how acupuncture works relies heavily on concepts unfamiliar to the Western scientific community. According to traditional Chinese theory, the basic energy or force of life, which flows through all living things, is called "Ch'i". When this force flows through the human body, it travels along twelve primary and two secondary channels or meridians. It is along these channels that the acupuncture points lie. Ch'i, traditional Chinese theory teaches, has two aspects to it: Yin, the negative aspect, and Yang, the positive aspect. The twelve primary channels through which the Ch'i flows are divided accordingly into six Yin and six Yang channels and paired. For each Yin channel, there is a Yang channel.

'Despite the reference to them as "negative" and "positive", as Yin and Yang are two aspects of the same force, one is no more desirable than the other. In fact it is a basic tenet of traditional Chinese theory that Yin and Yang must be in balance for Ch'i to flow freely and for all living things, therefore, to function properly. Thus, the theory teaches that it is when Yin and Yang are out of balance that the body is susceptible to pain and illness. Acupuncture treatment is designed to correct this imbalance. The skilled acupuncturist, by placing and manipulating the needles in the proper points, brings Yin and Yang back into balance. This allows Ch'i to flow freely and the body's natural defences to combat disease and pain.'

July/August 1981

Animal Liberation

PETER SINGER

YOU DON'T COME ACROSS many open racists nowadays. Though hidden racial feelings remain a problem, almost everyone now recognizes that the fact that we are white does not give us the right to exploit or enslave people of other races, or to use them as if they were objects designed for our use.

Yet we are all, or nearly all, open 'species-ists'. I use this term—and I admit it is not beautiful, but I haven't a better word—to refer to those who discriminate against beings who are of another species. Human speciesists think that the fact that we are human gives us the right to exploit and enslave beings of other species, and to use them as if they were objects designed for our use.

The logic of racism and the logic of speciesism are indistinguishable. If we reject discrimination on the basis of race—as of course we should—then consistency demands that we reject discrimination on the basis of species too.

Someone may object that racism is wrong because people of different races are in fact the same in important respects, like intelligence, the capacity to suffer, ability to communicate, and so on; while the various species of non-human animals are not equal to humans in these respects. Therefore, it may be claimed, we are entitled to treat other species as our inferiors, although we are not entitled to treat other races in this manner.

It cannot be denied that on average humans are more intelligent than other animals, and humans do have certain abilities that other animals do not have (including the ability to extinguish life from this planet). The point is, though, that the fact that one being is more intelligent than another does not entitle him or her to exploit or enslave the less intelligent being. If we really thought that it did, we would have had to allow Einstein to enslave us all.

The principle that all human beings are equal is not based on the idea that all humans actually are equal in intelligence or anything else. If it were, we would have to reject it, since it is obvious that humans differ in all sorts of ways. The principle of equality does not tell us what humans *are*: it tells us how humans *should* be treated. It requires us to give equal consideration to their interests, counting every individual's happiness and suffering as equally significant.

There is no real reason why the principle of equality should stop short at the boundaries of our own species. Over the centuries there has been a gradual expansion of our moral horizons: from the tribe to the nation, from the nation to the race, and from the race to all human beings.

If a being suffers, there can be no reason for refusing to take that suffering into consideration, counting it equally, so far as rough comparisons can be made, with a similar amount of suffering by any other being. Neither race nor species is a proper reason for disregarding suffering.

Some people say that we cannot know when animals suffer, because they cannot tell us about it. But babies can't talk either, and we can know when they are suffering. Similarly, it is not difficult to tell when a dog or a pig or even a mouse is in pain. Admittedly, the further down the evolutionary scale we get, the harder it is to know what a creature feels. An oyster has such a primitive nervous system that it may not be conscious at all. But animals with backbones, and mammals and birds especially, have nervous systems very like our own, and leading scientists agree that they are capable of feeling pain as we are.

What would the extension of the principle of equality to non-human animals mean in practice? It would not mean that we had to treat animals exactly as we now treat humans, nor even that we would have to regard the lives of animals as equally valuable to those of humans. For normal humans are different from animals, and these differences mean that they have different interests. So if it were to come to a choice between the life of a normal human being and that of an animal, it would not be a violation of the principle of equality to prefer the life of the human, because the human, with a greater awareness of what is going to happen, will suffer more before he or she dies; most likely it is the family and friends of the humans who will feel the loss more keenly; and finally, it would be the human who had the greatest potential for future achievements. On the other hand, where interests are strictly comparable—for instance the interest in avoiding physical pain—we should treat animals and humans equally. It is only where a human clearly has more at stake than an animal that we may favour the human.

Though extending the principle of equality to animals does not mean that we would treat humans and animals alike, it would still make a radical change in our everyday life. To see just how great this change would be we have first to look at some of the important ways in which we do not at present give animals anything like equal consideration.

Many of the worst and largest-scale cruelties to animals are unknown to the general public. When someone beats a dog or starves a horse, newspapers report it and people tell each other how terrible it is to treat an animal like that. Then everyone thinks how civilized and kind to animals they are, because they would never do such a thing.

In fact, these very people who condemn certain forms of cruelty participate every day in a more systematic form of cruelty that affects far more animals: the use of animals for human food.

Most city dwellers dine on the flesh of animals, in complete ignorance of what happened to their dinner while it was still a living animal. They may know, from having once driven behind a truck on its way to the slaughterhouse, that animals are transported in crowded, frightening conditions. They may guess that the animals, sensing something wrong, experience terror in the final moments of their lives. But they probably believe that these are just brief interludes in an otherwise pleasant experience.

The image that most people have of a farm is of calves grazing in the fields, pigs rooting around in the orchard, and a mother hen followed by chicks in stately procession across the courtyard. This image is now obsolete. Farming has become 'factory farming'. Animals are treated like machines that convert low-priced fodder into high-priced flesh or eggs. Anything that will reduce the cost of this conversion process is done. If confining animals indoors prevents them burning up food in 'wasteful' exercise, then they will be confined indoors. Cruelty is of no concern, unless it affects profits.

The hens that lay the eggs you buy in supermarkets have never walked outside, scratched the dirt, dust-bathed or tended their chicks. They spend their entire adult lives in long, dim sheds. Inside are endless rows of wire cages. The cages measure about eighteen inches by twenty inches (or the size of a single page of *The Times*). Each cage of this size holds five fully grown hens. They live in the cages for about a year, then their laying rate begins to decline, and they are thrown out to be made into chicken soup. These birds are never able to walk freely or even stretch their wings, for there simply isn't room. If you kept parrots or budgerigars in similarly crowded conditions you would be fined, but poultry farmers seem to be outside the normal laws against cruelty to birds. The hens are so crowded that they live under constant stress, and the stress leads to unnatural aggression. To stop the frustrated birds from pecking each other to death the farmer has to cut off most of their beaks in a routine operation known as 'de-beaking'.

Chickens raised to be eaten fare a little better, though their lives are shorter. They too are kept in windowless sheds, so crowded that they have to be de-beaked to prevent them from killing each other.

While the poultry industry is probably the most intensive form of animal raising today, the pig industry is not far behind, and hundreds of thousands of pigs are now being raised indoors. Veal calves are confined in narrow stalls and fed on a diet deliberately deficient in iron, because iron turns the flesh of the calves red, and the pale pink flesh from an anaemic veal calf fetches a higher price in the restaurant trade. Even beef cattle are being subjected to factory farming processes. In America most cattle are now fattened on an unnatural diet of grain in huge feedlots, holding tens of thousands of animals.

So we have a vast and growing industry, systematically exploiting other species to squeeze the maximum profit from them. And it is all utterly unnecessary. We do not have to kill animals to feed ourselves. We can live perfectly well— perhaps better—on a vegetarian diet.

In fact, intensive farming is actually a colossal *waste* of food, because we feed the animals on grains, soybeans and other products we could eat directly ourselves. The animals use most of the food value of what we feed them simply in living and breathing. When we finally kill them we get back only about one-tenth of the food value we put into them.

It has been calculated that the amount of protein wasted by being fed to animals in the affluent nations would be enough, if properly distributed, to end the shortage of protein in all the poorer parts of the world. No wonder that factory farming has been called 'a protein factory in reverse'.

All this cruelty, then, is not to provide us with food. It is to satisfy our taste for a certain kind of food. We are sacrificing the most vital interests of non-human animals in order to satisfy a trivial interest of our own. This is obviously a blatant violation of the principle of equal consideration.

There are many other things that would have to change if we gave up our bias in favour of our own species. Take, for instance, scientific experiments on animals. At least sixty million animals die every year in United States' laboratories and about five million in Britain. Many of the animals die painfully, and in experiments which are repetitious, poorly designed, or so trivial as to serve no important purpose. We would never dream of subjecting even a so-called 'human vegetable' to such experiments; yet we think very little of performing them on animals whose mental capacities may be far greater than those of a retarded human. This is another indication of our speciesism.

Then there are those speciesists who think they look elegant wearing a fur that has been ripped from the back of its rightful non-human owner; and those who take pleasure in shooting at anything that moves and isn't human; and those whose idea of a pleasant Sunday is to impale fish on a barbed steel hook, haul them out of the water and then let them flap around in the air until they suffocate. There are those who claim to adore their pets, but allow them to breed so that their offspring end up in a decompression chamber at the Lost Dogs' Home; and so on, and on.

With so much to be changed, the aim of extending the principle of equal consideration beyond our own species may seem utterly unrealistic. But the prospects for the abolition of human slavery must have seemed bleak to the first abolitionists. Change is possible if ordinary people show that they are capable of being moved by principles broader and more universal than those that consider the interests of our species alone. Every person who ends his or her own participation in the exploitation of animals brings the animal liberation movement one step nearer to its goal.

September/October 1977

The New Economics

Buddhist Economics

E. F. SCHUMACHER

'RIGHT LIVELIHOOD' is one of the requirements of the Buddha's Noble Eightfold Path. It is clear, therefore, that there must be such a thing as Buddhist Economics.

Buddhist countries, at the same time, have often stated that they wish to remain faithful to their heritage. So we read in Pyidawtha's *The New Burma*, 'The New Burma sees no conflict between religious values and economic progress. Spiritual health and material well-being are not enemies: they are natural allies,''We can blend successfully the religious and spiritual values of our heritage with the benefits of modern technology,' and 'We Burmans have a sacred duty to conform both our dreams and our acts to our faith. This we shall ever do.'

All the same, such countries invariably assume that they can model their economic development plans in accordance with modern economics, and they call upon modern economists from so-called advanced countries to advise them, to formulate the policies to be pursued, and to construct the grand design for development, the Five-Year Plan or whatever it may be called. No one seems to think that a Buddhist way of life would call for Buddhist economics just as the modern materialist way of life has brought forth modern economics.

Economists themselves, like most specialists, normally suffer from a kind of metaphysical blindness, assuming that theirs is a science of absolute and invariable truths, without any pre-suppositions. Some go as far as to claim that economic laws are as free from 'metaphysics' or 'values' as the law of gravitation. We need not, however, get involved in arguments of methodology. Instead, let us take some fundamentals and see what they look like when viewed by a modern economist and a Buddhist economist.

There is universal agreement that the fundamental source of wealth is human labour. Now, the modern economist has been brought up to consider 'labour' or work as little more than a necessary evil. From the point of view of the employer, it is in any case simply an item of cost, to be reduced to a minimum if it cannot be eliminated altogether, say, by automation. From the point of view of the workman, it is a 'disutility'; to work is to make a sacrifice of one's leisure and comfort, and wages are a kind of compensation for the sacrifice. Hence the ideal from the point of view of the employer is to have output without employees, and the ideal from the point of view of the employee is to have an income without employment.

The consequences of these attitudes both in theory and in practice are, of course, extremely far-reaching. If the ideal with regard to work is to get rid of it, every method that 'reduces the work load' is a good thing. The most potent method, short of automation, is the so-called 'division of labour' and the classical example is the pin factory eulogized in Adam Smith's *Wealth of Nations*. Here it is not a matter of ordinary specialization, which humankind has practised from time immemorial, but of dividing up every complete process of production into minute parts, so that the final product can be produced at great speed without anyone having had to contribute more than a totally insignificant and, in most cases, unskilled movement of the limbs.

The Buddhist point of view takes the function of work to be at least three-fold: to give a human being a chance to utilize and develop his or her faculties; to enable him or her to overcome ego-centredness by joining with other people in a common task; and to bring forth the goods and services needed for a becoming existence. Again, the consequences that flow from this view are endless. To organize work in such a manner that it becomes meaningless, boring, stultifying, or nerve-racking for the worker would be little short of criminal; it would indicate a greater concern with goods than with people, an evil lack of compassion and a soul-destroying degree of attachment to the most primitive side of this worldly existence. Equally, to strive for leisure as an alternative to work would be considered a complete misunderstanding of one of the basic truths of human existence, namely, that work and leisure are complementary parts of the same living process and cannot be separated without destroying the joy of work and the bliss of leisure.

From the Buddhist point of view, there are therefore two types of mechanization which must be clearly distinguished: one that enhances a person's skill and power and one that turns the work over to a mechanical slave, leaving the human being in a position of having to serve the slave. How to tell the one from the other? 'The craftsman himself,' says Ananda Coomaraswamy, a man equally competent to talk about the Modern West as the Ancient East, 'the craftsman himself can always, if allowed to, draw the delicate distinction between the machine and the tool. The carpet loom is a tool, a contrivance for holding warp threads at a stretch for the pile to be woven round them by the craftsmen's fingers; but the power loom is a machine, and its significance as a destroyer of culture lies in the fact that it does the essentially human part of the work.' It is clear, therefore, that Buddhist economics must be very different from the economics of modern materialism, since the Buddhist sees the essence of civilization not in a multiplication of wants but in the purification of human character. Character, at the same time, is formed primarily by a person's work. And work, properly conducted in conditions of human dignity and freedom, blesses those who do it and equally their products. The Indian philosopher and economist J. C. Kumarappa sums the matter up as follows: 'If the nature of the work is properly appreciated and applied, it will stand in the same relation to the higher faculties as food is to the physical body. It nourishes and enlivens the higher man and urges him to produce the best he is capable of. It directs his freewill along the proper course and disciplines the animal in him into progressive channels. It furnishes an excellent background for man to display his scale of values and develop his personality.'

If a person has no chance of obtaining work he or she is in a desperate position, not simply because of a lack of income but also because of the lack of the nourishing and enlivening factor of disciplined work which nothing can replace. A modern economist may engage in highly sophisticated calculations on whether full employment 'pays' or whether it might be more 'economic' to run an economy at less than full employment so as to ensure a greater mobility of labour, a better stability of wages, and so forth. The fundamental criterion of success is simply the total quantity of goods produced during a given period of time. 'If the marginal urgency of goods is low,' says Professor Galbraith in *The Affluent Society*, 'then so is the urgency of employing the last man or the last million men in the labour force.' And again: 'If . . . we can afford some unemployment in the interest of stability—a proposition, incidentally, of impeccably conservative antecedents—then we can afford to give those who are unemployed the goods that enable them to sustain their accustomed standard of living.'

From the Buddhist point of view, this is standing the truth on its head by considering goods as more important than people and consumption as more important than creative ability. It means shifting the emphasis from the worker to the product of work, that is, from the human to the sub-human, a surrender to the forces of evil. The very start of Buddhist economic planning would be planning for full employment, and the primary purpose of this would in fact be employment for everyone who needs an 'outside' job: it would not be the maximization of employment nor the maximization of production. Women, on the whole, do not need an 'outside' job, and the large-scale employment of women in offices or factories would be considered a sign of serious economic failure. In particular, to let mothers of young children work in factories while the children run wild would be as uneconomic in the eyes of a Buddhist economist as the employment of a skilled worker as a soldier in the eyes of a modern economist.

While the materialist is mainly interested in goods, the Buddhist is mainly interested in liberation. But Buddhism is 'The Middle Way' and therefore in no way antagonistic to physical well-being. It is not wealth that stands in the way of liberation but the attachment to wealth; not the enjoyment of pleasurable things but the craving for them. The keynote of Buddhist economics, therefore, is simplicity and non-violence. From an economist's point of view, the marvel of the Buddhist way of life is the utter rationality of its pattern—amazingly small means leading to extraordinarily satisfactory results.

For the modern economist this is very difficult to understand. He is used to measuring the 'standard of living' by the amount of annual consumption, assuming all the time that someone who consumes more is 'better off' than someone who consumes less. A Buddhist economist would consider this approach excessively irrational: since consumption is merely a means to human well-being, the aim should be to obtain the maximum of well-being with the minimum of consumption. Thus, if the purpose of clothing is a certain amount of temperature comfort and an attractive appearance, the task is to attain this purpose with the smallest possible effort, that is, with the smallest annual destruction of cloth and with the help of designs that involve the smallest possible input of toil. The less toil there is, the more time and strength is left for artistic creativity. It would be highly uneconomic, for instance, to go in for complicated tailoring, like the modern West, when a much more beautiful effect can be achieved by the skilful draping of uncut material. It would be the height of folly to make material so that it should wear out quickly and the height of barbarity to make anything ugly, shabby or mean. What has just been said about clothing applies equally to all other human requirements. The ownership and the consumption of goods is a means to an end, and Buddhist economics is the systematic study of how to attain given ends with the minimum means.

Modern economics, on the other hand, considers consumption to be the sole end and purpose of all economic activity, taking the factors of production— land, labour, and capital—as the means. The former, in short, tries to maximize human satisfactions by the optimal pattern of consumption, while the latter tries to maximize consumption by the optimal pattern of productive effort. It is easy to see that the effort needed to sustain a way of life which seeks to attain the optimal pattern of consumption is likely to be much smaller than the effort needed to sustain a drive for maximum consumption. We need not be surprised, therefore, that the pressure and strain of living is very much less in, say, Burma than it is in the United States, in spite of the fact that the amount of labour-saving machinery used in the former country is only a minute fraction of the amount used in the latter.

Simplicity and non-violence are obviously closely related. The optimal pattern of consumption, producing a high degree of human satisfaction by means of a relatively low rate of consumption, allows people to live without great pressure and strain and to fulfil the primary injunction of Buddhist teaching: 'Cease to do evil; try to do good.' As physical resources are everywhere limited, people satisfying their needs by means of a modest use of resources are obviously less likely to be at each other's throats than people depending upon a high rate of use. Equally, people who live in highly self-sufficient local communities are less likely to get involved in large-scale violence than people whose existence depends on world-wide systems of trade.

From the point of view of Buddhist economics, therefore, production from local resources for local needs is the most rational way of economic life, while dependence on imports from afar and the consequent need to produce for export to unknown and distant peoples is highly uneconomic and justifiable only in exceptional cases and on a small scale. Just as the modern economist would admit that a high rate of consumption of transport services between a person's home and place of work signifies a misfortune and not a high standard of life, so the Buddhist economist would hold that to satisfy human wants from far-away sources rather than from sources nearby signifies failure rather than success. The former might take statistics showing an increase in the number of ton/miles per head of the population carried by a country's transport system as proof of economic progress, while to the latter—the Buddhist economist —the same statistics would indicate a highly undesirable deterioration in the *pattern* of consumption.

Another striking difference between modern economics and Buddhist economics arises over the use of natural resources. Bertrand de Juvenal, the eminent French political philosopher, has characterized 'Western man' in words which may be taken as a fair description of the modern economist: 'He tends to count nothing as an expenditure, other than human effort; he does not seem to mind how much living matter he destroys. He does not seem to realise at all that human life is a dependent part of an ecosystem of many different forms of life. As the world is ruled from towns where men are cut off from any form of life other than human, the feeling of belonging to an ecosystem is not revived. This results in a harsh and improvident treatment of things upon which we ultimately depend, such as water and trees.'

The teaching of the Buddha, on the other hand, enjoins a reverent and non-violent attitude not only to all sentient beings but also, with great emphasis, to trees. Every follower of the Buddha ought to plant a tree every few years and look after it until it is safely established, and the Buddhist economist can demonstrate without difficulty that the universal observance of this rule would result in a high rate of genuine economic development independent of any foreign aid. Much of the economic decay of South-East Asia (as of many other parts of the world) is undoubtedly due to a heedless and shameful neglect of trees.

Modern economics does not distinguish between renewable and non-renewable materials, as its very method is to equalize and quantify everything by means of a money price. Thus, taking various alternative fuels, like coal, oil, wood or water-power: the only difference between them recognized by modern economics is relative cost per equivalent unit. The cheapest is automatically the one to be preferred, as to do otherwise would be irrational and 'uneconomic'. From a Buddhist point of view, of course, this will not do; the essential difference between non-renewable fuels like coal and oil on the one hand and renewable fuels like wood and water-power on the other cannot be simply over-looked. Non-renewable goods must be used only if they are indispensable, and then only with the greatest care and the most meticulous concern for conservation. To use them heedlessly or extravagantly is an act of violence, and while complete non-violence may not be attainable on this earth, there is none the less an ineluctable duty to aim at the ideal of non-violence.

Just as a modern European economist would not consider it a great economic achievement if all European art treasures were sold to America at attractive prices, so the Buddhist economist would insist that a population basing its economic life on non-renewable fuels is living parasitically, on capital instead of income. Such a way of life could have no permanence and could therefore be justified only as a purely temporary expedient. As the world's resources of non-renewable fuels—coal, oil and natural gas—are exceedingly unevenly distributed over the globe and undoubtedly limited in quantity, it is clear that their exploitation at an ever increasing rate is an act of violence against nature which must almost inevitably lead to human violence.

This fact alone might give food for thought even to those people in Buddhist countries who care nothing for the religious and spiritual values of their heritage and ardently desire to embrace the materialism of modern economics at the fastest possible speed. Before they dismiss Buddhist economics as nothing better than a nostalgic dream, they might wish to consider whether the path of economic development outlined by modern economics is likely to lead them to places where they really want to be. Towards the end of his courageous book *The Challenge of Man's Future*, Professor Harrison Brown of the California Institute of Technology gives the following appraisal: 'Thus we see that, just as industrial society is fundamentally unstable and subject to reversion to agrarian existence, so within it the conditions which offer individual freedom are unstable in their ability to avoid the conditions which impose rigid organization and totalitarian control. Indeed, when we examine all of the foreseeable difficulties which threaten the survival of industrial civilization, it is difficult to see how the achievement of stability and the maintenance of individual liberty can be made compatible.'

Even if this were dismissed as a long-term view—and in the long term, as Keynes said, we are all dead—there is the immediate question of whether 'modernization', as currently practised without regard to religious and spiritual values, is actually producing agreeable results. As far as the masses are concerned, the results appear to be disastrous—a collapse of the rural economy, a rising tide of unemployment in town and country, and the growth of a city proletariat without nourishment for either body or soul.

It is in the light of both immediate experience and long-term prospects that the study of Buddhist economics could be recommended even to those who believe that economic growth is more important than any spiritual or religious values. For it is not a question of choosing between 'modern growth' and 'traditional stagnation'. It is a question of finding the right path of development, the Middle Way between materialist heedlessness and traditionalist immobility, in short, of finding 'Right Livelihood'.

That this can be done is not in doubt. But it requires much more than blind imitation of the materialist way of life of the so-called advanced countries. It requires above all, the conscious and systematic development of a Middle Way in technology, a technology more productive and powerful than the decayed technology of the ancient East, but at the same time non-violent and immensely cheaper and simpler than the labour-saving technology of the modern West.

The Economics of Progress

LEOPOLD KOHR

AT A RECENT COCKTAIL PARTY, two middle-aged men became involved in conversation. One was a professor of economics at a major American University; the other was a professor of mechanical engineering at a famous Institute of Technology. Their talk touched upon both their fields. They discussed the economics of progress.

'How do *you* wash your nylon shirts?' asked the one.

'Very simple,' answered the other. 'I wash them with a nylon tooth brush. Nylon on nylon is very gentle. And it gets the smudges off collars and cuffs.'

They also discussed plumbing, floor polishing, and cooking, glorying in the fact that progress had so simplified matters that all these things could now be done by themselves. But in the end, one of them gave off an inadvertent sigh.

'Why the sigh?' asked the other.

'Well,' was the reply, 'I was thinking that fifty years ago we would have had maids. Instead of having to wash, plumb, and cook like unspecialized pioneers, we might have been better engineers and economists. Moreover, our shirts would have looked pressed, and our meals have tasted better. And instead of discussing housework at a party of scholars, we might have discussed our subjects.'

The experience of the two professors is shared by an increasing number of people. On the one hand, we witness the gigantic pace of progress and continuously rising output figures. But on the other hand we have the strange feeling that, instead of getting ahead in life, we have to give up every year something we could afford when, according to living-standard experts, we must have had less. When I was a student in the early thirties I drove a racy sports car. As a university professor with an income that ranges me according to my own text-books into the upper twenty per cent of the richest people on earth in the richest period of history. I drove, in 1955, a 1937 Lasalle, only to become a combination busrider-pedestrian in 1956. And the income classes above me have fared still worse. Mr DuPont, in a much publicized story a few years ago, had to abandon his palatial residence in Winterthur, Delaware. Now it is a museum, impressing the visitor with the high living standards of Mr DuPont's ancestors, not his own. Similarly in England, Lord Halifax at about the same time had to give up his castle and move into his stable. Though this was hailed as a great victory of democratic living, all the story demonstrated was the seemingly superior standards of the past, considering that the stable of then is found good enough to house a lord today.

However, it is said that while the living standards of the upper strata of society have admittedly declined those of the lower strata have risen. But have they?

43

Where are the persons who have become richer as a result of Mr DuPont having become poorer? On the contrary, most seem to be carried along the same road: downhill. For as those who previously lived in palaces now live in houses, many of those who lived in houses now live in smaller ones or in apartments. Those who previously drank wine with their meals now drink water, and those who had maids now have none.

As to maids, it is frequently said that their disappearance is precisely a sign not of declining but of rising standards. For maids of former days are now housewives or businesswomen. Quite. But why should maids have aspired to these higher levels except in the hope of having maids themselves? Yet, all they discovered was that, instead of escaping the chores of housework, they had to add to them. For progress had given them not leisure, but time to take on another job. As to housework, they must still do all themselves. Thus instead of having turned every maid into a housewife, progress seems to have turned every housewife into a maid.

And workers seem to have fared only outwardly better. True, they have record incomes and record quantities of goods to spend them on. But if all is taken into account, can they really be said to be better off than workers of earlier times? They can write and read. But what is their main literature? The funnies? They can send their children to college. But what has college education become under the levelling impact of intellectual mass production made necessary by the unprecedented numbers of those now able to afford it? Though the greater number of students has produced an ampler supply of professors, the very increase in teaching personnel has paradoxically become one of the principal causes not for the improvement but for the lowering of the level of academic offerings. As one of my colleagues, anxious to keep track of every development in his field, complained: 'I read journals day and night. But so much is being written these days that I have no time left to do any thinking myself.' And what does the worker gain by the higher education of which we are so proud? Almost nothing. With so many other workers going to school, higher education, already intellectually sterile, seems without added material benefit, having become the competitive minimum requirement for almost any job.

And so it is, not only with many intangible, but also with many tangible commodities which progress has showered on us. To an increased extent they have assumed the character of *remedial* goods whose possession, instead of improving conditions, merely prevents them from becoming worse. They are like aspirin tablets, whose invention has certainly improved our headaches. But have they improved our health? Hardly, if one considers that the less hurried and less progressive earlier periods seemed, along with fewer aspirin tablets, to have suffered also from fewer headaches.

As a result, what has actually risen under the impact of the enormously increased production of our time is not so much the standard of living as the level of subsistence. We swim in more water, but we are still in it up to our necks. In addition, along with the rising water level, many who previously enjoyed the luxury of the dry shore are now up to their neck in water too. Thus the question is no longer whether we would be worse off without our supermodern electronic gadgets, our cars, radios, or television sets. They have become our swimming equipment. The question is whether without them many of us could still exist at all. In other words, it would seem that we must produce the bulk of our famous progress commodities in such record quantities not for the sake of progress but for the same reason earlier ages needed to produce much less: just to live.

Up to this point, the presentation of what might be called our 'aspirin stand-ard of living' has, perhaps, been too sweeping to be acceptable as more than at best an exaggerated generalization to be disproved once further economic growth will have accomplished the full transition to higher levels. I might not even be permitted to plead with Diogenes who used to say that he followed the example of the trainers of choruses; for they too set the note a little high, to ensure that the rest should hit the right note. But even if it should be granted that there is a grain of truth in my portrayal of existing conditions, what about the dazzling nature of an array of recent production and consumption figures which convey so irrefutably the opposite impression?

It is because of these legitimate question marks that the study of the problem put forward here cannot be confined to surface manifestations. Its analysis must go to its roots. In particular, the cause must be found to explain why, in the first place, the asserted decline of living standards is merely a phenomenon of transition but the corollary of the very economic growth producing our dazzling output figures; and, secondly, why these figures may be correct, and yet convey a wrong impression.

In a superb study on the interrelationship of growth and form, *On Growth and Form*, W.D'Arcy Thompson has shown why nature puts a stop to the growth of things once they have become large enough to fulfil their func-tion. A tooth stops growing when it can effectively bite and chew. If it grew larger, it would violate its function. It would impede the organism it is meant to strengthen. Similarly a snail, after having added a number of widening rings to the delicate structure of its shell, suddenly brings its building activities, to which it seems by now accustomed, to a stop. For, as D'Arcy Thompson points out, a single additional ring would increase the size of the shell sixteen times. Instead of adding to the welfare of the snail, it would burden it to such an extent that any increase in its productivity would henceforth have to be consumed by the task of coping with the added difficulties created by the extension of the shell beyond the limits set by its purpose. This consequence is all the more pronounced as, along with the geometric growth of the physical structure, the resulting problems seem to have the tendency of growing likewise at a geometric ratio while the ability of the snail to catch up with them might, after a point, at best increase at an arithmetic ratio.

This is the fundamental philosophic reason why all growth, so beneficial up to a certain point, becomes the principal cause of difficulty once it goes beyond it.

But nature has not confined the mechanism of growth to biological organisms. In particular it has extended it to social organisms such as cities or states. The only difference is that in the case of the latter, human intelligence and technological progress have dulled the instinct of nature with the effect that the social application of the principle has not been grasped with half the lucidity with which its physical or biological applications have been recognized. True, many social theorists have begun to castigate the Roman cardinals for continuing to insist in the age of exploding populations on undiminished population growth merely because during the Middle Ages, when growth control was declared sinful, the cardinals were as right as their dogma. Indeed, any less radical concept would then, in ages ravaged by death, have lead to the virtual extinction of the human race. But the same people who castigate the continued growth obsession of the Church as a reactionary hangover from the Middle Ages, consider the analogous growth obsession of the cardinals of modern economic and political thought as the last in progressive attitudes, though they advocate the same principle: continued emphasis on undiminished growth and expansion in the midst of multiplying signs all around them, that the problem is also in *their* field, no longer one of how to *foster* growth, but how to *stop* it.

For just as the size of a tooth or a snail's shell, so is the size of a city or a state in the last analysis determined by the function they are meant to fulfil. This function may have different aspects according to whether we are collectivists or individualists. However, since living standards are meaningful only from the viewpoint of the individual person, we may dismiss the collectivist aspect from this analysis. And as to the individualistic interpretation, we need but repeat our earlier reference to Aristotle's idea that the function of the state is to provide the individual citizen with the substance of the good life, the *summum bonum*.

In other words, once a society has become large enough to furnish the convivial, economic, political and cultural needs of its inhabitants in satisfactory, though not necessarily gluttonous, abundance—leisure to think, taverns to debate, churches to pray, universities to teach, theatres to inspire, the arts to enchant—further growth can no longer add to its basic purpose. We have reached the point of diminishing living standards. Its function-determined location was already spotted by Aristotle when he suggested as the best limit of the population of a state the largest number which suffices for the purposes of life, and which can be taken in at a single view.

This does not mean that the position of the optimum limit of society is rigid, rather is it subject to modification in proportion to our ability to enlarge our administrative vision. In antiquity or during the Middle Ages, the Aristotelian optimum was probably confined to cities and states containing between 20,000 and 500,000 inhabitants (whose entire voting citizenship fitted into a single theatre and could therefore at all times keep itself fully informed of the affairs of state by means of orators whose voices were capable of reaching the furthest seat). In our time, the three size extending factors—education, administrative integration, and technological development—particularly in the field of communication—have enlarged this limit to include populations of perhaps ten to fifteen millions. But wherever the point of diminishing living standards may now lie, it is located within the relatively narrow boundaries set by human stature—by what we can take in at a single view. Once this point is passed, further growth of a community will add not to its individualistic function of providing a good life but to the collectivist function of maintaining itself for its own reason. And the individual, instead of being assisted by social growth, will henceforth be impeded by it.

Ancient Greece—which, with its emphasis on the individualistic purpose of existence, has given us the basic principle of our civilization—had its political instincts finely attuned to the question of optimum social size. As a result, whenever a state reached the point of diminishing living standards, something like this would happen. A delegation would be sent to the Delphic Oracle and, after the rendering of due sacrifices and the deposition of appropriate gifts, Apollo, through the mouth of his priestess, would communicate the following advice: Cut down trees in the forest, build ships, man them with your young men and women, then send them forth to found new cities across the seas. There growth could set in anew until the maturing societies could produce once again in creative competition with mother and sister lands the prerequisites of a good life—inns, theatres, universities.

In our time, however, the Greek way is no longer so easy to duplicate, considering that the world's supply of available territory has in the meantime nearly come to an end. As a result, human societies, instead of growing in the biological way of splitting and multiplying, have long begun to grow by unification and integration. Instead of becoming more numerous in order to keep the size of the state adjusted to the stature of man, they have become fewer and larger.

At first, this process did not greatly interfere with the continued development of higher personal levels of living, for the simultaneous advance of technology, accompanied in addition by improvements in techniques of social administration, made it possible for a time to keep abreast of the rapidly multiplying problems of unrestrained social growth. But with no *biological* law to check continued *social* growth, and with political instincts deteriorating in proportion as social complexes became larger and more difficult to encompass, the limit had sooner or later to be reached at which the different growth ratios governing social problems and human talent became caught in the same insoluble discrepancy which Thomas Malthus has assigned to the relationship between increasing populations and food supply. For, as in the case of a shell, once optimum size was exceeded, each arithmetic increase in the size of the community tended to produce a geometric increase in the magnitude and number of the community's problems, without being able to furnish a corresponding increase in technological facilities and administrative talent to keep up with them. Not even Oxford or Harvard could compensate for the pace at which, beyond a given social development stage, problems began to outrace their solutions.

There was only one way left by which, at least temporarily, the overgrowing political complexes of our time could be spared disintegration under the impact of their increasing growth problems. This was by reducing the share of the citizen's production which previously could be retained by him to serve his own *summum bonum*, and making it available instead to a government whose powers had to be increased in proportion as human administrative talent fell behind. The new *summum bonum* was therefore no longer that of the citizen but that of society as a whole, with the paradoxical result that, the more splendid the social apparatus became after having outgrown the form and size best suited for sheltering the individual, the poorer became the individual. The more he or she produced the less could be left for his or her personal enjoyment. For states are like skyscrapers. The taller they become, the larger becomes the *social* space (occupied by lifts, stairs, etc.) necessary for keeping the structure serviced, and the smaller becomes the *personal* space available for individual purposes. In the end, if a building were to rise on the area of a city block to a height of 400 floors, there would be no office or living space left at all since, as architects have calculated, the entire structure would then have to be occupied by lifts in order to transport the people who could live in it if the lifts had not pushed them out.

So much for the philosophical argument. It explains why the experience of a declining living standard felt by so many citizens of the seemingly most advanced and powerful societies is not a phenomenon to be conquered by further growth, but a phenomenon of growth which is aggravated by it. And it explains why the rate at which living standards decline varies from country to country. What was stated with particular reference to great powers such as the United States or Great Britain, is not half as manifest in smaller powers such as Canada. In fact, in the case of the latter, the descent to lower levels might be averted altogether if Canada should put a stop to the growth of her society before it exceeds the boundaries of optimum development. And it need not at all apply to such happy, smaller states as Switzerland, Iceland, or Denmark, whose narrow political boundaries automatically ensure optimum size as long as these countries resist the lures and dangers of unification.

But what about the figures? For, the philosophic deductions to the contrary, these show not only an increase of net national product proportionate to the increasing size and needs of great powers, but also an increase in national income and national consumer expenditures. And they still show these increases to a dramatic extent on a per capita basis, and after rising price levels and population changes have been taken into account. As a result it would appear that, though beyond a certain point of social expansion a continuously rising proportion of increasing national output may have to be diverted to the support of society as a whole, enough is left also to improve, even if only at a declining rate, the position of the individual.

And yet, in spite of the dramatic rise particularly in the field of per capita consumption, the portrait of improvement conveyed by it is highly misleading. Not that the figures are wrong, by any means. The error arises from the fact that they are not broken down into more significant and revealing categories. For not all consumer goods can be included in living standard computations. Many of them must actually be subtracted if they are to give proper information, since their increased consumption measures our multiplying complexities rather than our advance in well being.

A more realistic picture of living standards depends therefore on a new commodity breakdown. In the first place, we must distinguish between two general categories of goods: *social* and *personal* consumer goods. Social consumer goods—goods consumed by society to maintain its political and economic apparatus, and represented by government expenditures at all levels as well as by a large proportion of private investment expenditures—may, however, be largely discounted in this analysis since they measure not personal but social standards. In addition, being largely paid for by taxes, they are so clearly identifiable as not the fruit but the cost of existence that there is no danger of having their greater availability confused with greater welfare. Nevertheless they are indirectly of significance since their seemingly geometric rise with every arithmetic increase in the size of a state is responsible for the declining proportion of increasing output that can be diverted into personal channels. Since their ratio of increase depends on the increasing size and power of societies, social consumer goods might also be called *growth* or *power* commodities. They are remedial in nature. Their hallmark is that their production does not improve the status of the individuals producing them. Examples of such commodities are general government services needed to administer increases in power, safety, traffic, and police services; and particularly military expenditures whose geometric relationship to social size is clearly indicated if we compare, for example, the defence figures of various countries according to their size. The production increase accomplished by the United States between 1950 and 1951 in the area of power commodities alone, as expressed in government expenditures, amounted to no less than eighteen billion dollars, or seventy-two per cent of the much advertised twenty-five billion increase of the total national product of the same period. This means that nearly three fourths of the fruits of the production increase was consumed by the unparalleled needs of power.

The most important category of commodities for a living standard analysis is, however, the category of personal consumer goods. For if the latter registers an increase on a per capita basis, it becomes possible theoretically at least, to deduce that the standard of living has also risen. But even then the conclusion is not automatic, since greater personal consumption is not necessarily a sign of better living. If changed social conditions force a person to walk twice as far to work, the availability of a second pair of shoes can hardly be said to have made him or her any richer.

As a result, if we are to bring the problem into its proper focus, it is necessary to resort to a further breakdown of personal consumer goods into the well-known sub-categories of *necessities* and *luxuries*. But since the increase in necessary consumption merely reflects an increase in our needs, the only truly relevant category for living standard appraisals is that of *luxury commodities*. In other words, the goods measuring our welfare are therefore not goods within the subsistence level, but the changing quantities of goods available to us above it.

But here the principal difficulty sets in. For, what are luxuries? Mathematically, the answer would be simple. Luxuries are total personal consumer goods minus necessities, just as luxury consumption is total personal consumption minus subsistence level consumption. But mathematics does not tell us what is meant by subsistence level. For just as it cannot define the concept of luxury, so it cannot define the concept of necessity.

Where mathematics fails, however, logic may succeed. All that is needed to discern the elusive boundary between luxuries and necessities is to carry the process of categorization one step further. For necessities can again be subdivided into three kinds, two of them long familiar. In the first place, there are the biological necessities, such as food, clothes and shelter. Without them, physical survival is impossible. Secondly, there are the *cultural* necessities imposed by social environment, such as the *style* of food, clothes, and shelter. An example of the former, would be a coat or a raw chicken, of the latter a tie or a cooked meal. As writers such as Petty, Ricardo, Marx, Pigou, or Heller have pointed out, it is due to the changing nature of the second category that the socially imposed subsistence level may be pushed upwards, and that consumption may rise above biological requirements, without indicating a rise in living standards.

But there is a heretofore neglected third category whose existence explains why consumption may rise above both biological and cultural necessities, and still not entail a rise in living standards. The necessities of this third category, resulting from the technological difficulties caused by the scale and density of modern life, might be called *technological* necessities or *density commodities*. And these have become the most significant of all. For while cultural necessities were responsible for introducing the concept of a rising subsistence level, density commodities are responsible for the acceleration of that rise. It is primarily due to them that, in spite of the increase in overall consumption, the subsistence line, beyond which luxurious ease sets in, is constantly receding, and that the luxury margin, in spite of increased overall production, is constantly diminishing.

Typical examples of density commodities which, in contrast to the aforementioned power commodities, swell our personal consumption figures without adding to our welfare are: drivers' licences, signal lights on cars, urban parking space, commuter services, a large part of what *Punch* has called *stimulants for self,* not all but a major proportion of privately purchased legal and medical services, or replacement goods for wear and losses such as would never have occurred in less harassed smaller societies. To have an idea of the magnitude of the increasing consumption of unwanted density commodities, we need but bring a few facts before our eyes. Replacements rendered necessary in 1950 as a result of fire losses in the United States for example, amounted to almost $700,000,000. Those caused by the nine million casualties of the same year—of which 35,000 were fatal car accidents, more than the loss of life incurred in many a major war—to $700,000,000. Private medical costs amounted in 1953 to $10,200,000,000, though not all of them can be classified as density expenditures. And the annual repair work resulting from driving cars in the dense streets of the City of New York was reputedly in excess of one billion dollars at a time when the entire budget of the State of New York, the largest of the union, was still below that figure.

As a result of the preceding considerations it seems clear that the existing method of evaluating living standard changes has lost much of its usefulness. It was satisfactory as long as societies were within optimum size. Up till then, additional economic growth meant indeed that much of the new product could be made available for increased personal consumption not only within but also above the subsistence level. Once they developed beyond optimum to critical size, however, increased consumption ceased to reflect changes in living standard levels. It could now be just as well a sign of worsening as of improving conditions. If we are to obtain a correct picture of our wellbeing, a new measure must therefore be developed which emphasizes changes not in total consumption but in luxury consumption. For only changes in the latter reveal with precision whether we move upwards or downwards. Since it is luxuries which really count, the new living standard measure might therefore, in analogy to a thermometer, be called a *luxometer*. Relevant changes would be expressed in degrees of *luxes* rather than in percentages, a *lux* representing a unit of above subsistence level consumption.

But to arrive at a workable concept of luxury, it is important, we have seen, to subtract from total consumption not only biological and cultural necessities, but above all, the heretofore neglected category of technological necessities or *density commodities*. Unlike the other two categories, which are both needed and desired, they exert an undisguised depressing effect since they are needed without being desired. The only difficulty is one of definition. For most density commodities such as travel services, cars, or *stimulants for self,* set out as luxuries before social overgrowth transforms them into headache-producing necessities. And, depending on the density, integration, and technological development of a society, the transition from the one to the other category may take place at quite different times. A car may be a necessity for one region and a luxury in another, even within the same country. However, just as zoologists have no difficulty discerning when a caterpillar becomes a butterfly, so economists, psychologists, and statisticians should have no difficulty discerning the time and place at which goods turn from luxuries into necessities.

Once density commodities are properly evaluated, and a new breakdown of consumer expenditures on lines suggested in these pages is adopted, an entirely different picture of living standards will emerge. We may then be able to tell that, while consumption may have increased by, let us say ten per cent, our living standard may at the same time have declined by three *luxes*. Moreover, we shall be able to discover not only the functional but also the exact economic location of the point of diminishing living standards. It is reached whenever subsistence level consumption begins to rise faster than total personal consumption, or when *percentage* changes of personal consumption begin to move inversely with changes in *luxes*.

But will this not destroy many an illusion? Undoubtedly. This should however not deter us from introducing a new method of measurement. For once it provides us with facts instead of illusions, we may turn it to good account. Being able to discover a community's point of diminishing living standards, we shall be in a position to call a halt to further development instead of pushing it over the crest. This does not mean that stagnation should be cultivated. It merely means that, beyond that point, growth should be fostered along ancient Greek lines, in the biological way, through splitting, multiplication, duplication, not through integration or unification—the great modern ideals.

In a country like Canada, still endowed with vast unexploited regions, the conditions for such a development of growth without the danger of depressing living standards are still great. A tool such as the luxometer would therefore be a highly useful instrument, helping to determine when optimum size is reached in a given province, and when subdivision should take place. In countries such as most of the world's great powers, where the point of diminishing standards has apparently already been passed, the road of regional rather than centralized development, with the possibility of another era of rising levels, would be more difficult to pursue, since ingrained trends of thought have for too long stressed that salvation lies in the opposite direction.

But even there, the luxometer should prove a useful tool. For in spite of their love of integration, even the great powers have shown signs of awakening to the deeper designs of nature. Their giant firms have begun in some cases to abandon their monolithic structures in favour of smaller regional development. Co-operative enterprises have gained ground with their emphasis on local rather than national or world markets, and decentralization has again become a respectable slogan.

This indicates that great powers themselves have become mindful that union and integration are not the answer to everything. But there is as yet no firm policy behind their groping since, in the absence of a sharper analytical tool, the connection between growing social size and declining living standards is still far from being properly understood. The new measure would bring this into the open. But while it might not enable the great powers to move back to a position of rising standards, the information gained by it might lead to patterns of economic and political organization which could at least prevent further deterioration.

November/December 1966

Insane Work Cannot Produce a Sane Society

E. F. SCHUMACHER

'DANTE, WHEN COMPOSING HIS VISIONS OF HELL, might well have included the mindless, repetitive boredom of working on a factory assembly line. It destroys initiative and rots brains, yet millions of British workers are committed to it for most of their lives.'

The remarkable thing is that the above statement in *The Times*, like countless similar ones made before it, aroused no interest: there were no hot denials or anguished agreements; no reactions at all. The strong and terrible words—visions of hell; mindless, repetitive boredom; destroying initiative and rotting brains; millions of British workers, committed for most of their lives —attracted no reprimand that they were mis-statements or over-statements, that they were irresponsible or hysterical exaggerations or subversive propaganda. No, people read them, sighed and nodded, I suppose, and moved on.

Not even the ecologists, the conservationists, the doom-watchers and warners are interested in this matter. If someone had asserted that certain man-made arrangements destroyed the initiative and rotted the brains of millions of birds, or seals, or wild animals in the game reserves of Africa, such an assertion would have been either refuted or taken as a serious challenge. If someone had asserted that not the minds or souls or brains of millions of British workers were being 'rotted' but their bodies, again there would have been considerable interest; after all, there are safety regulations, inspectorates, claims for damages, and so forth. No management is unaware of its duty to avoid accidents or physical conditions which impair workers' health. But workers' brains, minds and souls are a different matter.

A semi-official report, published by Her Majesty's Stationery Office, bears the title *Pollution: Nuisance or Nemesis*. It contains no reference to man-made arrangements which destroy the initiative and rot the brains of millions of workers. Nor, indeed, would any reader even expect such references. We expect and find learned discussions of 'Some harmful pollutants'—DDT and PCB, metals, phosphates and nitrates, sulphur dioxide, etc.—and warnings of the modern perils—cancers, birth defects and mutations, that is all. We may fully share the authors' concluding hope when they say: 'We hope that society will be educated and informed . . . so that pollution may be brought under control and mankind's population and consumption of resources be steered towards a permanent and sustainable equilibrium. Unless this is done sooner or later—and some believe there is little time left—the downfall of civilization will not be a matter of science fiction. It will be the experience of our children or grandchildren.'

But it would hardly occur to the average reader that the destruction of initiative and the rotting of brains of millions of workers could be classed as the worst pollution of all, the greatest peril, and the most important danger for something to be done about to avoid the 'downfall of civilization'.

If it is thought that it may be a bit farfetched to deal with the rotting of brains under the heading of pollution, it will perhaps not be considered unreasonable to look for a treatment of this subject under the heading of *Natural Resources: Sinews for Survival* which is the title of a companion volume, also published by Her Majesty's Stationery Office. The most important of all resources is obviously the initiative, imagination and brain power of human beings. We all know this and are ready to devote very substantial funds to what we call education. So, if the problem is 'survival', one might fairly expect to find some discussion relating to the preservation and, if possible, the development of the most precious of all natural resources, human brains. However, such expectations are not fulfilled. *Sinews for Survival* deals with all the natural factors—minerals, energy, water, wildlife and so forth—but not at all with such immaterial resources as initiative, intelligence and brainpower.

Similarly, I might refer to the international report on *The Limits to Growth* prepared for the Club of Rome's project on the global predicament. This report caused a world-wide stir because it purported to demonstrate, with the help of a computerized world-model, that growth along the established lines cannot now continue for long without leading to inescapable breakdown. The authors therefore plead for policies which would lead to 'a desirable, sustainable state of global equilibrium'. They believe that 'much more information is needed to manage the transition to global equilibrium . . . The most glaring deficiencies in present knowledge occur in the pollution sector of the model . . . How long does it take for a given pollutant to travel from its point of release to its point of entrance into the human body?'

There is, here again, no reference to pollutants entering the human mind or soul. But the report does say this: 'The final, most elusive, and most important information we need deals with human values. As soon as society recognizes that it cannot maximize everything for everyone, it must begin to make choices. Should there be more people or more wealth, more wilderness or more automobiles, more food for the poor or more services for the rich?' We might say: what a collection of choices! Even in connection with 'human values' a choice affecting the rotting of human minds or brains finds no mention. And this is yet another example of the lack of interest in the vital question of human work and what the work does to the worker.

Considering the centrality of work in human life, one might have expected that every textbook on economics, sociology, politics and related subjects would present a theory of work as one of the indispensable foundation stones for all further expositions. After all, it is work which occupies most of the energies of the human race, and what people actually *do* is normally more important, for understanding them, than what they say, or what they spend their money on, or what they own, or how they vote. A person's work is unquestionably one of the most important formative influences on their character and personality.

However, the truth of the matter is that we look in vain for such presentations of theories of work in these textbooks. The question of what the work does to the worker is hardly ever asked, not to mention the question of whether the real task might not be to adapt the work to the needs of the worker rather than demanding of the worker to adapt to the needs of the work—which means, of course, primarily: to the needs of the machine.

It is not as if there were any lack of studies and reports on productivity, on workers' morale, workers' participation in management, and so forth. But they do not seem to germinate any fundamentally new thinking; they do not raise questions about the validity or sanity of a *system* which destroys initiative and rots brains. They all—although in varying degree—start from the implicit assumption that the *kind* or *quality* of work to be done in society is simply what it is: somebody has to do it; if it is soul-destroying work, that is regrettable but unalterable; if people do not like doing it, we pay them more and more until enough people like the money more than they dislike the work. But, of course, this economic solution of the problem—paying what the law of supply and demand prescribes—is no solution from our point of view; some people, as St Augustine observed, even take pleasure in deformities, and many are prepared—or they are forced—to ruin themselves for money. We are concerned with the fact that our system of production, in many of its parts, is such that it destroys initiative and rots brains, and inflicts this damage not on a few people by way of exception, but on millions of them by way of everyday routine. Why men or women tolerate it and accept it against pecuniary compensation is quite a different question.

We may remind ourselves of the teaching of the Church in this connection. 'No man,' said Pope Leo XIII 'may with impunity outrage that human dignity which God himself treats with great reverence, nor stand in the way of that higher life which is the preparation for the eternal life of heaven. Nay, more; no man has in this matter power over himself. To consent to any treatment which is calculated to defeat the end and purpose of his being is beyond his right; he cannot give up his soul to servitude; for it is not man's own rights which are here in question, but the rights of God, the most sacred and inviolable of rights.'

Let us ask then: How does work relate to the end and purpose of our being? It has been universally recognized, in all authentic teachings, that every human being born into this world has to work not merely to keep him or herself alive but to strive towards perfection. 'Be ye therefore perfect, even as your Father which is in heaven is perfect.' To stay alive, we need various goods and services, which will not be forthcoming without human labour. To perfect ourselves, we need purposeful activity in accordance with the injunction, 'Whichever gift each of you may have received, use it in service to one another, like good stewards dispensing the grace of God in its varied forms.'

From this, we may derive the three purposes of human work as follows:

First: to provide society with the goods and services which are necessary or useful to it;

Second: to enable every one of us to use and thereby perfect our gifts like good stewards; and

Third: to do so in service to, and in co-operation with, others, so as to liberate ourselves from our in-born egocentricity.

This three-fold function makes work so central to human life that it is truly impossible to conceive of life at the human level without work, which the Church declares, 'even after original sin, was decreed by Providence, for the good of man's body and soul'.

The kind and quality of work to be done is implicitly taken as given; somebody has to do it whether we like it or not. The time has come to question this implicit assumption and to attack this immobilism. Mindless work is as intolerable in a society that wishes to be sane and civilized as filthy air or stinking water, nay, it is even more intolerable. Why can't we set new tasks to our scientists and engineers, our chemists and technologists, many of whom are becoming increasingly doubtful about the *human relevance* of their own work? Has the affluent society nothing to spare for anything really new? Is 'bigger, faster, richer' still the only line of development we can conceive, when we know that it entails the perversion of human work so that, as one of the Popes put it, 'from the factory dead matter goes out improved, whereas men there are corrupted and degraded', and that it also entails environmental degradation and the speedy exhaustion of the earth's non-renewable resources? Could we not devote at least a small fraction of our research and development efforts to create what might be called a technology with a human face?

This 'human face' would reflect, to start with, in a certain way, the size of the human being: in other words, we should explore whether at least some organizations and some machines could not be made small enough to suit the human scale. Countless people long for a chance to become their own masters, independent and self-reliant—which they cannot become unless it is possible to be efficient on a small scale. Where is the small scale equipment, where are the mini-plants to give a chance to the people who can and want to stand on their own feet?

People say: it can't be done; small scale is uneconomic. How do they know? While the idea that 'bigger is better' may have been a nineteenth-century truth, now, owing to the advance of knowledge and technical ability, it has become—not all along the line, but over wide fields of application—a twentieth-century myth.

I have in mind, as an example, a production unit developed by the Intermediate Technology Development Group which costs around £5,000. The smallest unit previously available cost £250,000, fifty times as much, and had a capacity about fifty times as great. The makers of this large-scale unit were completely convinced that any smaller unit would be hopelessly uneconomic. But they were wrong. Think of it: instead of one unit requiring for its efficient operation a vast and complicated organization, we can now have fifty units, each of them 'on the human scale', each of them large enough for a few enterprising people to make an honest living, but none of them so large as to make anyone inordinately rich. Think of the simplification of transport if there can be many small units instead of one large one, each of them drawing on local raw materials and working for nearby local markets. Think of the social and individual human consequences of such a change of scale.

Admittedly, this kind of work was initially undertaken solely with a view to helping the developing countries where, on account of poverty, markets are small, unemployment is high, capital is scarce, and transport is generally difficult and expensive. But it quickly became apparent that the results of this work were of equal interest to many communities in the overdeveloped countries, because everywhere there are innumerable people who are excluded from the productive process in a validly human sense because organizations, capital requirements and machines have become so big that only people already very rich and powerful can get hold of them and all the others can merely be what might be called 'technological gap-fillers'.

A technology with a human face would not only favour smallness as against the current giantism; it would also favour simplicity over complexity. It is, of course, much more difficult to make things relatively simple again than to make them ever more complicated. I am not talking about the simple life as such—although there is much to be said in its favour: I am talking about processes of production, distribution and exchange, as well as about the design of products. Complexity, in itself often the result of excessive size and the excessive elimination of the human factor, demands a degree of specialization and division of labour which all too often kills the human content of work and makes people too specialized to be able to attain wisdom. It must therefore be seen as an evil, and it is the task of human intelligence—of R. & D. in the industrial context—to minimize this evil, not to let it proliferate.

All this, I believe, hangs together. All related to the human scale, all related to the humanization of human work, all conducive to the re-integration of the human being into the production process, so that he or she can feel alive, creative, happy—in short, a real person—even while they are working for their living.

If one thing stares us in the face, it is that insane work cannot produce a sane society. There is no reason to believe that today, with so much knowledge, so brilliant a science, and such astounding technological skills at our disposal, we should be incapable of extending the joy of creative productive work to those millions of people who are at present deprived of it.

A sane society cannot emerge if, as Paul Goodman called it, millions of youngsters are 'growing up absurd'; or if millions of men and women are condemned, most of their lives, to do work which destroys their initiative and rots their brains; or, indeed, if all—or most of—useful, productive, creative work is handed over to machines controlled by giant corporations, while people —real living people—are told to find their fulfilment in leisure activities.

May/June 1974

Think Globally, Act Locally

HAZEL HENDERSON

FUTURISM AND ITS GROWING ACCEPTANCE does imply this darker interpretation. The societies that embrace it are often those most rigidly enmeshed in past structures based on successful prior adaptations to past conditions and environments. There is an inevitable trade-off in evolution between adaptation and adaptability. Past success constrains future success. This is evolution's most interesting challenging riddle at many biological levels, culminating in that of human societies: growth creates structure, then structure inhibits growth. Nothing fails like success. Anthropologists would state it as the Law of the Retarding Lead: those cultures most successfully adapted to the past and present will be overtaken by those less committed and over-specialized. Religious views would restate the same proposition as The Last Shall Be First. However these concepts are stated, it is clear that a massive evolutionary shift is underway, based on a radically new set of environmental and resource conditions, and that these conditions are driving human societies into domestic transitions and a new configuration of global order. This New World Order is inevitable, even if the keepers of the old order in their fear of change and loss of their own power, try to stem the tide of change by means of violence and nuclear war.

Today we see the maturing industrial societies of the Northern Hemisphere caught in this oldest evolutionary trap, having developed socio-technical configurations superbly adapted to past conditions of vast, unexploited fossil fuel and raw material deposits and fertile or sparsely-populated lands. Today as countries such as Brazil try to emulate their specifically historic growth pattern, these older industrial societies of the North, whether capitalist, socialist or mixed, are in shock. They are almost totally unprepared for the rapid adaptations they must now make to survive in today's new environment and global resource conditions. We see vivid examples in the efforts to shore up sagging resource-intensive industries such as the automobile sectors of the US and British economies, while blaming the Japanese for making lighter more fuel-efficient cars. Similarly, the leaders of these stressed industrial societies urge each other to conserve energy or 'reflate' their economies to blow more air into the speculative bubble of undifferentiated GNP-measured economic growth. Leaders all sound alike in their expansionist, productivist approaches, re-doubling their efforts to play the old game, rather than reconceptualizing or rethinking their situation and redefining their problems and goals accordingly.

In most mixed industrial economies, there are two major parties offering a narrow, linear polarity of macro-economic 'management' policies. On what is called 'the right', there are parties, whatever their names, Republicans, Liberals, Conservatives, sympathetic to business and investors, who have their monetarists who know how to create recessions. On 'the left', there are parties, whether called Democrats, Labour, Socialist, sympathetic to labour and consumers. They have their Keynesians who know how to print money. Today neither will work, and the one-dimensional discipline of economics must give way to an era of post-economic decision-making, where policies are based on multi-dimensional, inter-disciplinary approaches and far broader public participation of all groups and perspectives in society to provide corrective feedback and 'feed-forward'.

Today we see fearful evidence that the leaders of these crisis-ridden industrial societies, instead of accommodating the necessary feedback and opening up their societies to adapt to changes, are rigidifying and redoubling their efforts to shore up their crumbling sectors and no-longer viable institutions by trying to augment the already unresponsive cumbersome machinery of centralized control. The crises of industrialism range from malfunctioning dinosaur technologies, bureaucratized decision-making, paralysis of over-centralization, information-handling bottlenecks, collapsing monetary and trading systems, proliferating pollution, domestic unrest, inadvertent weather and climate modification, overfished poisoned waters, vanishing agricultural land, loss of productivity and increasing vulnerability due to resource-dependencies. All this has culminated in increasing militaristic confrontations over resources and the now obvious instability of the existing international system based on the contradiction of mutual deterrence, polarization of the USA and the USSR based on nineteenth century ideological conflict between communism and capitalism (both now better seen as forms of industrialism itself). It is now clear that such an international system based on the institutionalized mistrust between competitive, expansionist, patriarchal nation-states and their mutual threats and machismo technologies can no longer operate on a finite interdependent, crowded planet.

One of the best indications of a generalized, systemic crisis is that continuing to apply conventional control mechanisms only makes matters worse, as for example when the traditional stop-go remedies of the monetarist and Keynesian economic planners leave industrial societies exhausted and 'stag-flated' with ever more pernicious unemployment. Even the question, 'Where is the new Keynes?' is wrongly posed, since the remedies lie beyond the discipline of economics. Today, we see many other instances where re-doubling old efforts and applying old mechanisms simply exacerbates old problems while leading to a score of new ones, as evidenced with our 'add-on' technological fixes. As Fritz Schumacher used to say, 'industrial societies now need a break-through a day to keep the crisis at bay.'

Take energy policies in most northern hemisphere countries. While paying much lip service to conservation, most are re-doubling their efforts to increase supplies of *non*-renewable energy, rather than reconceptualize their situation as one of energy and resource over-dependence, and address the real issues of redesigning their industrial processes and infrastructure for vastly greater thermodynamic efficiency, while committing their investments to an orderly transition to economies based on renewable resources managed for sustained-yield, long-term productivity. Instead of embracing and capitalizing on the inevitable dawning of a new solar age, most countries are still hurling their precious capital, research and development funds and human resources into yet another costly detour into non-renewable energy technologies. The Soviet Union, France, Germany and Britain are still backing into a nuclear future, looking through the rear-view mirror while the USA, its nuclear programmes stalled by wary Wall Street investors and insurance companies, has now committed $20 billion tax-funds into a wasteful, inept boondoggle in synthetic fuels from coal.

Meanwhile the so-called less-developed countries of the world's sunbelt are free to leapfrog the unsustainable technologies and proceed straight to the solar age. I recently attended the World Association for the Study of Social Prospects (Association Mondiale de Prospective Sociale) conference in Dakar, Senegal, where there was much discussion of these multiple crises of the industrial countries, as well as predictions that the next stage would be their stepped-up efforts to export all these crises to the Third World. If German, French and American citizens prefer safer, renewable energy to nuclear fission, then the electric power industry would step up its sales efforts in Brazil, the Philippines and Pakistan. If Americans are up in arms about toxic chemical dumps, such as that in Love Canal, New York, then the wastes must be dumped in Africa.

The case is even clearer in 'national security' policies where mutual deterrence depends on military threat, brinkmanship, posturing and confrontation. Continuing to apply these old mechanisms to maintain even an uneasy cold-war situation is clearly MAD (the acronym for mutually assured destruction), since deterrence is based on threat, which in turn, is only believable if occasionally carried out. But even short of war, these old-fashioned threat-systems of control are now simply bankrupting the countries that employ them, while their attempts to mitigate their own economic depletion by exporting weapons only spreads bankruptcy to other countries enmeshed in this global no-win power game.

The sales of military equipment in 1979 amounted to some $120 billion, larger than the national incomes of all but ten nations in the world, while US plans to build the ridiculously ill-conceived MX missile system will add several percentage points to its inflation rate, while forgoing a concomitantly inflation-reducing, fuel-efficient, mass-transit alternative that would provide transport for thirty-five million people daily, reducing dependence on imported oil. So much for 'national security'. In such cases, we see further indications of systemic crisis in that applications of old control mechanisms interact to create such vicious circles as the tragic interaction of energy and military policies. Thus the focus on energy *supply* rather than addressing the structure of *demand* creates similarly tragic absurdities, such as US threats to defend 'our' oil lifeline in the Mid-East, militarily if 'necessary', but at the cost of exacerbating domestic conflict by re-instating the military draft. Not surprisingly, a whole generation of young Americans, inculcated by advertising with the belief that their patriotic duty consisted of little more than buying a car to 'See the USA in Your Chevrolet', voiced misgivings and protest at the idea of fighting a war to preserve their parents' right to drive large cars and vacation in air-conditioned motor-homes. The most obvious contradiction in all this is the even more tragic absurdity that fighting wars over energy supplies wastes even more energy.

All human societies and other living species, for that matter, sustain themselves by taking ordered, low-entropy resources from their environments and discarding higher-entropy wastes. Thus all our extractions, production, consumption and recycling processes are entropic, and their true efficiency is best measured by their success at minimizing these rates of entropy and are better accounted in thermodynamic terms than by economics. In fact, the economists' mystification 'inflation' merely represents all the variables left out of economic models coming back to haunt us, and a good chunk of industrial economies' persistent inflation is the thermodynamic errors that economic models of efficiency encourage. Thus another symptom of the evolutionary bind of industrial countries is that all their redoubled efforts to continue on the historic course simply increase their inflation rates, since these resource-dependent societies are simply encountering the boundary conditions of the laws of thermodynamics. The harder they struggle, the deeper they will fall into the thermodynamic sink they prefer to call 'inflation'. Thus the contradictions of industrialism itself are now visible: the obsession with controlling and manipulating nature, exploiting resources in search of elusive 'security' and 'equilibrium' through managing ever more of the variables of human existence, together with frantic efforts to predict and reduce the fear of uncertainty—even though certainty and equilibrium are precise descriptions of death!

Paradoxically, these goals of 'certainty' and 'security' are pursued with ever-more desperate, destabilizing and violent technological means—all psychotically masked in the languaging of denial, reversal and projection: war is peace; big brother bureaucracies and corporations love us and take care of us; the proliferation of nuclear warheads is for our greater security—just as George Orwell warned us in his classic work of futurism, *1984*.

The most helpful model is that of the biological process of morphogenesis, extremely common in nature: the process, for example, by which a chrysalis turns into a butterfly. This kind of model of change allows us to see both the breaking down of old structures and the generation of new, often radically different structures occurring simultaneously. Other characteristics of morphogenetic change are that it is systemic, affecting all parts of the system in transformations, and that these processes of change accelerate, governed by exponential, positive feedbacks which amplify the changes and push the systems over thresholds into new states and structural forms.

This global metamorphosis can be seen in the altering of the Earth's atmosphere with increasing carbon dioxide levels, the mostly man-made changes in lands, oceans, forests as well as the swiftly changing, unmanageable societies of human beings, their technologies and values. In a real sense the whole world has changed, even in the past two years—once invincible dictators have toppled, leaders are confused and drowning in fragmented, useless data; hierarchies have become unmanageable; technologies backfire unpredictably and great nations are challenged from within by demands for ethnic, regional, cultural and political autonomy. Many decision-makers begin to generalize their own sense of loss of control, even panic, to the rest of us. But it is not the sky that is falling, it is they who are falling from their shaky pinnacles atop crumbling, unsustainable institutions. In times of rapid change, individuals learn faster than institutions, and it is always the dinosaur's brain that is the last to get the new message.

Order and chaos are two sides of the same coin, and imply an observer. For example the crises in the world monetary system look very different to a banker in New York or Zürich than a finance minister of a Third World country heavily in debt. However, like most other tightly-linked systems in our crowded, interdependent world, the monetary system is so delicately interwoven (nothing more than an information system operating globally at computerized speed) that it *requires* co-operation, as it is enmeshed in its own feedback. Although the rules of the game were set by industrial countries, they have now transformed the system with their own technology and belief in endless paper profit, which flouts the basic laws of physics and commonsense. Multinational companies can make more paper profits by trading currencies than by putting up a real factory to produce real goods in the real world, while private investors look for ever higher paper returns or flee to gold.

Those who live by the monetary illusion may die by the monetary illusion, since they have mistaken money symbols for real wealth. In such a chaotic system, any significant group of Third World debtor countries could bring the whole house of cards crashing down, by simply declaring bankruptcy together, reminding the bankers and financiers of a similar happening when Germany defaulted after the First World War. Thus, there already *is* a 'New International Economic Order', since the relationship between debtor and creditor countries is no longer hierarchical in reality, but one of mutual dependence—and only mutual respect and re-writing the rules to fit the new facts allow a peaceful evolution of the world's monetary and trading system. Thus the task is to correct the inequities and imbalances perpetuated on paper, and re-write the charter of all global monetary institutions to reflect full participation of all factors in all decision-making: debtors and creditors alike. Thus debtor countries now see their power to 'call the bluff' of those who have controlled the monetary system, by declaring that they will no longer play the game by an outmoded set of rules that have led to imbalances now verging on disaster for all players.

Thus we must call the bluff of many other keepers of the old order who cannot see what is being born. They say, in effect, 'we have created such a dangerously unstable system that you must keep us in power since only we know and can manage the dangers we have created.' Thus one can never expect new alternatives to emerge from dominant cultures and their elites. Those who see the new possibilities are usually from groups subordinated and manipulated by the conventional wisdom. This 'protection rule' logic of the keepers of the old order must at last be debunked, if we are to see beyond it and create alternative futures for human societies.

These alternative futures are already visible to the rest of us with little stake in the dinosaur industries and the government agencies that cater to them. In the painful birthpangs of global transition we see what is being born: the planetary societies of the new solar age, more communitarian and co-operative, based on sustainable technologies and renewable resources, on multiple leadership at all levels, on information-sharing and networking, on heterarchy (not hierarchy), firmly rooted in biological science and specific, regional ecological and cultural resources, all linked by pluralistic communications media, diverse patterns of regional co-operation, trade and exchange and regulated by global treaties and principles for the use of oceans, space and all common heritage resources, and for enforcement and peace-keeping.

As growing enclaves in Northern industrial societies are developing and spreading their concepts and activities (in what I have described as the emerging 'counter-economy', and others have called the 'informal economy', the 'dual economy', the 'household economy' and the 'convivial economy'), they look to the more balanced, traditional communities of the Third World for inspiration. Traditional, communitarian, village lifestyles and values have always been despised by the Eurocentric, industrial societies—viewed as 'inefficient' by both capitalists and Marxists. All fell under the spell of progress, 'efficiency' and monetization, the basic coefficient by which all was to be judged. Even today, economists ignore the fact that well over fifty per cent of all the world's production, consumption, maintenance and investment is not monetized, indeed, eighty per cent of all capital-formation is not monetized. Yet today the world's monetized systems are in shock precisely because they have ignored the basic rural, village, agricultural production sectors on which they have been parasitic. They have likewise cannibalized these co-operative, non-monetized sectors, destroying their very roots and the bedrock on which they rest. Today, then, we must ask 'Will the Real Economy Please Stand Up?'

Contrary to economists' beliefs, the informal sectors of the world's economies, in total, are predominant, and the institutionalized monetized sectors grow out of them and rest upon them, rather than the reverse. Even in the industrialized nations, this submerged and surprising reality can be documented—although the bias of economic statistics virtually precludes this type of analysis. In France, for example, a 1975 study calculated that while forty-three per cent of the total working hours of the French population were devoted to formal employment, fifty-seven per cent of the working hours were in the informal sector. While it is clearly necessary for any society to have both an institutional and an informal sector in its total economy, the danger has arisen in industrialism's focus on 'economic efficiency', measured by money and values derived thereby, that the overgrowth of the institut- ionalized sector has created huge imbalances which now threaten to destroy the informal sector which is the bedrock of all societies. This cannibalizing of the informal sectors, where the monetized sectors' social costs have been buried is most visible in the most 'advanced' industrial societies, and luckily is providing an important object lesson for other countries who want to avoid the same trap. Thus the task is that of re-balancing of societies so that informal sector values and functions are revived and restored, while the institutionalized economy and its money values are limited and put back in their place.

The drive for economic growth can be seen as a crucial vehicle for oppression, domination and exploitation, and not only of women, by designating house- hold, community and all co-operative work as low-status and unpaid and by its accompanying economic reasoning which abets the subordination of minor- ities in all countries by designating vital but non-specialized, non-academic, non-bureaucratic work as 'less productive'. Similarly the economically power- ful countries can dominate and downgrade the role in the world economy of so-called 'less developed' countries, and justify the role of multi-national corporations and capital investment, as well as the world trade game they have designed under the guise of the 'free market system'.

A re-balancing of the dual economies in societies is really the only way to reduce centralism, big-brotherism, bureaucracies, mindless hierarchies and bottlenecks, as well as the accumulations of power and wealth they always cre- ate—which in turn, have always led to expansionism, institutional aggrandize- ment, military adventures, technological mischief, fantasies of omnipotence and control, and the inevitable exploitation of subordinated groups and the environment. Such clearly-achievable re-structuring of the patriarchal ordering of societies could defuse these dangerous imbalances.

To devise workable ethics for the solar age will require that we begin the co-operative, global task of inventorying all of the world's value-systems, religious beliefs and cultures, past and present, assessing these behavioural outputs and hardware configurations they produce. In this task we will come to appreciate that human value-systems are resources, just as real as coal or oil; highly-sophisticated regulatory mechanisms that put governments' cum- bersome, overt regulatory efforts to shame. Similarly we see that traditions and myths of all cultures are the most efficient encoding of our collective historical experience, our 'cultural DNA'. This grass-roots documentation of cultural resources is now a viable task, using current computer technology and its greatly reduced cost, due to micro-processor innovation. Then it will be neces- sary to assess which value-systems have been most inter-personally harmonious and just, as well as environmentally-attuned and sustainable for the longest periods, and review all historical evidence as to why they may have failed.

Here, we must be aware of the terrible trap of all history—that it records events not only with the distortion inevitable in the perceptions of the chronicler, but also of the record-keepers of the culture, and what was deemed 'important' to record. Thus most conventional history is that of human ego, pride, power, and conquest; ignoring all but fragments of the story of the humble production and activities of ordinary people. Furthermore, what have usually been deemed the historical 'failures' of some cultures because of their conquest by a more 'powerful' or wealthy culture, may have simply reflected the sheer luck of geographical location and rich veins of mineral and energy resources available. But these caveats should in no way prevent us from addressing such tasks.

The outlines of the ethics for the solar age, summed up in the edict of Thinking Globally and Acting Locally, are visible today, not only in the principles and declarations mentioned, but in the actions of citizens in thousands of groups and networks now linked in budding planetary coalitions.

Models abound, from that of the international postal system run out of a small brownstone house in Switzerland, to global telephone linkages. If even a small fraction of what is spent on armaments were channelled into the serious study and development of such global organization forms and functions, spectacular new successes would surely follow. General formulae for the Thinking Globally, Acting Locally model would seem to imply keeping production, consumption and institutional participation in economic and political life as close to the local level as possible. Global information and laterally-designed communications systems of all kinds, based on user-controlled, random-access principles, and two-way representation and reciprocity and exchange of experience, ideas and planetary learning.

Thus in general terms, there are five basic principles on which the New World Order must be built:

—the value of all human beings;
—the right to satisfaction of basic human needs (physical, psychological and metaphysical) of all human beings;
—equality of opportunity of self-development for all human beings;
—recognition that these principles and goals must be achieved within ecological tolerances of lands, seas, air, forests and the total carrying capacity of the biosphere;
—recognition that all these principles apply with equal emphasis, to future generations of humans and their biospheric life-support systems, and thus include the respect for all other life forms, and the Earth itself.

The new scientific understanding of *interconnectedness* and the fundamental processes of *redistribution* are accompanied by the emerging paradigms of *interdeterminacy, complementarity* and *change* as basic descriptions of nature. These five principles operate not only at the phenomenological level of our every-day surface realities and in our observance of nature, but also at the sub-atomic level of phenomena of quantum mechanics.

Thus the new world order can be founded both on scientific *and* ethical principles. We are *discovering* the new world order in science and *remembering* that we know it already, since these same five principles are found in all religious, spiritual traditions. Ethical principles have become the frontiers of scientific enquiry. Morality, at last, has become pragmatic; while so-called idealism has become realistic.

But it is equally clear that the needed global transformation will either occur amid increasing human resistance and social rigidity, or it will be accommodated and encouraged by more enlightened and flexible social policies and shifts in human values and behaviour. Thus the global politics of reconceptualization involves the emergence of pragmatic strategies, new coalitions and what might be termed 'a new proletariat': not only workers, as Marx preached, but all people who have been tyrannized by arbitrary symbol-systems and social designations of their roles, for example, all the world's people whose work has not been monetized, and therefore not valued: rural, subsistence farmers, lower-caste workers; ethnic people in all nation states who have been ghettoized in some way, such as the Native American Nations, the Aborigine of Australia, the Ainu in Japan, who have been driven off their ancestral lands into reservations; and all people undervalued by discrimination because of colour, sex, race, or religion. In the same way, countries and regions have been subordinated to the tyranny of the global monetized economy and their contribution to the world's development and human culture thereby devalued.

We now see in the emerging paradigms in science, that *all these issues flow from erroneous abstract drawing of boundaries where none exists in nature.* Yet the bringing to human consciousness of these errors is a *political* task, *requiring* that these issues and existing power centres be confronted. This planetary consciousness-raising activity must be militant, reasoned and non-violent.

〰〰〰〰〰〰〰〰〰〰〰〰〰

November/December 1980

[From a talk given at the Global Conference on the Future, held in Toronto in 1980]

Childhood & Education

Education or Manipulation

VINOBA BHAVE

THE IMPORTANCE OF FORMAL EDUCATION has been exaggerated beyond all reason, and as a result our methods of education have become ridiculously unnatural and harmful. If a child appears to have a quick and retentive memory, he or she is pushed excessively to learn. Parents and teachers wonder how much can be rammed into the child's head. If the child is slow he or she is often deliberately neglected. Clever pupils manage somehow until they reach college, but then many of them fall behind. If they do not lose ground in college, they frequently fail to achieve anything worthwhile in after-life. This is because their immature minds have been loaded with too heavy a burden. When a horse is lively and runs well there is no need to whip it along. You can see that it is a good runner, so why not leave it alone? When you use the whip, what happens?—the horse shies and falls into a ditch, and brings down the rider with it. This kind of pressure is barbarous, and should be done away with as a method of education.

As soon as the pupil begins to feel: 'Now I am learning,' something is wrong with the educational machinery. The best form of physical training and development of the body for little children is play. The child never feels: 'Now I am training my body.' While the child is playing the outside world does not exist. Children at play are absorbed in one undivided experience. They are not aware of comfort or discomfort, they feel neither hunger nor thirst, neither pain nor weariness. For them play is a joy, not duty; it is pleasure, not physical training. This principle has to be applied to all kinds of learning. Instead of the artificial idea that education is a duty, we must foster the natural and inspiring idea that education is a joy. The feeling among schoolchildren is that education is punishment. As soon as the restless energies of the child begin to develop, as soon as there is a tendency to independence, the family decide that it is time for them to be shut up in a school. The meaning of school is—a place for shutting children up! Teachers who set their hands to this work are merely school jailers.

The teacher should be free from the professional attitude—'Now I am teaching my pupils.' Unless the *guru* is a single-minded, natural teacher, the pupils cannot learn naturally. Whenever you find yourself saying that 'we are teaching by the Froebel, or Pestalozzi, or Montessori method,' you may be sure that this is empty verbiage, the meaningless copy of some method or other; it is a ghost, it has no life. Education is not like algebra, it is not a matter of applying the formula and getting the answer ready-made. Education is a well-spring within, overflowing naturally into the outer world. Even though this natural education may have its faults, it is workable. What must never be tolerated is the orderly doling out of ignorance by slaves who follow a fixed method, which is nothing but systemized ignorance. Herbert Spencer, the educational philosopher, has commented that 'education has no power to fashion an outstanding personality.' What value then can be attached to educational techniques? These systems must be able to make the promise that by knowing this you will grow wise and your work will be fulfilled. Any educational technique that cannot give this undertaking is simply an organized effort to throw dust in the eyes of ordinary people. Did Shakespeare study any theory of drama? Has anyone been made a great poet by learning by heart the rules of rhetoric? There is no great meaning or value in the words 'system' and 'method' in themselves. They are a delusion.

Those seers who were gifted with the deepest insight made it abundantly clear that they did not know how education is given. As is said in the *Kena Upanishads*, 'He knows who says: we do not know.' Method, syllabus, timetable—those are all meaningless words. They are nothing but self-deception. Education is to be had only from living deeds. When some separate activity, unconnected with the work of life, is given the name of education, this 'education' has a poisonous and unhealthy influence on the mind, just as some foreign substance entering the body usually has evil consequences. Unless we are exercised in work we have no hunger for learning, and when learning is forced artificially upon someone who has no appetite for it, the digestive organs have no power to digest it. If wisdom were to be had by cramming books, the library cupboards would be wise indeed. But learning which is forcibly crammed in is not digested. Mental dysentery sets in and intellectual powers are atrophied and die. Let us therefore define education as 'that which, without method, builds itself up into a methodical and ordered whole, that which no *guru* can give and which nevertheless is given.'

The true teacher does not teach, yet one may educate oneself at his or her side. The sun itself *gives* its light to no one, yet all, in the most natural and easy way, receive its light.

Anything which is cut off from life loses its power to teach. The attempt to divide education from life and its problems is like putting off the thought of death. In reality we are dying every moment, and the day of death is only the final stroke. The person is truly free who 'dies before their death', by facing the fact of death with open eyes. Anyone who can accept the steady approach of death as part of experience will find death gentle. Anyone who tries to escape from that experience, to tear it out of life, will find death sits like a nightmare on their shoulders. The blind man knows that there is a pillar in his path only when he strikes his head against it; the man who sees it ahead of him avoids the crash.

Teaching must take place in the context of real life. Set the children to work in the fields, and when a problem arises there give them whatever knowledge of cosmogony, or physics, or any other science, is needed to solve it. Set them to cook a meal, and as need arises teach them chemistry. In one word, let them live. The children should have someone with them, but that someone should not belong to a special category called teacher, he or she should be someone living an ordinary life in the practical world. Anyone who is to guide children should conduct their life intelligently and be capable of explaining the processes of life and work to the children as opportunity arises. It is not education to fill students' heads with information, but to arouse their thirst for knowledge. Teacher and pupil both learn by their contact with each other. Both are students. True education is that which is experienced, tested and digested. What can be counted and recorded is not education. Education cannot be doled out; it cannot be weighed and measured.

In the *Upanishads*, the praises of ignorance are sung side by side with the praises of knowledge. We need not only knowledge, but ignorance too. Knowledge alone, or ignorance alone, leads us into darkness, but the union of fitting knowledge with fitting ignorance is the nectar of eternity. The world is so filled with the matter of knowledge that we would go mad if we were to attempt to cram all of it into our heads. The ability to forget is just as necessary to us as the ability to remember.

Many people would agree about the importance of self-reliance in education. Self-reliance has a very profound meaning. There must be economic self-reliance through manual labour. Everyone must learn how to use their hands. If the whole population were to take up some kind of handicraft it would bring all sorts of benefits; class divisions would be overcome, production would rise, prosperity and health would improve. At the very least this measure of self-sufficiency must form part of our education programme.

Education must be of such a quality that it will train students in intellectual self-reliance and make them independent thinkers. If this were to become the chief aim of learning, the whole process of learning would be transformed. The present school syllabus contains a multiplicity of languages and subjects, and the student feels that in every one of these he or she needs the teacher's help for years. But a student should be so taught that he or she is capable of going forward and acquiring knowledge for him or herself. There is an infinite sum of knowledge in the world, and each one needs some finite portion of it for the conduct of their affairs. But it is a mistake to think that this life-knowledge can be had in any school. Life-knowledge can only be had from life. The task of the school is to awaken in its pupils the power to learn from life.

Most parents are anxious for their children to complete the school course so that they can get a salaried job and lead an easy life. This is the wrong way to look at education. Learning has value in its own right. The purpose of learning is freedom. Freedom implies not only independence of other people but also independence of one's own moods and impulses. The person who is a slave to their senses and cannot keep their impulses under control is neither free nor self-sufficient.

The question 'What shall we teach our students?' is raised in the *Upanishads*, and the answer given is that we should teach them 'the Veda of *Vedas*'. We teach the *Vedas*, but omit the *Bible*; we teach the *Bible*, but omit the *Qur'ān*; we teach the *Qur'ān*, but omit the *Dhammapada*; we teach the *Dhammapada*, but omit science; we teach science but omit political economy. Where are we to stop? No, we have to give them instead the *Veda* of *Vedas*, that is to say, the power to study the *Vedas*, and everything else for themselves. We have to put into their hands the key to knowledge.

The things we set children to learn are bound to be forgotten; they are not worth remembering in full. And because we know this, we allow them to pass if they get thirty-three per cent of the marks. A pupil who gets thirty-three per cent of the marks is sixty-seven per cent a failure, but we have to pass them because we know that they cannot remember the things we have taught them. It is of no use to remember them, and so we give this much margin. On the completion of their education students ought to have confidence in their own powers. This is what matters, not a supply of miscellaneous information and a degree.

The goal of education must be freedom from fear. In the *Upanishads*, when the *guru* is teaching his disciples, he says to them: 'O my students, whatever good conduct you find in me, that follow; whatever you do not find to be good, that do not follow.' That is to say, the *guru* gives students freedom, tells them to use their own judgement in deciding what is right and what is wrong. They are not to think that whatever their *guru* says is wholly right. It is certainly true that the *guru* is endeavouring to live by the truth, otherwise he would not be *guru*; but he nevertheless cannot claim that his every action will be in harmony with truth. And so he tells his students to be alert, to use their intelligence and examine his conduct, and to disregard whatever seems to them wrong. And by this means he enables his students to grow in fearlessness.

Fearlessness means that we should neither fear anything, nor inflict fear on others. Both these things are parts of fearlessness. A tiger cannot be called fearless, it may not be afraid of any other animal, but it is afraid of a gun, and it also inspires fear in other creatures. True fearlessness neither enslaves, nor does it slavishly submit to another.

The only sufficient basis for such fearlessness is the knowledge of the self. This self-knowledge is the foundation of education. But the education which children get today is the direct opposite of this. If a child commits some fault we slap it, and it begins to obey us because it is afraid. But we have taught it nothing of truth by our action. Until education is really based on fearlessness there is no hope of any change in society. We ought to teach children never to submit to those who beat and strike them. The pity is that even fathers and mothers do it. God has given them a child who trusts their every word, who has complete confidence in them. God has put into the parents' hands a completely trustful disciple, who yet gets beaten. We have to begin the teaching of fearlessness in the family and continue it in the school.

The fountainhead of all the world's conflicts is that knowledge has been separated from action. They have been separated intellectually by faulty psychology; they have been separated in life by faulty sociology; and they have been assigned different market values by faulty economics. There is no such thing as knowledge divorced from action. There is only one exception to this rule, and that is the knowledge that 'I am, I exist'; the knowledge of the self *is* divorced from action. It is beyond action. But all other knowledge is linked with action. There is no knowledge without action and no action without knowledge. The two are one, this is not a question of technique, but is a fundamental principle of Basic Education. People ask—if children have to work for two or three hours every day, how are they to learn anything? It seems to me an extraordinary question. What we should really be asking is how they are ever going to learn anything if they spend three or four hours a day poring over books. It is amazing to think what three or four hours of reading really means. In three hours a child might read sixty or seventy pages of a book but does he really *learn* anything? The muscles of his eyes no doubt get some exercise. We never seem to have any doubt that by reading the child is obtaining knowledge, and that reading is in fact the direct road to knowledge. It is nothing of the sort; on the contrary, book-learning is like a curtain that shuts us off from the real world.

There is a book called *The ABC of Bee-Keeping*, in which every possible piece of information about bee-keeping is to be found. Having read it I thought: 'Now we can do something; let us get hold of some bees.' But I did not get them without many days of running around, and when I had got them it took two full months more to win their confidence. Everything was written in the book and the book was certainly of some help, but the main road to knowledge is direct action. Reading and study are supplementary to action, they are tools. It is like saying 'That man has no spectacles, how can he see?' The eyes, not the spectacles, are the organ of sight, though if the eyes are weak, spectacles can certainly assist them.

The separation of learning from labour results also in social injustice. Some people do nothing but study and others nothing but hard labour, and as a result society is split in two. Those who earn their bread by manual labour form one social class and those who do only intellectual work form another. In India manual labourers are paid one rupee a day, intellectual workers are paid twenty-five or thirty rupees. A very great injustice has been done by rating the value of manual and intellectual work so differently. And it is the abolition of such injustice that must be the goal of our education.

Even if these differences are done away with, that is not enough. The more closely we can live in harmony with nature, the greater our welfare and happiness will be; the more we are cut off from nature, the less contented we shall be. The smallest possible percentage of our population should be employed in agriculture, and the largest possible percentage in other productive kinds of work. But at the same time the life of the whole population should be closely in touch with agriculture. If a single person is cut off from the life of the fields, their life will lack completeness. Everyone needs to be in touch with the land, to be rooted in the soil. Human lives are like trees, which cannot live if they are cut off from the soil which nourishes them. Therefore, everyone must have the opportunity to tend the soil, but at the same time the business of agriculture must be done so efficiently that the smallest possible number of people are tied to the land. These two principles may seem to be mutually contradictory, but they are both parts of Basic Education. It is a basic need of humanity to be in touch with the earth, and any nation or civilization which is cut off from it slowly but surely loses its vigour and degenerates.

Basic Education is bound up with nature; how can any such education be carried on in our large cities? It is a great misfortune for the cities to be cut off from the earth, for human life could suffer no greater loss. When I was in jail everyone got the impression that I was enjoying myself. One day the jailer said to me: 'You seem to be very content; is there nothing that you miss?' 'Yes,' I said, 'There is one thing.' 'What can it be?' he asked. 'Why don't you guess?' I said. 'I will give you a week to do it.' He thought it over for a week and then he said, 'I don't know what it is that you miss.' I told him. 'I am very content with everything else, but I am sad that I can never see the sunrise and sunset.'

How much joy there is in being able to go out in the open air, among the natural objects of creation! City-dwellers cannot know this joy, so what do they do, poor things!—they get a flower pot and put paper flowers in it, and hang pictures of sunrise and sunset on the walls. So artificial has their life become that at night they cannot see the stars. How can our cities be blessed with the sight of the starry heavens in the midst of all their artificial lighting? What is left, I sometimes wonder, for these people to burn? They have burned up even the darkness, the darkness of night, which was given to us for peace, rest, and quiet thought. This means that the task before education is to change the whole system of values and way of life that is current in our cities. No joy is to be compared with this joy of the free life. There is a word in Sanskrit for this boundless joy, the word *sukha*, well-being and contentment. In Sanskrit the primary meaning of *sukha* is 'the wide and boundless sky'. Happiness is to be found beneath the open sky. It is hard to find it where life is artificial and the sky is cramped.

If a man's house is full of medicine bottles, we infer that the man is probably ill. But if his house is full of books, we conclude that he is intelligent. Surely that is not right? The first rule of health is to take medicine only when it is absolutely necessary. By the same token, the first rule of intelligence ought to be to avoid, as far as possible, burying one's eyes in books. We consider medicine bottles to be the sign of a sick body; we ought to consider books, whether secular or religious, as the sign of a sick mind!

Examinations seem to me to provide a most disgusting picture of the old educational system. When we take an examination, a supervisor has to be appointed to watch us, to see that no student steals from another by copying. It is to me a very saddening spectacle. For if it is possible to suspect us of being capable of stealing, then, as students, we have already failed. What is there left to examine?

I have no real knowledge of the subjects in which I have had to take examinations, but I do know well things in which I have never been examined. My own experience, therefore, does not lead me to attach any value to examinations. Examinations are exactly like the purgatives that people take to cleanse the stomach—one takes an examination and all one's knowledge is cleared out! There is no reason why we should fall into this trap which the pedagogues have set for us.

If I want to teach children about doors and windows I will ask them what windows are for. Then, when they have seen clearly why we need windows and doors, I will say: 'Now tell me, what windows and doors have you got in your own bodies?' Eyes, ears, mouth and nose are all called 'doors' in Sanskrit. I will then ask the children to draw a window, an eye—there comes practice in drawing. After that I will tell them about various kinds of windows that people have made—there is history. Can these old windows be seen anywhere in the world today?—I will take them to Lapland and in that connection tell them about the life of the people there. In short, one should tell children about the way of life of different countries in connection with some such natural interest.

China like India is an ancient country with a wealth of population and intensively cultivated; why is China so productive? What do they do to maintain the fertility of the soil? In this connection I will tell the children about manures. We have to learn from China in particular how to make use of human excreta. This is very widely used in China and thanks to it the soil maintains its productivity even though it has been farmed for so many years.

An American has written a book called *Farmers of Forty Centuries*, describing the agriculture of China. In it he says: 'How thriftless we Americans are! We possess fifteen or twenty acres of land a head, and we have farmed it for only four centuries at most. Yet we use all kinds of chemical fertilizers to make it productive, and these ruin the soil, while we allow a valuable manure like human excreta to go to waste.'

If it rains very heavily the children should be given a holiday and enjoy themselves playing in the rain. The teacher too should take his clothes off and play with them. We in India get a holiday when it rains, but in England they get a holiday when the sun shines. Why?—because there the sky is usually dull and overcast, so when the sun comes out there is a holiday. In this way, while they are playing and enjoying themselves, I can give them some idea of the climate of England.

But this kind of extensive knowledge should never be given apart from a natural context of interest. It will not do for the teacher simply to get up and talk about Lapland; let the natural opportunity arise. It is the teacher's task to seize the natural opportunity to widen the children's knowledge.

A young man said that he wished to do some good work for society. 'Tell me,' I said, 'what kind of work do you feel you could do well?'

'Only teaching, I think,' replied the young man, 'I can't do anything else. I can only teach, but I am interested in it and I feel sure I shall be able to do it well.'

'Yes, yes, I do not doubt that, but what are you going to teach? Spinning? Carding? Weaving? Could you teach any of these?'

'No, I can't teach those.'

'Then tailoring? or dyeing? or carpentry?'

'No, I know nothing about them.'

'Perhaps you could teach cooking, grinding and other household skills?'

'No, I have never done any work like that. I can only teach.'

'My dear friend, you answer "No" to every question, and yet you keep saying you can only teach. What do you mean? Can you teach gardening?'

The would-be teacher said, rather angrily, 'Why do you ask all this? I told you at the beginning, I can do nothing else. I can teach literature.'

'Good! Good! I'm beginning to understand now. You mean you can teach people to write books like Tagore and Shakespeare?'

This made the young man so angry that he began to splutter.

'Take it easy,' I laughed. 'Can you teach patience?' That was too much. 'I know what you mean,' I said, 'You can teach reading, writing, history and geography. Well, they are not entirely useless, there are times in life when they are needed. But they are not basic to life. Would you be willing to learn weaving?'

'I don't want to learn anything new now. Besides I couldn't learn to weave, I have never before done any kind of handwork.'

'In that case it might of course take you longer to learn, but why should you be unable to learn it?'

'I don't think I could ever learn it. But even supposing I could, it would mean a lot of hard work and a great deal of trouble. So please understand that I could not undertake it.'

This conversation is quite enough to enable us to understand the psychology and characteristics of far too many of our 'teachers'. To be 'only a teacher' means to be completely ignorant of any kind of practical skills which might be useful in real life; incapable of learning anything new and indifferent towards any kind of craftsmanship; conceited; and buried in books.

'Only teaching' means being a corpse cut off from life.

Teachers should give up the mistaken notion of 'only teaching' and take upon themselves the responsibility for their own living, just as the workers and peasants do. They must let their pupils share fully in this responsibility and make their whole environment a means of education: that is, they must let the education come about of itself.

The teacher in the school should be the inspiration of the whole town, and the school should be the centre of service. If the community needs medicine, it should be supplied through the school. If the streets need cleaning, the school should initiate the work. The people should turn to the teacher to help them settle disputes. The school should make plans for the observance of festivals. In this way the school should become the centre of the community; it should develop whatever is of value and introduce the things that are lacking.

The most important thing for the students is to preserve the independence of their minds. If anyone has a right to full freedom, it is the student. Knowledge cannot be had without trust, but it is equally essential that the student should have intellectual freedom. Many people think that trust and intelligence are incompatible, but that is a mistake. The ear and the eye are different senses, but they do not contradict one another, and it is the same with trust and intelligence. Without trust it is impossible to learn anything. The mother points to the moon and says: 'Look, my little one, that is the moon.' If the child had no faith in its mother, if it were to say to itself: 'Who knows whether what she shows me is really the moon or not?' it would learn nothing. So that trust, or faith, is fundamental to learning. Knowledge begins in faith, but it is perfected, completed, in independent thought. Students therefore must never let go their right to freedom of thought. A teacher who tries to compel the students' assent is no teacher. We must not allow our independence of thought to be interfered with, and we must guard the privilege of freedom.

I want to warn students that their right is in danger of being lost in the modern world. An attempt is being made, in the name of 'discipline' to force all students' minds into the same mould. In the name of discipline we are imposing mechanical uniformity, and this causes injury to students' minds.

Throughout the world education is under the control of governments. This is extremely dangerous. Governments ought to have no authority over education. The work of education should be in the hands of men of wisdom, but governments have got it in their grasp; every student in the country has to study whatever book is prescribed by the education department. If the government is fascist, students will be taught fascism, if it is communist, it will preach communism; if it is capitalist, it will proclaim the greatness of capitalism; if it believes in planning, the students will be taught all about planning. We in India used to hold to the principle that education should be completely free from state control. Kings exercised no authority over the *gurus*. The king had absolutely no power to control education. The consequence was that Sanskrit literature achieved a degree of freedom of thought such as can be seen nowhere else, so much so that no less than six mutually incompatible philosophies have arisen within the Hindu philosophy. This vigour is due to the freedom of education from state control.

The status of teachers has sunk so low that they feel themselves to have no authority at all. They must follow whatever path the government directs. They are under orders, the servants of authority. They may perhaps modify the government schemes by a comma here or a semi-colon there, but they cannot do more than that. Today there is an attempt to expand education and the number of schools and of teachers is being increased, but the spirit of the true *guru* is not there. A good teacher means one who is a good servant; a bad teacher means a bad servant; good or bad, he remains a servant.

The 'knowledge' which is purchased for money is no knowledge at all; knowledge bought for cash is ignorance. True knowledge can only be had for love and service, it cannot be bought for money. So when wise teachers, travelling from place to place, arrive at a village, let the people lovingly invite them to remain a few days, treat them with reverence and receive from them whatever knowledge they have to give. This is quite a feasible plan. Just as a river flows of itself from village to village, serving the people; just as cows graze in the jungle and return of themselves with full udders to give the children milk; so will wise teachers travel of themselves from place to place. We must re-establish this institution of the wandering teacher. In this way every village can have its university, and all the knowledge of the world can find its way into the villages. We must also re-invigorate the tradition of the *vanaprasthashram* (a state of freedom from worldly responsibility) so that every village gets a permanent teacher for whom no great expenditure will be incurred. Every home must be a school, and every field a laboratory. Every *vanaprastha* must be a teacher and every wandering *sannyasi* a university. The students are the children and young people who want to learn; in every village there will be people who give an hour or two to learning and spend the rest of the day working. This seems to me to provide a complete outline of education from birth to death.

The purpose of this education is that the village as a whole solves the problems of its life by its own strength. The wealth and resources of the village must therefore belong not to individuals but to the village itself. Only then is it possible to plan for all children to have an equal chance of education. If we cannot even give them all their share of pure and nourishing food, how can we give them an equal education?

If you ask someone what they are drinking they may answer 'tea'. There may also be sugar in it, but they never mention the sugar, never say they are drinking tea-and-sugar. The sweetness of the sugar permeates the tea, but the drinker drinks and says nothing about it. Education must be like the sugar, doing its work in secret. We can see that hands, nose, ears and tongue are active, but no one can see what the soul is doing. Our ears appear to be listening, our tongue appears to be talking. No matter what the appearance may be, it is not *only* the tongue that talks. In spite of appearances, it is not only the ears that hear. That which speaks and hears is the spirit within. And the spirit is invisible. The best education is similarly invisible. The more it is seen, the more imperfect it is.

January/February 1974

A Teacher's Tale

ROGER KIRK

IT IS EASY TO BE WISE with hindsight, to see the pattern in the events that at the time were distinct and unrelated. When people ask what caused the injury, I find myself repeating the last part of the pattern as if it explains the whole; rather as if someone asked you what a novel was about and you told them in detail about the last chapter and nothing else. It's not enough. It doesn't really answer the question.

So where is Chapter One? I find myself wanting to talk about a childhood and schooling where succeeding (cramming for 11+, access to successful grammar school) meant persistent hard work, a driving sense of needing to make an impression in an all-male environment. Schoolwork and early exam entry meant abandoning outside activities and focusing life exclusively on school— sports and study. Doing was everything. If you had a spare minute it 'ought' to be filled. The assumptions went right through school to university to job. Who was there to say that equal attention to *being*, as opposed to doing, mattered?

By the time I left my first teaching post, I was known as the Basil Fawlty of my school, the man with the manic energy, with two briefcases and three distinct job titles. Looking back, those recurrent stomach pains at twenty-five were probably an ulcer.

Job number two on paper looked easier—a single task to undertake. But there are a thousand ways of getting involved and expanding one's areas of activity and I tried them all. Besides work there were activities with the children, clubs and societies, DIY, allotment gardening. I got a buzz out of being known as the man who could handle it all, who was in his element, never content unless he was doing something. 'Why don't you ever sit down?' my wife Anne would say in exasperation as I restlessly picked up a cloth to clean the windows.

Going to the USA in 1984-5 only stoked the furnace higher: a new situation, new friends to make, new places to go, new activities to try. It seems I was made for the USA and bathed in the plaudits of friends and colleagues who commended my more than American get-up-and-go. True, on my return to England I took up yoga, conscious that there was more to life than incessant activity, trying to do something which deliberately looked inwards (whilst enjoying a new and strenuous physical challenge . . .). But job number three in Devon with a new house and garden to get on top of provided plenty of opportunities to be the old self. By the end of the first year we had all but redecorated the entire house.

Only now do we come to the final chapter, the bit I usually relate to 'explain' what happened. I spent a week at the end of October cutting down diseased fruit trees in the steeply sloping back garden. Looking back at this week, Anne said, 'You didn't stop once.' She would make tea for me and I would pick it up an hour later stone cold. I felt driven to complete the task in the time I had defined it should take, to make use of good weather and to return the borrowed chain saw. The children saw little of me that week. I banished them—and the dog—from the garden for safety reasons. In efforts to save time, I toiled uphill with logs big enough to make my back creak with effort. And I pressed on.

I took satisfaction in the speed of progress, felt a macho achievement in handling the saw, in raising a heavy sweat. There was no stopping me for five days solid. Hubris. By the end I felt very tired and sore, but not in great pain. It was to take the next two months to add the straws which would break the camel's back. With each new straining activity my back got stiffer and the warnings to rest more clear. But I 'couldn't'. Each task—relaying a train set, humping large sheets of chipboard upstairs, building huge bonfires, rehearsing for a play where someone jumped unexpectedly on my back, travelling long-distance for Christmas, drilling a hole in a kitchen work-top to fit up a Christmas present— was *necessary*. And had to be done then. Meanwhile I was trying to exercise away my stiff back. The Gods had their way finally and I received my come-uppance. Returning from Christmas with relatives, I could scarcely climb the stairs and the next day I could not move without acute pain. This began two months confined to bed, including two separate ten day spells in hospital. I am now fit enough to return to school, having missed an entire term. What kind of recovery I shall finally make only time will tell.

From having 'no time' to mull things over, to read, to converse at length with friends, there was now nothing else to do. I learned with a refreshing shock the extent of people's love—family, friends, professional health-workers. Reading sent me on long journeys. In *The Dancing Wu-Li Masters*, the account of traditional Chinese medicine seemed to make sense. The back is Yang, male; the front Yin, female. I had much over-used the one at the expense of the other, over-used it and damaged it. For a while there could be no doing, only being. Part of becoming whole again involves a reassessment of roles, expectations, priorities, purposes. Family life has had to change. Work will be different. I've turned an unexpected corner in life and have to make sense of the landscape that I now see. I'm looking forward to it.

September/October 1988

Children of the Future

MICHEL ODENT

ONCE, IN A GARDEN, Maria Montessori saw a two-year-old Hindu child looking intensely at the ground on which he seemed to be tracing a line with his finger. There was an ant there which had lost two legs and could only walk with difficulty. The child was trying to be helpful by making a track with his fingers. Another child approached, saw the ant, put his foot out and crushed it.

This story suggests how deeply rooted a positive or negative attitude to life can become. Anyone with a good knowledge of two-year-olds knows that, by this age, their respect for life can be strong or it may already be weakened. How can this respect for life be kept intact?

From its introduction by Haeckel in the eighteen sixties up to the middle of this century, the word 'ecology' referred to a well-defined scientific discipline. Ecological science was the study of the interrelationship between plants, animals and their environment.

It was only in the nineteen-fifties that some voices started to claim that, by appropriating nature to our own ends and our own needs, we were destroying the planet. The world 'ecological' was associated more and more often with awareness, consciousness, crisis and even shock.

Ecological awareness triggered new questions: 'How can we stop destroying the planet?' In order to achieve this goal, the word 'ecological' was paired with some unwonted terms. A number of authors wrote about an ecological society, others introduced the concept of ecological philosophy, and others still talked about an ecological technology.

I became convinced that the word ecological should be attached to the word 'humanity' and tried to introduce the concept of an ecological man and woman. What we need is a new respect for all life.

When I wrote my first book I called it *Genèse de l'homme ecologique* but on both sides of the Atlantic all the publishers felt that the word 'birth' would attract readers, while nobody would care about the genesis of an 'ecological humanity'.

The main point I developed was the link between the baby-mother relationship and that of humanity with mother-earth. This lead to a study of the bonding process, the process of attachment.

Scientific studies of the process of attachment started in the middle of this century with the works of the ethologists. Everybody remembers the goslings of Konrad Lorenz who remained attached for their whole life to the first large body that they met. These studies stumbled on the importance of sensitive, critical moments; of short periods of time which will never happen again. Since these preliminary studies the concept of sensitive periods has been used with reference to different species of birds, mammals, primates.

After witnessing thousands of normal, undisturbed births, either at home or in a home-like hospital at Pithiviers, I became convinced that the first hour following birth is an important period for the bonding process among humans. By normal birth I mean a spontaneous birth in an atmosphere of privacy and spontaneity, in semi-darkness, with as few people as possible.

During this hour many mothers are still in a very special state of consciousness. They are able to forget what they may have learned and what they had planned. They can forget that they had planned to bottle-feed their baby. But, on the other hand, they know instinctively how to hold their newborn, and how to make the exact gesture which facilitates its early sucking at the breast.

Kittie Frantz, a well-known leader of the La Leche League, a breastfeeding counsellor, spent many years helping young mothers who had difficulties in breastfeeding. After years and years of observation and analysis of attitudes, she understood how some positions, some gestures, some ways to place the hands could make sucking easier.

She told me that she had the opportunity to watch a film made at the Pithiviers hospital. A short time after the birth a young mother, still transported, took the baby in her arms and discovered within seconds all the details of position the breastfeeding advisers had learnt after years of careful study. This first hour is also a time when most babies express the 'rooting reflex' and have a special ability to find the breast. When a baby is able to do this within two hours following birth it is almost a guarantee of easy and happy breastfeeding.

We are just starting to understand what might be the hormonal basis of the process of attachment. From simple observation one can guess that during the first hour following birth, mother and baby have not yet eliminated the hormones they had to secrete during the process of birth. These hormones seem to play a part in the process of attachment, in particular the endogenous opiates (endorphins). We know the properties of opiates to create habits, dependency, and to trigger affectionate, care-giving behaviour. When two people are in close contact and are, at the same time, impregnated with endorphins, it is the beginning of a habit, of an attachment.

Most of the cultures we hear of through anthropologists and historians found excuses to control the process of birth and to disturb the first contact between mother and baby. The most common cross-cultural excuse is that colostrum ('pre-milk') is bad for the baby.

Our technological society has its own ways to disturb deeply all the physiological processes in the period around birth. The main one is over-control by medical institutions. Our society as a whole cannot understand the need for privacy of the woman in labour.

One may well wonder why most of the cultures we know of imposed frustrations upon the newborn baby, and even violence such as circumcision. Perhaps in the power struggles between civilizations, the winners have been those who knew the best ways to develop their potential for aggression. These attitudes had a meaning at a time when the watchword was for humans to dominate the world and master all the animals and plant species.

When the day dawns that the genesis of 'ecological humanity' is a priority we will first have to rediscover that we are mammals and that all mammals hide themselves, isolate themselves to give birth and welcome their offspring.

Our western society has many specific ways to weaken mother-infant bonding. We invented the pram or the push-chair. In all the other cultures we know of, the baby used to be carried by the mother. During the night the baby was not sleeping in a crib but with the mother.

From my own observations I understood that the period of weaning is an important time for the future of the relationship with living creatures as opposed to the relationship with things. D.W.Winnicott talks about the transitional object; that is, the object a young child becomes strongly attached to. It may be a piece of a blanket or a teddy bear. Even if this object gets damaged or dirty, nothing can replace it. Some studies have demonstrated how common this phenomenon is. Winnicott insisted that the adoption of a transitional object is a normal stage of human development. Several observers confirmed that it is frequently associated with a good relationship with people. On the other hand, the studies of Provence and Lipton suggested that the children who spent the first year of their life in a 'depriving institution', with a lack of love and stimulation, had no transitional objects.

I made some enquiries regarding one hundred children who had been breastfed longer than a year. None of them had a transitional object. My interpretation is that this phenomenon is a healthy reaction to a special situation, to a situation which is particular to our society—weaning before the age of twelve months. Most of the experts who write about the human infant forget to warn us that they only know babies who were born in a hospital, who do not sleep with their mothers, and who are weaned before they are a year old.

Modern science knows that the primitive part of the brain, the emotional-instinctive brain, reaches its maturity early in the life of the individual; before the age of two. This is a way to understand that, in fact, the whole lifestyle during infancy is important. What is the future of a young child who has no contact at all with animals and plants? What is the future of a child whose relationship with water develops only in the utilitarian context of the bathroom?

After infancy it is the role of education to cultivate and take advantage of a positive attitude to life. At the age of elementary school, children are sensitive to moral values. They are able to feel that it is wrong not to care about those who will live on this planet during the next centuries, and not to care about trees and animals. At the age of secondary school, adolescents can develop a sense of different scales of time. They can anticipate and realize the long-term consequences of the actions of technological 'civilization'.

The development of such a capacity comes up against a huge difficulty because where a vision of the future is concerned we are genetically as short-sighted as the hunter-gatherer. But the actions of the hunter-gatherer had only short-term consequences in the scale of the history of the planet. As a matter of fact, the hunter-gatherer probably had an implicit trust in natural processes. The Pygmies say, 'Never cut the trees.' Pygmy babies continue to nurse for about five years, when sleeping at night their only blanket is their mother.

Although the genesis of 'ecological humanity' is the most important topic one can imagine at the end of this millennium, it is not a common topic. The rare eloquent voices who gave useful answers to our questions expressed themselves before the age of ecological awareness. Jean Jacques Rousseau is undoubtedly the great precursor. A century before Darwin he considered human beings as belonging to the animal kingdom and was conscious of the interdependency of living creatures. His contemporary, Voltaire, could not understand his work and was ironic about his *discours sur l'inégalité*: 'One desires to go on all fours when reading your book.' Rousseau knew how deeply rooted are our attitudes to life. He claimed that human beings are fundamentally good at birth and, if proper development is fostered, natural goodness of the individual can be protected. He wrote about the importance of breastfeeding. In his *Confessions* he found it important to point out that he had never been cruel with animals when a little boy. In *Emile*, a book about education, he recommended that children should be brought up in the country.

At the beginning of this century, Maria Montessori knew how to teach ecology before the word was commonly known. She wrote that 'life of all kinds form a whole in relation with each other.' She gave great importance to the first contact between mother and baby.

Wilhelm Reich studied human nature from new angles. He looked at what we now call the process of desertification. It is the emotional desert in us that creates the desert in nature. Reich's concern at the end of his life was the children of the future who 'will have to clear up the mess of this twentieth century'. In his attempt to analyse the origin of the 'emotional plague', that is to say, the current negative attitude to life, he always came back to the newborn baby. He dreamed of a time when we would stop 'killing nature in every newborn child'. 'Civilization will commence on the day when the well-being of the newborn baby will prevail over any other consideration.'

January/February 1989

Positive Peace

Peace is a Way of Life

IVAN ILLICH

VIOLENCE NOW LURKS in many key words of the English language. John Kennedy could wage *war* on poverty; pacifists now plan *strategies* (literally, war plans) for peace. In this language, currently shaped for aggression, I must talk to you about the recovery of a true sense of peace, bearing in mind always that I know nothing about your vernacular tongue. Therefore, each word I speak today will remind me of the difficulty of putting peace into words. To me, it seems that each people's peace is as distinct as each people's poetry. Hence, the translation of peace is a task as arduous as the translation of poetry.

Peace has a different meaning for each epoch and for each culture. This is a point on which Professor Takeshi Ishida has written and, as he reminds us, within each culture area peace means something different at the centre and on the margins. At the centre, the emphasis is on 'peace-keeping'; on the margin, people hope to be 'left in peace'. During three so-called Development Decades, the latter meaning, people's peace, has lost out. This is my main thesis: Under the cover of 'development', a worldwide war has been waged against people's peace. In developed areas today, not much is left of people's peace. I believe that limits to economic development, originating at the grassroots, are the principal condition for people to recover their peace.

Culture has always given meaning to peace. Each *ethnos*—people, community, culture—has been mirrored, symbolically expressed and reinforced by its own *ethos*—myth, law, goddess, ideal—of peace. Peace is as vernacular as speech. In the examples chosen by Professor Ishida, this correspondence between *ethnos* and *ethos* appears with great clarity. Take the Jews; look at the Jewish patriarch when he raises his arms in blessing over his family and flock. He invokes *shalom*, which we translate as peace. He sees *shalom* as grace, flowing from heaven, 'like oil dripping through the beard of Aaron the forefather'. For the Semitic father, peace is the blessing of justice which the one true God pours over the twelve tribes of recently settled shepherds. To the Jew the angel announces 'shalom', not the Roman *pax*. Roman peace means something utterly different. When the Roman governor raises the ensign of his legion to ram it into the soil of Palestine, he does not look towards heaven. He faces a far-off city; he imposes *its* law and *its* order. There is nothing in common between *shalom* and this *pax romana*, though both exist in the same place and time.

In our time, both have faded. *Shalom* has retired into a privatized realm of religion, and *pax* has invaded the world as 'peace', *paix, pace*. Through two thousand years of use by governing élites, *pax* has become a polemical catchall. The word was exploited by Constantine to turn the cross into ideology.

Charlemagne utilized it to justify the genocide of the Saxons. *Pax* was the term employed by Innocent III to subject the sword to the cross. In modern times, leaders manipulate it to put the party in control of the army. Spoken by both St Francis and Clemenceau, *pax* has now lost the boundaries of its meaning. It has become a sectarian and proselytizing term, whether used by the establishment or by dissidents, whether its legitimacy is claimed by the East or the West.

The idea of *pax* has a colourful history, in spite of the fact that little research has been done on it. Historians have been more occupied filling library shelves with treatises on war and its techniques. *Huo'ping* and *shanti* seem to have meanings today which are not unlike those of the past. But between them there is a gulf; they are not comparable at all. *Huo'ping* of the Chinese means smooth, tranquil harmony within the hierarchy of the heavens, while *shanti* of the Indians refers primarily to intimate, personal, cosmic, non-hierarchic awakening. In short, there is no 'identity' in peace.

In its concrete sense, peace places the 'I' into the corresponding 'we'. But in each language area this correspondence is different. Peace fixes the meaning of the first person plural. By defining the form of the *exclusive* 'we' (the *kami* of the Malay languages), peace is the base on which the *inclusive* 'we' (*kita*) can arise. This distinction between *kami* and *kita* of the Malay languages comes naturally to most speakers around the Pacific. It is a grammatical difference utterly foreign to Europe, and completely lacking in western *pax*. Modern Europe's undifferentiated 'we' is semantically aggressive. Asian research cannot be too wary of *pax*, which has no respect for *kita*. Here in the Far East it should be easier than in the West to base peace research on what ought perhaps to be its fundamental axiom: war tends to make cultures alike whereas peace is that condition under which each culture flowers in its own incomparable way. From this it follows that peace cannot be exported; it is inevitably corrupted by transfer; its attempted export always means war. When peace research neglects this ethnological truism it turns into a technology of peace-keeping: either degraded into some kind of moral rearmament or perverted into the negative polemology—war science—of the high brass and their computer games.

Peace remains unreal, merely an abstraction, unless it stands for an ethno-anthropological reality. But it would remain equally unreal if we did not attend to its historical dimension. Until recently war could not totally destroy peace, could not penetrate all levels of peace, because the continuation of war was based on the survival of the subsistence cultures which fed it. Traditional warfare depended on the continuation of people's peace. Too many historians have neglected this fact; they make history appear as a tale of wars. This is clearly true of classical historians, who tend to report on the rise and fall of the powerful. Unfortunately, it is equally true of many of the newer historians who want to act as reporters from the camps of those who never made it, who want to tell the tales of the vanquished, to evoke the images of those who have disappeared. Too often these new historians are more interested in the violence rather than the peace of the poor. They primarily chronicle resistance, mutinies, insurgencies, riots of slaves, peasants, minorities, marginals; in more recent times, the class struggles of proletarians and the discrimination battles of women.

In comparison with the historians of power, the new historians of popular culture have a difficult task. Historians of élite cultures, of wars waged by armies, write about the centres of cultural areas. For their documentation they have monuments, decrees engraved in stone, commercial correspondence, the autobiographies of kings and the trails made by marching armies. Historians from the losing camp have no evidence of this kind. They report on subjects which often have been erased from the face of the earth, on people whose remains have been stamped out by their enemies, or blown away by the wind. The historians of peasantry and nomads, of village culture and home life, of women and infants, have few traces to examine. They must reconstruct the past from hunches, must be attentive to hints which they find in proverbs, riddles and songs. Often the only verbatim records left behind by the poor, especially women, are the responses made by witches and rogues under torture, statements recorded by the courts. Modern anthropological history, the history of popular cultures, *l'histoire des mentalités*, has had to develop techniques to make these odd remnants intelligible.

This new history often tends to focus on war. It portrays the weak principally in their confrontations with those against whom they must defend themselves. It recounts stories of resistance and only by implication reports on the peace of the past. Conflict makes opponents comparable; it introduces simplicity into the past; it fosters the illusion that what has gone before can be related in twentieth century uniquack. Thus war, which makes cultures alike, is all too often used by historians as the framework or skeleton of their narratives. Today there is a desperate need for the history of peace, a history infinitely more diverse than the story of war.

What is now designated peace research very often lacks historical perspective. The subject of this research is 'peace', purged of its cultural and historical components. Paradoxically, peace was turned into an academic subject just when it had been reduced to a balance between sovereign, economic powers acting under the assumption of scarcity. Thus study is restricted to research on the least violent truce between competitors locked into a zero sum game. Like searchlights, the concepts of this research focus on scarcities. And they permit the discovery of unequal distributions of scarcity. But in the process of such research, the peaceful enjoyment of that which is not scarce, people's peace, is left in a zone of deep shadow.

The assumption of scarcity is fundamental to economics, and formal economics is the study of values under this assumption. But scarcity, and therefore all which can be meaningfully analysed by formal economics, has been of marginal importance in the lives of most people through most of history. The spread of scarcity into all aspects of life can be chronicled; it occurred in European civilization since the Middle Ages. Under the expanding assumption of scarcity, peace acquired a new meaning, a meaning without precedent anywhere in Europe. Peace came to mean *pax economica*. *Pax economica* is a balance between formally 'economic' powers.

The history of this new reality deserves our attention, and the process through which *pax economica* monopolized the meaning of peace is especially important. This is the first meaning of peace to achieve worldwide acceptance. And such a monopoly ought to be deeply worrisome. Therefore, I want to contrast *pax economica* with its opposite and complement, popular peace.

Since the establishment of the United Nations, peace has been progressively linked with development. Previously this linkage had been unthinkable. The novelty of it can hardly be understood by people under forty. The curious situation is more easily intelligible for those who were, like myself, adults on January 10, 1949, the day President Truman announced the Point Four Programme. On that day most of us met the term 'development' for the first time in its present meaning. Until then we had used development to refer to species, to real estate and to moves in chess. But since then it can refer to people, to countries and to economic strategies. And in less than a generation we were flooded with conflicting development theories. By now, however, most of them are merely curiosities for collectors. You may remember, with some embarrassment, how generous people were urged to make sacrifices for a succession of programmes aimed at 'raising per capita income', 'catching up with the advanced countries', 'overcoming dependencies'. And you now wonder at the many things once deemed worthy of export: 'achievement orientation', 'atoms for peace', 'jobs', 'windmills' and, currently, 'alternative lifestyles' and professionally supervised 'self-help'. Each of these theoretical incursions came in waves. One brought the self-styled pragmatists who emphasized enterprise, the other would-be politicians who relied on 'conscientizing' people into foreign ideology. Both camps agreed on growth. Both advocated rising production and increased dependence on consumption. And each camp with its sect of experts, its assembly of saviours, always linked its own scheme for development to peace. Concrete peace, by thus being linked to development became a partisan goal. The pursuit of peace through development became the over-arching unexaminable axiom. Anyone who opposed economic growth, not this kind or that, but economic growth as such, could be denounced as an enemy of peace. Even Gandhi was cast into the role of the fool, the romantic or the psychopath. Worse, his teachings were perverted into so-called non-violent strategies for development. His peace too was linked to growth. Khadi was redefined as a 'commodity', and non-violence as an economic weapon. The assumption of the economist, that values are not worth protecting unless they are scarce, has turned *pax economica* into a threat to people's peace.

The linkage of peace to development has made it difficult to challenge the latter. Let me suggest that such a challenge should now be the main task of peace research. The fact that development means different things to different people is no obstacle. It means one thing to TNC executives, another to ministers of the Warsaw pact, and something other again to the architects of the New International Economic Order. But the convergence of all parties on the need for development has given the notion a new status. This agreement has made of development the condition for the pursuit of the nineteenth century ideals of equality and democracy, with the proviso that these be restricted within the assumptions of scarcity. Under the disputes around the issue of 'who gets what' the unavoidable costs inherent in all development have been buried. But during the seventies one part of these costs has come to light. Some obvious 'truths' suddenly became controversial. Under the ecology label, the limits of resources, of tolerable poison and stress, became political issues. But the violent aggression against the environment's utilization value has so far not been sufficiently disinterred. To expose the violence against subsistence which is implicit in all further growth, and which is veiled by *pax economica*, seems to me a prime task of radical peace research.

In both theory and practice all development means the transformation of subsistence-oriented cultures and their integration into an economic system. Development always entails the expansion of a formally economic sphere at the cost of subsistence-oriented activities. It means the progressive 'disembedding' of a sphere in which exchange takes place under the assumption of a zero sum game. And this expansion proceeds at the cost of all other traditional forms of exchange. Thus development always implies the propagation of scarcity— dependence on goods and services perceived as scarce. Development necessarily creates a milieu from which the conditions for subsistence activities have been eliminated in the process of making the milieu over into a resource for the production and circulation of commodities. Development thus inevitably means the imposition of *pax economica* at the cost of every form of popular peace.

To illustrate the opposition between people's peace and *pax economica*, let me turn to the European Middle Ages. In so doing I emphatically do not advocate a return to the past. I look at the past only to illustrate the dynamic opposition between two complementary forms of peace, both formally recognized. I explore the past rather than some social science theory to avoid utopian thinking and a planning mentality. The past is not, like plans and ideas, something which might possibly come about. It is not something which ought to be. The past has been. It allows me to stand on fact when I look at the present. I turn toward the European Middle Ages because it was near their end that a violent *pax economica* assumed its shape. And the replacement of people's peace by its engineered counterfeit, *pax economica*, is one of Europe's exports.

In the twelfth century, *pax* did not mean the absence of war between lords. The *pax* that Church or Emperor wanted to guarantee was not primarily the absence of armed encounters between knights. *Pax*, or peace, meant protecting the poor and their means of subsistence from the violence of war. Peace protected the peasant and the monk. This was the meaning of *Gottesfrieden*, of *Landfrieden*. It protected specific times and places. No matter how bloody the conflict among lords, peace protected the oxen and grain on the stem. It safeguarded the emergency granary, the seed and the time of harvest. Generally speaking, the 'peace of the land' shielded the utilization values of the common environment from violent interference. It ensured access to water and pasture, to woods and livestock, for those who had nothing else from which to draw their subsistence. The 'peace of the land' was thus distinct from the truce between warring parties. This primarily subsistence-oriented significance of peace was lost with the Renaissance.

With the rise of the nation-state, an entirely new world began to emerge. This world ushered in a new kind of peace and a new kind of violence. Both its peace and its violence are equally distant from all the forms of peace and violence which had previously existed. Whereas peace had formerly meant the protection of that minimal subsistence on which the wars among lords had to be fed, henceforth subsistence itself became the victim of an aggression, supposedly peaceful. Subsistence itself became the prey of expanding markets in services and goods. This new kind of peace entailed the pursuit of a utopia. Popular peace had protected precarious but real communities from total extinction. But the new peace was built around an abstraction. The new peace is cut to the measure of *homo economicus*, made by nature to live on the consumption of commodities produced elsewhere by others. While the *pax populi* had protected vernacular autonomy, the environment in which this could thrive and the variety of patterns for its reproduction, the new *pax economica* protected production. It ensures aggression against popular culture, the commons and women.

First, *pax economica* cloaks the assumption that people have become incapable of providing for themselves. It empowers a new elite to make all people's survival dependent on their access to education, health care, police protection, apartments and supermarkets. In ways previously unknown, it exalts the producer and degrades the consumer. *Pax economica* labels the subsistent as 'unproductive', the autonomous as 'asocial', the traditional as 'underdeveloped'. It spells violence against all local customs which do not fit a zero sum game.

Secondly, *pax economica* promotes violence against the environment. The new peace guarantees impunity—the environment may be used as a resource to be mined for the production of commodities, and a space reserved for their circulation. It does not just permit, but encourages, the destruction of the commons. People's peace had protected the commons. It guarded the access of the poor to pastures and woods; it safeguarded the use of the road and the river by people; it reserved to widows and beggars exceptional rights for utilizing the environment. *Pax economica* defines the environment as a scarce resource which it reserves for optimal use in the production of goods and the provision of professional care. Historically, this is what development has meant: starting from the enclosure of the lord's sheep and reaching to the enclosure of the streets for the use of cars and to the restriction of desirable jobs to those with more than twelve years of schooling. Development has always signified a violent exclusion of those who wanted to survive without dependence on consumption from the environment's utilization values. *Pax economica* bespeaks war against the commons.

Thirdly, the new peace promotes a new kind of war between the sexes. The transition from the traditional battle for dominance to this new all-out war between men and women is probably the least analysed of economic growth's side-effects. This war, too, is a necessary outcome of the so-called growth of productive forces, a process implying an increasingly complete monopoly of wage labour over all other forms of work. This too, is aggression. The monopoly of wage-related work entails aggression against a feature common to all subsistence-oriented societies. Though these societies be as different from each other as those of Japan, France and Fiji, one central characteristic is common to all of them: all tasks relevant to subsistence are assigned in a gender-specific way, to either men or women. The set of specific tasks which are necessary and culturally defined vary from society to society, but each society distributes the various possible tasks to either men or women, and does so according to its own unique pattern. In no two cultures is the distribution of tasks within a society the same. In each culture, 'growing up' means to grow into the activities characteristic there, and only there, of either man or woman. To be a man or a woman in pre-industrial societies is not a secondary trait added on to genderless humans. It is the most fundamental characteristic in every single action. To grow up does not mean to be 'educated', but to grow into life by acting as a woman or as a man. Dynamic peace between men and women consists precisely in this division of concrete tasks. And this does not signify equality; it establishes limits to mutual oppression. Even in this intimate domain, people's peace limits both war and the extent of domination. Wage labour destroys this pattern.

Industrial work, productive work, is conceived as neutral and often experienced as such. It is defined as genderless work. And this is true whether it is paid or unpaid, whether its rhythm is determined by production or by consumption. But even though work is conceived as genderless, access to this activity is radically biased. Men have primary access to the paid tasks which are viewed as desirable and women are assigned those left over. Originally, women were the ones forced into unpaid shadow work, although men are now increasingly given these tasks, too. As a consequence of this neutralization of work, development inevitably promotes a new kind of war between the sexes, a competition between theoretical equals of whom half are handicapped by their sex. Now we see a competition for wage labour, which has become scarce, and a struggle to avoid shadow work, which is neither paid nor capable of contributing to subsistence.

Pax economica protects a zero sum game, and ensures its undisturbed progress. All are coerced to become players and to accept the rules of *homo economicus*. Those who refuse to fit the ruling model are either banished as enemies of the peace or educated until they conform. By the rules of the zero sum game, both the environment and human work are scarce stakes; as one gains the other loses. Peace is now reduced to two meanings: the myth that, at least in economics, two and two will one day make five, or a truce and deadlock. Development is the name given to the expansion of this game, to the incorporation of more players and of their resources. Therefore, the monopoly of *pax economica* must be deadly; and there must be some peace other than the one linked to development. One can concede that *pax economica* is not without some positive value—bicycles have been invented and their components must circulate in markets different from those in which pepper was formerly traded. And peace among economic powers is at least as important as peace between the warlords of ancient times. But the monopoly of this elite peace must be questioned. To formulate this challenge seems to me the most fundamental task of peace research today.

September/October 1981

[A talk given at the Asian Peace Research Conference in Yokohama]

Deep Peace

JOHN-FRANCIS PHIPPS

THE DEVELOPMENT of a deep philosophy of peace that defines strength in moral and metaphysical rather than macho and military terms is something the defence establishment could do without. Current nuclear strategy has an obvious vested interest in maintaining the old otherworldly, weak and negative definitions of peace that have prevailed for so long in our culture. The conventional definition of peace as mere absence of war is essential to military strategy. Once the whole concept of strength is equated with armed might, any alternative views of peace are bound to seem weak, flabby, naïve, prone to appeasement.

Compared to other cultures, ours would seem to be unique in its dualistic perception of time: the traditional division between the profane and finite time of this world and the sacred and eternal time of the next. Our everyday language reveals this split: 'temporal' is taken to mean a form of time that is anything but eternal, while 'eternal' is generally understood to mean non-temporal—an infinitely vicious circle if ever there was one.

A certain morbid stiffness became associated with peace—to 'be at peace' is one of our many euphemisms for death, the implication being that death is the only passport to real peace. War was seen as something exciting and dynamic (it still is, by some otherwise quite intelligent people). Peace was thus assumed to be something static and deadly dull, not of this world.

Our culture has grown so used to these dualistic divisions that it tends to treat them as fixed and immutable points of reference. Some of our hopelessly inadequate definitions stem from this underlying attitude towards time, and until this is sorted out we shall continue to operate on the basis of dualistic misperceptions.

Since the time of this world was traditionally perceived as something shoddy and second-rate compared to the time of the next world, it is hardly surprising that the idea of peace became associated with something otherworldly, sublime, too good to be true. The idea that peace might one day actually break out would spread alarm and despondency in certain quarters. The 'peace virus' would be seen by some as something far more dangerous than AIDS. For those of a strategic disposition, peace has to maintain its cadaverous associations, it has to remain safely outside the realm of the living.

One can conduct an interesting perceptual experiment with time by seeing this world in terms of the values and attributes traditionally ascribed to the next. The fact that we might not be sitting on clouds playing harps should not discourage us from conducting this experiment as a form of imaginative visualization. Moreover, we would find ourselves in illustrious company.

A notable exception to the familiar old western dualistic two-timeworld view was the seventeenth century Dutch philosopher, Baruch Spinoza. He saw everything 'under the form of eternity' and for him this world was just as eternal as the next one. Spinoza was really more of a visionary than a philosopher in the strictest sense and there is something noble and inspiring about his vision, even if one cannot get to grips with his philosophy, or necessarily agree with some of the statements he makes.

Moreover, he lived by his philosophy and suffered as a result of it: he was excommunicated by his own Jewish community and declared heretical by orthodox Christians. He declined worldly honours, turned down a profes- sorship and remained all his life a grinder of optical lenses, never living to see the publication of his *magnum opus*, the *Ethics*. It seems most fitting that he earned his living as an optical craftsman, clarifying vision. It also seems rather significant that a person with such a spiritual view of the world should also happen to be one of the very few western thinkers to have supplied a positive definition of peace. He wrote: 'Peace is not the absence of war; it is a virtue born out of the strength of the heart' (*Tractatus Politicus*). The original Latin reads: *ex animi fortitudine*—'fortitude of soul'. Inner strength from a deep level is the main feature of this definition.

Clearly, a person who perceives *this* timeworld as being in some sense eternal and therefore sacred would be extremely well motivated to preserve the planet. Such a person would be morally and metaphysically incapable of contemplating for one split second the idea of allowing such an infinitely precious world to be destroyed. Such destruction would be perceived as the supreme act of blasphemy and desecration, de-sanctification. But if this physical world is merely seen as a rather large lump of matter, with absolutely no timeless values or eternal attributes, then there is no morally compelling reason to preserve it. Maurice Ash is surely right when he says that our concern for the environment in itself marks the restoration of a spiritual dimension in our lives. In this respect, the green perception could be regarded as the re-emergence— or, more appropriately *resurgence*—of a vision similar to Spinoza's. There is certainly nothing new, least of all trendy, about this vision. It is timeless, part of the perennial philosophy and therefore not subject to transient whims, passing fads and fashions. Herein lies the deep strength of the vision, which provides foundations for a philosophy of peace based very much on *this* world.

At its deepest level, peace is a mystery, a paradox. Our western philosophical tradition has tended to be prejudiced against the very idea of paradox and our secular-scientific ethos tends to see mysteries as problems that have to be solved. In an essay aptly entitled *The Secret of Peace*, John Gardner explores the symbolic significance of the first three numbers in relation to peace. He observes that 'war is a function of those who think in twos; peace is made by those who think in threes.' The number two represents the 'fall' into dualism, from the initial primal unity. Here everything is perceived in straight, non-paradoxical, either/or terms: good/evil, light/dark, time/eternity, left/right, east/west and so on. This state of dualism is characterized by cerebral cleverness as opposed to wisdom—the intellect operating in a manner dissociated from deeper feelings and intuitions. This is often mistakenly described as 'rational' and all other feelings, sensations and intuitions are consequently seen as 'irrational'. So whenever anybody proposes a restoration of spirituality to metaphysics, such a proposal is seen as 'an assault against reason'. But the original philosophical concept of wisdom was far closer to mystical awareness than to cerebral cleverness.

According to Gardner, the peace-maker stands between two extremes and consequently needs inner strength, fortitude of soul, in order to avoid the war-prone confrontation of dualism: 'Every virtue stands under the three. But when the good is perceived as the preferred half, of a *duality*, war will be not only likely but in the long run sure. The art of life is to achieve the good by walking the middle way.' As long as one is centred, one can regard opposing powers as potentialities for good. Dualism involves the denial of one's own shadow elements and their projection onto an enemy figure. The fury against the other is, as the sages have always told us, rooted in that which we hate and cannot accept in ourselves. The third way is the way of integration, where both light and dark aspects of our personalities are accepted.

A culture that has been immersed for centuries in a dualistic worldview is thus apt to define everything in terms of opposites. Consequently we have lost sight of our own western equivalent of *ahimsa*, which is something very much more positive than a mere absence of violence. It is a sort of 'soul-force', something flowing from the deepest levels of our beings. We therefore need a language of soul-strength that can touch this inner sanctum, this holy of holies that dwells in each and every one of us, thereby releasing untapped latent potentials for creative growth.

It can sometimes be helpful to see things in terms of temporal rather than religious language. This can have the effect of restoring vitality to overused and misused religious terminology. For example, when we see the varieties of religious experience in temporal terms—as experiments with time—we thereby perceive more clearly that such experiences involve the perception of a different order of time in *this* world and include temporal attributes traditionally assumed to belong exclusively to the next world.

In virtually all the main spiritual traditions, the present moment is regarded as a potential 'door to the non-temporal': 'The present, man's most precious gift, is the point where time and eternity meet; it symbolizes hope and joy. It is the moment of faith and the door towards the non-temporal. Time itself is impregnated by the eternal in such a way that every moment of time is a gate to the eternal, practically all the traditions of the world speak with the same tongue concerning the present moment, the instant, the present now, the eternal now.'

We tend to stand in awe of great luminaries like Spinoza and Blake, but often what they are actually talking about is something we can all relate to in everyday life, in moments of stillness and contemplation. The present moment can hardly be regarded as something inaccessible, restricted only to great thinkers and visionary poets. It depends, of course, how we perceive it; perception is the key. The fact that we may not write a learned treatise or wax lyrical about our own particular timeless moments should not be construed as implying that we all perceive time in exactly the same way.

Thousands of people from all walks of life, from different religious backgrounds and many who would describe themselves as agnostic, have sent in accounts of their moments of illumination to the Alister Hardy Research Centre at Oxford. Recent surveys indicate that at least one third of the populations of Britain and America would claim such experiences.

The political implications of this nobler, more joyful, unitive and life-affirming aspect of human experience need further exploration. For this is a form of liberation that goes deeper than other more familiar forms and can properly be called metaphysical liberation. Of what value are other forms of liberation if at a deep level we remain metaphysically repressed, spiritually imprisoned? Metaphysical liberation is the most powerful form of liberation. Nothing can prevail against it, no bombs, no state authority and all its armed might, no defence industry. For the human spirit is, as the women of Greenham have reminded us, free and strong and you can never kill it.

There is a great wellspring of creativity and life-affirming spirituality simply waiting to manifest itself. There are now countless sects and groups of every conceivable variety, but many, if not most, suffer from political apartheid—they impose a dualistic division between the realm of the spirit and the affairs of this world. This separation is based on a false perception of the actual nature of politics. If we are talking about inner power (which we are), then we are discussing politics. On the other hand, many political activists suffer from the illusion that metaphysical liberation is of no relevance to politics, whereas in reality this inner freedom could form the basis of a more honest and relevant form of politics based on mutual trust and co-operation rather than antagonism and confrontation.

Only connect, only connect. The inner-outer connection has only just got under way and has yet to attain socially significant proportions. The emphasis is on quality, not quantity, the inner and invisible, more paradoxical processes rather than outward and visible, non-paradoxical facts and figures. A strong and deep philosophy of peace could provide the necessary bridge between the inner and outer realms, promoting a new (yet timeless) form of contemplative activism rooted in the vision that there is in reality only *one* timeworld and that this one world is sacred and therefore of infinite value.

January/February 1986

The Deterrent Myth

E. P. THOMPSON

GEORGE KENNAN HAS WRITTEN, 'To my mind, the nuclear bomb is the most useless weapon ever invented. It can be employed to no constructive purpose. It is not even an effective defence against itself.'

Immoral or insane, the weapons are now here in super-abundance. They condition our consciousness and expectations in innumerable ways. The consequences of their use defy our imagination, but at the same time the dismantling of all this weaponry, down to the last nuclear land-mine, by the mutual agreement of both blocs, would require such a total realignment of strategy, resources, direction, ideologies, diplomacies—such an unprecedented investment in agitation, negotiation, and conversion—that this also exhausts our imagination. In confronting this threat to civilization we are, in the end, confronting ourselves, and we turn away from the mirror exhausted and self-defeated. We will pass the problem on, unresolved, to the next generation or the generation that follows. If any generation does.

This is, essentially, the political meaning of contemporary deterrence theory. In its pure form, that of MAD or Mutual Assured Destruction, it proposes that war between the super-powers and their allies may be indefinitely postponed because nuclear weapons make any alternative unthinkable or unacceptable. I emphasize 'postponement'. The theory does not propose the victory of one 'side' over the other 'side', neither does it propose the resolution of those differences between the two parties which might bring them to war. On the contrary, by maintaining each party in a posture of menace to the other, it fixes indefinitely the tension which makes the resolution of differences improbable. It transfixes diplomacies and ideologies into a twilight state; while postponing war it also postpones the resolutions of peace.

This would be so even if we were to succeed in reducing weaponry to a level of minimal deterrence: let us say six delivery-systems on each side. But we are not reducing weaponry. Over the past two decades this has been steadily increasing, not only in gross destructive power—as Mr Kennan has said, 'levels of redundancy of such grotesque dimensions as to defy rational understanding'—but also in the quality and accuracy of delivery-systems. Hence the theory of deterrence now legitimates not Mutual Assured Destruction but Mutual Aggravated Destruction. And to the degree that menace is aggravated with each year, the resolution of differences by means short of war becomes less probable. There is no longer an even-handed postponement both of war and of peace; terminal war becomes more likely, the terminus of peace recedes from any agenda.

Is such a consequence inherent in the premises of the theory itself? On the one hand, it can be argued that this need not necessarily be so. A rigidly-enforced state of minimal deterrence, policed by some international authority, need not be subject to the law of aggravation. On the other hand, it has been argued persuasively that deterrence is inherently addictive, and hence must lead to aggravation. In 1979, shortly before his death, Gregory Bateson addressed his own University of California with the plea that the university renounce any part in the research or development of nuclear weapons. Employing analogies from biological systems transferred to social psychology, he argued that 'the short-time deterrent effect is achieved at the expense of a long-time cumulative change. The actions which today postpone disaster result in an increase in strength on *both* sides of the competitive system to ensure a greater instability and greater destruction if and when the explosion occurs. It is this fact of cumulative change from one act of threat to the next that gives the system the quality of *addiction*.'

Bateson is reminding us that we are not just dealing with weapons in a medium of pure theory, where one threat balances and cancels out the other. These weapons operate in the medium of politics, ideology and strategy; they are perceived as menacing and are intended to be so perceived; they induce fear and they simultaneously enhance and frustrate feelings of aggression. Nor need aggravation pursue a steady linear advancement: in the vocabulary of mathematical catastrophe-theory civilization may already be tipping over upon the overhanging cusp between fear and aggression.

That is more than enough about deterrence as theory. It is in truth a most pitiful, lightweight theory. It is espoused, in its pristine purity, only by a handful of monkish celibates retired within the walls of centres of Strategic Studies. It cannot endure any intercourse with the actual world. It is at heart a very simple, and simple-minded idea, which occurred to the first cave-men when they got hold of clubs (it is this very simplicity which gives to it a certain populist plausibility). If I have a club, that will deter him from clobbering me. The thought has gone on, through armies and empires, dreadnoughts and gas; all that a historian can say is that sometimes it has worked for a while, and sometimes it has not, but always in the end it has broken down. All that is new about it now is that the clubs of today, the technology of destruction, are so immense as to defy any rational exercise.

But it is not an *operative* theory: that is, it does not direct any nation's behaviour. It appears always as a gloss, as an *ex post facto* apologia, as a theoretical legitimation of actions which are taken for quite different reasons. The first atomic weapons were not developed because some theorist invented deterrence and *then* scientists were commissioned to invent a bomb. The bombs were invented to blast the German and Japanese antagonists into submission. Thermonuclear weapons were not developed to deter anyone, but to demonstrate United States military superiority, and because it seemed to be a sweet new device worth developing. It was only *after* the Soviet Union also developed thermonuclear weapons that the theory of deterrence came into vogue, and on both sides.

Deterrence theory has become the ideological lubricant of the arms race. Its theories can be turned to use by arms manufacturers or by military lobbies; or they can be brought in afterwards to justify anything. To be anything more than that it would have to be fleshed out with some empirical substance, it would have to engage with the full historical process; and, at the end of all its worst-case predictions, it would have to envisage some way forward to an ultimate better case—to proffer some little advice as to policies which might possibly advance the better and forestall the cumulative worst.

And how do deterrence theorists suppose that this race will ever end? Short of a final nuclear war, I suppose there are these alternative scenarios. Soviet ideologists may suppose that, in the end, Western capitalism will collapse, with conjoint recession and inflation, shortage of energy resources, internal insurrection and revolt throughout the Third World. Western ideologists suppose that the Soviet economy will collapse under the burden of increasing arms allocations, with internal nationalist and dissident movements, and with insurrection or near-insurrection throughout Eastern Europe.

But these theorists need only cross the corridor and knock on the doors of their colleagues in History, Politics or Sociology to learn that these scenarios might provide, precisely, the moment of the worst case of all. Each of these developments could bring the continent, and ultimately the world itself, into the greatest peril. Each could provide the conditions not for the peaceful reunification of Europe, but for the rise of panic-stricken authoritarian regimes, tempted to maintain the discipline of their peoples by recourse to military adventures. The breakdown of East or West, in a situation of massive military confrontation, would tend to precipitate the resolution of war. And, indeed, already the military and political élites, both East and West, who are now sensing gathering difficulties within their own systems, are showing that they need the Cold War—they need to put not only their missiles but also their ideology and security systems into good repair—as a means of controlling internal dissent.

In doing this, these élites find deterrence theory to be of increasing service. We pass into a new, exalted stage where deterrence theory becomes the astrology of the nuclear age. It is a peculiar situation. In the case of internal ideological systems, the public normally have some experiential means of checking the ideology's veracity. Thus monetarism may appear as a superbly logical system, but we still know what prices are in the shops, which of our neighbours are unemployed, and who has gone bankrupt. But in the case of deterrence theory, the ideologists control both the intellectual system and the information input. None of us has ever seen an SS-20, nor can we count their numbers; none of us can check out the throw-weight or circular error probable of a Trident missile. We have no experiential means of critique whatsoever. The information itself is pre-processed within an ideological matrix (the intelligence services) and is presented with intent to prejudice.

Militarization in the advanced world today has these contradictory features. It is distinguished by the very low visibility of some of its activities and the high visibility of others. The actual military presence, in most parts of Western although not in all parts of Eastern Europe, is very low. This is not a time, as were the jingo days before World War I or as was Hitler's Germany in the late 1930s, of ostentatious parades, rallies, tattoos, and the ubiquitous recruiting sergeant. The actual weapons are invisible, at Grand Forks, North Dakota, or on the Kola peninsula, or at sea. The attendant communications and security operations are screened by official secrecy. The militarization of nuclear warfare is science- and capital-intensive; it does not require a huge uniformed labour force, nor does it necessitate conscription or the draft. The growing retinue of 'deterrence' is more likely to be in mufti: in manufacture, research and development; we may exchange small-talk with them in the university common-room—easy-going, civilian, decidedly unmilitary types.

But at the same time militarization as ideology has an increasingly sensational visibility. It is presented to us on television, in the speeches of politicians, as the threat of the other: the backfire bomber, the ss-20, the hordes of Soviet tanks. It is necessary—and on both sides—to make the public's flesh creep in order to justify the expense and the manifest risks of 'our deterrents'. With the break-up of the Cominform, and the weakness and disarray of Western Communist movements, no one is much impressed today with the story-line of the first Cold War: the threat from within (this story-line still works to more effect in the East). What then must be imprinted upon the public mind is the escalating threat from without. Deterrence theory is elevated to the Chair of Propaganda.

The other contradiction is this. None of these weapons—*none* of them—can ever be used, except for the final holocaust. As Mr Kennan has told us: 'The nuclear bomb is the most useless weapon ever invented. It is not even an effective defence against itself.' From some time around 1960, each additional weapon has been useless. They might as well not exist. The significance of these weapons is symbolic only.

I say 'symbolic only'; but as a social historian I have often offered the view that symbolism is a profoundly important component of historical process. Symbolic confrontations precede and accompany confrontations by force. The rituals of state, the public execution, the popular demonstration—all carry symbolic force; they consolidate the assured hegemony of the rulers or they demystify that hegemony and challenge it with numbers or ridicule. Symbolism is not a mere colour added to the facts of power; it is an element of societal power in its own right.

New generations of nuclear missiles are not less dangerous because they are only symbolic. They are carriers of the most barbarous symbolism in history. They spell out to our human neighbours that we are ready, at any instant, to annihilate them; and that we are perfecting the means. They spell out also the rejection of any alternative means of resolution of differences. That is why we must resist the temptation of being drawn within the premises of deterrence theory. The weapons are useless, except for the final event; they exist, today, only as symbols of human self-defeat; they must be rejected.

What should properly command our attention today is not the theory of deterrence but the social and political *consequences* of its working over two decades. From one aspect these consequences are merely absurd. Anthropologists will be familiar with the potlach—the ritual and ceremonial destruction by primitive peoples of their surplus food and resources. From this aspect, the nuclear arms race is nothing but a gigantic potlach. From another aspect, matters are perilous. It is not only that these weapons do actually exist; their function may be as symbols, but they remain there, on their launch-pads, instantly ready. The weapons have been consumed in no potlach, only the human resources have been consumed. And there are now new and devilish strategies which propose that they might actually, in 'limited' ways, be used.

But the greater peril does not lie here. It lies in the consequences of a course of action which has frozen diplomatic and political process and has continually postponed the making of peace. Deterrence theory proceeded by excluding as irrelevant all that was extraneous to weaponry. But no theory can prohibit economic and political process from going on. Through these two decades, frustrated aggression has fed back into the opposed societies; the barbarous symbolism of weaponry has corrupted the opposed cultures; the real and material bases of the weapons-systems—the military-industrial complexes of both sides—have enlarged and consolidated their political influence; militarism has increased its retinue of civilian retainers; the security services and security-minded ideologies have been strengthened; the Cold War has consolidated itself, not as between both parties, but as an indigenous *interest* within each one.

Deterrence theory proposed a stationary state: that of MAD. But history knows no stationary states. As deterrence presides, both parties change; they become addicted; they become uglier and more barbarous in their postures and gestures. They turn into societies whose production, ideology and research is increasingly directed towards war. 'Deterrence' enters deeply into the structure, the economy, and the culture of both blocs. This is the reason—and not this or that advantage in weaponry, or political contingency—why nuclear war is probable within our lifetime. It is not just that we are preparing for war; we are preparing ourselves to be *the kind of societies* which go to war.

I doubt if there is any way out, although increasing numbers are searching for it. Since the weapons are useless and function only as symbols, we could commence to behave as if they do not exist. We could then resume every possible mode of discourse—inter-personal, scholarly, diplomatic—designed to break up the unnatural opposition of the blocs, whose adversary posture lies behind the entire operation. But the melting of the blocs can never take place upon terms of the 'victory' states, but in good part *against* the states of both sides. This means that we cannot leave the work to politicians, or to the employees of states, to do on their own. There would have to be an unprecedented investment of the voluntary resources of ordinary citizens in threading a new skein of peace. In this work, scholars and intellectuals would find that they had particular duties, both because of their specialist skills and opportunities, and because of the universal humane claims of their sciences and arts. I am not inviting them to 'go into politics'. I am saying that they must go *ahead* of politics and attempt to put European culture back together, or all politics and all culture will cease.

January/February 1982

[From a paper presented at the British Association meeting in New York]

The Poet and the Bomb

ELSA MORANTE

THERE'S NO DOUBT that the most important fact today, the one nobody can ignore, is that we of the civilized nations in the twentieth century live in the atomic age. Everyone is so aware of it that the word 'atomic' is everywhere, even in our jokes and our comic strips. Most people still protect themselves from the full meaning and impact of the word by keeping it (quite understandably) at a distance, and even those few who recognize the real menace and are tormented by it—and so are considered neurotic, if not mad—are more preoccupied with the consequences of the phenomenon than with its hidden causes and, so to speak, its biographical origins. Few, in short, question their own consciousness (and perhaps the real atomic centre lies in each individual consciousness) as to why this essential secret (perhaps *the* secret of nature) has only been located and cracked in this present age when we know that right from antiquity, highly developed peoples in various places and epochs, all hungry for knowledge, knew of its existence. It won't do to reply that the sirens of science have replaced those of the imagination in our great intellectual voyage; that may seem to be the answer, but our question remains, and it makes the problem even more pressing.

Now no one will be prepared to believe that it is a matter of chance—that humanity has reached this global crisis merely because at this point human intelligence, ever on the lookout for new adventures, chose this particular dark path out of so many others and discovered the secret, thanks to its scientific wizards. No, we all know by now that in collective as in individual life, what seem to be accidents are nearly always due to the results of unconscious will (which, if you like, we can call *destiny*) and therefore of choice.

Our bomb is the flower, the natural expression, of our contemporary society, as Plato's dialogues were the flower of the Greek city state; the Colosseum of Roman imperial power; Raphael's Madonnas of Italian humanism; the gondola of the Venetian nobility; the tarantella dance of certain rural populations in the south of Italy; and the death camps of petit bourgeois bureaucratic culture, already infected with the insanity of atomic suicide. To sum up in a few, now much-abused words: contemporary society is experiencing the secret desire to destroy itself.

People will say that the fatal first seed of this desire was sown at the birth of the human race and has grown up with it, so whatever's happening today is only the inevitable crisis of this development. But this theory only supports our proposition. Nowadays it is common knowledge that the life instinct (Eros) and the death instinct (Thanatos) coexist in the human psyche, and with regard to the second of these it is theoretically quite possible for someone to read the holy scriptures of all religions and conclude that bliss can only be attained through final annihilation. Some psychologists even speak of the 'Nirvana instinct' in man. However, while the Nirvana promised by religion is won by a life of contemplation, self-renunciation and universal piety—by the unification of consciousness—its wicked petit bourgeois surrogate is attained by the exact opposite: disintegration of consciousness by means of injustice and organized insanity, by degrading myths, by feverish and savage alienation. Finally, there are the famous bombs, those gigantic whales sleeping in the best-protected quarters in America, Asia and Europe. Attended, guarded and cherished in idleness like a harem by totalitarian and democratic regimes alike, they are the treasure of our nuclear world. They aren't so much the potential cause of our destruction as the necessary expression of the disaster already active in our consciousness.

I don't want to burden you with a millionth account of the everyday social evidence for this disaster; it is so pervasive and relentless that even our poor domestic fellow creatures (dogs, cats, not to mention the wretched chickens) can feel the tension.

Still less do I want to deliver a propagandist sermon against the bomb. And besides, I am a citizen of the contemporary world myself, and perhaps swayed by the universal desire too; I'll do better not to boast so much until I feel wholly immune.

Yet, at the same time, it is my good fortune and honour to belong to the writing species. I can say that I was passionately devoted to this art—or rather, to art itself—from the moment I started to speak, and I hope it's not too presumptuous of me to claim that I've learned one thing at least from my long experience and labour, and that is an obvious and simple definition of art (or poetry, as for me they are synonymous).

Here it is: *Art is the opposite of disintegration*, simply because its *raison d'être* and justification (now and in the future), or to put it another way, its *function*, is to prevent the disintegration of human consciousness in its wearing and *alienating* daily contact with the world, and to be a constant witness, in the unreal, disjointed and stale confusion of external relationships, to the integrity of the real, or in one word, to reality. Reality is always vivid, bright and actual; it cannot be damaged or destroyed, nor can it decay. In reality death is only a different development of life. Reality is wholeness, integrity itself: it is inexhaustible in its protean restlessness, so its exploration is infinite.

So if art reflects reality it would be, to say the least, a contradiction in terms to call specimens or productions of disintegration 'art'.

Then one must ask oneself what role art can have within the disintegration system if its *raison d'être* is integrity. The answer is: *none*. If the world in all its vast momentum is hurtling towards destruction as its supreme goal, what is there left for the artist to do, because if he really is an artist, he tends towards integrity (i.e. reality) as the only liberating and joyful condition of his consciousness? He must make a choice.

He can come to believe that he is wrong and that reality as an absolute, as that unique, secret wholeness of things (i.e. art) is only a self-produced phantom— a trick of Eros to keep the whole farrago going. In which case he will feel that his role is hopelessly discredited: it will seem empty and he will stop writing.

Or he can come to believe that the fault doesn't lie in him but with the great mass of his contemporaries—that not Eros but Thanatos the illusionist is at work, forging his monstrous visions to terrify and bewilder consciousness, perverting it from its only happiness, turning it away from the real explanation. So people are reduced to an elementary fear of existence, evading themselves and therefore evading reality, for people get used to unreality as they do to drugs, and unreality is the bleakest degradation of all. They are alienated even from true negation, for the way of unreality leads not to the wise men's Nirvana but to its exact opposite, which is Chaos, the most abject and anguished regression.

In this second case, if he realizes the plague of madness isn't 'his' but in the collective unconscious, the writer will find he has a further choice to make. He may consider that the collective disease is too far advanced to be stopped: he can already detect the first signs of infection in himself in any case, and is incapable of resisting it, so it would be better to save himself and run away, to a forest or a south sea island or wherever he likes—perhaps to a desert of pillars where he can copy Saint Simeon Stylites. And whatever the demagogues, courtiers and apostles of disintegration say, it is a fact that one real person—even a sole survivor—sitting on top of a pillar, thinking, is better for the health and life of the universe than yet another chap dressed up, televised and shining for the bomb. By an intuitive logic of events, the atomic bomb will be hard put to go off as long as he resists and goes on writing poetry on top of his pillar.

The other and happier possibility is that the writer will find he still has some faith in collective liberation, together with the certainty that he himself is, as yet, safe from the disaster and capable of resistance. In this case there is no doubt that he will see his *function* as a writer as not only vitally useful to society, but more necessary than ever before in man's history: faced with the obscene invasion of unreality, art, coming to restore reality, can represent almost the only hope for the world. Where a crowd of people is being cheated, the mere presence of one person who won't let himself be cheated can be the first step to rescue, but if that person is a writer this step will be multiplied by a thousand, a hundred thousand fold. Whether he knows it or not, the writer is destined to expose fraud, and once a poem is let loose it never stands still: it spreads and multiplies, reaching places and people the poet himself had never dreamed of.

Naturally the poor poem will have to suffer if it is to command any attention in the gloomy market places of our alienated world, amid the furious din of official business, dedicated to the boredom of its alienated victims—for among the many more severe trials that resistance entails, the clamour of boredom is exhausting. Sometimes the writer will want to send them all to the devil with their newspapers, their singers and their cyclotrons, and to sail away for ever, like Rimbaud, or even go to the desert to keep his friends company on top of their pillars. But he won't. Or if he does, he comes back after every flight; for it is his nature to need others, especially those who are different from him; without others he's a broken man.

Now for goodness sake don't misunderstand me and deduce that art's mirror is an *optimistic* one. On the contrary, great art in its profundity is always pessimistic because the real essence of life is tragic. Great art is essentially tragic. And if a writer distorts the real tragedy of life when it has opened its heart to him in order to preserve *good feeling* and please *refined spirits*, he commits the sin which the New Testament calls the worst of all sins, the *sin against the Holy Ghost*, and he would no longer be a writer at all.

The purity of art does not consist of dodging the aspects of nature which the social law in its muddled proceedings censures as dirty and wicked, but in restoring them spontaneously to the dimension of the real, where they are natural and therefore innocent. Art is inherently liberating, so it is always revolutionary. Any passing experience becomes a religious one when the poet gives it his attention, and in this sense one *can* talk about optimism. Whatever befalls him in life, even if he's reduced by misfortune to the naked limits of horror, as anyone may be, until he feels sure that this horror is ruling his mind, it won't be his destiny's last word. If his consciousness does not sink into unreality, and even the horror becomes a real answer (i.e. poetry) for him, he will be performing an optimistic action the instant he puts pen to paper.

Of course, the disintegration system has its own officials, courtiers, secretaries and hangers-on, and they all try to weaken the writer's resistance in various ways, either in their own (misconceived) interest, or because they have been genuinely taken in.

They might try to win him over, to draw him into the system by corrupting him with popular success and grotesque publicity, turning him into a star or a playboy. Or they might do the opposite by making out that his opposition to the system is treacherous or sinful, or moralizing, or immoral, or sheer weakness. They will say, for example, that he's not modern. Of course not! In their eyes, being modern means being disintegrated. True writers cannot live within the system, but there are plenty of people who write and publish books, and to distinguish these from the genuine article I shall call them *hacks*. Some of them are mere tools of the system, of very secondary importance compared to the nuclear scientists, and their rooms and offices can be described as the least significant branches of the real nuclear establishment.

The true writer usually likes to venture among people of all sorts, but he inevitably prefers the *dominated* to the *dominant* classes, not on humanitarian grounds, but because of the fatal law that always rules his life. And indeed the domination of one person over another has always been evil and is now steeped in unreality.

This is why, in his social and political life, the writer always feels drawn to revolutionary movements, whose declared aim is the ending of all domination of one person over another.

And in the end the writer nearly always finds his truest friends among the young, even among children, for they alone still recognize and dwell in reality. The great poet Umberto Saba said that a poet can be many things, but he is above all a child who marvels at what happens to him when he grows up. He marvels, but, if I may add, he also enjoys himself; luckily he derives some enjoyment from his absurd and desperate fight with the dragon.

Finally, what sort of novel or poetry should our writer choose to 'pursue his struggle', as the newspapers might put it? The answer is simple: he will write what he honestly believes. To quote Saba again: 'The poets' task now is to write honest poetry.'

But it would be enough to say, 'to write poetry', for if it is poetry it cannot be anything but honest; a poet of whatever sort can never be insincere. As history has shown, he might be ugly and deformed, he might be addicted to the worst vices, he might be a drunkard, a ne'er-do-well; he might be dirty and he might smell. This is and always has been his own affair. But insofar as he's a writer, these are the necessary conditions he must always meet: attention, honesty, disinterestedness.

I've tried to explain what reality is, but sadly I doubt that I have been successful because it is something one understands only when one experiences it, and when one experiences it there is no need for explanations. A novice once asked a wise man from the East, 'What is the Absolute?' The sage answered readily, 'The shrub at the bottom of the garden.' And when the boy, still doubtful, asked, 'And who is the one who understands this truth?' the old man replied, giving him a tap on the head, 'A lion with a golden coat.'

November/December 1986

[An edited extract from one of Elsa Morante's remarkable talks translated from the Italian by Betty Romary and Mark Thompson]

The Greening of Germany

PETRA KELLY

EMMA GOLDMAN ONCE WROTE: 'The true emancipation begins neither at the polls nor in the courts, it begins in women's soul. History tells us that every oppressed class gained true liberation from its masters through its own efforts. It is necessary that women learn from that lesson, that they realize that their freedom will reach as far as their power to achieve their freedom reaches.'

The true essence of Emma Goldman's feminist vision was that women should start taking responsibility for their own lives instead of trying to improve or purify the lives of men. Emma Goldman explained that male egotism, vanity and strength in the patriarchal sense, operated to enslave women. It was partly, she argued, because women themselves often idolized those qualities in men, creating a self-perpetuating system. Women must change their consciousness, break from the patriarchal circle and free themselves from such ill-suited ideals as those of the masculine, patriarchal and nuclear society. All too long we have been told that to gain equal chances and equal opportunities, we must accept the equal rights and equal duties of men. But it cannot be emancipation to stand beside men in the various national armies and learn to shoot and kill. It cannot be emancipation to learn how to operate a nuclear reactor or sit behind the control panel of a nuclear silo.

The development of women, their freedom, their independence, must come from and through themselves, by asserting themselves as a personality, as human beings and not as sex commodities; by refusing the right to anyone over her body; by refusing to bear children unless they want them; by refusing to be a servant to the state, society, husband, family; by making her life deeper and richer.

I begin with this vision of the strong women in history, because without emancipation of women, and without the emancipation of men, we cannot build a non-violent, ecological and non-military green republic. The women of the 'Pentagon action' of November 1980 explained that: 'We are in the hands of men whose power and wealth have separated them from the reality of daily life and from their imagination. We are right to be afraid.'

There is fear among the people, and that fear, created by the industrial militarists, is used as an excuse to accelerate the arms race. 'We will protect you,' they say, but we have never been so endangered, so close to the end of human time. Women are gathering because life on the precipice is intolerable. We want to know what anger in these men, what fear which can only be satisfied by destruction, what coldness of heart and ambition, drives their days. We want to know, because we do not want that dominance which is exploitative and murderous in international relations and so dangerous to women and children at home; we do not want that sickness transferred by the violent society through fathers to sons.

On Monday, 6th August 1945, a totally different era in human history opened. The forces which held together the constituent particles of the atom had been harnessed to man's use: on this day, men used them. By a decision of the American military authorities, made in the wake of the protests of many of the scientists who had worked on this project, an atomic bomb was dropped on Hiroshima. Two thirds of the world's population today were born after the bombs on Hiroshima and Nagasaki. I was born in 1947, after the bombs on Hiroshima and Nagasaki. Many of us were born in this atomic age and have grown up with the bomb, with many irresponsible leaders, often infantile old men, whether they be in the White House or in the Kremlin, and we have been made to believe that we can live with the bomb and can continue to watch the politicians and military personnel build up their stock of overkill war toys. But in 1976 and in 1981, I went to Hiroshima and to Nagasaki, and I will not forget the atomic victims still suffering today in the atomic hospitals in Japan and elsewhere in the Pacific. I cannot forget watching the children bring their coloured paper cranes to the Memorial Park in Hiroshima and I cannot forget the many women and men of the Pacific Islands, of the Bikini atoll, of Micronesia, the Indians of the United States and the Aborigines in Australia—all victims of the nuclear industry, all victims of the militarization and nuclearization of this planet Earth which has no emergency exit.

I have also seen the luxurious air-conditioned and thick-carpeted rooms of the European Economic Community in Brussels where I have worked for the past nine years, and I have seen them at NATO, and I have seen them within the Pentagon. There such terms and such unholy language as 'body-count', 'collateral damage', 'escalation control' and 'targets of opportunity' are used. There people work whose speech and behaviour suggest that what they are doing needs to be done and is therefore right. Why can they not stand back from their day-to-day computerized killings and begin to examine the implications of their work? How can these human beings be converted? Albert Einstein and Bertrand Russell, just before the former's death, issued an appeal in which they said: 'Shall we put an end to the human race; or shall mankind and womankind renounce war? Most of us are not neutral in feeling, but as human beings we have to remember that, if the issues between East and West are to be decided in any manner that can give any possible satisfaction to anybody, whether Asian, European or American, whether White or Black, then these issues must *not* be decided by war.'

'Wars will cease when men refuse to fight'—this has attracted many to the pacifist philosophy which is an integral part of the Green Party, the party for which I speak, the alternative party and non-violent movement which I have helped to build up since leaving the Social-Democratic Party in 1978. The Green Party, a non-violent, ecological and basic-democratic anti-war coalition of parliamentary and extra-parliamentary grassroots forces within the Federal

Republic of Germany is, at the moment, the only hope I have to change not only the system of structural and personal violence but also to find a way out of the insane policies of atomic deterrence. The Green Party to which I have dedicated my efforts and all my energy in the past three years, is committed to basic democracy, to ecology in the broadest sense of the term, to social justice and to non-violence.

The Green Party has an underlying concept which states clearly that human-kind must not consider the land and what it supports in terms of real estate. We are all temporary custodians of the land—it is entrusted to us for pass-ing on *unimpaired* to future generations. We argue that the most urgent and most straightforward disarmament measures required from an ecological standpoint are the absolute prohibition of all atomic, biological and chemical weapons and a complete demilitarization and conversion to protective sta-tus of ecologically important regions. Nuclear states now comprise a large part of the world's population. There is for me only one way out—com-plete unilateral disarmament. The bilateral step-by-step approaches have failed. Arms control talks and the present hypocritical talks in Geneva and the so-called zero-option of Mr Reagan have also failed. We propose unilateral and calculated first steps towards complete disarmament as a solution not only for the Federal Republic of Germany, but for all European countries, for all countries in the world. Each of our governments must take that first step which it expects the other government to take. And if governments do not take these first steps, we shall take these first steps for them. We must work towards a disarmament race. The only war we seek should be the war against humankind's ancient enemies—poverty, hunger, illiteracy and preventable disease.

We need increased trust in world relationships. We must shed our Western paranoia in regard to the possible threats posed by the Soviet Union. This paranoia, this new hysteria in our established media and in government circles has prepared once again the ground for 'just wars' to be fought against the so-called red menace. But in both blocs, in the bloc of NATO and in the bloc of the Warsaw pact, lie many corpses, many strangulated and tortured men, women and children, in El Salvador, in Turkey, in Vietnam, in Chile and in Afghanistan. We speak about 'limited nuclear wars'. We speak of 'victory that is possible', we speak of megatons and megadead.

We can only kill thousands because we have first learned to call them the enemy. Wars commence in our culture first of all because we kill each other in euphemisms and abstractions long before the first missiles have been launched. It has never been true that nuclear war is unthinkable. It has been thought and has been put into effect. It was done in 1945 in the name of the Allies—it was done by professing Christians, when a victory against the Japanese was certain. What is unthinkable is that nuclear war could happen to us. So long as we can support the idea that this war will be inflicted on 'them', the thought comes easily. We think each other to death.

Within the logic of 'deterrence', millions are now employed in the armed services, in the security organs and military economy of both blocs. Here is also the driving rationale for expansion programmes in unsafe nuclear energy (programmes with a military pay-off), while the urgent research into safe, renewable, soft energies is neglected. The so-called capitalist and the state-socialist powers compete to feed into the Middle East, Africa and Asia more sophisticated means of killing and they compete for markets for arms and weapons.

All over the world people from the grass roots, from below, are saying 'no' to the games of the superpowers. They are coming in the thousands and in the hundreds of thousands tomorrow. Women were arrested on November 17th 1980 at the end of a two-day civil disobedience action at the Pentagon. Women were recently arrested outside the missile base at Greenham Common in Great Britain, for they had protested non-violently for several months in a peace camp. And on September 9th 1980, a group called 'Plough-shares Eight' (among them the Berrigan Brothers) walked into the General Electric Re-entry division plant at King of Prussia, Pennsylvania, hammered on two nuclear warhead cones and poured their blood on the damaged cones and on documents and desks until they were stopped by guards and arrested. On March 6th 1981, they were found guilty of burglary and criminal conspiracy.

At the Montgomery county court in Wellstown, Pennsylvania, Daniel Berrigan, a dear friend of mine, stated that 'The struggle to prevent nuclear war is a struggle for the soul and heart and minds of people. I believe that with all my heart. I believe that the crime of nuclear catastrophe is already on the way. Even if, as we all hope and pray, there were never to be another nuclear explosion against human life, I believe that the intention to use the bomb is signified by having the bomb around.'

We in Europe must do all we can to prevent an Euroshima. We must resort to non-violent blockades, sit-ins, die-ins, hours of silence, fasting periods, information campaigns, discussion with the police and with military personnel. We must rejoice with the many reserve officers who have handed in their reserve passes and with the many thousands of war resisters. We must also resist any attempt by the statesmen and politicians of East and West to manipulate this movement to their own advantage. Our objectives must be to free Europe from confrontation and to lead this Europe out of *both* blocs.

One day the great military alliances must be dissolved by the people in both blocs. And so we must continue to agitate non-violently for the expulsion of all nuclear, of all ABC-weapons and bases from European soil. I am ashamed of the present state of affairs, whereby my country, the Federal Republic of Germany, has become the sixth largest weapons exporter in the world. Over seventy per cent of all West German arms exports go to the developing countries of the Third World. We export weapon components, U-boats and tanks to South American military dictators and to apartheid regimes.

The anti-war and anti-nuclear movement does not mean negative protest: it is necessarily pro-environment, pro-woods and pro-fields, pro-rivers and oceans, pro-plants and animals, pro-solar energy, pro-clean air and above all, pro-people. It is a planetary vision, a planetary moral standard, for hungry people, poor people, women, youth, the handicapped, the old people, the Amazon tribes, the Aborigines, the inner-city slum dwellers, the oppressed minorities everywhere—we are all in this together. We *are* in fact the realists, we are not only the dreamers of brother- and sisterhood, of non-violence and of survival.

When I think of the non-violence that we need, not only in the course of politics but as a way of life, I think of the native Americans, the American Indians, who have a reverence for life, respect human dignity and understand the interconnection of all things to an extent that has yet to be surpassed. The genocide perpetrated by the United States on the Indian tribes and cultures —a pattern which still continues today—remains one of the most crucial indictments of the white civilization. In 1854, Chief Seattle, leader of the Suquamish tribe in the Washington territory delivered this prophetic speech to mark the transfer of ancestral Indian lands to the Federal Government: 'This we know. The Earth does not belong to man; man belongs to the Earth, this we know. All things are connected like the blood which unites one family. All things are connected. Whatever befalls the Earth, befalls the sons of the Earth. Man did not weave the web of life, he is merely a part in it. Whatever he does to the web, he does to himself.'

This is perhaps another way of saying that we must build up the power of the people which will be a power different from the power of the state. We need to restructure and overhaul the entire social fabric. I want both peace and a non-violent revolution. If we want peace then, as Mahatma Gandhi has said, the only way to peace is peace itself. We have to prove that non-violence and peace have the power to revolutionize society. If this is proved, violence will cease to be the indispensable adjunct of the past. Society can be saved. Non-violence is a relatively new idea which differs considerably from religious pacifism. While pacifism refers to the traditional belief that all killing, particularly in war is wrong, contemporary non-violence concerns itself with the implications of this belief in the whole social fabric. Non-violence has for me a broader definition of what causes and constitutes violence. It takes the initiative against the existing system of dominance and privilege and gives more conscious attention to the building of an alternative social structure.

For me, non-violence in the tradition of Martin Luther King and Mahatma Gandhi and Bertha von Suttner is a natural element which relies on the power of truth rather than the force of arms and flows from a sense of the underlying unity of all human beings.

At the same time, there can be no sustained non-violent struggle on a massive scale until social institutions based on non-violent principles are built up. While non-violent resistance and direct action are an extremely important part of this movement on a European and worldwide basis, at the root of non-violence is unity based on love and the desire for justice and voluntary constructive work which will build up the structure of the new global society.

Conscience must become stronger than custom, and personal risks must be taken to better the common lot. I think at this stage especially about the brave initiatives of the Catholic bishops in the United States, on the question of nuclear disarmament. I think of Bishop Raymond Hunthausen who has been initiating a tax-strike since April of 1982 with the consequence of perhaps having to go to jail. I think of Daniel Ellsberg and the many men and women who sat on the railroad tracks in Rocky Flats to stop a plutonium train. I think of the farmers in Comiso, Italy, who are trying to help buy the property to prevent the siting of Cruise missiles which will point at Libya. I think of the 'other America', which is now engaged in the Freeze Campaign, and I think of the many Japanese sisters and brothers who together with our friends in the Pacific are marching for a nuclear-free world.

We must learn much more about the pacifist tradition, the roots of non-violence and the struggle for freedom of conscience. And as a woman I must reiterate that especially my sisters must demand that the psychological, physical and economic violence perpetrated by men against women be recognized and ended and that social institutions be changed so as to no longer reflect the pattern of dominance and submission. We must turn towards encouraging a more human, loving standard of behaviour instead of relationships steeped in aggression, competition, exploitation. We women are so intimately close to our oppressors and this sometimes has made me pessimistic. We must explore new forms of relating.

The feminist vision, which is also an ecological one, abandons the concept of naming enemies and adopts the concept familiar to the non-violent tradition: naming behaviour that is oppressive, naming abuse of power that is held unfairly and must be destroyed, but naming *no person*, one whom we are willing to destroy. Barbara Deming has written: 'If we can destroy a man's power to be violent, there is no need of course to destroy the man himself. And if the same man who behaves in one sense as an oppressor, is in another sense our comrade, there is no need to fear that we have lost our political minds or souls when we treat him as a *person* divided from us and from himself in just this way.' We must always judge the social role and see behind that role the human being.

As Gandhi said, the non-violence of the weak must become the non-violence of the brave. I believe that unarmed truth and unconditional love will have the final word.

~~~~~~~~~~~~~~~~~~~~~~~~~~~

September/October 1983

[Extracts from a speech delivered
on her acceptance of the Right Livelihood Award in Stockholm]

The Guernica Inside Us

KEN SPRAGUE

IT WAS THE FIRST MEETING of its type for twelve years. The regime banned all such exchanges of opinion.

The conference began by the one thousand delegates standing in silence in memory of a therapist who lived in Buenos Aires and was arrested in the middle of a hospital session. All his patients were tied up and beaten and he then disappeared. He has never been seen since. He was one of five thousand who disappeared.

Even under Hitler there were some records kept, but in Argentina opponents, or people thought to be opponents, of the military just ceased to exist.

My partner Marcia Karp and I attended this international encounter of Psychodrama and Group Psychotherapy for two reasons: firstly to represent and show our work as therapists, therapeutic trainers and educators here in England; secondly and perhaps more specifically, to run a workshop in Argentina's biggest city, open to all who wanted to attend, on the Falklands/Malvinas conflict.

The idea for such a grassroots investigation and sharing began during the conflict itself. Many young men sent to the South Atlantic were from Devon, the county in which we live. Some in the ships from Plymouth died there.

Marcia and I opposed the war from the start; we regarded it as a murderous mission that allowed both sides to divert attention from enormous problems at home. For Galtieri, the head of the Junta, it was a last desperate gamble to bolster his hideous regime. For the English Prime Minister it allowed her to build popularity based upon rekindling dreams of imperial glory. Dreams from the past that are the Achilles heel of the British people.

At the same time we were living among people whom we love, whose sons were out there killing or being killed. Those neighbours suffered through each and every day.

One mother, the wife of our postman, saw her son on television armed and landing in the Falklands—she had been unaware that he was a combatant. When we asked her what her feelings were about the war she replied that she didn't know, but she had to believe that her son was a hero, risking his life for his country. That was the only way she could cope with it.

In this way the people of both countries were used by the politicians. It became clear to me that the people of both countries must bypass the politicians. This was the beginning of the idea of the Buenos Aires Workshop.

The idea became more concrete when, in our kitchen in 1984, a visiting doctor from Argentina was speaking of how Picasso's painting Guernica, so much part of the European tradition, had suddenly become relevant in

Argentina. We shared our different encounters with that painting. Each of us, the doctor, Marcia and I, had seen the painting differently, at different times in different places. Yet for each of us the effect had been lasting. We agreed that the disruption and murder that the painting cries out against was now commonplace, a part of everyday experience for some people, somewhere in the world. Television even brings it into our living rooms. With the mountainous growth of nuclear weapons, Guernica experience hangs over us all. Since we remake Guernica perhaps we could begin to unmake Guernica?

We decided to call our workshop 'The Guernica Inside Us'. The majority of those attending the workshop were from Argentina, several from Brazil, a couple from Columbia and one from Germany.

We began by giving everyone a large photocopy of Picasso's painting. I told of my boyhood memories of the actual event when the town of Guernica was bombed on April 26th, 1937. It had been the first mass air attack upon an open city. Hitler had sent dive bombers to do the savage work in support of General Franco.

Picasso painted his great picture in protest. During the Nazi occupation of Paris a German officer, seeing the painting in the artist's studio asked, 'Did you do that?' Picasso replied, 'No, you did.'

I explained that the painting had deeply affected my own development as an artist, and that in two shops close to my hotel in Buenos Aires big reproductions were on sale.

The group divided into fives, each person carefully choosing who they worked with. They discussed their feelings and reactions and then gave an action presentation of the similarities between Guernica and their own recent life experiences. The horror of the military control and the disillusion and bitterness of the Malvinas was enacted. Personal creativity stimulated and released collective creativity. In some cases the presentations were remarkable. Our knowledge and perceptions were enlarged, our emotions were touched, and we understood that we were all more alike than different.

Then the group sat together and watched slides we had prepared of the front page of British newspapers. The slides showed differing attitudes to the war. The headlines included 'God be with you' above a picture of warships sailing out of Plymouth; 'Pope demands Peace' with an appropriate picture; 'Go get 'em lads' above an artist's impression of advancing Royal Marines; 'Stop the War' beneath a huge bomber dropping its deadly cargo.

Only six slides were shown, but immediately there was discussion about the media and the way that both governments used it to brainwash their people.

This discussion again added to our knowledge of each other and led directly to group members assuming the roles of Thatcher, Galtieri, the Press, the military and the parents of the soldiers. They interacted, confronted one another, changed roles and relived the experiences that had so deeply affected them. Slowly the stage area cleared leaving Thatcher and Galtieri to be confronted by each person taking the opportunity that life hadn't given them to express feelings of sadness, disappointment, disgust and optimism.

The session ended in a circle, simply sharing our humanity. It was a very small step towards sanity.

However, the second small step occurred almost immediately. People who had not attended the workshop stopped us in the corridors, on the conference steps and in the street. Language differences often meant that we couldn't understand their words but there was no mistaking their meanings. Some apologized for not attending because they were still fearful or unable to face their own pain. One said he was unsure of us, the imagined enemy. His friends had been killed by the British. He spoke with tears in his eyes, yet hugged me warmly before he left. Our interpreter also lost dear ones and had an English boyfriend sent to the Malvinas as an Argentinian soldier (there is a large English community in Argentina).

We addressed larger gatherings at discussion forums and attended other workshops studying the effects both psychological and social of the military terror.

We spoke to the entire conference in its final session, and the friendship of those thousand people was electrifying for all present. The flood of collective outpouring was given strength and greater depth by many individual contacts —in particular a developing friendship with a couple whose son had been in the Malvinas. The father is a doctor and psychodramatist, the mother a university lecturer who uses the psychodramatic method.

During the period of the war, twelve fathers, patients of our friends, had suffered heart attacks. Each had a son in the conflict. Some of the boys were killed. The doctor connected these attacks to stress and unexpressed grief. He said that 'if you don't express your emotions—you explode!' The fathers were the products of a macho culture.

At the height of the war he placed an advertisement in a newspaper inviting soldiers' parents to come together to share their concern. Seven hundred parents came.

They met regularly, formed support groups and shared information, like the fact that the soldiers had no identification tags. Many made their own, scratched on scraps of metal or written on pieces of wood. At some meetings lists of the dead were read out. There was small relief for those whose sons were still alive. Among them, even sitting next to them, were devastated mothers and fathers.

The doctor asked, 'What kind of parents are we that we allow our children to be brutalized and massacred?' It is perhaps a question that parents across the whole world should be asking.

Slowly the parents realized that the great majority of their sons were eighteen years old with only two months' training. They were fighting crack British troops with recent combat experience in Northern Ireland. The Argentinians had been raised as Catholics under the commandment, 'Thou shalt not kill'.

Within two months the soldiers had to replace those eighteen years with 'You must kill'. Their own élite troops stayed at home to police a regime that was already tottering.

The young soldiers who survived returned home as non-heroes in a fallen regime. The doctor and his wife work in their respective areas to rehabilitate these young men. Twenty-five of them have committed suicide. Many have turned in hatred on the military that betrayed them. All face the dilemmas of a country in deep social crisis.

The current rate of inflation in Argentina is 1,000 per cent, plus. The International Monetary Fund has the country in a firm grip. Interest alone on the national debt is considerably larger than each year's national product. There is a growing demand within Latin America for an end to international usury. Each day we cleared our wallets of worthless paper money. Heaven knows how working people and the poor manage.

It's an uneasy position. The conference received two bomb threats. The extreme right still manoeuvre for power. Galtieri has been overthrown but the society that produced him is still there.

On our flight home the stewardess gave us copies of the *Observer*. The headlines proclaimed Britain's problems: unemployment, MI5 blacklisting, cuts in social services. There are many similarities between our two countries.

As we left Argentina we were given a book, recently published. It is about the young men who suffered in the Malvinas/Falklands disaster. Inside the front cover the author had written: 'For Marcia and Ken with love and friendship. It was a beautiful encounter. Wish Galtieri and Thatcher could have seen it.'

November/December 1985

The Fence

ROSALIND BRACKENBURY

THE EXISTENCE OF THE FENCE. This is what strikes me first: there it is, we have heard about it, it is famous. On this side of it, parked cars, buses, marquees planted in mud and grass, the tents for lavatories and creche, the stalls selling hot drinks, chilli con carne, baked potatoes, vegetable curry; banners, balloons, people in thick jackets and scarves and hats, ponchos, anoraks, cloaks, people warmly and decoratively wrapped, women, a few men, children strapped and packed or kicking in push-chairs, small portable insulated children, larger children, dogs, all these, all of us, on this side of the fence, and the milling to and fro, the greeting of friends, the smell of food, the gloved hands passing coffee, the steam rising, the warm breath in the chill air, the glances in sunshine, shouts, embraces; all this, on this side of the fence. Women are already plaiting rushes and bracken, weaving the signs of peace into the mesh of the fence. There are webs of coloured wool, there are collages of shining silver paper, doves and dancing figures and suns and moons, there are balloons with faces and postcards and letters from children and streamers and holly and crosses and carols and woolly babies' hats and poetry and songs. On this side of the fence it is Christmas and carnival time and a children's party and Hallowe'en and birthdays and a gypsy camp. It is hot dogs and blowing paper. It is blown red noses and cold fingers clutching. It is everything. We are in it, quite suddenly, we are it, it is us, there is nothing else.

To start with, the fence is just this surface upon which the decorations spread and flower, it is there to be embroidered, an empty canvas, space for women to fill. You can do what you like. It is freedom, better than finger paints, bigger than a blank wall. And the day stretches ahead, full of hours for invention.

When I begin to look at the fence it is green, it is wire mesh covered with plastic, it is ten feet tall, it is between fixed concrete posts that curve over like pictures of concentration camps, it is topped with barbed wire. It goes on. On and on and on. We walk beside it, keeping it on our left, for mile after mile. Suddenly it becomes possible to see it, beyond the decorations, the webs and the embroidery. It is a fact upon which fictions flourish. But it is. And, looking at a green wire mesh fence, you look immediately beyond it. There it is, marking a boundary, and beyond it what? At first it looks like nothing. Only, absence of trees, absence of people, absence. A bare stretch of ground, green-brown, grass short, curls of wire made sharp with a million little razors. More fences. But nothing else. And life mills up to the outside edge of the fence, it seems, and stops there.

There is a notice—Down with de fence! But it looks permanent from here.

Then there is a stir of movement in that watchtower. It is a man, not a machine, a young man. He looks down. We wave. But he stares down at the ground within the fence, as if we were not there. We sing and play fiddles, flutes, guitars, penny whistles, saucepan lids, cymbals, maracas, combs, spoons. There is the grand roll of a drum, and a woman stroking its taut skins alive. We stretch our cheeks and holler like Indians. In each of us there is a small hooligan rampaging, enjoying the sheer noise. We shout and sing and wave and the pale young man on the watchtower looks down, shifts his weight, is alone there. Policemen lean against the fence in twos and threes, looking as if someone has told them to chat among themselves. They chat among themselves. It is a play, with scripts. The young men who line up on the other side of the fence do not speak yet, but look straight ahead. We get out our mirrors and they flash in the sun, we press them up against the fence. The fence is mirrored, and the blue sky, and the close-shaven young faces, and the khaki, and the bearded police faces dip from time to time into the reflection. We chant and sing now—All we are asking is: give peace a chance. We press up hard against the fence, presenting the reflections: look, this is you. All we are asking—

The fence may be standing between us, but everyone can hear. Suddenly, a ripple comes, a tremor down the line, a growing shout of triumph out of the singing, and the fence shakes. Suddenly, out of nowhere, there is a police car and running policemen and a white-faced woman grabbed, held, shoved into the car. Shouts, blows, a head ducking, a child in tears, women up close around the car, preventing it, and then the car moving away, the crowd closing up again. Word comes down the line: the fence has been cut. A soldier runs up with a new roll of barbed wire under his arm. Now, there are soldiers elbow to elbow in there, their faces white-looking. There are police, their backs to the fence, pushing women away—get away from the fence!

All we are asking: Whose fence is it? Who shall decide whether it shall stand or fall? For a moment, there is no passing of biscuits and peppermints to and fro, there is no chat or joking, but a stunned silence. Then: 'All we are asking is: give peace a chance.' But the fence is breached. The police have their backs to it. There are new figures, on the inside. USAF in their blue overcoats and peaked hats. And there is not nothing in there, but watchtowers, sheds, cars rushing to and fro, hangars, a runway, silos, missiles, death.

Ten miles, walking beside that fence, getting to know it. We walk, my cousins, my friends and I, and there are moments of pure festivity, when we meet and greet people we know in the passing crowd and moments of deep conversation and moments of silence and moments of terror. The fence runs along beside us on one side, and on the other, all the people we ever knew, the jokes we shared, the food we ate, the moments we had of delight and fear, everything that had ever happened to us. The trees and houses and churches and pubs and roads and animals and encounters of real life. The men we have loved, the children we have borne, all our memories, all that has made us. Sometimes we sing songs, join in with others, do dances, yell slogans, chat about nothing, hold hands, look at the sky, eat biscuits, munch apples, stop to pee, laugh, start unfinished sentences, blow whistles, beat drums. We walk, one behind the other, or in twos, in threes. The policemen see us pass. We are all women, they are all men, or so it seems, but at the same time this becomes irrelevant. Which side of the fence are you on? The policeman who laughs and accepts a sweet is on our side of the fence for a moment, but faces us, faces the same way as the soldiers, outwards. We are facing in. We are clamouring up against the fence, pressing against it, talking through it, singing through it, staring in through it like people at the zoo, offering peanuts, bananas. Do not feed these animals, they are dangerous. But the animals, as well, look cold and sad.

A woman runs along the fence, whispering: make a diversion, some women are going in! And the fence sways, rocks, it is a long ripple of movement and sound, the concrete posts rock in their foundations, and it gives, it gives: the long ripple of sound echoes, the hands of the women grip the wire, the soldiers on the inside have long sticks and are beating at the wire, at the hands of the women, there are shouts, screams. As dusk begins to fall there is a turmoil of movement on both sides of the fence, and then it is down. The fence is down. Men with dogs line up on the other side, policemen line up on this side, the rolls of spiked wire are still in place, the women reel away with hands bleeding; but there is no fence.

Down with de fence! And suddenly there is open space between the men on the inside and the women on the outside, no fence, only the breath of the dogs and a stretch of mud. It feels as if nobody quite knows what to do. Close by there is a van, and women are bundled into it. A shout goes up—Take the toys from the boys! Take the toys from the boys! The woman in the van looks out calmly, as if she expected it. The music and the shouts grow around her, and fade as she is driven away. And the fence is down.

In many places, of course, it still stands. Mile after mile after mile of it, keeping in, keeping out. We march on along its perimeter as night falls. And the candles are lit, the thousands of candles, in the hands of marchers, at the foot of the standing fence. The dusk is blue, and the night in the woods is lit with a hundred fires and a thousand, ten thousand, candles. The woods are alive with fires and with people, standing around them, warming themselves, cooking, singing. The bare birch trees grow close together, the woods are beautiful. Inside the fence, the soldiers stamp their feet and stare out. At their feet, candles; and the glow cast up into their faces, like that of Christmas. We march through the woods, with difficulty following each other now: branches slash back into our faces, and underfoot is mud and slush. There is still a long way to go.

And again, out of the peace and stillness, suddenly there comes fear. It is like a wave on the air, reaching us. We are at the Green Gate, pressed up close in the crowd, when suddenly the horses appear: men on horses, policemen, towering over us, and the horses trotting fast into the crowd, skidding on the mud, dancing, foam flying from their bits. Suddenly we are in it, the fear. We

press together, our backs up against the trees. If the horses barge into us we
have no escape. Somebody is hurt; the crowd parts and a siren wails and an
ambulance comes rushing, blue light flashing in the dusk, and the gates open
suddenly and it rushes into the base. The gates close again. The horses plunge
and slip. People are close to their hoofs. We dive out, the five of us, and run
away through the trees, going parallel to the fence, following a hat, a white
jacket, a pair of striped socks, marking each other in the darkness. We are
close, we are necessary to each other: we hold on to each other and shake
from head to toe. It is as if fear flowers suddenly and without warning, as if
the violence comes out of nowhere, as if, quite suddenly, it is materialized in
a stick, a policeman's hands, a horse's flying hoofs, and then dies away again,
goes out of sight. The fence shivers and shakes, registering it like a seismograph.
We cling on to it in places, to help us through the mud. In many places it is
ripped, hastily patched, stitched together again; in many others it is right down,
trampled into the mud. It bellies and swoops over our heads, its barbed wire
dipping. It is rickety, collapsing, collapsed.

It lies crushed in the mud, the barbed wire torn from the posts. The posts
were not in deep, only inches after all. In many places, the green wire dangles.
But, on the other side still, the men in close ranks now and the furry-eared dogs,
like something put there for us to admire. On the hour, again, the sounds swell
from the crowd, the voices pitched as high and as loud as they can, the whistle
and drumbeat, the clash of tin. The singing rises and dips, the songs change.
The Red Indian ullulation more pronounced now, as if everyone has got into
the swing of it. Nice girls do not make a noise. And inside there's a kind of
frenzy; the cars and vans dash to and fro, the men stride, lights flash, it is all
activity, all vigorous male activity; but to what end?

My cousin leans on the fence, talking to a policeman. She gestures towards
the United States flag, hanging there on British soil. She says—Ah, yes, but
there was a time, wasn't there, when we weren't afraid to go it alone. You and
I remember that. Don't we?

Three soldiers stand still, in the darkness they are so still, like a picture, and
the candles glow at their feet. Somebody says—Look, the three wise men.

I'm leaving the army in February, he says; ask me what I think then.

In an isolated place, where the fence has been ripped with wire cutters, a
policeman leans, puts his arm through, hands something, a sweet or a piece of
chewing gum perhaps, to one of the soldiers. From the outside to the inside,
where once was impossible. Ah, holes have their uses.

And further along, where we stumble on through the dark, through pine
woods now, the smell of wood smoke in our nostrils and snow falling white
as ash, we find a policeman in a helmet making something out of wire; from
his helmet dangles a CND sign made of Christmas tree tinsel. He hangs what
he has made carefully on the bare branch of a tree. What are you making? It's
the male symbol, he says; well, there are enough of you here. And hangs it like
a decoration, carefully, and steps back to see the effect.

A policeman holding a long wax candle, so that it will not drip, hardly looks like a policeman. We take our lights from him and process on, teasing. He says, it's police issue, don't get me wrong!

The soldiers, bored, begin to call out as they did not earlier. What a waste of women! And we call back cheerfully—What a waste of men!

Up against the fence, where it is still standing, a young woman in a red beret stands leaning, talking intently to a soldier. In the darkness, as if they were courting. She talks and talks and perhaps he listens. She is all leaning and intense and absorbed. His face is white, hers hidden. She leans, unaware as in an attitude of love.

The day has moved on, become night. In the woods there are small fires everywhere, between the trees. There is the smell of woodsmoke and pine resin and figures bob against the light and cast huge shadows; the woods are alive, peopled as they have not been for centuries. There is food cooked and children fed and wiped. Far into the woods the glowing signs of human habitation. Small fires and faint music between the trees. Further away, on the roads, the buses are already beginning to fill with people, to set off again, back across the country, east, west, north and south. We walk on and on and the fence seems never-ending. It becomes like a dream. You walk, and repeat what has already been; your feet go mechanically, weighted with mud. There is a steep hill, a stream to cross, trees that whip your face, a place where the fence is torn down and hangs, sagging, another place where a soldier suddenly stands against the whitening ground, and then there is a steep hill, a stream to cross, trees that whip your face—

> Old and strong
> She goes on, and on and on,
> You can't kill the spirit,
> She is like a mountain—

We have walked right round the base now, following the fence, keeping it close, observing it. We have seen it rip, shake, fall. It is no longer the impermeable, the real, the solid thing it was. They can put it up again, mend it, try to reinstate it in all its green impressiveness; but thousands of us, now, have seen it down. We have seen the babyfaced khaki soldiers staring out across it, quite baffled, with only their dogs for company; we have talked to them, passed them sweets, asked them what they thought, while the fence in tatters lay between us. We know, and they know now, that women can pull it down, yes, with our bare hands.

July/August 1984

Not Guilty

IAN LEE

ON THE 18TH OF SEPTEMBER, in the small village of Shrewton on the edge of Salisbury Plain at about midday, we were expecting Cruise support vehicles to start dispersing from Greenham Common in small groups as advance parties to a big convoy the following night. They go ahead to make the camp and set up security. There may be as many as fifty vehicles dispersed from Greenham in small groups of five or six, all leaving at different times from different gates on different routes to avoid detection, getting themselves mixed up with all kinds of other military traffic. We spend many days following them and trying to sort which are which. On that particular day some of us just knew it was going to happen. It was amazing to see on the roads around Newbury that day cars with Greenham women, cars with Cruisewatch men and women, all acting on some sort of telepathy.

I'd followed a group of Dodgerams, which are the American equivalent of Landrovers except that they're combat vehicles and quite a lot bigger, carrying about eight men and their kits. I'd followed these five vehicles along the A4 to Hungerford and Marlborough. They were going by the back roads trying to avoid being followed. They're quite speedy, having 7-litre engines, so they got away from me quite often, me chugging along in the vw. But I had an idea about where they were headed and I took short-cuts and kept managing to come out in the road just ahead or just behind them. I followed them on to Salisbury Plain and came down the hill into the village of Shrewton. Ahead of me on the road, completely unplanned, were five women; all in front of the military vehicles. It was a busy sunny day on a main road, with a lot of traffic, lots of shoppers standing and gawping while the women held the whole lot up. I parked and walked up to the vehicles; most of the windows were open so I could talk to them. I asked them questions like 'Why are you spending so much of your lives practising for murder on a massive scale?', 'If you're asked to press the button tonight you've got to decide not to do it, it'll be up to you,' and 'You can't protect your family by threatening other families, and you can't protect your children by threatening to murder other children.'

Unfortunately they heard very little of that because they immediately wound their windows up, swore and sneered, then turned their backs and faced each other inside so that I couldn't even see their faces. So I got out of my pocket a white marker pen and wrote on all the windows the messages I wanted them to read, like the things I'd said and some more. I did this and drew peace symbols on every vehicle. During the course of this RAF men got out of the vehicles and started to pull me around, and each time I managed to calm them down and made them let go of me and carried on writing.

Soon the vehicles began to move off, those who were left behind began to jog after them. Some of the women and myself began to jog along with them talking with them. The Americans were trying to pretend we were not there, but we were puffing along three or four abreast and quite a lot of communication took place. Up ahead the vehicles had pulled into a layby for the men to catch up and here the whole process was repeated; they climbed into their cabs and slammed the doors and I started writing on the vehicles again. At this point lots of Ministry of Defence police and RAF motorcyclists arrived. They all saw the sorry state of the vehicles but seemed too fazed to do anything about it, so they held us back while the Americans drove off.

About two hours later a policeman came along, asked me if I was Mr Lee, and said that he was arresting me on suspicion of criminal damage. I went to get a book, but he said not to worry as I would only be there an hour or so; in fact they held me there for twenty-two hours. I immediately made a voluntary statement taking responsibility for what had happened and explaining why I thought there was nothing wrong with it. But still they held me for twenty-two hours. Of course, they were holding me until the convoy had come out.

I was charged with criminal damage and asked to appear in court on Monday 16th February in Devizes where I pleaded not guilty. I had insisted on all the prosecution witnesses being there and said that I wouldn't accept any of their statements being read as evidence, I wanted the men and women there to be cross-examined by me. We've come into contact a lot with Devizes Magistrates Court recently and had some pretty bad treatment. I suppose, because it's a small market town, the only crime that it's used to is a bit of drunkenness, some petty thieving, a few kids wrecking bus shelters. Suddenly along come us, crazy people who persistently break the law and who cheerfully say, 'Yes, we did it, and we'll do it again.' The magistrates there, after an initial honeymoon period in which they were quite lenient with us because they thought of us as poor saintly fools, finally lost their patience and decided they wouldn't tolerate it and gave us heavy fines. So I decided I was going to risk everything by negotiating with them so that I could start off on an equal footing, and I asked for a 'MacKenzie' (a friend who can sit with you and advise you, give you support emotionally or practically), which they said I could have. Then I said that I wanted a table and the same facilities as the prosecution.

I said that I wanted the table to be the same distance back so that we could all be equidistant. The magistrate said, 'Yes, certainly; he does seem to be rather on top of us, doesn't he?' I then said I wanted to know all their names before we started, and they all looked surprised; why did I want to know that? I said that it was just a matter of common courtesy, they all knew my name, I would like to know theirs. So they all introduced themselves. The Chairman of the Bench said sarcastically, 'Well, now we're all acquainted, Mr Lee, perhaps we can start.' 'There is just one other thing,' I said, 'I know the American witnesses are not here alone; they have a legal observer here, and if that person is in court I'd like her to be identified and asked what her purpose is.' The magistrates looked dumbfounded at this, so I explained that six months earlier I'd been at Banbury Magistrates Court where there had been such a legal observer, and I had been certain that this person had been indicating the answers to certain questions to the USAF witnesses. I had watched this going on for about an hour, and when I'd pointed it out I was dragged out of court. I simply wanted to prevent any possibility of that happening again. The magistrate told me that this was a public hearing and that anyone had the right to be there provided they behaved themselves. I pointed out that I didn't object to the woman being there, I just wanted her to sit out of the line of sight of the witnesses. The prosecutor jumped up and said, 'The woman Mr Lee is referring to is simply the driver, she brought the three American witnesses here.'

I then pointed out that since the three Americans had managed to drive enormous vehicles around at dead of night, it seemed very strange they couldn't drive themselves to Devizes in the middle of the day, and that for a driver she was very well-dressed and had an attaché case full of files; but perhaps USAF drivers are really well qualified these days. The point went home and she was asked if she wouldn't mind sitting outside.

Then we got started and the prosecution called in the witnesses; three USAF men, one RAF man and three police. After the prosecution had asked them questions I cross-examined them. They were all about twenty and not one of them would look me in the eyes. I managed to draw attention to this once by hesitating in my questioning and saying, 'Can you hear me?' His eyes flickered towards me and he said, 'Yeah.' I said, 'Well I just wondered because you weren't looking at me, will you please look towards me when I speak to you?' He didn't reply but his eyes swivelled away as though there was an oil on water effect; his eyes just would not stay on me; it looked really shifty on their part. I asked the RAF man if he was the only RAF man there. He replied, 'There was one of us in each vehicle.' So I asked what had happened when they were stopped, he said, 'All the RAF got out.'

'Was that one of your duties?'

'Yes.'

'Why?'

'It was one of our duties to come between you and the Americans.'

'One of your jobs is to protect the Americans from coming into contact with the British?'

'Yes.'

'Whose command were you under at the time?'

'I was under the command of an American.'

'Does British military law apply to you when you're under American command?'

He looked confused and said he didn't know. This was amazing—the fact that he admitted that he was under USAF command. We had known this for some time, that parts of the RAF were under direct American control, but it had always been denied; this was the first time we'd had official confirmation of it. He then went on to say, 'The Americans didn't get out of their vehicles because they had no jurisdiction.'

'If you were under USAF command then what jurisdiction did you have?'

Again he just looked confused. I asked the USAF men the same sort of questions. Why wouldn't they get out of their vehicles; were they afraid of having contact with us or were they told not to speak to us, could they look at us? The security guard who'd been driving just glared at me: 'We got orders, we ain't even to acknowledge your existence.'

The magistrates looked pretty shocked at this. I kept asking the witnesses about why they were there and all their answers to this were evasive. The prosecutor kept standing up to say it was irrelevant and political. The magistrate said, 'Yes, you must restrict yourself to the facts of the case,' and I replied, 'Well, the facts of the case do include the convoy, what it was part of and what it was preparatory to. My defence later on will be based on the nature of the convoy, what its intention was, and I will show that that justifies what I did; so I must elicit this information.' I managed to ask about half the questions I had wanted to.

'You were an advance party for the Cruise convoy coming out that night, weren't you?'

'I have no knowledge of this.'

'Well, you know that a Cruise convoy did come out that night.'

'Maybe.'

Another had said, 'I can't tell you for security reasons.'

'Surely you can tell me whether other vehicles joined you.'

'No.'

I went through this routine with all the men and after a while the magistrate interrupted wearily, 'Mr Lee, I think everybody knows that a Cruise convoy came out that night.'

'Well, in that case, why do these men keep denying it?'

He just said, 'Professional ignorance, I suppose.'

Then the police witnesses came in and I cross-examined them. I asked the investigating officer whether he took my voluntary statement as an admission of 'guilt', and he said, 'Yes.' So I asked, 'Does that mean your investigations were complete by the time you had my statement?'

'More or less, yes.'

'Do you know of any reason why I should be kept for twenty-two hours when I'd made that statement within two hours of arriving at the police station.'

'No.'

That went home to the magistrates. All this was happening in the morning, and I realized that if I wasn't careful I'd end up with half an hour before lunch and they'd say, 'Right, present your defence', and it would all have to be squeezed into a corner and they'd rush to make a decision, so I started to go really slowly and got them to agree to adjourn for lunch.

After lunch I started off on my defence, and I said that I didn't consider it to be damage really, and if it was then it was trivial; certainly the USAF didn't seem to consider it major. The paint can easily be removed with a paint scraper. My main defence, though, was that I had a lawful excuse, and to explain this I would have to refer to the Criminal Damage Act 1971, Section 5, which defines lawful excuse, and the four criteria necessary to this, namely:

1. An act must be to protect property, and that property could be any-one's, not just mine;
2. That property must be in need of immediate protection;
3. The means of protection must be reasonable in all the circumstances;
4. This must be my honestly held belief.

I distributed copies of the Act and indicated where these criteria were written into it, and gave them copies of a legal textbook which amplified and explicated these criteria so that they could be in no doubt as to what it meant.

I then explained how my actions had fitted the criteria. The first was that such an act must be to protect property, so I explained first of all what I was protecting that property from, which was the destructive effects of Cruise. I explained how destructive Cruise was, how many Hiroshimas: that it was part of a first strike policy of the US government. I talked in more detail of the consequence of using these weapons, not just the immediate effects but also the long term environmental consequences of using them. Thus I was protecting by my actions property in Eastern Europe and Russia, which I assumed the missiles were targeted at. I was also protecting my own property and that of my friends, since the Soviets had said that they would respond to such an attack by a massive all out nuclear retaliation. The use of those missiles would thus set up a train of events which would result in the destruction of my property.

I went on to the second criterion: that the property must be in need of immediate protection. I said that in my evaluation the danger was indeed immediate as I had watched those Cruise convoys for the last three years and I was certain that this was an advance party for a full Cruise convoy coming out later that night which would be protected by masses of police and I would have very little chance of getting close to the drivers or their vehicles; thus effectively that small advance party was my last chance to intervene in the train of events and alter them. The need was immediate because I had no way of telling what was practice and what was real. The example of the US raid on Libya had shown us how a routine military exercise could turn into the real thing halfway through. Since Cruise is a first strike weapon there might be no prior warning, no signs at all. The launching of a Cruise missile would *be* the first thing to happen. I asked the magistrates to consider what I had said about the destructive effects of Cruise and the consequences that would follow from using Cruise, and then to consider what I had done: writing with a fine white pen on a few windows. I asked them whether or not, in all the circumstances, my actions seemed reasonable or not. Were they not restrained, extremely reasonable? I went on to give an example: if I knew of a man who intended to commit a murder, and I had seen him leave his house with a weapon, and I wrote on his windscreen: 'Don't commit murder,' then nobody would accuse me of criminal damage. They might even accuse me of not taking enough steps to prevent him committing murder. In which case why was it so different when murder was being prepared on a vast scale by many men?

Finally I dealt with the last criterion, and quoted the parts of the Act and the textbook which made it clear that this all came down to my beliefs. I told them that I hadn't come to this position lightly, quickly or easily. I had come to it after many years of working and raising a family, and that it was my sincerely held belief that what I had done was necessary.

One of the things that had brought me to this position was a journey I went on to Germany as part of my work, visiting medical companies, talking to doctors about publishing medical papers. One particular doctor who was on the point of retirement started chatting with me about Britain and Germany. He asked me, 'Do the British still hate the Germans?' I remember feeling quite embarrassed about that question and I replied, 'Of course not, except maybe in kids' comics.' He replied, 'You should do, because it was our fault. Not just the Nazis, it was the fault even more of people like me.' He went on to say that I probably couldn't imagine what it was like in Germany in the thirties. It was just after he'd graduated from medical school and Hitler had come to power. He said, 'Hitler wasn't a dictator you know, which is how everybody thinks of him. He was elected to power and he had massive public support.' He described how many people, his friends and colleagues, had a really sickening feeling in their guts, that something awful was being prepared without knowing what, 'but we all ignored it, we didn't speak of it, if it came up at a dinner party there would be a silence and then it would be passed over. What allowed Hitler to build the concentration camps and for many years to prepare and carry out a policy of genocide was millions of ordinary people like me not having the courage to act.' He said that the world today was like Germany in the 1930s and the genocide was on a global scale instead of a national or a continental scale. He said, 'If I were in better health I'd be out there with the Greens tearing down the nuclear plants. There is nothing better you can do with your life.'

I told the magistrates that that had stayed with me, but that I had come back and kept my work for another eight years; but it had stayed with me and linked with other things and it had got to a point where I simply couldn't turn over in bed and keep my fingers crossed. I said, 'You may not agree with me, though I hope you do, at least in part, but please do not insult me by doubting my sincerity and the responsibility and the care with which I acted.' I asked them to think of all the things I could've done—crashing a car into the convoy, smashing the windows, ripping the tyres, attacking the men—I did none of these; I did the most restrained and peaceful thing I could think of to dissuade the men from what they were doing, I wrote my appeals for peace on the windows.

I was aware that, when in different cases, not peace cases, this defence had been used in the past it had been disallowed when the damage caused had not been to actually prevent something but had been a gesture to draw attention to a state of affairs, so if I had set light to a hedge to draw attention to a passing convoy then I would not have had lawful excuse. So I explained that I perceived the dangerous aspect to be the men themselves and not the machines, and I was trying to speak with them to change their minds. I explained that writing on the windshields was part of the same act, not a mere gesture but an act of protection. I asked them why on earth it was necessary for those machines to come out twice or three times a month. I said that I had come to the conclusion that it couldn't be simply to test the machinery, to make sure the wheels went round and the missile tubes went up and down, since the machinery was not that unreliable. The real reason was to drill those men into blind obedience, so that by the time they were told to perform an unimaginable act they would have practised it so many times that it would have lost its significance for them. Even if the convoy wasn't to be used that night I was still interrupting the numbing effect that was systematically being exerted on those men.

This was about two hours' worth, and that was it. I said they should find me not guilty, not so much because it mattered to me personally, but because it mattered very much both generally and morally. Because the decision to prosecute me was American, the main witnesses were American. We even had an American legal observer. Was it right that the magistrates should deny to another British person a legal defence actually written into the Act simply because it was an American genocide convoy that was involved? I also reassured them that what I had said didn't mean that it was a free-for-all and that anyone could do anything and get away with it, simply by saying, 'Oh, it was my honestly held belief.' The criteria I had mentioned were really quite strict. Also in another part of the Act it makes clear that these criteria only apply to actions which do not endanger life and are not likely to. This was not opening the floodgates.

I seemed to have established strong links between the magistrates and myself, so that everything else seemed to be side-lined, and perhaps the prosecutor felt this too. The Chairman of the Bench, who was the headmaster of the local public school, had been looking at me in the morning as at a sixth-former who'd been getting out of line and might need slapping down, but by the afternoon he was just taking it all in, not taking his eyes off me and looking extremely disturbed. One of the magistrates just sat back and closed her eyes part of the way through. Her imagination had taken hold of her. The other magistrate was fiddling with a pencil and he fiddled more as time went by. I thought he would interrupt me, but he too was drinking it in.

After the prosecutor had finished, the magistrates went out and we sat there quietly waiting to see. I had no expectation that I would be found 'Not Guilty'. I simply hadn't considered that possibility. Everything had been focused on me being able to say what I wished to say. I was pleased I had done it and it was now an academic matter of waiting to see how long it would take them to find me 'Guilty' and how much they would fine me. I had already decided I would not pay the fine. About twenty minutes later they came back and said, 'We've decided to dismiss the case. Do you want any costs?' I just didn't have the heart to accept costs, it would be like rubbing salt into a wound.

The prosecutor was gibbering afterwards, saying, 'I'm sure the Crown Prosecution Service will appeal. They can't let this stand. They can't.'

We couldn't laugh or smile or be jubilant until ten yards down the pavement; then we found ourselves jumping up and down. I looked at the sign I'd written on my van—'They will protect us they say, but we have never been as endangered as now.'

September/October 1987

[Reprinted from Threads, *the newsletter of the Interhelp network]*

The Tax Strike

ROGER FRANKLIN

MY 'TAX STRIKE' arises out of a conscientious objection to war, and particularly to genocidal nuclear war. The right of conscientious objection to serving
in the armed forces is now widely accepted. But nations are now preparing
for wars fought by machines, not against soldiers, but largely against innocent
populations. My conscience will not allow me any longer to make a willing
payment to help the building of this genocidal machinery, however much it is
disguised as a 'deterrent that keeps the peace through mutual fear'. Arms races
may, for a while, delay war breaking out, but in the end they always provoke it.
This final war will be all the more terrible for the longer time of preparation.
What we now face is the total extermination of humanity, and possibly the end
of all life on this beautiful planet.

For a long time now the military has not needed our bodies, except as victims
and hostages, but they have needed our consent to spend the nation's money
on ultimate destruction—all, of course, in the sacred name of 'deterrence'. So,
at long last, I am withholding that consent. This is not much, considering that
the money can be taken anyway, but it is one more thing that I feel I can and
must do. And it may help, if only a little, to sway the balance back towards
sanity and survival.

So, in the face of the British government's policies that 'seriously endanger
the continuation of life on Earth', I can no longer bring myself voluntarily to
'render unto Caesar' by signing cheques to the Inland Revenue. I realize that the
government can appropriate the money, and can impose various financial and
other penalties. None the less, I cannot bring myself to make further payments
as though the expenditure for which I am contributing had my approval. It must
be clear that the government is taking my money against my will.

Over the years I have paid many thousands of pounds to the Treasury,
much of which has been spent on the race to extinction which I deplore. I
therefore feel that a total tax strike now, rather than a diversion of a 'nuclear'
or 'military' proportion, is quite justified. I have helped policies of annihilation quite enough.

I am, though, more than willing to pay the amount of the tax demand, and
more, to any organizations, whether government-controlled or not, that help
to promote peace, or to remove poverty and injustice. I do contribute to

---

*This is the text that Roger Franklin presented in court. As a result of his tax strike,
he was declared bankrupt by a judge in chambers in the High Court in London. The
tax demand was eventually settled at considerable extra cost through the Bankruptcy
Office in Gloucester.*

such organizations, but I would gladly add to such contributions the money I am now being asked to pay the government, much of which will be used in preparing for a terminal war. I have provided the tax collector with a list of some such organizations, and I have the list here in court.

For a year or so now I have been carrying on a 'tax go-slow', not taking any notice of tax demands and related court hearings. While on 'go-slow', I retained the hope that a change of British policy on nuclear weapons would allow me to revert to my previous grudging conformity to the tax laws. But I am now resolved that I shall not end my 'tax strike' until a British government abolishes all nuclear weapons controlled by or based in this country.

However, the more I ponder my 'tax strike', the more I wonder what on earth I have been paying for—aside from nuclear and non-nuclear so-called 'defence'. I pay rates that cover local education, policing, fire and emergency services; I pay to the DHSS a regular contribution to the health service and pension funds; I pay taxes on my petrol and car to provide the roads, and other transport is on a pay-as-you-go basis, rarely subsidized. Just what does the central government do to justify its demands for money other than pay itself, the elected representatives and the non-elected employees (Civil Service). There is much to recommend the anarchist view—although certainly not the violence of a few who once held it.

Tax-gathering has always been a difficult business. But with mesmerized populations, modern states have developed it to a fine art, they have 'engineered consent'. Nearly everyone now has taxes paid before they see any wages or salaries; they can sometimes beg a bit back. Most taxes are now gathered as VAT and other taxes on trade. But there remains this anachronism, this small loophole for protest, on income from investments. I understand that it may soon be blocked off. So I see it as my duty now to make clear, on behalf of many who cannot, that I am not any more willing to hand over to the state monies to pay for our extermination. It is like being asked to dig burial trenches before being shot, or to build gas ovens.

As the taxes will probably be taken from me anyway, it might appear that I am making a lot of fuss merely to draw attention to myself in some way. This is not so. I do it very reluctantly, and as a last resort. I do it now, and I should have done it much sooner, for we are living on borrowed time already, so as to draw attention in one more way to the extreme danger of a nuclear catastrophe. This danger is still being ignored by so many people. If there were a large number of big guns pointing at your house, you would be constantly terrified. But because nuclear missiles are further off and out of sight, and threaten everyone's houses (and lives), most people seem to try to forget them, or to say 'there's nothing *we* can do', or 'we must be safe because our missiles are pointing at them and they wouldn't dare.' Yet, at the same time, we know that our military and theirs are being paid handsomely to find a way to hit without being hit back. Sooner or later they'll think they've found one.

Shouldn't I be patient and use only legal, democratic means of persuasion? I have been patient. I've tried legal means for nearly forty years. And the state has continued for that long to build up the danger.

It may be said that we live in a democracy, and policies can be changed by political means. I have done my share of 'politicking', but I could point out that I have never yet been in a position where my actual vote has counted for anything. Without proportional representation, a vote in a firm Tory constituency makes no difference in the short-run, and but little in the fore-seeable future. Government policies supported by the media tend to become self-perpetuating.

I have occupied myself for many years in a variety of ways to resist the nuclear arms race. This 'tax strike' is but one more attempt to help save our species from extinction. I have written politely (and sometimes angrily) to politicians and to the press; I have been on many marches and vigils and to countless meetings; I have helped to organize talks and films. More recently, I have taken part in blockades at Burghfield and Upper Heyford (and been arrested). I have participated in Cruisewatch and trespassed at some risk on MoD land in search of the not-so-elusive missiles that could massacre half a million people at a time. I have even been arrested for attempting to recycle on my tree plantations some discarded wire from Molesworth. So it certainly seems high time that I resisted paying for the military madness.

I have spelled out before in many an article or letter to the press just what I see as insane and immoral about nuclear policies. There are now huge numbers of people, both 'ordinary' and 'influential' who agree with this view—from Bruce Kent and Paul Oestreicher (both tax-resisters) to Enoch Powell, and including, somewhat hopefully, Neil Kinnock. I am therefore hopeful that my 'tax strike', which is a response to inspiration from others, who have taken a similar stand in the distant or more recent past, may move still others to take whatever steps are open to them to help block the insane race to nuclear destruction.

In 1849, Henry David Thoreau spent one day in jail for non-payment of a small tax. This was to resist his government's policies which included an unjust war and the continuation of slavery. In resisting an even more disastrous government policy, one heading towards the extermination of humanity, I am refusing to pay a rather larger sum, although it is insignificant com-pared with the total that is used for armaments. It is a sum that the gov-ernment could certainly spare towards peacemaking and famine relief, where I would gladly re-direct it.

By refusing to sign a cheque, I am presumably in rebellion against the state. Whatever 'the state' is, it is behaving immorally, and indeed seems increasingly insane. No individual would get away with plotting mass murder, amounting also to organized suicide, and putting extermination on a hair trigger. People must now show they want to survive, they want at all costs to stop the insane rush to extinction. International laws against genocide, natural laws of self-defence, indeed common sense and common decency, all take precedence over archaic national laws that demand loyalty and obedience all the way to a universal grave. A state that is actively participating in a plot to destroy the world loses all legitimacy.

You, sir, represent 'the law'. The law says I must pay taxes to 'the state', which is something run by 'the government', which is a lot of people elected and appointed to organize the affairs of the nation.

But I was born a human being, a result of natural biological processes and I feel there is a natural law that all human beings should hold to, which takes precedence over any laws drawn up by groups of men and women. The main concern of that natural law is the right to life, to live and let live. There are many other aspects, such as justice, liberty and so forth, most of which are incorporated in various national and international laws. But the right to life takes precedence, hence the abhorrence of murder.

Now I stand here as one small part of a threatened species. My right to life, and yours, and everyone's, is now threatened at every moment by terrible weapons prepared under the organizing power of the state. It is true that my life, and yours, and everyone's in this country may actually be extinguished by weaponry launched from another state, over which we have no control. But we are surely provoking the people of the other state, and terrifying them with our so-called 'deterrent'. Thus we hold a terribly precarious peace through mutual terror.

States go on like little children, each blaming the other for 'starting it'. Yet the weapons are not sticks and stones, but machinery for extermination, totally out of proportion to any conceivable quarrel. If my right to life is to be preserved, I must deny the state, which is thus behaving so foolishly, if not totally irrationally, any further support.

What has developed is a kind of super-Mafia, a protection racket. States condition their citizens to believe in an 'enemy' that wants to destroy them. But not all the time. One could list over a hundred states that threaten the lives of no one, at least outside their own borders. But super-states, and super-alliances tend to go over the top and bring about wars. People living under such states or alliances have a duty under natural law to regain control of the mechanism that will otherwise destroy them.

How to regain control is the question. Resort to violence would make the problem worse, as well as breaching natural law. But other forms of resistance —protest and withholding of support—need to be developed. I am at this point using the money mechanism to make a point of resistance. It is no more than a protest, since the state has ways of taking the money; but at least it must be taken under protest, and I can point out that the state is misusing much of its money in ways that breach natural law and threaten my life, and most other lives.

The judge in Arthur Windsor's case (Gloucester, April 12, 1985) said that, whatever his feelings, he felt obliged to act as an administrator and an enforcer of the law—i.e. he had to do his job.

I want to ask you to look at your own conscience in this desperate matter which concerns and affects us all; all our lives and those of our fellow human beings, present and future, on this unique and beautiful planet. As I see it, you *do* have a choice. You can act as a mechanical agent for the law, or you can act as a human being, equally endangered as I am, and we all are, and make a different decision.

I ask you to allow me to pay the tax due to organizations that are helping to bring peace, rather than to pay it to a government that is prepared to commit genocide. I ask this, even though the preparations for genocide are excused as 'deterrence', for they none the less describe a willingness to take a futile vengeance on millions of innocent people in a distant land, and to prevent future generations ever enjoying the experience of life.

If you cannot bring yourself to allow this, then at least you can order the money taken from me, clearly against my will, and take no punitive action against my person. Imprisonment would surely be counterproductive. It will make us all and 'the state', which you represent, that much poorer. Certainly it will give some more employment to gaolers (prison officers, nowadays). But things must have come to a pretty pass in this country if we have to make employment by locking each other up unnecessarily.

Prisons I can accept as places where people are held who would otherwise do serious harm to other people or to property. I cannot accept them as places for the punishment of an act of conscience; used to punish or deter disobedience, as it were.

Furthermore, there is a curious 'Catch 22' dilemma should you try to coerce my conscience by putting me in prison. If I go to prison, the state will need to spend some of the taxes it takes from me on keeping me there, rather than on other purposes, including preparations for nuclear war. At the same time, I shall not need to support myself, and I shall be able to give more from my investment income as contributions to organizations that promote peace.

I suggest that you would be doing your full legal duty in this case by ordering my money to be taken 'forcibly', that is from my bank; plus a fine to cover the costs of this case. But I hope you will not do this, but will see your duty as a human being take precedence over your duty to the state, in this situation. In that case you will allow an alternative use of my tax money in ways that will help, rather than hinder the cause of peace and human survival.

If locked up, I shall be a political prisoner, incarcerated because I believe a true patriot wants his country, and, of course, humanity, to survive, rather than be utterly destroyed in the absurdity of a nuclear holocaust. After all other means of protest have had little effect, I have finally resorted to a total withdrawal of support for a government that is so dangerously deluded about the safety of its policy of nuclear deterrence. In 1958, Martin Luther King Jr said, 'To accept passively an unjust system is to co-operate with that system, thereby the oppressed become as evil as the oppressor.' Non-co-operation with evil is as much a moral obligation as is co-operation with good. Today I feel a moral obligation of non-co-operation with nuclear insanity.

If you describe my tax strike at this time as a crime, it is surely a political crime: I feel forced to reject the demands, not of an evil state, but of a state that is doing evil, indeed criminally insane things. I note, however, that if the danger I am protesting about comes to pass, it appears to be the state that could survive, but precious few of the people. I am making this stand on behalf of the people, as the state has become a danger, indeed an enemy. People have often been described as 'enemies of the state'; I am pointing out that the state has now become the enemy of the people.

I have respect for law, but not for a state that has started to administer the law in a way that protects its policies at the risk of genocide of millions of innocent people. I do not hold such a state in contempt, but rather I feel pity for it and for its innocent victims. The state has not merely lost its way, it has lost its reason entirely. I only wish to help in a small way to show a way back towards sanity and survival, before it is too late.

We daily see government warnings that 'Cigarettes can seriously damage your health'. I want to issue a warning that government nuclear policies are seriously endangering your life. Paying taxes to nuclear-armed governments is thus a form of risk taking far greater than those taken by tobacco smokers, or excessive drinkers. And the risk is not confined to one's own life, or that of bystanders, it is a risk to all humanity, all living beings. We have no right to take such a risk, and by paying taxes to such governments we are as guilty as those we condemned at Nuremberg—although our excuse may be more understandable, since the general ignorance of the threat remains profound.

September/October 1985

Jonah and the Bad Guys

ANNE HERBERT

THIS IS THE STORY OF JONAH, the guy who lives in the Bible about halfway between Elijah and Luke. A lot of you probably think that Jonah is the story of a man and his whale. That's not actually true. Jonah is the story about the joy of hatred. Jonah is the story about that exhilarating feeling you get when you discover someone who is really more morally reprehensible than you are. Jonah discovered that joy, and Jonah's basic thing was hating Ninevites. Ninevites lived far away from him, and he'd never met any of them, but he had a lot of data about them.

Now, hating Ninevites was not like hating Jews, Catholics, Black people, etc. Hating Ninevites was like hating American Nazis, builders of nuclear reactors, and tuna fishermen. It was a rational, well-researched hatred based on the actual behaviour of the hatees. Jonah had a lot of data on Ninevites, and he was building a career on them. He had just had a story about the relationship of Ninevites, the Mobil Oil Corporation, and saccharine on the cover of *Mother Jones*. He was hitting the junior college circuit with a speech about Ninevites, and he was hoping to make the Ivy League soon.

So he was not surprised when one day God came to him to talk to him about the Ninevites. He had never spoken to God before, and he wasn't really a God groupie, but he figured God knew who the expert was, right? So God came to Jonah, and said, 'Jonah, I'm going to destroy all the Ninevites.' And Jonah said, 'Wow, you must have read my article.' God said, 'Before I destroy them, I want to warn them. It seems only fair. Since you know so much about them, I want you to go to Nineveh and tell them I'm going to destroy them, so they'll have a chance to change their ways and save themselves.'

Jonah said, 'No way in hell. I don't want to go there, they're creepy people, and besides that, what if they change?' So Jonah took off. He took the Greyhound bus to the most distant point available, only it wasn't a Greyhound bus at that point in time, it was a boat. He got on the boat, and thought he would skip town and all would be cool. He did not know he was dealing with a Whole Earth God.

God followed him in the boat and started a very large sea storm. The captain of the boat was extremely upset about the storm. He was an experienced captain who knew a theological sea storm when he saw one. So he said, 'Someone on this boat is not on speaking terms with their god. Let's draw straws and see who.'

Jonah said, 'Ah, we don't need to do that, I'm the one. I'll jump overboard because it seems like the only way I'm going to win.' Now it turned out that God knew, as well as any civil rights legislator knows, that the only way to overcome hatred is with brute force. And God doesn't give up easy.

So when Jonah jumped over the side of the boat God had a whale there to catch him. Jonah landed in the whale, stayed in the whale with rotting fish and whale digestive juices for three days. Jonah was a stubborn man of principle—it took seventy-two hours of an unusual smell for him to change his mind. Finally he said, 'Oh heck, God, I'll go to Nineveh.' The whale barfed him up on shore near Nineveh and he headed for the world capital of badness.

When he got to Nineveh, he was pleased to see that everything he'd ever thought about the Ninevites was true. I mean they were right there on the streets using sweatshop labour to run a nuclear reactor that powered an ITT plant that made neutron bombs, whale trawlers, and saccharine. He was naturally appalled. So he got into his street-beggar mode, which he had used to support his Ninevite research, and started mumbling things way down low against his chest. He shuffled down the street, leaned against the walls and muttered, 'Repent. Repent. In forty days you will be destroyed if you don't repent.' You had to be walking right by him to hear him but the very first person who happened to walk by him happened to be bored with his job as a nuclear reactor janitor and he said, 'You're right! This is really awful! Let's all repent!'

And that guy started yelling Jonah's message and it turned out that a lot of people were bored with their jobs as neutron bombadiers and saccharine cane cutters and they went to the president of the country and said, 'We've been gross and awful. We're going to repent, and you have to, too.' They took off their fine polyester clothes and put on sackcloth and ashes and burlap and dirt. They turned their nuclear reactor into a solar generator and they all planted organic gardens and Jonah was *pissed*. He was just furious and said, 'OK, God, are you gonna be conned by these hypocrites? Do you think just because they're behaving differently they're better?' God said, '"Fraid so. Behaviour counts. You lose.'

Jonah stomped to a hill outside of town and sat under a tree praying for the Ninevites to show their true nature and for God to fry them alive. All that happened was that God destroyed the tree Jonah was sitting under so he got a sunburn.

Jonah said, 'God, how come you destroyed this tree? This tree never did nothing.' He did a ten minute rap about the tree and how trees are important and you can't just destroy them for no reason. And God said, 'How come, Jonah, how come, wherefore, why is it, that you care so much about that tree, when you have no pity at all for Nineveh, a city that has a whole lot of folks in it, and some children and animals and you wanted me to kill them all? How come you didn't care about them?' And that's the end of the book in the Bible. You're left there with the question. You never know what Jonah said.

Arts of Imagination

The Language of the Soul

JOHN LANE

ON ONE OF THE PAINTED WALLS of the Lascaux cave, surrounded by those haunted, exquisitely shaped and coloured animals, there is an almost childish stick-like figure of a man, a huntsman, who having cast his spear into the guts of a bison, is now weaponless and vulnerable, poignantly frail, exposed and incomplete. A modern American poet, Wendell Berry, has commented that 'the message seems essentially that of the voice of the whirlwind in the book of Job: the creation is bounteous and mysterious, and humanity is only a part of it —not its equal, much less its master.'

Fifteen to twenty thousand years after these caves had been painted, another poet, Goethe, visiting the Sistine Chapel, remarked that no one who had not seen Michelangelo's ceiling frescos 'can have a clear idea of what a human being can achieve'. Had he seen Lascaux, perhaps the most astonishing of all our recollections of the past, I have little doubt he would have expressed his admiration in not dissimilar terms. For here at the so-called dawn of consciousness humankind was already capable of an aesthetic sophistication which, I suggest, is amongst the finest in our entire history. Perhaps art, as Whistler thought, since it begins with the infinite, cannot progress.

What are these artistic needs and emotions which our hunting ancestors experienced and which we still know when we feel them? What is beauty and its antithesis, ugliness? What is the aesthetic dimension, the inner vision, and what happens when it is, as it is in our own age, stunted or withdrawn?

We do not know how nameless artisans—carpenters, wheelwrights, potters, plasterers—were once capable of producing beauty; nor how, before the world was stripped of almost every sanctity, everything people made for their own use—bowl, textile or house—was endowed with a harmony so immaculate and so exquisitely wrought that only our finest artists can now emulate these achievements. Yet it seems, for all its faults, that the culture of the past, the culture of traditional, pre-industrial societies, was harmonious—something not only whole in itself but a wholeness or equilibrium that included both what was known and what was not known.

A healthy culture is an integrated pattern; a communal order of memory, insight, value, work, reverence. It reveals the human necessities and the human limits. It clarifies our inescapable bonds to the earth and to each other. And it permits, or encourages us, to embody aspects of the truth which we can never otherwise know. Thus it is that in all those cultures before the machine metaphor was allowed to usurp and wipe from consideration not merely some values, but the very *issue* of value, our labouring ancestors were, almost every one of them, as Coomaraswamy would have said, not labourers but artists, 'special kinds of artist'. There was then, of course, no word for 'art' in the sense in which we use it now—art was all that was well and truly made. But in that the aesthetic and the practical had not been divided the work of these men and women, as its beauty still testifies, was a responsible and qualitative skill; the practical understanding of value; the enactment or the acknowledgement or the signature of responsibility to the mystery heard at Lascaux still to be heard today.

In point of fact all traditional pre-industrial cultures had (or have) a complex metaphysical doctrine governing all their various arts and crafts, including the most basic of all, agriculture—for true farming depends as much on character, devotion, imagination and a sense of structure as the painting of an icon. Each was seen not merely as a means of producing material necessities but as a paradigm of the cosmogonic act; a meditative path, a support of contemplation. In such societies the skill, be it baking bread, refining the lines of a chair or weaving a blanket, was a vocation in the true sense of the word: an inseparable part of the maker's being, an inseparable part of a life in which expression and beauty were integral to the pattern of life as a whole. We find this corroborated in many artefacts, folk stories and myths: in the chants of the Navajos:

> In beauty I walk
> With beauty before me I walk
> With beauty above me I walk
> It is finished (again) in beauty
> It is finished in beauty.

It is typical of the mentality of our own age that we cannot conceive of such beauty except in terms of the past, of money or, most sadly of all, of the work of someone else. We cannot conceive of it as 'the outward and visible sign of an inward and spiritual grace'; the leaves and blossoms of the tree as pattern or cycle, orderly process, reverence.

In our culture the wholesale denial of the spirit, the death of the soul—name as we will the withdrawal of the inner vision from the outer world—has gone so far that even matter has been coarsened, made base; far from exalting it, it is now abused and treated with contempt. From the suburbs of Dagenham to the outskirts of New York, Mexico City or Hannover, a growing number of people now live in an environment less personal, more featureless, than any that a civilization has built in the past. A growing number of people now work for organizations which deny them responsibility not only for what they do but for the kind and quality of what they make (for, as Ruskin said, our so-called manufacturing units produce everything except men). Ugliness and disorder, one might say, have become a way of life. 'It is,' as D. H. Lawrence wrote in the thirties before the dehumanizing effects of the Cartesian mechanistic philosophy had reached its climax, 'It is as if dismalness had soaked through everything.'

Yet if our culture is disordered and divided—'all out of shape from toe to top' as Yeats described it—the sacramental wisdom of the intuitive or creative mind, the response to harmony, order, wholeness, rhythm, even reverence, have not been totally expunged. In timeless moments we individually respond to the call of the beautiful where the pattern is complete. Sometimes it is that these sudden peaks of experience—these posts in a field, this wasp on an ivy flower, this frost-white landscape under a winter sun—provide us with an immediate apprehension of life as life. They give us the ability to see the real nature of the things that are before our eyes, of the people we know here and now in this world, of all creation, of ourselves. Thrown back upon the last and richest of human resources—the fertile solitude of the deep self—our heart responds to meet the world; it dances to the slow tune of the hills, crawls with the wasp, skis down the rainbow, praises the sentient flower. Speaking of a bluebell Gerard Manley Hopkins says, 'I know the beauty of our Lord by it'; a great and simple affirmation but one, I fancy, meaningless to those now under the spell of materialism.

Such experiences of exalted consciousness—impossible to convey in words —occur more frequently in our lives than we would sometimes admit. The experience may be brief, spontaneous, and unexpected, but of a clarity in which all is minutely perceived as if by finer sense. And then it is that quite simply we know in a different and much finer kind, from the all-too-familiar everyday mode which places yang over yin, activity over contemplation, natural knowledge over intuitive wisdom, science over religion and seems increasingly incapable of labouring for their integration. Such *knowing*, aesthetic knowing, the predominant experience of seeing with the inner eye, the eye of the heart, the eye of love, is one of the means, if not the predominant means by which we may realize the *oneness* of all things: of non-duality. 'The light of the body is the eye,' says Matthew, 'if therefore thine eye be single, thy whole body shall be full of light. But if thine eye be evil, thy whole body shall be full of darkness.' Surely these enigmatic words remind us that to know in the full sense is *to see*, to be full of light, not to walk in the dark.

What is happening in these little moments, so fleeting, and yet so significant in our lives? Can they be explained? And if so, how?

The idea that our conscious self is by no means our entire self is nowadays familiar. There is an immense array of evidence suggesting that not only do unconscious processes make up a great portion of mental activity, but also that this activity itself covers a vast spectrum ranging through dreaming, habitual behaviour, pattern recognition, conceptualization, creative imagination, intuition and religious experience. Consciousness, then, as Kathleen Raine has said, 'is like a small circle of light beyond which lie regions of memory, some recoverable at will, some not; and beyond our personal memories, archetypal configurations and unknown energies of the psyche. Beyond everything we can still, however remotely, call ourselves, there is what the mystics have called the divine ground, the presence in, and to the human soul, of what can only be named God.'

The mystery goes by many names: *nous* for the Greeks, *mens* for the mystics, *pneuma* or spirit for St Paul, who described this presence in the deepest and most central part of the human psyche, as the living breath of God by which all things are continually sustained and created. Although this presence is sometimes called the supraconscious or the 'higher' or trans-personal self— as contrasted with the limited, conscious, personal ego-self, the kingdom, as Blake puts it, of 'Satan the Selfhood', to which it is entirely opposed—I myself prefer to use the name by which it is most hallowed, the soul.

A not dissimilar interpretation of the divinity of all is to be found in that classic of Sanskrit literature, the *Upanishads*, where the words *Brahman*, the ground of universal being, and *Atman*, the ground of personal being, respectively describe what may perhaps be translated as the Holy Spirit and its living, indwelling presence in each one of us. For the momentous truth may be that God must not be sought as something far away, separate from us, in a Heaven to which we may ascend only after our death; but rather as something close at hand, forever and forever in the inmost of us: more interior to us, as Thomas Aquinas says, than we are to ourselves. Thus 'the holiness of life is not something predicated, as an attribute, but inherent in the divine nature of the ground,' the divine spirit of humanity.

Such reflections are, I believe, confirmed every time we respond to beauty, love, or some aspect of the truth which moves us, as the sea itself is pulled, by an invisible force of spiritual gravity. But never more so than in those moments of singular intensity, rarer and of a different order of consciousness from perception of the beautiful, when we catch exalted glimpses of the perfection of the everlasting Now; when, for example, not looking at the budding sycamore in the hedge, but living it, we are pure Being. Then, indeed, in this confrontation of the temporal with the eternal, the 'I' of the Soul and the 'thou' of the tree are united in a timeless hymn of praise for the flow of life in the sap and cells, the crackling buds against the sky, the leaping choreography of branch and grass and beast and hill: the one in many and the many in one.

The joy of this union is described by St Teresa in words which remind us of the *Upanishads* two thousand years before. It is, she writes, like 'water falling from heaven into a river or fountain, when all becomes water, and it is not possible to divide or separate the water of the river from that which fell from heaven; or when a little stream enters the sea so that henceforth there shall be no means of separation.' Such experiences of the ultimate unity are aesthetic, for at such moments face to face with a Giotto, a Rembrandt, the sycamore tree, there is no subject-object distinction, all individual identity is lost, dissolved in the greater Soul, and we and nature are one. This, of course, is the real renunciation which is always demanded, the renunciation of 'I' and 'mine'.

I used to wonder if this transformation of consciousness could be achieved through standard or pedagogical education. I fear not. Direct insight, the truth of the Soul, cannot be reached by abstract reason but solely by transcending the ego, the centre of all conscious thought, through struggle, suffering, love, contemplation or, not least, through art. If the logic of this transition from divinity to art is not immediately apparent it is a measure of the disrepute into which the arts have (on the whole deservedly) fallen that their mention in the context of humanity's spiritual enlightenment may seem strange. None the less what we now call the arts are important, supremely important, because they are (or can be) the embodiment of imaginative truths which man cannot otherwise know.

There is, of course, the obvious point that the arts and crafts of different cultures are themselves different in content, style and tradition; as divided one from another as the various races of the earth. Yet surely these differences, important as they are, are but the dialects of one and the same language of the spirit. Holding with Heraclitus that the word is common to all, and that wisdom is to know the will by which all things are steered, I am convinced that there is a 'common universe of discourse' transcending the differences of tongues. Even the works of ages or civilizations remote from our own—ages like the prehistoric, of which we have the most meagre knowledge—speak to us directly, more directly in fact, than those works of our own time ungrounded in the Imagination. For Imagination is of the timeless Soul, fashion is not. So understood the arts, as the products of vision, are the very food of our humanity, whose nourishment is, as Jesus reminds us, the 'word of God'; the words and sounds, the symbols and myths, the images and forms spoken from Soul to Soul across time and space, across culture and medium, the living language of the Imagination.

The Imagination is the very essence of human life, the principle of oneness in us, the principle by which we may perceive, value and imitate order beyond our rational understanding. It is, indeed, the only faculty with the power of bridging the chasm between subject and object and of seeing, with extreme clarity, the reality or essential form. This reason cannot do. By its nature it is restricted to the finite and material; but Imagination, having no such limitations, can. It can, in fact, perceive the Infinite in everything, and in that moment of recognition give entrance to the other mind beyond the mind of the personal ego. It is therefore no surprise to find that art flourishes or decays according to the adequacy of our ideas of the transcendent; flourishing in those cultures or individuals which possess, however unconsciously, a sense of the numinous; withering in those which have lost the power of seeing spiritual truth. Such a culture is our own. For the separation of the soul from the body and from the world is in us no disease of the fringe, no aberration, but a fracture that runs through our mentality like a geological fault.

There is nothing equivocal about this point. This rift, this fault, is a flaw in the mind that runs deep into the heart of matter, 'affecting or afflicting substance neither by intention nor accident, but because, occurring in the Creation that is unified as a whole, it must; there is no help for it.' Spirit and body cannot be divided; their mutuality, their unity is inescapable. The

Creation, any creation, is not the freeing of the spirit from the flesh, from matter; it is their marriage, their union, their reconciliation in harmony. No wonder then that Henri Bergson has compared the love of God for his Creation to the love for creation that moves the soul of the artist. 'This is my conclusion,' he writes, 'to which the philosopher who accepts the mystical experience must come. The whole creation will thus appear to him as a vast work of God for the creation of creators, for the possession of beings co-workers with Him and worthy of His love.'

In every civilization the artist (the artist, that is, in each of us) has borne authentic witness to the mind of the Creator of whom he or she is the earthly representative. Thus art acts as a metaphor as well as a preparation for the greatest art of all, the art of giving form and meaning to existence. Making use of matter in a holy or a wholesome way—by working with it playfully or lovingly, or by eating and drinking it joyously—the artist in us consecrates it, lifts it close to the light of mystery. In the Cabalistic phrase we 'cause the sparks to fly'.

Thus we see that whenever the creative imagination is present, whenever we live in the knowledge that our very existence rests upon the immediate creation of every moment that we live by this God within, then matter may become inspired (from the Latin *in spire*, to breath into); and the potter's clay, the weaver's wool, the painter's colours, the carpenter's wood may be spiritualized, made sacramental—a grace bestowed solely on those who have found freedom from all selfish attachment. Yet all things on earth, by the incomplete workings of the human mind, may easily become snares. Even the mineral whose contemplation can give us, through the intuitions of the cosmic imagination, a living experience of non-duality—a living experience which goes deep down to the very roots, the very breath and rhythm of life—may be reduced to an object of intellectual interest or possession, an object of greed by means of which we may feel ourselves to be greatly magnified. Thenceforward we become chained to matter, tied to time, victims of an attachment to impermanence which it is the Buddhist's aim to renounce or remove. Only too easily we fall and our works denigrate not only life but our own souls.

This seems naturally to bring us back to our own age, the age of materialism at whose nadir we have perhaps arrived. The first principle of this age is that the primary reality, that by which all else is evaluated and measured, is matter. Matter which can only be described from empirically based and publicly verifiable knowledge of the sense-perceived world; matter which can be analysed, re-combined and utilized in such a way that we may, in Francis Bacon's words, 'be enabled to enjoy without any trouble the fruits of the earth and all its comforts.' On the surface materialism may appear beneficial, and might indeed be so were it not for its implicit assumption of a separation between mind and matter which has inaugurated an expanding series of divisions, bringing into existence a universe devoid of life, a desacralized nature outside which each one of us stands alone, as (in Descartes' words) a 'Lord and Master'.

But that is not all. Another more inscrutable repression drives the engine of urban-industrialism. For if matter is the prime reality, quantitative measurement is all. Whatever escapes the net of numbers must, almost by definition, be regarded as unproven; the left-over realm of mind and spirit, of 'secondary qualities'—the ghostly country of art and religion that has come to be regarded as less and less habitable during the last three hundred years.

That is what stands behind the contradictions of modern society. That, too, is what stands behind the appalling ugliness of our contemporary environment and the growth of what the poet Schiller called 'the disenchantment of the world'—the dying out of the magic of things, the slow, inexorable, drying out of ancient springs. No wonder there exists a feeling that something has been stolen from us; that, as Gregory Bateson put it, we are no longer responsive to 'the pattern that connects'. No wonder, too, that as Lord of Creation we may have conquered the earth, split the atom, walked on the moon, yet know that we have become, as Paul expressed it, 'as sounding brass or tinkling cymbal'. Momentous signatures of desolation and emptiness darken our skies. We are approaching the terminal phase of a civilization which dates back to the end of the Middle Ages and, in spite of the evidence of transformation, are still a long way from any large scale regeneration. A precarious moment 'between a death and a difficult birth'.

There are in fact a growing number of indications that the way out of this monstrous pathology—the pathology of arrogance and emptiness which characterizes our culture—can only in the end be corrected by a reversal of the premises upon which post-Renaissance civilization rests. For the pattern of renewal shows that the renewal of life comes out of what we have consciously despised and rejected—just as, for example, in the Christian story, the great renewal begins in the despised stable with the Son born of a scorned race. If this is so—and there are many intimations that it is—then it is mind or spirit, not matter, which may soon be considered the first principle of the universe, the ground of reality. To me this is the awakening, supremely to be desired. This is the 'new theme' we should try to live.

I began with a mystery, Lascaux, and would end with another, Quarr. Not a Catholic, not even a Christian, every year I go for a few days to a Benedictine monastery on the Isle of Wight where most of this paper was written. I go there for a number of reasons, but chiefly to experience something which I can find nowhere else. The painter Marc Chagall sums it up: 'In our life,' he writes, 'there is a single colour, as on an artist's palette, which provides the meaning of art and life. It is the colour of love. I see in this colour of love all the qualities permitting accomplishment in other fields.' It is this colour, and the resulting accomplishments, which I experience at Quarr.

Quarr, in fact, is important to me because it bears witness to a way of life which is the opposite of the materialist picture of reality. And if, as I believe, our first priority is to recognize and develop spirituality, to reclaim the lost world of the spirit until it is once again rich for cultivation, then Quarr may be one of the places in the Western world where we can still discover a wholeness of being. Not that, for a moment, I would have us all become monks—or Catholics or Christians or believers of any faith; vital religion must spring not from propositions which are the outcome of abstract speculations, such as doctrinal statements, but from the immediate and imaginative apprehension of love, beauty, mystery.

On the contrary, Quarr is important because the company of men who live there are trying to give corporate witness by their life as a community to a harmonious—and therefore responsible—pattern; a pattern which is healthy because the parts are joined harmoniously to the whole. They are not, of course, alone. Only recently I discovered the same sanity in San Francisco in the Zen Centre, where several hundred young men and women have created an environment not just of the welfare of the spirit, but of a larger harmony, including the immediate environs of the city itself. Here too the spirit has enfleshed itself in the materiality of the world, producing food, shelter, worship, well-made artefacts emblematic of the best and most responsible care. 'Art' as such does not exist; the aesthetic dimension is integral. 'Education' as such does not exist; it grows naturally from a passion for excellence and order that is handed down to young people by older people whom they respect and love. 'Work' as such does not exist; it is an essential part of practice, a way to realize the nature and needs of environmental and social existence.

It is difficult to convey the qualities of a community in which a human being's whole nature and its capacities can be fulfilled. But at Quarr and the Zen Centre everyday work, worship, the reverence for life, the sense of a group of men all-of-a-piece within themselves and with a holy order within each one of them, all this can bring heart and mind into some faint intimation of a human order that accommodates the various concerns of culture to each other. If they are anything to go by the integrated life is an attainable ideal.

Meanwhile we must live in the world where the task before us is formidable. Faced with bankruptcy, we need to rediscover, and rediscover swiftly, so much. We have to rediscover a life of meaning and purpose, no longer moving away from the centre. We have to discover the importance of Creation, the imaginative act, without which we cannot be human. We have to discover art and life as one; art, that is, as an act, not an object; a ritual, not a possession. We have to rediscover that we can all be involved one with another in a seamless web of kinship, love and responsibility. We have to rediscover the unity of all things, that the spirit moves in all created things—God and beast and human beings and star and plant—that spirit without matter is no less a thing than its opposite. Nothing less will do, and nothing will be more difficult to bring about.

September/October 1980

In the Serpent's Mouth

JOHN MOAT

I'LL BEGIN, LIKE THE GREEKS, with time. In time there is nothing fixed
—everything is subject to change. Principalities and powers, trade unions and
empires; the role of kings, the role of priests. The role of the poet.

Time, and the way we view time, is at the back of our regard for life, our
belief in history, our estimate of the meaning of creation. To those Greeks,
fathers of the Western mind, time was the hideous Cronus who devours his
own children. Perhaps it was the tick of this same Cronus, an apprehension
deep in the inherited mind, that influenced the Christian church when it came
up with its chronometry—another child-devourer, only this time the one who
'bears all his sons away' does not exactly resemble an ogre but, perhaps equally
forbidding, is 'like an ever-rolling stream'.

Such a view sees time as linear and consequential, and it is a view which,
it seems, our culture has this last thousand years been disposed to accept.
Almost as if our disposition, one largely egocentric and dominated by the
mind, requires that alpha and omega be set poles apart so that, across the
gulf fixed between, time can be drawn as a narrow thread, a tyrant way where
options are closed and where deviation, or momentary loss of balance, threaten
with absolute perdition.

There are though, mercifully, other ways of looking at time. To the Hindus
time is Kala who fetches us back to our beginning, irresistible, an implacable
adversary—unless we go with him willingly, and then he is tantamount to
a lover. Maybe none of us can say he knows that creation is a sustained
revolution, that powers of every kind must wax and wane, but in one part
of us there is, currently eclipsed or out of fashion, an informed intuition that
senses it must be so. This faculty, contemplating time, perceives two things
outstanding. First, time is not linear, it is cyclic. The old green serpent with
his mouth full, feeding on his own tail. There is nothing in creation exempt
from his formula of beginning and end, growth and decline, death and rebirth.
And second that time is a contrivance of double aspect—simply because, being
a dimension of creation, it must reflect the duality of creation, that union of
two. Two aspects then. Call them the sun and the moon—those two in single
revolution. That is the marriage. There must be this marriage in time. That is
the dichotomy of the Great Year.

The sun is brightest at midday and midsummer. The moon has her twenty-
eight phases. There is the full moon and the dark of the moon. In any complete
cycle these two luminaries, the one of the day the other of night, will each have
its ascendancy. Always the two are in single revolution, each moving in accord
with and counter to the rotation of the other; always, in precise balance, making

153

way for, or replacing the other's ascendancy, the other's decline. Two thousand winters (and now I'm getting to the heart of this briar-patch), that's what Yeats gave to one complete gyre.

Each luminary brings to the whole its own character, but (as is similarly expressed by the graphic yang-yin) a character in every detail complementary with that of the other. So in any year, with the increase of the solar influence and the corresponding failure of the lunar, one behaviour or disposition or bias becomes assured. Then the consequences are predictable. The ascendancy of the sun-god, the hero-god, monotheism, male sovereignty, the rule of reason, of *logos*, of all that Robert Graves has given us to understand by the Apollonian mind. Its zenith, it may be, is the high point of civilization. For a moment it may even seem that the dream of the utopian city has been realized on earth. But when that moment has passed, and the power begins to withdraw from the patterns and institutions and formulations of the solar culture, and to recharge the lunar properties so that the latter's *hylic* or material aspect begins to reassert itself, then this transition in turn shows its rash of predictable symptoms. First the solar dictate hardens to dogma, and out of that dogma all the soulless -*isms* begin to appear: hubristic humanism, bleak totalitarianism, determinism, positivism, self-annihilating materialism. These are the jingles of the ageing sun. They have no true authority because authority is elsewhere; it is shifting, in transit to the moon. This is the hour between one coherence and another, when 'the best lack all conviction'.

The Christian church is very much an example, almost a prototype, of the solar/sun-god formulation. From this point of view it is interesting to read again Dr Edward Norman's 1978 Reith Lectures. In these he analyses the state of the church and suggests how, having lost effective contact with its spiritual authority, it is for its own credibility drawing increasingly on the tenets of temporal humanism, and in some instances even aligning itself with Marxist materialism. He makes this comment: 'Politicization of religion means the transformation of the faith itself, so that it comes to be defined in terms of political values; it becomes essentially concerned with social morality rather than with the ethereal qualities of immorality—the temporal supersedes the spiritual.' This observation, it seems to me, is unassailable; and to a churchman who conceives of time as linear this predicament of the church must be cause for alarm. But according to the cyclic view what Dr Norman describes are merely the standard symptoms of a sun-credo, not invalidated, but whose operative power is spent. One that is approaching its eclipse, and the midnight moment of its own rebirth.

And all the time, in constant compensation, hardly observed maybe, the lunar cycle also is under way. As the hold of the sun-god weakens and his voice grows brittle, increasingly frantic, ultimately insane, so all the time is the stirring of the other wisdom: the manifold deity, magic, the heart's constraint of the mind, the rule of rune over reason, everything that is feminine and fluid, the power of instinct and sensation, of image over dictate. The abiding wisdom of mother earth and mother nature.

But, and it must be stressed, this should not be seen as a formula of conflicting black and white. When (as now) that happens, we break faith with time and merely engineer between essential complements a vapid opposition and, as if the two lobes of the brain were in conflict, insanity. At no moment is the one independent of the other. Just as in the year no season is independent, so here too are the apportioned ascendancies and equinoxes. Every moment is unique and uniquely involved with every other—so, although the two equinoxes might appear similarly composed (a similar compromise between midsummer and midwinter) they are by their place in the rotation as different as spring is from autumn.

Within this revolutionary whole the two elemental dispositions in turn bear the focus of power, the expression of Divinity. Here then is my burden—and it is not often in the wheel of time one could say such a thing and not risk one's skin. Those two aspects of the divinity, upon whose intercourse the creative wholeness of the year is founded, each has its appointed human celebrant. And not just a celebrant but, at zenith, its officer, its mediator, the one who on earth can point and demonstrate and, in certain circumstances, even command its respective, the positive or the negative, power. The solar is served by the priest. The lunar by the poet.

The priest (and because I speak in mythological terms the generalization is not totally ludicrous) is devotee of the *unspoken* word, of the disembodied singularity of God. He must therefore be at odds with the picturehouse of existence, with Maya and the mesh of the senses. Asceticism and self-denial are his way: the shortest route to atonement. But the celebrant of the lunar aspect, the poet, is in everything contrary to the priest. His testimony is the triumph of the *spoken* word, the incarnate word; his grail the perfect heartbreak, the *I am* self-expressed in myriad transient form. He is the seer who by his fined senses beholds and magnifies the creator in the adornment of creation. The poet becomes an eye and tongue of love whereby love may, through contemplation and utterance, comprehend itself in the unbridled wonder of the beloved.

Are these two then in opposition? The answer to this is the answer to every question of existence: yes and no. That answer signifies the two contentions, that simplicity of two upon which all existence is founded. Yet to wisdom they are no more opponents than the seasons, and what is seen in a moment, at midsummer say, as disproportion appears to vision that can scan the full year as the proof of order. So each has its hour, but no matter how great its domination may appear it is never anything but the essential complement of the other. Then for each as the term of office is accomplished that role simply passes from the light, not into obscurity but into another light, the diurnal light of the secular. So the priest becomes the scientist and ultimately the technician; and the poet becomes the writer, ultimately the commentator. Seen in this light one might expect the revolution could be bloodless!

A thing that is drawn out in history is caught by myth in a moment. Jung saw it, how under the growing tyranny of the sun-god the medieval mind looked for compensation and sanity in legend. Parsifal is the sun-struck Christian hero, and who is his dark brother but Merlin, yes, the lunary, son of the devil and a pure virgin, the type of the bardic mage? The hour is Parsifal's, and Merlin and his voice have gone from the world. Dead? Or does he after all live on in the forest? His cry is still heard, a night-cry, full of warning and dismay. It disturbs the people terribly, but they can no longer understand it. Disowning it they have disowned and banished from consciousness a living part of themselves. The dark disowned becomes blackness, the words evil and demon change their meaning. Just as the pregnant virgin cast out becomes a witch, so the banished bard becomes the black magician.

Now, with the Parsifal legend as the lens, take a look at literature these last thousand years.

In self-assured Celtic society the poet was esteemed above everyone except the king and the queen. No idle dignatory, they had demonstrable power. They commanded the language which was the life and lineage of the people. Their role and significance are not easy for our moon-starved minds to imagine. The poet was the sorcerer with power of word to command and alter life (both Taliesin and Valmiki could couplet a man to death). The poet was seer and mage, the muse was the moon—and because the moon was in the ascendant this power was toward, it was pertinent, it was particular and compelling.

As the ascendancy of the moon began to wane, so the emphasis in due course shifted to the sun-god, the rule of the fiery *logos*. For convenience and mythological tally we'll say that the throes of this can be traced to the first thousand years after the birth of Jesus. Slowly the priest replaced the poet as ruling celebrant—and it should be understood that even in the myth there is only a moment, that hour of eclipse at the full or the dark of the moon, when the two do not in some measure share each other's attributes, or when their specific power is unmitigated. What then happens to the poet? Look at Merlin, increasingly an irrelevance, an outcast, divided from his shadow and cut off from all but a vestige of his power, he becomes finally a being of pretension grubbing the fashions of the secular courts for any sort of a living.

That didn't happen immediately. For a while, clinging to the chair of office, the poet hung about the church, contrived to please both the new order and his muse with crafty lovesongs, allegories where lip-service to the bridegroom conceal a profane interest in the bride. Even an epic like Beowulf, seeming at first of such dark lunar majesty one marvels at how it could have been hatched in a monastery, reveals to second thoughts a sinister, tell-tale strain. One sees emerging the Christian hero who by his act of killing the dragon, that phenomenal configuration of bright energy, the guardian of ancestral gold, somehow associates him with Grendel and the brood of Cain. The sun-god is back with a vengeance.

Gradually the poet, the sanctuary sealed, lost power in the world of action and was shoved out further and further into the secular periphery. So even great poets like Chaucer and Spenser seem barely conscious dissidents, serving up the mysteries in a form acceptable, or else that will escape the notice of an army of occupation, couching knowledge in the evasive conventions of allegory.

There in the night, suddenly at its most stark and much too close for comfort, is the cry of the lost Merlin. What else is that power that so disturbs us, that gleams time and again with a kind of dreadful spectral light? The tension becomes unbearable, and all that is forgotten and unconscious of the teeming medieval lunar life cries out against a new consciousness, the censure and disgust of solar puritanism. At heart there is only ever the one conflict, which is precisely why Shakespeare's plays are universal. Born at the right moment maybe, but his power ensured he was in at the kill.

There comes a point, somewhere near to the autumnal equinox, when the sun's glare is softened by the re-emergent moon, but its control not over-ridden nor yet hardened into reflex; and when the lunar is fully responsive but without that *femininity* yet showing pent signs of repression. It is a time when the spoken word achieves maximum coherence and articulation is capable of strange beauty, a marriage of control and passion. The so-called metaphysical poets, John Donne especially, evidence this both in style and content. To my mind the high moment, the hour of perfect equinox, where no strain between conscious and unconscious, between control and spontaneity, between logic and song, can any longer be detected is in the poems of Andrew Marvel.

The hour passed. John Milton was there, like the official receiver. The old conflict that rang through Shakespeare is now set as the war in heaven, and the outcome is assured. Paradise lost. The puritan rule. How on earth could the poet have contrived it so majestically? The sense of strain is incredible, and, one fears, the personal cost.

In the eighteenth century, with the moon gathering momentum, the mind must now fight for control. To keep the crack from the façade, form and structure hardened are *formalized*, and strength borrowed from old classical design. Inspiration can barely filter through, until suddenly Blake. In such a strenuously reasonable age the voice of the bard can only be heard where the hold is super-human at the very fringe of sanity. The suppression is so violent something simply snaps. Blake is like a haemorrhage that breaks clean through the cranium.

With the Romantics one feels some crisis is past. The calm after a fit, all conscious power spent. Coleridge dopes the habitual mind, and then goes sounding in the unconscious. And what emerges of the moon in Shelley and Keats is like the dream of a lost hiker sleeping in a barn. There is a stillness which touches one, in Keats especially. It is I think the dream of the before-dawn sleep:

>   Already with thee! tender is the night,
>   And haply the Queen-moon is on her throne,
>   Cluster'd around by all her starry Fays;

Maybe what we see then, in Tennyson or later the pre-Raphaelites, is a false lunar-dawn, soon snuffed by the bone-dust blowing in the solar wind. An unformed conviction, a mere harping back.

>   'I am half sick of shadows,' said
>   The Lady of Shalott.

But clearly the heat has gone from the sky, the thousand eyes of night have begun to peer through.

What then of the poets of our present time? In that crowd (because for certain there's no shortage), two faces maybe. One is the face of those who cling to what they, still living under the skeletal solar thumb, see as the development of literature. They include academics, social commentators, entertainers, mynah birds, the tide-followers, the criers of the demotic revolution, and the string-puppets of the market-trends. Almost unbelievable is the impoverishment of the language they weave with—hardly surprising then if they, along with politicians and theologians of the old order, should be disregarded, as if there no longer exists the ear upon which their voices can register.

The other is the face of the renascent. Those who, making under some impulse the orphean descent into their own underworld, are coming up with the moon; who are thereby discovering not the shadow but the actual world of myth and legend, and who are experiencing how the current is coming back to the language.

The predictable symptoms of such a time are these. The breakdown of the utopian dream, the gradual failure of the power of abstraction, and of faith in a bureaucratic solution. The decline of humanism (both its negative and, alas, its positive face) and of the hold of the standard or egalitarian principle. The full revolution, probably violent, of repressed femininity. And finally the departure of that fantasy which is the sun's favourite intoxicant, the dream of the absolute subjection of the lunar dominions, nature and matter.

At the same time one is likely to see a resurgence of the self-expressive life, organic and instinctive design. Multiplicity, self-determination, decentralization, these will manifest themselves not in the catch-cries of the urban politician, but as natural order. Already there are signs of the return to Earth: the uncomfortable primitivism in art, a naïve interest in the occult, in the potencies of nature and animals, in folklore. Slowly Pan revives. And as he does, the seasons become again the rubric and the four ages of humanity the order of office.

A paradise regained? No, not at all. A new dark age? Perhaps. The hour of the full moon has as many nightmares and pitfalls, precisely as many as the shadowless tyranny of midday. Besides if we have no love for the solar, merely dismiss it, we make the same deadly mistake again—we disown a half of ourselves, and are sentenced once more in time to tear ourselves apart, the same old schizoid delusion. To discredit the past is to unfound the future. Only by coming to terms with time can we end this war in ourselves. This means that we can look to the next sure equinox only out of our regard for the last. The next, in the lunar spell, is the vernal; that is spring, the hour of impregnation. As we sow, so shall we reap. And looking back to the last equinox, the autumnal, was the harvest so poor?

So for my specific prediction. It is in these present circumstances that the poet is likely to attain his true tenure; Merlin come out of the wood, no longer in monkish brown but wearing the six-coloured cloak of office. With the change of aspect once again the supreme custodianship passes to him (remember how Jesus on the cross entrusted his Mother not to Peter but to John, or how Sita, when Rama lost his reason, was cared for by Valmiki?); and now by the poet's word the canon and ceremony of common life, cradle, marriage-bed, hearth and grave, will gather its deep-questing meaning and be hallowed.

There are signs that this is already happening. Before many years we will find the bardic colleges reconstituted. Places where poets will get their training in all the arts of the word and the will, in the command and control of the mind, and in the responsibilities that accompany power. Here the great lunar mysteries, the Eleusinian mysteries of death and rebirth will be celebrated; and here the incantations and the exacting hymns of life will be appropriately rehearsed.

September/October 1979

The Sacred Principles

KEITH CRITCHLOW

OUR ARCHITECTURAL PRACTICE is different because we deliberately choose to embrace a deeper perspective, what you might call a metaphysical dimension; things other architectural practices either feel unnecessary or haven't the time to research. We are particularly fortunate in having spent so much of our lives investigating the more subtle effects of architecture; I mean the sacred traditions which have left both documentary evidence and the magnificent forms behind—the crystallized wisdom of past ages. Because I am also a teacher and what is known as an academic, I have been able, over the past twenty-five years to conduct a research programme into the geometry of the sacred or, as you might say, the metaphysical basis of geometry that underlies all the great traditions of humanity.

Surely there are profound differences between, say, the Temple of Heaven in Peking, Khajuraho in India, and Salisbury Cathedral; yet the evidence is that there are four universal languages which all three of them were concerned with. These are the languages that all people can agree upon—the objective basis of experience. Arithmetic or pure number is the first, followed by geometry or the direct relationships of order in space. This is followed by the principles of music or harmony, and lastly the objective evidence of the night sky and the rhythms of sun and moon which we call cosmology or astronomy. Once you take all these into account your architecture becomes different—you are dealing with more than mechanical or 'functional' criteria.

I believe that architecture can be designed and built with a sense of caring and sacredness rather than being ruled by economic force or any other abstract element. The return to an awareness of sacredness will come through people being aware of their own sacredness and their inter-dependency upon all aspects of the planetary environment—the body of the world, one's community and one's own body. One Chinese philosopher said, 'Whether you concern yourself with the big or the small, you start with your own body.' Architecture is the next bodily envelope after one's clothes.

Our present projects include the Lindisfarne Chapel in Colorado, a pavilion for the Municipality of Riyadh, Saudi Arabia, a Buddhist retreat centre and a holistic health centre, which we also consider to be a task of sacred architecture in the very truest sense. This centre is going to be built in Lanzarote in the Canary Islands. It will not be for sick people who need hospitalization, but for people who need to de-stress and learn more about themselves and to understand how they can work most efficiently, both for themselves, their immediate colleagues and for the world at large. So, in a way, it will be more like a 'Health Hotel'. We have designed it on traditional principles. It will have in it all the allopathic, herbal, homoeopathic, acupuncture and many other modern, as well as the traditional ways of healing.

Then there are the more traditionally 'religious' projects. Besides the Lindisfarne Chapel which is a non-denominational ecumenical space, I have been asked to work primarily for the Buddhist and Islamic traditions, both of which are a great privilege. I have been designing a monastery for the Tibetans in Colorado. I have also designed a mosque in Tehran and now one in Kuwait. I have been asked to design a rather interesting neo-sacred project —a prototype kindergarten school. The Arab people are very concerned about the continuation of their tradition. Also they are very concerned about being in the twentieth century. I have been talking to them about the fact that it is not particularly wise to have kindergarten schools which are designed on international or what I would call anonymous principles; acultural buildings make for acultural people. So, if they want a continuity of their sacred traditions then they need to have traditional geometric forms and cultural forms integral with their buildings.

It has been very interesting to go to Kuwait and study Islamic art and design, and to have an audience there interested to hear what I have to say. I run a venture called SURAT, which in Arabic means image. This we have done to promote Islamic design, even to the point of making traditional Islamic tiles. I consider this, in a way, to be architecture; a single tile is as much architecture as the whole building is, because often the piece of geometry in a tile can actually express the layout of the building. And the final surface is the one the user reads in any architecture. Hence a tile is a microcosm.

We in the West have always tended to treat Islamic Art as decorative, inferior to 'fine' art like Rembrandt and so on. To my mind it is in no way inferior to Rembrandt. The reason that Islamic buildings are often made from small pieces is extremely practical. They did not have large trees. Most often they had small, very twisted little trees, so they had only little bits of wood. Thus to make a door you have lots of little bits of wood, which you put together as cleverly as you could. It was very good because the joints were never glued, they were able to breathe with the change of temperature. So there is an immensely practical aspect to Islamic design as well as the symbolic allusions to the cycles of the sun and the planets. There is no lecture given. The eye is attracted to beauty and the beauty speaks for itself—through symmetry and light.

The body of the building is a reflection of a healthy body. If the body of the building stands out and is well poised, that helps you the user to be healthy. If you go into a beautiful building, the first thing it does is draw you up, and as you look it opens your chest, you breathe better. If it is a Gothic cathedral you look up at the vaults and you take in a deep breath—that's the secret of a sacred building. It makes you realize your own ability, it puts you in touch.

I have been working in Colorado for Lindisfarne Chapel which we call the Grail. We have been working on it for four years. We decided that the people who build it, the way it is built and the building itself are all of equal importance. Therefore you must design by sacred principles. There are laws of beauty and harmony and those laws must also point to the ultimate goal of humanity. The making of the building is done with people who understand that the act of building is the act of building oneself. The Grail is a universal chapel. Anybody can go there and sit and be quiet or meditate or pray towards Mecca, or hold a Mass. It's a circular building with seventy-two seats in it. It has a millstone in the middle which is a symbol of the turning of the universe. As I say, it is really evidence of an approach, an attitude.

The Indian wisdom of building domestic houses of organic material with not too solid or permanent a structure was a spiritual reminder that we are transitory beings and the only permanence should be in the temple, or possibly the palace, which is really the permanence of governing the physical plane by the mandate of heaven. Any good ruler can rule only because they are ruling by the great principles. So the palace and the temple surely can be permanent because they are representing permanent principles. The Lindisfarne Chapel is itself made of woven beams of timber with a more permanent outer skin of copper tiles: a way of indicating both levels of permanency and impermanency.

It is part of the technology of modern days that the citizen himself can't build his or her own house. Why? Because we don't teach building at school. But some very good experiments have been taking place in the West where a group of people together who pool their financial resources, include an architect in a community of maybe ten or twenty families and then build a little set of houses using the skill of the architect. All sorts of different skills within that group get together. That, to me, is a very good collective way of trying to break down the barrier between specializations. You make a small selection of people who can actually get together and build their own houses. The bricklayers can teach the other people, and the architect can show everybody where the decisions come which are not specialist.

In modern education we are told that specialization is the most important thing, yet this is just the opposite of developing a *whole* view, and the biggest threat is the specialization of computers because it not only isolates by subject but also from human contact and interaction. It is *the* amoral tool. In other words, we are all made to feel impotent unless we can speak a computer language which, of course, is a tragedy. I was very pleased to hear the Queen in her Christmas speech say that we can't programme compassion into a computer.

I would never be against having good tools, but tools for what? Unless we develop a psyche and a relationship to the nature of unity, the tools will always lead us to more confusion. In other words, tools are absolutely valuable to live a physical life and nourish the planet as best as we can. If we need computers then fine, as long as we know what we need them for. If it is just to direct more and more atomic warheads, forget it. Tools are tools, and it doesn't matter how sophisticated they are, it is the motivation behind using them which is so important.

Architecture is also a tool, but far more than merely a mechanical tool. Le Corbusier did an immense bad service by saying the house was a machine for living in—because it became just a machine and we all forgot what *living* was. Now the task is to acknowledge the miraculousness of life, the preciousness of life, and the vast beauty of what we do not know about life and the living.

To treat life, ourselves, our neighbours, our land, our green life, our architecture, as sacred teaches us to be careful, appreciative and sensitive—from here on it is up to each one of us how we build.

July/August 1984

[From an interview by Satish Kumar]

The Mystery of the Wild Man

ROBERT BLY

HISTORICALLY, THE MALE has changed considerably in the past thirty years. Back then there was a person we could call the fifties male, who was hard-working, responsible, fairly well disciplined; he didn't see women's souls very well, though he looked at their bodies a lot. The fifties male was vulnerable to collective opinion: if you were a man, you were supposed to like football games, be aggressive, never cry, and always provide. But this image of the male lacked feminine space. It lacked some sense of flow; it lacked compassion. The fifties male had a clear vision of what a man is, but the vision involved massive inadequacies and flaws.

Then, during the sixties, another sort of male appeared. The women's movement encouraged men to actually *look* at women, forcing them to become conscious of certain things that the fifties male tended to avoid. As men began to look at women and at their concerns, some men began to see their own feminine side and pay attention to it. That process continues to this day, and I would say that most young males are now involved in it to some extent.

Now, there's something wonderful about all this—the step of the male bringing forth his own feminine consciousness is an important one—and yet I have the sense there is something wrong. The male in the past twenty years has become more thoughtful, more gentle. But by this process he has *not* become more free. He's a nice boy who now not only pleases his mother, but also the young woman he is living with.

I see the phenomenon of what I would call the 'soft male'. Sometimes when I look out at my audiences, perhaps half the young males are what I'd call soft. They're lovely, valuable people—I like them—and they're not interested in harming the earth, or starting wars, or working for corporations. There's something favourable toward life in their whole general mood and style of living.

But something's wrong. Many of these men are unhappy. There's not much energy in them. They are life-preserving, but not exactly *life-giving*. And why is it you often see these men with strong women who positively radiate energy? Here we have a finely tuned young man, ecologically superior to his father, sympathetic to the whole harmony of the universe, yet he himself has no energy to offer.

It seems as if many of these soft young men have come to equate their own natural male energy with being macho. Perhaps it's because back in the sixties, when we looked to the women's movement for leads as to how we should be, the message we got was that the new strong women *wanted* soft men.

I remember a bumper sticker that read: 'Women say yes to men who say no.' The women were definitely saying that they preferred the softer receptive male: nonreceptive maleness was equated with violence and receptivity was rewarded.

These changes didn't happen by accident. Young men for various reasons wanted harder women, and women began to desire softer men. It seems like a nice arrangement, but it isn't working out.

One of the fairy tales I'm working on for my *Fairy Tales for Men* collection is a story called *Iron John*.

As the story starts, something strange has been happening in a remote area of the forest near the king's castle: when hunters go into this area, they disappear and never come back. Three hunters have gone out and disappeared. People are getting the feeling that there's something weird about that part of the forest and they don't go there anymore.

Then one day an unknown hunter shows up at the castle and says, 'What can I do around here? I need something to do.' And he is told, 'Well, there's a problem in the forest. People go out there and they don't come back. We've sent in groups of men to see about it and they disappear. Can you do something?'

Interestingly, this young man does not ask for a group to go with him—he goes into the forest alone, taking only his dog. As they wander about in the forest, they come across a pond. Suddenly a hand reaches up from the pond, grabs the dog, and drags it down. The hunter is fond of the dog, and he's not willing to abandon it in this way. His response is neither to become hysterical, nor to abandon his dog. Instead, he does something sensible: he goes back to the castle, rounds up some men with buckets, and then they bail out the pond.

Lying at the bottom of the pond is a large man covered with hair all the way down to his feet, kind of reddish—he looks a little like rusty iron. So they capture him and bring him back to the castle, where the king puts him in an iron cage in the courtyard.

Now, let's stop the story here for a second. The implication is that when the male looks into his psyche, not being instructed what to look for, he may see beyond his feminine side, to the other side of the 'deep pool'. What he finds at the bottom of his psyche—in this area that no one has visited for a long time —is an ancient male covered with hair. Now, in all of the mythologies, hair is heavily connected with the instinctive, the sexual, the primitive. What I'm proposing is that every modern male has, lying at the bottom of his psyche, a large, primitive man covered with hair down to his feet. Making contact with this wild man is the step the modern male has not yet taken; this is the process that still hasn't taken place in contemporary culture.

As the story suggests, there's a fear around this ancient man. After a man gets over his initial skittishness about expressing his feminine side, he finds it to be pretty wonderful. He gets to write poetry and go out and sit by the ocean, he doesn't have to be on top all the time in sex anymore, becomes empathetic— it's a beautiful new world. But Iron John, the man at the bottom of the lake, is quite a different matter. This figure is even more frightening than the interior female, who is scary enough. When a man succeeds in becoming conscious of his interior woman, he often feels warmer, more alive. But when he approaches what I'll call the 'deep male', that's a totally different situation.

Contact with Iron John requires the willingness to go down into the psyche and accept what's dark down there, including the sexual. For generations now, the business community has warned men to keep away from Iron John, and the Christian church is not too fond of him either. But it's possible that men are once more approaching that deep male.

Freud, Jung and Wilhelm Reich are three men who had the courage to go down into the pond and accept what's there, which includes the hair, the ancientness, the rustiness. The job of modern males is to follow them down. Some of that work has already been done, and in some psyches (or on some days in the whole culture) the Hairy Man or Iron John has been brought up and stands in a cage 'in the courtyard'. That means he has been brought back into the civilized world, and to a place where the young males can see him.

Now, let's go back to the story: One day the king's eight-year-old son is playing in the courtyard and he loses his beloved golden ball. It rolls into the cage, and the wild man grabs it. If the prince wants his ball back, he's going to have to go to this rusty, hairy man and ask for it. The plot begins to thicken.

Notice that in this story the boy is eight. We all lose something around the age of eight, whether we are girl or boy, male or female. We may spend the rest of our lives trying to get the golden ball back. The first stage of that process, I guess, would be accepting that the ball has been lost.

So who's got the golden ball? In the sixties, males were told that the golden ball was the feminine, in their own feminine side. They found the feminine, and still did not find the golden ball. The step that both Freud and Jung urged on males, and the step that men are beginning to undertake now, is the realization that you *can't* look to your own feminine side, because that's not where the ball was lost. You can't go to your wife and ask for the golden ball back; she'd give it to you if she could because women are not hostile in this way to men's growth, but she doesn't have it.

After looking for the golden ball in women and not finding it, then looking in his own feminine side, the young male is called upon to consider the possibility that the golden ball lies within the magnetic field of the wild man. Now, that's a very hard thing for us to conceive; the possibility that the deep nourishing and spiritually radiant energy in the male lies not in the feminine side, but in the deep masculine. Not the shallow masculine, the macho masculine, the snowmobile masculine, but the *deep* masculine.

And I think that today's males are just about ready to take that step; to go to the cage and ask for the golden ball back. *Some* are ready to do that. Others haven't gotten the water out of the pond yet—they haven't yet left the collective male identity and gone out into the wilderness alone, into the unconscious. You've got to take a bucket, several buckets. You have to do it bucket by bucket. This resembles the slow discipline of art: it's the work that Rembrandt did, that Picasso and Yeats and Rilke and Bach all did. Bucket work implies much more discipline than many males have right now.

And of course it's going to take some persistence and discipline, not only to uncover the deep male, but to get the golden ball back. It seems unlikely that this 'un-nice' wild man would just hand it over.

What kind of story would it be if the wild man answered: 'Well, okay, here's your ball—go have your fun'? Jung said that in any case, if you're asking your psyche for something, don't use yes-or-no questions—the psyche likes to make deals. If part of you, for example, is very lazy and doesn't want to do any work, a flat-out New Year's resolution won't do you any good: it will work better if you say to the lazy part of yourself, 'You let me work for an hour, then I'll let you be a slob for an hour—deal?' So in *Iron John* a deal is made: the wild man agrees to give the golden ball back if the boy opens the cage.

At first the boy is frightened and runs off. Finally, the third time the wild man offers the same deal, the boy says, 'I couldn't open it even if I wanted to, because I don't know where the key is.' The wild man now says something magnificent: he says, 'The key is under your mother's pillow.'

Did you get that? The key to let the wild man out is lying not in the toolshed, not in the attic, not in the cellar—it's under his mother's pillow!

In the West our way has been to enter the soul by consciously exploring the relationship with the mother—even though it may grieve us to do it, even though it implies the incest issue, even though we can't seem to make any headway in talking with her.

In the story, the mother and father are away on the day that the boy finally obeys the wild man. Obviously, you've got to wait until your mother and father have gone away. This represents not being so dependent on your own mother. There are very few mothers in the world who would release that key from under the pillow, because they are intuitively aware of what would happen next—namely, they would lose their nice boys.

And then we have a lovely scene in which the boy succeeds in opening the cage and setting the wild man free. At this point, one could imagine a number of things happening. The wild man could go back to his pond, so that the split happens over again: by the time the parents come back, the wild man is gone and the boy has replaced the key. He could become a corporate executive, an ordained minister, a professor; he might be a typical twentieth-century male.

But in this case, what happens is that the wild man comes out of the cage and starts towards the forest, and the boy shouts after him, 'Don't run away! My parents are going to be very angry when they come back.' And Iron John says, 'I guess you're right: you'd better come with me.' He hoists the boy up on his shoulders and off they go.

I think the next step for us is learning to visualize the wild man. And to help that visualization I feel we need to return to the mythologies that today we only teach children. If you go back to ancient mythology you find that people in ancient times have already done some work in helping us to visualize the wild man. I think we're just coming to the place where we can understand what the ancients were talking about.

In the Greek myths, for example, Apollo is visualized as a golden man standing on an enormous accumulation of dark, dangerous energy called Dionysus. The Bhutanese bird men with dog's teeth are another possible visualization. Another is the Chinese tomb-guardian: a figure with enormous power in the music and the will, and a couple of fangs sticking out of his mouth. In the Hindu tradition this fanged aspect of the Shiva is called the Bhairava: in his Bhairava aspect, Shiva is not a nice boy. There's a hint of this energy with Christ going wild in the temple and whipping everybody.

These are all powerful energies lying in ponds we haven't found yet. All these traditions give us models to help us sense what it would be like for a young male to grow up in a culture in which the divine is associated not only with the Virgin Mary and the Blissful Jesus, but with the wild man covered with hair.

May/June 1988

[From Challenge of the Heart: Love, Sex and Intimacy in Changing Times, *published by Shambhala, USA]*

Art in Nature

ANDY GOLDSWORTHY

THE SINGLE SOURCE FOR EVERYTHING THAT I DO is the land. The land is big, it covers a lot of things. When I say land I mean something far wider than most people's concept of it. For me nature is the driving force behind everything, it is in everything, in people and in the land.

It's the places that are nearest to where I live which are the most important. Even though I travel the world and see many different places, I get less sense of change by travelling than in working my own patch day after day throughout the year. I need the excitement and stimulus of the first snowfall or the first frost, the first leaf; these are very important occasions in my work and in my life. Travelling round the world you lose all that—flying to Japan, stopping off at Moscow. My first snow this year was in Moscow—a brief view out of an airplane window—when you arrive in Japan it is getting warmer again. That really throws off a lot of the rhythms and flows I get when I work in a particular place.

When I'm working with material it's not just the leaf or the stone, it's the processes that are behind them that are important. That's what I'm trying to understand, not a single isolated object but nature as a whole—how the leaf has grown, how it has changed, how it has decayed, how the weather's affected it. By working with a leaf in its place I begin to understand these processes.

Some people get very angry with the fact that I use nature, that I actually touch nature. With an exhibition of stone or wood carving they wouldn't even have made the connection. I take responsibility for what I do. I am honest about the fact that I touch nature. I celebrate that and I am careful. If you recognize the relationship between the material and the source you are far more careful and concerned about that source. The best conservation is where people have been so strongly linked with the place and the material that both have sustained the other.

I feel a particular need to come to terms with the urban environment, for nature doesn't stop at the city or town boundary. It is everywhere. I've done obvious things like working in green places in the city trying to recognize how rich and important green places are. Some of the most desolate places I worked in have turned out to be incredibly exciting. A very rich place was the Holbeck Triangle just outside Leeds City Station. It is a very scruffy bit of ground. I worked there for a couple of weeks and I found a certain wildness. I like wild places but they don't have to be up on mountain tops. Wilderness can often be in the middle of the city. A week or so after that I spent some time in the Lincolnshire countryside but I found it a most barren place. The small pockets of wood were heavily gamekeepered. I was only there for a week but I got very difficult feelings about that landscape. I got on much better in the city.

As well as working with the wild bits of the city I also want to work with the city as an entity. The best work that I've done in urban places has been where I've dug holes in buildings to expose the earth beneath. I'm trying to touch the earth in the building, the nature of the building, to recognize that this is earth. We have this crazy idea that buildings just spring up out of nowhere, just appear.

The moves that I've made over the years—from Morecambe to Ilkley to Cumbria to Dumfriesshire—have been very stimulating. When I was at college I started working outside in Morecambe Bay. I'd go back to Leeds during the summer holidays where I worked in a woodland. After working on the beach the smell of the wood was so potent. That was just one of the senses that was heightened because of the change and the differences between the two places. Looking closely at one environment and then another was a very rich source of understanding. A change of environment can be good, but I felt a strong need to find somewhere where I was going to be able to live for as far as I could see— if not for the rest of my life. So my attitude towards Penpont in Dumfriesshire has been very different from other places—which have been kind of 'passing through' places. With Penpont I looked for a place where I could put down my roots. I decided this is the source from which I will draw, this is the source to which I can return and this will give me strength to do the things abroad.

There are continual pressures on me as interest grows in my work, like going to Japan and not having a work for an exhibition in a month's time. But that kind of pressure is nothing compared to the daily pressure I experience due to the weather changing or the tide coming in or it beginning to rain on something that I don't want it to rain on. These pressures are far more important.

I still make things in Penpont that don't last a day, but I've begun to think more long-term and make things that will continue to change and grow and be in the landscape for many years. This is what I'm doing with the Stonewood land, which is an area of scrub and woodland near Penpont. When Common Ground initiated the Trees, Woods and the Green Man project, an idea that had been swimming round in my head came to the fore. I decided that I wanted to do something that was far closer to the energies of a wood, in that the wood is a growing thing and very long-term, trees taking many, many years to grow. I wanted to start something, to plant a seed if you like, of a project that would last many years.

At Stonewood I'm making things that have a great personal significance to me. This wood is a place where I'm making things that relate very strongly to the place and the growth of trees in it.

The first work that I made is a dome of stones with a hole in the top. I planted hazel around it which I'm going to stool. There are going to be thin saplings, like a cage around this work, which you have to peer into. I'm very concerned about the relationship of the work to the land and the way time will flow over it, the way the colours will change and how the trees will grow into it or around it. I will be placing things very much in relation to the trees and planting trees in relationship to the stones that I use.

I still don't know exactly what's going to happen. When I go home now and go to work I see how things have grown, and when I'm away I'm aware that things are going on whilst I'm not there, which is fantastic. When I was in Japan I used to think of the stones which I've placed on this plot of land and because I've worked with those stones and laid them I feel very intimate and very close. I feel I'm in that place and this helps me enormously when I'm away from home. That is my own spiritual connection with the place.

Japanese culture is rooted in nature—as with all cultures. When I was in Japan I was working with the land. Many of the forms that I used there were ones that I used in Britain, and a lot of the things that were made there can be traced back to things that I discovered in our own landscape. In Japan there was more understanding of things being placed in a landscape, and hence a great enthusiasm. They went crazy over the balanced rock works. The balanced rock has enormous significance in Japan. They make these piles of rock, and if they put one on that causes the pile to collapse it's really bad luck. They're often found around temples or in special places. I could make balanced things in Japan which I know would never get knocked down, whereas in Britain they would just become targets.

Although I say that the area around my home is important I do enjoy going to very grand and spectacular places such as the Lake District, where I recently completed a residency. But it was a difficult thing to take on because I realized I would be there touching and doing all the things that they really don't like you doing in a National Park. One of the reasons I went in winter was because I knew I'd be working with snow which would melt. I also worked in the slate tips where there is a lot of useful material and debris. I gave a talk to some National Park workers and I showed them a slide of a particular work that I made and they said, 'Oh, can we protect it somehow?' If I had proposed to make anything in a National Park in wood or stone that was going to last it would have caused such a backlash and resentment from the people who, once it was made and had been there a few years, would be wanting to protect it and put a fence around it. Those are the most difficult people to deal with because their attitude and their reactions affect those of us who are sensitive to putting things in the landscape and who recognize the importance of places and of the relationship between people and the land. I get very confused because one side is saying don't touch and the other people are saying, 'Oh, how can you just let it be destroyed?' It's a sad situation if we feel the land must be fenced off or that we can't change or add to it. The land is a changing thing—to try and stop change really is changing it.

I think that the most difficult thing with conservationists is that they tend not to take the people into account alongside the place. It's like a woodland or a bit of waste ground in the inner city which is full of dens. Kids have played in it and there's been a bit of damage and it's a bit of a mess—but these experiences are so important to a child. A conservation group comes along and they turn it into a nature reserve, and tidy it up—then the kids can't go in there. It's a very difficult issue. Obviously we don't like trees being damaged but I think it is very important for children to have those very strong experiences in these places. These scruffy little places are wonderful for that. Making dens is an important experience for a child. It was for me, and it was through that that I learnt to care.

There is an emphasis in my work on commonplace materials—dandelions, sycamore, hawthorn—the often neglected plants and trees that many ecologists don't like. Because they are so common and so successful I can use them and crop them. There is no way I'd take the last flower. I wouldn't touch anything that looked particularly rare. I tend to use windfall or common materials and I'm careful about the effect of what I do. Some things I just don't touch. Everywhere is important and everything has significance. For me the significance of what I do is that it makes everything sacred.

July/August 1988

[From an interview by Neil Sinden of Common Ground]

Perennial Wisdom

Right Relationship

SATISH KUMAR

RELATIONSHIP IS AN ALL-EMBRACING SUBJECT. I cannot think of anything which does not come within the domain of relationship. It is a very important, fundamental and basic factor of our existence. If we can understand what is right relationship we will be able to understand everything else through it. The only thing we need to know is: How to Relate. We cannot live without relationship.

Living in this mechanistic world we have developed a way of relating with others which is a mechanistic way. 'What am *I* getting out of this relationship?' 'Are you using me?' That's the beginning of mechanistic thinking. I am *Me*. You are *You*. I want to get something for me. So do you. Thus we are *divided*. 'I will go my way and you go your way,' but we will have marriage so that we can *have* certain things from each other. This is the idea of equality between man and woman which is mechanistic.

The organic relationship is a way of unity. In marriage a woman and a man are one, not two equals but one. The idea of *unity* between man and woman is organic: when I am united with you I say, 'I am here, use me, it's my pleasure, use me as you like.' And then the other says: 'Wonderful, and I am here to be used as well. We are united.' In marriage I and you are no more separate individuals. We have gone beyond those individual personalities of me and you. We have become one. And the symbol of that unity is a child. Unless we are totally united, emotionally, spiritually, ideologically, intellectually and physically there is no true marriage. A child is the most beautiful organic symbol of that relationship.

The mechanistic mind thinks: 'I am to get my pleasure, if I don't get enough pleasure with you, you are no good as a partner, so I will go and seek somebody else'—we can go on seeking new partners but we are never going to experience the real pleasure, unless we unite in love which completely diminishes our ego —'me' melts, 'you' are no more. This is unity despite duality.

If we look around at our industrial relationships—the workers, the nurses, the doctors, the civil servants, the miners, the railwaymen and the bosses—they are always trying to find a mechanistic way of working together, and they never succeed. We can have Tory Party after Labour and Labour Party after Tory, and if you don't like either of them go Liberal, or create an SDP. But we will never have a relationship which works because we are thinking that we can create a set of rules, or regulations, or a code of conduct, a 'social contract', a 'national feeling'. But it cannot work.

Because our view of relationship is industrial, professional, hierarchical, analytical, rational and divisive, we have cultivated a habit of linear thinking

—we want to travel on a straight line from A to B and this will be fine if we can learn to balance it by holistic, compassionate and humane qualities, if we can accept that sometimes there is no straight road to success. We have to go in circles and cycles. After all the analysis we have to seek the value of synthesis, of unity, of co-operation. After all our passion for progress we have to learn to respect the traditional and the indigenous ways of doing things.

When we are dominating less able people and silent nature we have to realize that without those people and without the flourishing nature our own survival will be in danger. We have developed a fancy theory of survival of the fittest, but the result of that theory is that we have more strife, more class struggle, more pollution, and the whole fabric of our society is under threat.

We try to meet our mechanistic problems by mechanistic solutions, by more technology, by more politics, by new social theories and by more money. We can pay workers ever more money, yet still it is not going to bring them the sense of fulfilment, satisfaction and contentment which is required; money cannot give it, status cannot give it, comfort cannot give it. Even the idea of equality, justice and fairness cannot give it. If these mechanistic theories alone were able to give that sense of satisfaction, Britain should be one of the most happy societies in the world. I come from India, and by comparison we are very poor. We are well below all the European countries in the economic league. My people have no cars, they don't earn £100 a week, but my family is united, my folks are less greedy. India is still rural and organic. England is one of the richest nations in the world; but I find more and more loneliness here, more and more strife.

Relationship in the West is lost in the mechanistic jungle. We try to buy industrial peace with money. The bosses and the workers do not believe in unity. For the bosses the workers' welfare does not come first and the workers see their bosses as the oppressors. This is no way of organic togetherness.

Not only have we turned mechanistic in our human interaction, we have also lost the organic approach to nature and to our environment. Just take the example of our milk industry. We treat cows as if they were only milk-machines, as if they had no life in them. I live in Devon where we have many dairy farmers and I see them every day. I can hardly call them farms—they are industrial units where cows have lost their charm. I know what a beautiful and charming creature a cow is, because I live on a smallholding of two acres. Our family's needs of milk, butter and cheese are met by Hazel, our cow. Every morning my first act of worship is to milk my cow. I have a close relationship with her. We understand each other and we like each other. I get a very special feeling in my hands when I touch her udder. While I am milking she is totally relaxed—so relaxed that sometimes she goes to sleep. I have heard her snoring. I learn from her how to breathe. The deep—Buddha—breathing is very natural to her. I cannot establish such relationship if I milk hundreds of cows in industrial style. Our factory farming has no place for relationship with animals or with plants.

The modern farmer thinks: 'How much can I get out of this land as quickly as possible?' whereas a traditional farmer respects the earth as mother earth. We all come from it and all return to it. If we have such unity we will not have problems of pollution, nor of resource depletion. But mechanistic society is only interested in high living standards for itself. It is interested in animals, in land, in plants, in forests only to raise its own living standards. Therefore it will use all the land, all the oil, all the minerals to gain short-term advantage.

By no means is this mechanistic society homogeneous. It is divided into blocs, the Western Bloc and the Russian Bloc, and there is a huge competition to dominate not only the human world but also the natural world. The Russians are trying to get access to the Middle East oil and to the Indian Ocean and Red Sea. We always condemn the Russians. We say they have gone into Afghanistan and they are slowly heading towards the sea, they want to create an annexe to the Gulf. We say: 'They are Communists, they are awful.' But they are saying: 'All the Arab oil is controlled by the Americans and the Western Europeans; can't we have a share of that cake?' So they are trying to get there. When you have only few resources and everybody wants to get them, you have to have armies; you have to have a Rapid Deployment Force to maintain your dominance. Armies and weapons are only by-products of the mechanistic relationships in the world.

You cannot have peace if you have a mechanistic relationship. You have no peace within your heart or within your marriage, you have no peace within your family or within your community, you have no peace within your union or within your job; and you have no peace within your nation and no peace within your world. Lack of peace is a sure sign that we are living in a mechanistic world.

It is our social responsibility to create a climate where organic relationship is possible. Unfortunately our schools have become the breeding ground for mechanistic relationships. The children of my village, Hartland, have to travel by bus one hour every morning to a school fifteen miles away, a school of 1,600 children; all crammed into prefabricated buildings, awful classrooms, impersonal teaching. The children have to be there every day from nine to four and then endure a one-hour journey back to the village in the evening. This kind of schooling is not conducive to organic education nor to organic relationship.

Hartland is one of the most beautiful, attractive and culturally rich English villages. I am fortunate to live there. There is a baker, there are pubs, there are chairmakers, there is a cabinetmaker, there are three potters, there are farmers, there is a printer, there is a blacksmith, there is a brass band, there are three churches. There is a primary school but no secondary school in the village. So we said: Why can't we have a secondary school which is homely and where parents, teachers and children can relate to each other? Relationship of this kind cannot exist if we have a school of 1,600 children, all crammed in together. Where you have ten or fifteen children you can relate to each other—you know their names, you know their background, you know their capacity, you know how much they need and what they need. Each child is different, but if you are all pushed into one large classroom you cannot see the difference. What is important for you in such a situation is, how many of those 1,600 children will get 'O' levels and 'A' levels and get to a university. Only eight per cent of the children go to university. But the rest of the ninety-two per cent of children have to go through the torture of all those exams and all that pushing so that they can get into university and their school will get a name for how many per cent got into Oxbridge.

If this is the foundation upon which the life of our children is built we have no hope of an organic society and peace between people. If the children of a village begin to commute at the age of eleven what do they think of the village? They think that it cannot educate them. And when they leave school the village cannot give them work. They lose respect for the village. Then they go to Bristol or to London or Birmingham. How can you have a happy society when people have no roots in the soil, in the village, in the community? Our education makes children rootless from the age of eleven. They come home and what can they do apart from watch television? And then we hope that our children will grow in goodwill, in love, in peace, and in compassion. These all will remain pious words. Unless we have our roots in the village, in the community, in the family, in the soil, we will never be able to cultivate an organic relationship. The urban, industrial, mechanistic civilization has totally rejected the value of village culture and has concentrated all education in the city and for the city. This is a great pity.

We have to live in a small community if we want to have organic relationship, where men and women and children and older people are part of an organic family, where everybody understands each other, helps each other and needs each other. In the industrial system all our needs are fulfilled by commercial and professional sources—if we are ill, go to hospital; if we have mental problems, go to a psychologist; if we are unemployed, go to an unemployment office, if we are poor go to a Social Security Office; we don't need our family, we don't need our community, we don't need our village.

The most important change starts in our mind, in our heart, and in our consciousness. The same husband and the same wife will look different if you have a new mind and new eyes. All debates, quarrels and competitions between husband and wife will seem meaningless when the fixed minds have been transformed into flexible minds. Fixed mind is a stiff mind. Stiff mind is a dead mind, like dead wood. Flexible mind is a living mind like a living tree. A fixed mind cannot bend and so it breaks the marriage. It thinks that if I break out everything will be wonderful. Well, thousands and thousands of stiff people have come and gone, have broken their marriages, and still haven't found peace. The grass is greener on the other side of the fence—but we don't know what the problems are on the other side. In fact the problems are inside us. We carry them with us wherever we go.

There are some water-like people and some boat-like people. If you meet a water-like person, become a boat and sail through that person. If you meet a boat-like person, become water and let that person sail through you and over you; don't complain that 'somebody has walked all over me'. If you meet a boat-like person and you stay a boat there will be a crash; you will have holes in both boats and both will sink. Even a small hole can sink a boat. As one little match can destroy the barn full of hay, one little argument can destroy a lifelong relationship. So care has to be taken at the very beginning. If we dwell on disagreements they will only increase. We want to talk and talk or go to a psychoanalyst and talk further, and go to a therapist and talk further and so on. Talking doesn't solve problems; understanding the other does. When we accept the other as part of ourselves a miracle happens: when we are not pressing our own personality on the other we get everything.

When we give in, we win—what a paradox. It is considered to be cowardly, unmanly to give in—'you must stick to your guns'; but the Tao says 'when you give in, you get everything'. Giving in is the most comfortable thing to do. Just give in. Give in to your child. Give in to your mother, to your father, to your brother, to your sister, to your wife. Give in. Give in to the workers if they are asking for a rise in their salary. The moment you give in, they will say: 'We don't want it,' and *they* will give in too, like a living tree gives in to the wind. The bamboo is a very strong tree because it is a very supple tree. The suppleness is the source of its strength. If the wind blows from the east the bamboo bends to the west, if the wind blows from the south the bamboo doesn't resist it either. Look inside the bamboo. It's hollow, it has no ego, still bamboo is the most useful tree. We can eat bamboo shoots, we can make furniture with it, we can build houses with it. A Zen monk learns the lessons of relationship from the bamboo: supple, egoless and at your service.

Furthermore a Zen monk learns from the water the art of organic relationship. Water finds the most humble, the most lowly way to its destination, the sea. If it meets a rock it does not fight, rather it turns to the side. At times it disappears in the ground, maintains a low profile. If it meets other streams it becomes united to travel together. Even by falling down it derives positive strength. By its softness water breaks the rock. The softness of water is so soft that we can put it on our eyes. Water always keeps cool. Even when we force it to boil, water quickly starts to cool down. Water teaches us to be cool, soft and satisfying.

If we have this kind of impersonal society, spiritual and moral values are the victims. Spiritual values cannot exist in a vacuum. They cannot exist in books, in seminars and in discussions. They have to exist in real life. Religion has to be reflected in how we cook, how we eat, how we talk, how we walk—that is where spiritual values have to be experienced. We can cook as a chore or an act of worship. Our mundane activities can be transformed into an act of art if that activity is performed with love, care and flair. It is easy to talk about good ideas and publish them, very easy. I lived in London and published *Resurgence* from an office, and I found how mechanistic a way of producing a magazine it was, so I moved out of London to where, when I am editing the magazine, I can smell cow dung!

~~~~~~~~~~~~~~~~~~~~~~~

September/October 1983

[From a talk given at the World Goodwill Conference,
Royal Commonwealth Society, London, 1983]

Pursuit of Reality

YEHUDI MENUHIN

FOR A LONG TIME our senses failed to perceive, let alone to be outraged by, the image of a flat earth; today our senses confirm the image of a spinning sphere. It is the relative truth of the image which determines our perception, our assumptions and our behaviour.

Shakespeare said 'there is nothing either good or bad but thinking makes it so'; however, there is good or bad thinking. Human reality is not alone the observable, measurable and affecting circumstance of our life, rather it is as well our mental interpretation of this data which determines the real world we make.

In short, the idea is the ideal, the projection of a hope, of a dream. When you are in love with someone your dream becomes substance, a particular person with a name. Sometimes when we are very lucky and our dreams are good—when our thoughts, feelings and desires are determined as much by and for the benefit of the beloved object as by the loving subject—then the beloved and our dream may turn out to be identical and we will be in love forever afterwards.

When I prepare a concert and finally walk on to the stage to make music, I too go out to meet my dream, my love, to substantiate it into living sound, the living message I have trained myself to create and to achieve which I have dedicated many decades, for I share my world with an audience to whom my message and my premise are intelligible.

We are thus not merely slaves driven by circumstances, economic and physical, but we are in equal measure drawn on and on, irresistibly enticed beyond ourselves by the vision we conceive in our mind's eye, the design we weave out of the active and passive materials we find in and about us. But the catch is that our images can be wrong, our thinking bad, and the resultant scale and sense of values utterly false. False images may offer some immediate gains, undemanding intellectually, cheap and convenient; almost everyone thinks they understand, they are usually solvents for conscience and shame; forgers of mobs. The false image may achieve all this, but in the long run simply cannot work. Factional strife, wars, disease, corruption are proof enough that we pursue delusions.

We are trapped like mice. We are encouraged in this age-old negative exercise by both advertising and propaganda, which trap us in the same way that we trap mice—by a tempting promise, isolated in context and addressed to some widely-held, secret and comforting image, shaming to the individual but, when collectively exposed, achieving a general release of energy, a suspending of inhibition and discipline.

The image may be one of success, revenge, hate, sex, power, violence, ambition, or money. Moses may have repeatedly shattered the pagan idol, the golden calf, three or four thousand years ago at the foot of Mount Sinai, but here we are still nurturing in our heart of hearts false images, worshipping false gods.

There is a close relation between every image we carry, every word we think or utter and every act we perform.

Take our motorcars, their names and shapes. If we are of modest circumstances, obliged to transport a small family for the least expense, we buy a mini-car—charming, well designed and soon, I hope, to be electrically driven; but given half a chance we parade as pirates in Corsairs or Buccaneers, as bankers and property-developers in Eldorados and Palm Beaches, as ruthless plastic cowboy heroes in Avengers, or as show-offs, and on the road we are in fact as much of a menace as if we were indeed pirates and property developers.

You might well ask how does one distinguish the false image from the true? As soon as we supplant one image with a truer one, our new direction is confirmed by the fact that our motion is smoother, that we meet less which is unaccountable or surprising; we achieve inner harmony, we lose fear, we acquire confidence and excellence in our fields whilst our conscience reports that we have enough value to give and to help others with in order to make our existence desirable and worthwhile in their eyes. A further criterion for distinguishing between false and true images and their resultant behaviour or actions is the following; any which leave in the subject or the object a residue of unspecified tension—like a motor idling at too high a speed; or any which generate impatient or violent reactions instead of good purpose, gratitude and harmony are by definition false.

Hateful and fearful images are altogether paralysing. Even the images of relentless work, drudgery and of course self-inflicted torture are defeating. What is left you will ask? Everything, I answer. With faith and patience, with the analysis of every detail of every joint, limb, motion and thought in body and mind, and finally through the cultivation of true images, we search for the true image of the digital, physical, structural, respiratory, intellectual and emotional sensations, the patient build-up of correct and corrective images and the memory of effective sensations.

Each step which brings one nearer the truth, however microscopically, is measurable and rewarding. There are thus progressive degrees of truth and progressive degrees of falsehood. By making ourselves sensitive to the direction we are going in we can effectively guide our progress.

We know that the more distant our guiding star, the more accurate our measurement and our control of direction. Dead-reckoning yielded to the magnetic compass, which in turn yielded to checking the distant star as with the sextant. In the same way our thoughts and our actions continuously require assessment in terms of a bigger, larger dimension by which the smallest and minutest are measured: birth and death, the mystery of life and the dimensions of the universe, the continuous recycling of matter into energy, the consciousness and spirit of that energy; the limits of our life-span, the breadth of our intellectual and spiritual capacities, the borrowing of our life and body against repayment, our use of our time and energies with particular relation to the happiness and wellbeing of those about us and to future generations of living flora and fauna, and to our own mental and physical health.

These are a few of the compass points against which individual progress or drift can be measured and defined. These compass points of reference represent a dimension comparable to religious inspirations and concepts. You will find them all originally in the great religions, but institutionalized religion, and bureaucratic government, impose strait-jackets on profound belief and on democracy respectively. The many religious attempts to create the images and thoughts, the visionary and the intellectual worlds, the forms and structures which govern behaviour, were certainly never quite as successful in execution as in conception; yet the great religions remain repositories of treasure, truth and wisdom. People are notoriously bad interpreters of the given word or of musical notes, because for the most part they are expressing themselves and their failings and not the spirit of the word or the music.

I believe we are now living on the threshold of a new revelation of truth, or shall we say of the truer (one step nearer *absolute* truth), which will provide an acceptable hypothesis, a common ground for all to share, and will bring its own definitions of good and bad, of right and wrong, of infinity and eternity of spirit, life and matter, organic and inorganic, and of what is holy. It will express a continuation and an evolution of humanity's searchings and findings, valid for our and our children's future, undogmatic yet flexibly principled. It will recognize the interdependence of all life and matter, as well as the one spirit which seems to inhabit and animate all organic and inorganic matter.

Our chief defence as well as our strongest attack will come from that dawning awareness of the greater truth. These maturing attitudes will provide the framework for restored and renewed evolution of commonly held convictions and will widen human affiliations to include not only our region and our country, but the existence and well-being of life beyond our gates, the respect for all living forms—human, animal and vegetable—in that great ecological unity of all organic matter.

The other effect of these maturing attitudes will be a new sense of proportion, balance, restraint and responsibility. Work is not confined to one job and to working hours, for it must include public obligations and hobbies as well; nor is leisure time to waste and to cast off responsibilities; nor is play banished to off-hours, for all life is a play (my children always said: Daddy! why *he* never works, he only plays!) and that even while engaged in earnest activities, a sense of humour is not necessarily out of place—witness taxi-drivers, musicians and good teachers.

Look at China where dams are built in people's spare time at no expense, and where so-called white collar workers (now in blue denim) go off to factory and farm periodically. I would not mind at all if for two hours a week I were to trot, drawing a rickshaw in urban pedestrian precincts, nor were I to join hands working with a professional and expert garbage or sewer worker, who, as experienced guide, would lead recruits—a modest team of say artists, accountants and property-developers—in their unaccustomed tasks. We must re-establish links and contacts with our fellow human beings and voluntarily impose restraints and disciplines on our own misused liberties.

In the competitive society so much of our satisfaction derives from our position relative to where we came from, relative to others, and finally relative to our own driving energy. Too small a fraction of our satisfaction derives from self-improvement, independent of relative and incidental yardsticks. I speak about the satisfaction of acquiring a skill—painting, singing, playing an instrument, improving our physical and mental responses; extending our knowledge and appeasing our curiosity in archaeology, chemistry, literature, languages, not for money, but for pleasure and for the benefit of society. Fulfilment means not buying or dominating everything we can lay hands on, but rather in bringing out of ourselves and of others everything we are capable of.

Considering the growing polarization between beauty and ugliness, compassion and crime, sensitivity and brutality, repose and tension, and considering that a growing proportion of our population is both surrounded and inhabited by ugliness and brutality, by obsessive and false images, is it not high time we tried to refurnish their minds, hearts and their environment? Their entertainment, reading, dwelling, occupational environment, food, hobbies and self-expression too leave much to be desired.

Now we are reaping the whirlwind, but it is not too late to escape the dire consequences—if we embody a change of heart, a change of mind, a new set of images, if we see with new eyes and hear with new ears. When I was a boy of thirteen and played with the great conductor Bruno Walter, I was struck when he expressed so passionately his wish that he might hear again the symphonies of Beethoven played for the first time.

July/August 1975

The Yin Yang Balance

FRITJOF CAPRA

DURING THE PAST THREE YEARS my work and my life have been profoundly influenced by three books, each of which I have read several times. They are—in the order in which I read them—*Of Woman Born* by Adrienne Rich, *Creating Alternative Futures* by Hazel Henderson, and *Nuclear Madness* by Helen Caldicott. I think it is no accident that all three authors are women. Although only Rich is considered a feminist author, all three books represent for me important aspects of the feminist movement. They all deal with crucial elements of our current cultural crisis, and they made me realize that a feminist perspective will be essential to overcoming it.

When we talk about the current crisis we have to realize, first of all, that it is complex, global, and multi-dimensional; a crisis whose facets touch every aspect of our lives. Its various manifestations include the lethal threats of nuclear weapons and nuclear power, the misery and starvation in the Third World, the deterioration of our natural environment through the effects of our technology, the shortage of energy and natural resources, the threats to our health through pollution and chemical poisoning, the increase in social pathologies—violent crimes, accidents, suicides, and drug abuse—and the economic anomalies of global inflation and massive unemployment that seem to defy all efforts of our leading economists and politicians. It is important to understand that all these problems are but different facets of one single crisis. They are systemic problems, which means that they are closely interconnected and interdependent, and cannot be understood within the fragmented approach that is characteristic of our academic disciplines and government institutions.

Further reflection shows that the roots of our problems seem to lie in a profound imbalance in our culture—in our thoughts and feelings, our values and attitudes, and our social and political structures. It is an imbalance between two modes of consciousness which have been recognized as characteristic aspects of human nature throughout the ages. They are usually called the rational and intuitive modes, and have also been described by various other terms—scientific/religious, linear/non-linear, and so on. The terminology which I have found most useful for discussing our cultural imbalance is the ancient Chinese system of *yin* and *yang*.

The Chinese saw reality, whose ultimate essence they called *Tao*, as a process of continual flow and change. In their view, all phenomena we observe participate in this cosmic process and are thus intrinsically dynamic. The principal characteristic of the *Tao* is the cyclical nature of its ceaseless motion; all developments in nature—those in the physical world as well as those in the psychological and social realms—show cyclical patterns. The Chinese gave this idea of cyclical patterns a definite structure by introducing the polar opposites *yin* and *yang*. They are the two poles which set the limits for the cycles of change. According to an ancient Chinese text: 'The *yang* having reached its climax retreats in favour of the *yin*; the *yin* having reached its climax retreats in favour of the *yang*.'

In the Chinese view, all manifestations of the *Tao* are generated by the dynamic interplay of these two archetypal poles which are associated with many images of opposites taken from nature and from social life. It is important, and very difficult for us Westerners, to understand that these opposites do not belong to different categories but are extreme poles of a single whole. In the Chinese view, nothing is only *yin* or only *yang*. All natural phenomena are manifestations of a continuous oscillation between the two poles, all transitions taking place gradually and in unbroken progression. The natural order is one of dynamic balance between *yin* and *yang*.

The terms *yin* and *yang* have recently become quite popular in the West but are rarely used, in our culture, in the sense originally intended by the Chinese. Most Western usage reflects cultural preconceptions which severely distort the original meanings. In the classical Chinese terminology, *yin* corresponds to all that is contractive, responsive and conservative, whereas *yang* implies all that is expansive, aggressive, and demanding. It is important to note that *yin* and *yang* have never been associated with any moral values in Chinese culture. What is good is not *yin* or *yang*, but the dynamic balance between the two; what is bad or harmful, is imbalance.

From the earliest times of Chinese culture, *yin* was associated with the feminine and *yang* with the masculine. This ancient association is extremely difficult to assess today because of its re-interpretation and distortion in subsequent patriarchal eras. In human biology, masculine and feminine characteristics are not neatly separated but occur, in varying proportions, in both sexes. Accordingly, the Chinese believed that all people, whether men or women, go through *yin* and *yang* phases. The personality of each man and of each woman was seen not as a static entity, but as a dynamic phenomenon resulting from the interplay between feminine and masculine elements. This view of human nature is in sharp contrast to that of our patriarchal culture which has established a rigid order, where all men are supposed to be masculine and all women feminine, and has distorted the meaning of those terms by giving men the leading roles and most of society's privileges.

In view of this patriarchal bias the frequent association of *yin* with passivity and *yang* with activity is particularly dangerous. In our culture women have traditionally been portrayed as passive and receptive; men as active and creative. This imagery goes back to Aristotle's theory of sexuality and has been used, throughout the centuries, as a 'scientific' rationale for keeping women in a subordinate role, subservient to men. The association of *yin* with passivity and *yang* with activity seems to be yet another expression of patriarchal stereotypes;

a modern Western interpretation which is unlikely to reflect the original meaning of the Chinese terms.

Some insight into the traditional Chinese view of activity can be gained from
the ancient term *wu wei* which is frequently used in Taoist philosophy and
means literally 'nonaction'. In the West, this term is usually interpreted as
referring to passivity. This, however, is quite wrong. What the Chinese meant
by *wu wei* was not abstaining from activity, but abstaining from a certain *kind*
of activity—activity that is out of harmony with the ongoing cosmic process.
Wu wei does not mean being passive but rather means refraining from action
contrary to nature. If one refrains from acting contrary to nature, one is in
harmony with the *Tao* and thus one's actions will be successful. This is the
meaning of Lao Tzu's seemingly so puzzling words 'By nonaction everything
can be done.'

In the Chinese view, then, there seem to be two kinds of activity—activity in
harmony with nature and activity against the natural flow of things. The idea
of passivity, of complete absence of action, is not entertained. Therefore, the
frequent Western association of *yin* and *yang* with passive and active behaviour
does not seem to be consistent with Chinese thought. In view of the original
imagery associated with the two archetypal poles, it would seem that *yin* can
be interpreted as corresponding to responsive, consolidating, co-operative
activity; *yang* as referring to aggressive, expanding, competitive activity. *Yin*
action is conscious of the environment, *yang* action of the self.

These two kinds of activity seem to be closely related to the two modes of
consciousness mentioned above. The rational and the intuitive are complementary modes of functioning of the human mind. Rational thinking is linear,
focused, and analytic. It belongs to the realm of the intellect whose function
it is to discriminate, measure, and categorize. Thus, rational knowledge tends
to be fragmented. Intuitive knowledge, on the other hand, is based on a
direct non-intellectual experience of reality arising in an expanded state of
awareness. It tends to be synthesizing, holistic, and non-linear. From this
it is apparent that rational knowledge is likely to generate self-centred, or
yang, activity, whereas intuitive wisdom is the basis of ecological, or *yin*,
activity.

This, then, is the framework that I shall use in my discussion of cultural values
and attitudes. In Chinese philosophy and science, the polar opposites *yin* and
yang are associated with a wide variety of images, but for our purpose it will be
sufficient to use the following associations.

YIN / YANG

feminine / masculine; contractive / expansive;
conservative / demanding; responsive / aggressive;
co-operative / competitive; intuitive / rational;
mystical / scientific; synthesizing / analytic;
holistic / fragmented.

Looking at this list of opposites, it is easy to see that our society has consistently favoured the *yang* over the *yin*—rational knowledge over intuitive wisdom, science over religion, competition over co-operation, exploitation of natural resources over conservation, and so on. This one-sided emphasis has led to the profound cultural imbalance which lies at the very root of our current crisis. The consistent preference for *yang* values, attitudes, and behaviour patterns has resulted in a system of academic, political, and economic institutions which are mutually supportive and have become all but blind to the dangerous imbalance of the value system that motivates all their activities. According to Chinese wisdom, none of the values pursued by our culture is intrinsically bad, but by isolating them from their polar opposites, by focusing on the *yang* and neglecting the *yin*, we have brought about the current sad state of affairs.

Our culture takes pride in being scientific; our time is referred to as the Scientific Age. It is dominated by rational thought and scientific knowledge. That there can be intuitive knowledge, or awareness, which is just as valid and reliable is generally not realized. This attitude of 'scientism' is widespread, pervading our educational system and all other social and political institutions.

The emphasis on rational thought in our culture is epitomized in Descartes' celebrated statement '*Cogito, ergo sum*'—'I think, therefore I exist'—which forcefully suggested to Western individuals to equate their identity with their rational mind rather than with their whole organism. The effects of this division between mind and body are felt throughout our culture. We have cut ourselves off from our organisms and have retreated into our minds. Thus, we have forgotten how to 'think' with our bodies, how to use them as agents of knowing. In doing so, we have also cut ourselves off from our natural environment and have forgotten how to commune and co-operate with its rich variety of living organisms.

The division between mind and matter has led to the view of the universe as a mechanical system consisting of separate objects which, in turn, were reduced to fundamental building blocks whose properties and interactions were thought to completely determine all natural phenomena. This Cartesian view of nature was extended to living organisms which were regarded as machines, constructed from separate parts. Such a mechanistic conception of the world is still at the base of most our sciences and continues to have a tremendous influence on many aspects of our lives. It has led to the well-known fragmentation in our academic disciplines and government agencies and has served as a rationale for treating the natural environment as if it consisted of separate parts, to be exploited by different interest groups.

It is now becoming apparent that the overemphasis of the scientific method and of rational, analytic thinking has led to attitudes that are profoundly anti-ecological. In fact, the understanding of ecosystems is hindered by the very nature of the rational mind. Rational thinking is linear, whereas ecological awareness arises from an intuition for non-linear systems. Ecosystems sustain themselves in a dynamic balance based on cycles and fluctuations, which are non-linear processes. Linear enterprises, such as indefinite economic and technological growth or the storage of radioactive waste over enormous time spans, will necessarily interfere with the natural balance and, sooner or later, will cause severe damage. Ecological awareness will only arise when we combine our rational knowledge with an intuition for the non-linear nature of our environment.

From this short survey of cultural attitudes and values, we see quite clearly that our culture has consistently promoted and rewarded the rational, or *yang*, elements of human nature and has disregarded its intuitive, or *yin*, aspects. The relevance of feminism to this analysis becomes apparent with the recognition that the *yang* values and attitudes favoured by our culture are associated with male patterns of thought and behaviour. Whether the basis for this association is biological or cultural is irrelevant to this discussion. The fact is that our society is dominated by men who consistently suppress women—both by overt force and by subtle cultural rituals and traditions—and who have established self-assertive, masculine, behaviour as the social norm.

Excessive self-assertion, which is characteristic of the *yang* mode of behaviour, manifests itself as power, control, and domination of others by force; and those are, indeed, the patterns prevalent in our society. Political and economic power is exerted by a dominant corporate class; social hierarchies are maintained along racist and sexist lines, and rape has become a central metaphor of our culture—rape of women, of minority groups, and of the Earth herself. Our science and technology are based on the seventeenth-century belief that an understanding of nature implies domination of nature by 'man'. Combined with the mechanistic model of the universe, which also originated in the seventeenth century, and with an excessive emphasis on linear thinking, this attitude has produced a 'macho technology', as Hazel Henderson likes to call it; technology that is both unhealthy and inhuman.

This technology is aimed at control, mass production and standardization, and is subjected, most of the time, to centralized management which pursues the illusion of indefinite growth. Thus the self-assertive tendency keeps increasing, and with it the requirement of submission, which is the reverse side of the same phenomenon. While self-assertive behaviour is presented as the ideal for men, submissive behaviour is expected from women, but also from the employees and executives of companies who are required to deny their personal identities and adopt the corporate identity and behaviour patterns.

The promotion of competitive behaviour and neglect of co-operation is one of the principal manifestations of our *yang*-orientated society. Competition is seen as the driving force of the economy, the 'aggressive approach' has become the ideal of the business world, and this behaviour has been combined with the exploitation of natural resources by creating patterns of competitive consumption.

Aggressive, competitive behaviour alone, of course, would make life impossible. Even the most ambitious, goal-orientated, individuals need sympathetic support, human contact, and times of carefree spontaneity and relaxation. In our culture, these needs are provided by women. They are the secretaries, receptionists, hostesses, nurses, and homemakers who perform the services that make life more comfortable and create the atmosphere in which the competitors can succeed. These services all involve *yin* activities, and since they rank lower in our value system those who perform them get paid less. In fact, many of them, like mothers and housewives, are not paid at all.

The association of self-assertive, *yang*, values and behaviour patterns with the patriarchal character of our society shows that a feminist perspective is essential for an understanding of the deepest roots of our cultural crisis. At the same time, the rise of feminist awareness is turning into a major force for cultural transformation. If we shift our focus from the notion of static social structures to the perception of dynamic patterns of change, our cultural crisis appears as an aspect of transformation and we become aware of a tremendous evolutionary movement. As the Chinese text says, the *yang* having reached its extreme retreats in favour of the *yin*. The sixties and seventies have generated a whole series of philosophical, spiritual, and political movements which all seem to go in the same direction. They all counteract the overemphasis of *yang*, masculine, attitudes and values, and attempt to regain a balance between the masculine and feminine sides of human nature.

There is a rising concern with ecology, expressed by citizen movements that are forming around social and environmental issues, pointing out the limits to growth, advocating a new ecological ethic, and developing appropriate 'soft' technologies. They are the sources of emerging counter-economies, based on decentralized, co-operative and ecologically harmonious lifestyles. In the political arena, the antinuclear movement is fighting the most extreme outgrowth of hard technology and, in doing so, is likely to become the most powerful political force of the eighties.

At the same time, there is the beginning of a significant shift in values— from the admiration of large-scale enterprises and institutions to the notion of 'small is beautiful', from material consumption to voluntary simplicity, from economic and technological growth to inner growth and development. These new values are being promoted by the 'human potential' movement, by a number of new psychotherapies and various holistic approaches to health and healing, and by spiritual movements that re-emphasize the quest for meaning and the spiritual dimension of life.

All these movements are part of a major cultural transformation, of a 'paradigm shift' involving a profound change in the thoughts, perceptions, and values that form our vision of reality. The paradigm which is now shifting has dominated our culture for several hundred years, during which it has shaped our modern Western society and has exerted a significant influence on the rest of the world. This paradigm comprises a large number of ideas and values which have been associated with various streams of Western culture, among them the Scientific Revolution, the Enlightenment, and the Industrial

Revolution. They include the belief in the scientific method as the only valid approach to knowledge; the view of the universe as a mechanical system, the view of life in society as a competitive struggle for existence, and the belief in unlimited material progress, to be achieved through economic and technological growth. During the past decades, all these ideas and values have been found to be severely limited and in need of radical revision.

As a physicist, I am particularly interested in the role that physics can play in the current re-examination of cultural values. Ever since the seventeenth century, physics has been the shining example of 'hard' science, and has served as the model for all the other sciences. For two and a half centuries, physicists developed and refined the mechanistic world view that was adopted by the other sciences and became the scientific basis of the dominant cultural paradigm. In the twentieth century, however, physics went through several conceptual revolutions which clearly revealed the limitations of the mechanistic world view and led to an organic, ecological, view of the world which shows great similarities to the views of mystics of all ages and traditions. The universe is no longer seen as a machine made up of a multitude of separate objects, but appears as a harmonious indivisible whole; a network of dynamic relationships that include the human observer and his or her consciousness in an essential way.

The fact that modern physics, the manifestation of an extreme specialization of the rational mind, is now making contact with mysticism, the essence of religion and manifestation of an extreme specialization of the intuitive mind, shows very beautifully the unity and complementary nature of the rational and intuitive modes of consciousness; of the *yang* and the *yin*. Physicists, therefore, can provide the scientific background to the changes in attitudes and values that our society so urgently needs. Modern physics can show the other sciences that scientific thinking does not necessarily have to be reductionist and mechanistic; that holistic and ecological views are also scientifically sound.

In my current work, I attempt to provide a scientific basis for a new conceptual framework which, I hope, will help the various movements of the sixties and seventies to recognize the communality of their aims. So far most of these movements still operate separately and have not yet realized how their purposes interrelate. Thus, the human potential movement and the holistic health movement often lack a social perspective, whereas spiritual movements tend to lack ecological awareness, with Eastern gurus displaying Western capitalist status symbols and spending considerable time building their economic empires. However, coalitions between some movements have recently begun to form and are likely to be strengthened during the coming decade.

I believe that feminism will play a pivotal role in the coalescence of philosophical, spiritual, and social movements. The rise of feminist awareness, originating in the women's movement, will make ever larger numbers of people realize that the deepest roots of our cultural imbalance lie in our patriarchal value system. For men, the most radical contribution we can make to this collective awareness will be to get fully involved in raising our children from the moment of birth. John Lennon, who was always a step ahead of his time, did just this during the last five years of his life. His contribution to our culture as a father and 'househusband' were as revolutionary as his artistic contributions and stand out as a shining example and inspiration to all feminist men.

While men will become more active as fathers, the full participation of women in all areas of public life, which will undoubtedly be achieved in the future, is bound to bring about profound changes in our attitudes and behaviour patterns. Thus feminism may well become the catalyst that will allow the various cultural movements to flow together and form a powerful force of social transformation. The beginnings of this development can already be seen. It is no accident that women play important roles in the contacts that are now being made between environmental groups, consumer groups, ethnic liberation movements, and various feminist organizations. Helen Caldicott, who has provided the anti-nuclear movement with a sound scientific basis together with a sense of urgency and compassion, and Hazel Henderson, who has lucidly analysed the shortcomings of the Cartesian framework in current economic thinking, are examples of women in leading positions who are forging coalitions of such a kind.

Among these coalitions, the one between the ecology movement and the women's movement was the first to occur, as could be expected from the age-old identification of woman with nature. Books like *Women and Nature* by Susan Griffin and *The Death of Nature* by Carolyn Merchant show convincingly that, throughout the ages, the exploitation of nature has gone hand in hand with that of women. From the earliest times, nature—and especially the Earth —was seen as a kind and nurturing mother, but also as a wild and uncontrollable female. In pre-patriarchal eras, her many aspects were identified with the numerous manifestations of the Goddess.

Under patriarchy the benign image of nature changed into one of passivity, whereas the view of nature as wild and dangerous gave rise to the idea that she was to be dominated by man. At the same time women were portrayed as passive and subservient to men. With the rise of Newtonian science, nature became a mechanical system which could be manipulated and exploited, together with the manipulation and exploitation of women. The ancient association of women and nature thus interlinks women's history and the history of the environment and is a source of natural kinship between feminism and ecology.

The view of man as dominating nature and woman has been supported and encouraged by the Judaeo-Christian tradition which adheres to the image of a male god as the personification of supreme reason and source of ultimate power. In questioning these patriarchal metaphors and modes of thought, together with the sexism that is evident in most religious organizations—East and West—feminism is becoming the source of a new spirituality; a spirituality which is intimately connected with ecological awareness and makes it clear that true ecology is spiritual in its very essence.

These are but a few examples of the philosophical, spiritual and social developments that are taking place as we move into the eighties. To me they show convincingly that the feminist movement is one of the strongest cultural currents of our time. Our ultimate aim, as feminists, is nothing less than a thorough redefinition of what it means to be human, which will have the most profound effect on our further cultural evolution.

May/June 1981

Evil and the Apartheid of Good

WILLIAM IRWIN THOMPSON

THIS WEEK I HAVE HEARD some of the clergymen here at the Cathedral Church of St John the Divine defend the singular calling of the Christian Church from the threat of New Age ecumenicalism and planetary cultural pluralism by quoting the familiar scripture of John, 'I am the way, the truth and the life, no man cometh unto the Father, but by me.' It is a scripture I have often heard quoted before, especially by fundamentalists in Colorado, when the orthodox wish to convince me that paths like Yoga or Zen are demonic and partake not of the Christ but of the antichrist.

This separation of Christianity from all the other cultures and religions of the world creates an apartness of Christ, an *apartheid* of good in which the purity of Christianity is to be protected from the dark contaminations of other religions, other cultures.

Over and against this orthodox view is an attitude that is known as 'New Age', a point of view that sees the Christ as *in* and *with* the diversity of the world. It is a theology closely akin to an ecological perspective of life, a vision that sees the singularity of the sun energizing an enormous diversity of life. How can we be true to that singularity of vision when, if we are truly honest with ourselves, we see it reflected, not in a *creed*, but in an *incredible* diversity of life. Jesus also said, 'I am come that they might have life, and that they might have it more abundantly.' If the Christ is life, and life in its abundance, how can we contain Christianity within a creed that demands uniformity when nothing in abundant life reveals that rigid uniformity but the *rigor mortis* of death itself?

So this tension arises between the singularity of religion and the multiplicity of life, and this tension creates conflict, conflict within ourselves as we struggle to decide the right way through Christ to the Father, and conflict within our world as we fight to keep the *apartheid* systems of orthodoxy.

And it does take quite a struggle, for no sooner has one separated Christianity from the other religions of the world than one needs to struggle again against other sects within Christianity. It would seem that the very mentality of seeing divisions only creates more of them. Church divides against church, congregation against congregation, until the calling to singularity ends up in a condition of purity in which only one single person is right and all the others are wrong. It ends in the war of each against all, and the abundance of life becomes the abundance of death in Beirut, in Belfast.

I feel a personal childhood connection to this particular problem of religious violence because conflict is my patrimony. My father, though born in the United States, was Northern Irish and Protestant; my mother, though also born in the United States, was Southern Irish and Catholic. For the illicit union of their marriage she was disowned by my maternal grandfather, and by Canonical Law I was born in bastardy as the illegitimate child of two Christian traditions that should never have been brought together. They were meant to be kept apart in Chicago. They are meant to be keep apart in Belfast. They are meant to be kept apart in Beirut, in South Africa. They are meant to be kept apart.

By Canonical Law my mother's marriage was not Catholic, and by the Torah my children are not Christian but Jewish. The Jewish mother of my Jewish children was far from the reach of Hitler in Los Angeles, but somehow evil has its imaginative reach, so even in a sunlit backyard in Los Angeles at the age of two she would hide to escape the purifications of the Aryan Race.

How deadly this impulse to perfection can become when one adopts a creed that allows one to believe that only one way is right. We all long to be lifted up out of the mire of confusion and multiplicity to know the simple truth. We wish to commit ourselves to high ideals. As a people, we Americans are nothing if not idealistic. We want to be loved and we wish to see ourselves being loved by the world in visions of GIs liberating Europe and giving Hershey bars to adoring children, or in visions of volunteers giving grain to the starving people of Africa.

How hard it is, then, for us, when we rise to our ideals to bear witness to the truth and condemn the wicked, when the world refuses to see it our way. We see ourselves as exemplars of the Truth, but the world sees us as exemplars of power. We are the model for Brazil and South Africa of a dynamic, charging, modernizing industrial nation moving forward into world power as it eliminates its indigenous population through use of the army. And when the South Africans or the South Americans reflect our own image back to us, we are shocked into silence and shrivel up like a sea anemone. Only in a naive idealism can we Americans be extroverted and expansive. If the complexity of thought and ambiguity touches us we fold in upon ourselves in isolationism, bitterness, and resentment that the world does not love us in the way we need to be loved.

How then shall we act? How can we begin to feel ourselves as the good pitted against the powers of evil? The best of us becomes silent as the worst of us begins to scream in fanaticism, for that has always been one way of eliminating ambiguity and complexity. As Yeats said during the Irish Troubles of another generation: 'The best lack all conviction, while the worst are full of passionate intensity.' Out of this passionate intensity our idealism flips over into a pouting cynicism, and we get the punks who say that it all doesn't matter for the world is going to get nuked anyway. We get the yuppies who say it doesn't matter, and that before it all goes up in smoke they are going to get it while the getting is good. Both punks and yuppies are the two sides of a coin, the common currency of our era of anti-idealism and aggressive materialism. A simplistic idealism flips over into its opposite and becomes a simplistic cynicism. Extreme right and extreme left flip back and forth. Now already people begin to anticipate the return of the idealism of the sixties in the nineties, but in the meantime the idealists of the sixties observe the fanaticism of the fundamentalists and the indifference of the punks and yuppies and wonder when the greed and the violence will come to an end.

When is the murder going to end? As a child in Chicago, I heard my mother say, 'Black as Cromwell's heart'. It is a long time from Drogheda in the seventeenth century to Chicago in the twentieth, but still the murder goes on in Ireland. Cromwell's troops killed 3,500 men, women and children and then called on God to bless the holy work of the day in killing the Papists. Cromwell too thought that his Christ was the only way and that all other ways were of the Devil. The spirit of Cromwell lives on in Northern Ireland and the murder continues. When will it end? When will it end in Belfast, in Beirut, in Iran, in Sri Lanka, Amritsar and Assam?

It will end when we no longer bless our violence with sanctity, ortho-doxy, and divine self-election. The fundamentalist of any conviction, Christian, Marxist, or Muslim gives himself a licence to kill. When we lose this singularity of vision, we will begin to understand the battle of good against evil in a different way.

How shall we ever act again when complexity only seems to paralyse us? How can we, or should we even try to, regain that innocence of feeling ourselves to be the forces of good pitted against the forces of evil? Whose side is God on? And what is God doing in all this violence? If God is omnipresent, then how is He present in evil?

Perception itself, the very structure of seeing and knowing, is suffering. It is the system of limitation, the arising of knowing that breaks being into things. Wordsworth said, 'We murder to dissect,' but this poet's wisdom is true not simply of the scientific method, but of perception itself, for perception is the wrenching of something out of its context in Being. We *see* the part, and therefore we suffer. If you are being tortured, and if you withdraw your mind from the torture, you will not suffer. You will no longer be perceiving. Perception is the fixing of attention to limits, and that structure of limitation is suffering; it is the crucifixion of the body to the crossing of time and space.

Because we have more to us than a mere central nervous system, a mere perceptual mechanism triggered by thresholds of difference, there are ways to escape suffering. There is a gnosis, a yoga of *pratyahara*. It is humanly possible to walk on fire; it is possible, in the trance of a dervish, to impale yourself with a spike and not bleed. There are yogic techniques and gnostic forms of escape from the fixing of limits of the soul in incarnation. So, if you are being tortured, you can move off the cross, and in the Docetist heresy some gnostics said that Jesus did allow himself to escape and never truly suffered on his cross.

Although one can withdraw consciousness from the perceptual mechanism, from the structure of consciousness that is another name for suffering, com-passion calls for a passing-with, a participation in the being of others that does not allow us the gnostic escape of blocking the pain, of eliminating suffering, not by connecting the part with the whole but by disconnecting the part from the part, disconnecting the perception from the mind. A feeling of connection, a sense of participation of beings in being, would endeavour to rejoin the part to the whole; it is not an escape but a coming to presence with, a compassion. Escape is an intensification of the process of fragmentation; if this time and space hurts, change to another: transcend.

So some kinds of psychic meditation can be simply an escape, a release in which pain flips into its opposite in ecstasy. This kind of meditation can become an escape into further separateness, further apartness, the apartheid of a transcendent perfection. For meditators of this persuasion the world is divided into two classes: those who are 'on the path of spiritual evolution' and those who are not. It is the karma of the second group to suffer, and the dharma of the first to escape suffering, to transcend it.

Although all of this may sound terribly foreign and oriental, there have always been two very different orientations to historical reality in our own Judaeo-Christian tradition as well. There is Abraham and there is Melchizedeck; there is Aaron and there is Moses; there is Peter and there is St John the Divine. In one orientation we stand within the centre of history, caught up in the body and the body politic; in the other we stand at the edge of history within a horizon of myth, the place where another reality impinges on the body and society with all its weighty institutions. Let us call one orthodox and the other gnostic. The orthodox believer carries the heavy burden of tradition and responsibility, but the gnostic says: 'Ah, but I know esoteric secrets; I know how to fly. I know how to walk on fire, to raise the serpent on the staff; I know the mysteries of the other seven churches that are in Asia.' Each orientation has its light and shadow, and it would be a simplistic error to think that the orthodox is right and the gnostic wrong. Both can be taken over by spiritual pride and arrogance, but at their best, one expresses the materialization of spirit, the other, the spiritualization of matter. The place where these two different directions meet is at the cross. There we suffer the weight of the body, and we watch ourselves in suffering, knowing that we are not only a body nailed to the crossing of time and space.

If we observe our suffering, if we stay present, we begin to sense the presence of God in suffering, in evil, in limitation. Eventually, as our crises multiply, we begin to see that goodness is basic to life, and that evil is the shadow-side to form, to individuality, to perception. But the consequence of this perceiving of limits is not to limit being with perception but, rather, to limit perception with being. If we see the part but are immersed in the feeling of the whole we are immersed in being, and we come to a new awareness of our perceptions. In some Buddhist legends there is a story of a saint who is having his arm cut off by the king, but all the while the saint talks to the king as he is being hacked to pieces: 'You know, this isn't really good for *you*. I'm a yogi and can watch my suffering, but you are really going to have a much harder time with this bad karma you are creating. I would advise you, for your own sake, to stop carrying on like this.' This is one way of being present in one's suffering, a yogic way, but it is also the compassionate commitment of Christ to his cross. The saint limits his perceptions with being, the rest of us limit our being with perception.

Meditation can teach us how to limit our perception with being, and as we learn, we become different beings. Those who seek to eliminate suffering through struggle and angry combat against the forces of wickedness only increase suffering. If out of some fanatical ideology we try to kill evil, we become evil killers. Those who have limited their own being with perception are not in a good position to help others: a person who doesn't know how to swim and still tries to save a drowning person is likely to go down with the other, each one grasping at the other in a confusion of lifting and climbing.

When one limits being with perception, one perceives oneself as an isolated individual, and the little box in which this individuality is contained becomes like a rectangular frame that cuts across all the relationships that exist connecting the part to the whole. Aloneness, alienation, and the fear of death are the forms of suffering that come built into this structure of perception we call consciousness. But when, by contrast, one limits perception with being, one begins to feel all the relationships that connect one being to another in being. This passing through time with one another is com-passion, and compassion is the basic sense of relationship, of what it means to be.

With the growth of compassion, consciousness becomes not a wall of exclusions but a membrane through which many relationships pass. A membrane provides us with the basic definition of a living system, an identity, and at this level we can recognize that a membrane is not an object but a relationship, a structured relationship between an inside and an outside, a this side and a that side. At this basic level, we can recognize that religion, *religare*, is another word for life, for biology, for *bios* and *logos*.

Religion is cosmic life. Imagine the soul before its incarnation in time as a perfect sphere in which the entire inner surface is a mirror. It is all pure light, but vacant, without imagery, without content. It is the gnostic's consciousness without an object, a pure *samadhi* without a sensory object or construction. Then the sphere descends and passes through the plane of space and time; this plane of form is like a template that imprints its world of objects into the sphere. Now there is content and imagery everywhere reflected on the inside of the sphere. As the sphere continues its descent it passes entirely through the plane of space and time and moves out of incarnation again, but as it does it begins to turn inside out, and the reflecting, mirroring surface is no longer inside the sphere but has now become its outer surface. Now imagine all these reflecting spheres, all these mirroring monads, coming together, each mirroring the other, each reflecting its unique experience universally in all the others. Think of it as a holograph or a vessel of spherical facets that could be called the Grail, the Mystical Body of Christ. In the Chinese tradition of Hwa Yen Buddhism, the sphere would be called a jewel, and the lattice of jewels would be called Indra's Net. Each of us is a jewel in Indra's net.

To envision what I have just described one must use imagination, and imagination is one means we all have of expanding our perceptions into the realm of being. This kind of awareness cannot come from simply reading books or going to church on Sunday. It comes from the imagination, from the capacity to relate the unique to the universal. And to enrich and extend our imagination we need the gifts of the Holy Ghost, the gifts of other traditions, other cultures, other religions. There is the unique Christ fixed to the cross, but above the cross in our Christian iconography is always pictured the Holy Ghost. As Gerard Manley Hopkins has expressed it: 'Because the Holy Ghost broods over the wide world with warm breast and with ah! bright wings.' He broods over the *world*, and not merely over the Christian church.

Christ came to give us life more abundant, and life abounds in dirt and variety. Purity withdraws in horror into the sterilization of its abstract perfections in doctrine, into its *apartheid* of goodness; but life invades, increases, and multiplies; no place is too lowly, or too imperfect for its bacterial abundance.

The perfection of life into a perfect doctrine would make of the world one large Beirut. So if we would see religion as doing good to one another, then let us not inflict goodness on one another, but let us be generous in the sharing of our common life.

〰〰〰〰〰〰〰〰〰〰〰〰

July/August 1986

*[From a sermon given
at the Cathedral Church of St John the Divine, New York City]*

A Christian Cosmology

STRATFORD CALDECOTT

IT IS SOMETIMES SAID that our present ecological crisis is the fault of Judaism and Christianity. Certainly Christians are in it up to the neck. After all, the industrial worldview was born in the Christian West, not the Hindu or Buddhist East. It was a Christian, Descartes, who fathered modern philosophy, and who is at least partly to blame for our present state of alienation from the rest of nature. Animals, he said, are mere machines without consciousness. For those who followed him, their own intellectual consciousness became like a ghost in the machine of the human body, its feelings reduced to symptoms of chemical or hormonal imbalance.

If the crisis is largely the fault of Christians, does this mean we should abandon Christianity? It seems to me that much of what we have seen since Descartes can hardly be called Christianity at all. In answer to the question, 'What do you think of Western civilization?' Gandhi replied, 'It would be a very good idea!' A genuinely Christian civilization might well be a good idea. But what would such a civilization look like, and how would it regard the earth?

According to the book of Genesis, God placed men and women at the centre of Creation, 'in his own image', to have 'dominion over the fish of the sea, and over the birds of the air and over the cattle, and over all the earth, and over every creeping thing that creeps upon the earth.'

Dominion, according to the Old Testament, does not mean the right to pollute, oppress and destroy. Originally it did not even mean the right to eat the other animals. God gave to humankind, along with other animals, the plants for food: no animal was given the right to eat another until after the landing of Noah's ark, in another age of the world. It was clear from the start that human dominion over the rest of nature was to be strictly controlled by a higher order: the law of God's love and wisdom. Human beings were to 'order the world according to equity and justice'. That is, we were to rule the earth not as a tyrant, but as a steward of the *true* owner, the one who created it and who continually holds it in being.

This was the meaning of the 'jubilee' in the law given to Moses. Every seven years the land was to lie fallow: 'it shall be a year of solemn rest for the land.' Similarly, the fiftieth year was to be a jubilee. And 'The land shall not be sold in perpetuity, for the land is mine,' the Lord said. How could the land belong to God when he had given it to the Israelites? Only by belonging to the Israelites as representatives of the true owner, and as subject to his laws.

The other Semitic religions—Christianity and Islam—share with Judaism a fundamental obligation to respect God's creation, and to administer it wisely. It is only when faith in God grows pale and thin that members of these religions lose the sense of obligation to respect some higher law than our own selfish greed and will to power.

The Eastern religions, of course, have their own ways of describing this fundamental obligation, sometimes not involving reference to a personal God at all. But the principle remains the same. For them, too, humanity is in some sense central to creation, while at the same time subject to a higher law: the Dharma, or Tao. 'Man follows the laws of the earth; Earth follows the laws of heaven; Heaven follows the laws of Tao; Tao follows the laws of its intrinsic nature.'

Christ claimed not only to reveal, but to *be in his own person* this higher law or Tao. 'I am the Way, the Truth and the Life.' To Christians, as well as being God, he is the exemplar of true humanity, along with his mother Mary. It is to him they look to find a revelation of what the Taoists call 'the true man', and the Sufis 'universal man': the axis of the universe in human form. Just as it is to Mary that they look to find the sage who 'keeps the Tao'. As for the rest of us, we are only central to Creation ('made in the image of God') to the extent we conform to the image or structure of the Tao.

All animals, vegetables and minerals, and even all angels, devas and gods, reflect aspects of the Being who creates them; they are all living icons, or sacramental symbols. But only when you take them all together, and balance the lions against the peacocks, the sharks against the eagles, the galaxies against the fields of corn, Gabriel against Raphael, that you obtain a composite image, a multi-faceted panorama which projects in all directions from the single divine command, 'Be!'

This cosmic panorama, echoing through endless dimensions like reflections in a palace of crystal, sweeps in a whirlwind of light through the narrow channel of a single human life. 'He is the image of the invisible God, the first-born of all creation; for in him all things were created, in heaven and on earth, visible and invisible, whether thrones or dominions or principalities or authorities— all things were created through him and for him. He is before all things, and in him all things hold together.'

A vision of the whole world redeemed in Christ completely excludes the destruction of nature for economic benefits. Since every part of the natural world is a mode of the presence of God, a sign of his love and an extension of his Incarnation, the world is sacred. 'The universe is sacred. You cannot improve it. If you try to change it, you will ruin it. If you try to hold it, you will lose it.' The opposite mentality to this reduces everything to a banal level, and refuses to admit mystery. Its ultimate expression—transcending even the sacrilege of industrial pollution and massive deforestation—is twofold: nuclear and genetic engineering. The horror of the first is already apparent in the threat of nuclear war. The genetic horror, whether from germ warfare, industrial accident or commercial eugenics, is just as real.

March/April 1986

Native Cultures

Bulldozing The Poor

ANIL AGARWAL

THE FOOD NEEDS OF THE WESTERN WORLD have played havoc with the lands of the Third World. Despite the worldwide process of decolonization, there is today many times more land being used in the developing world to meet the food needs of the western countries than in the 1940s, before the process of decolonization began. More than a quarter of all Central American forests have been destroyed since 1960 for cattle ranching; eighty-five to ninety-five per cent of the beef produced as a result has gone to the US, while domestic consumption of beef in Central America has fallen dramatically. In the US this beef has been mainly used to make tinned and pet food and cheap hamburgers, because the Central American beef is half the price of the grass-fed beef produced in the US. The price of the Central American beef does not represent its true ecological cost. Cattle ranching has proved to be the worst form of land use for the fragile soils on which these tropical moist forests existed. Within five to seven years their productivity dropped dramatically and the cattle ranchers have had to move on.

The Sahelian drought of 1968-74 which hit the world headlines and claimed the lives of approximately 100,000 nomadic people was caused by nothing less than the French colonial policy to drive these countries into peanut farming to secure its own source of vegetable oils. Through heavy taxation policies, the French colonial authorities forced the West African peasants to grow groundnuts at the expense of subsistence crops. Groundnut cultivation rapidly depleted the soil. It soon spread to traditionally fallow and forest zones and encroached on land previously used for grazing, upsetting the delicate balance between the farmers and the nomadic herders. The expansion of groundnuts was encouraged by artificially high prices, but when the US soya production began to hit the European market and vegetable oil prices began to fall, the newly independent West African countries had no alternative but to increase the groundnut area to keep up their foreign exchange reserves. As this area increased by leaps and bounds under the pressure of government policies, the nomads were slowly pushed further and further north into the desert, for which they were not prepared, their traditional relationships with the settled farmers having been totally disturbed. When the long period of drought set in and thousands of animals and human beings began to die, the nomads and their over-grazing were blamed. Nobody blamed the French or the Sahelian elite which had worked hand in glove with the French.

The current over-fishing off India's coasts, as off the coasts of almost all south-east Asian countries, is taking place because of the heavy demand for prawns in Western and Japanese markets. This over-fishing is leading to considerable tensions between traditional fisherfolk and trawler owners, and violent encounters between the two are regularly reported. Recently, Indonesia completely banned the operation of trawlers from its coastal waters, and several countries including India have set up regulations to prevent trawler operators from fishing in the first few kilometres from the coast. This zone is reserved for the traditional fisherfolk. But policing trawlers over such an extensive coastline is an expensive proposition and regulations are, therefore, seldom observed or enforced.

The pattern of environmental exploitation that we see on the global scale simply reproduces itself on the national scale. Exactly what the Western industry does to the Third World environment, Indian industry does to the Indian environment. Nearly half the industrial output in India is accounted for by industries which can be called biomass-based industries: cotton textiles, rayon, paper, plywood, rubber, soap, sugar, tobacco, jute, chocolate, food processing and packaging. Each of these industries exerts an enormous pressure on the country's cultivated and forest lands. They need crop lands, they need forests, and they need energy and irrigation.

The Indian paper industry has ruthlessly destroyed the forests of India. Paper companies in Karnataka, having destroyed all the bamboo forests, are now getting their raw materials from the last major forested frontier of India: the North-east. The government's own public sector paper companies are coming up in the North-east itself. The Andhra Pradesh government has meanwhile set its sights on the forests of Andamans and Nicobar Islands for a paper mill that it wants to build in Kakinada. The shortage of raw materials for wood pulp has already forced the government to liberalize import of pulp for the country's paper industry, thus, adding to the pressure on the forests of other Third World countries.

The first lesson is, therefore, clear: the main source of environmental destruction in the world is the demand for natural resources generated by the consumption of the rich (whether they are rich nations or rich individuals and groups within nations) and because of their gargantuan appetite it is their wastes that contribute most to the global pollution load.

It is the poor that are affected the most by environmental destruction. The experience shows clearly that eradication of poverty in a country like India is simply not possible without the rational management of our environment and that conversely environmental destruction will only intensify poverty. The reason is simple though seldom recognized. The vast majority of the rural households meet their daily household needs through biomass or biomass-related products, which are mostly collected freely from the immediate environment. In short, they live within nothing other than a biomass-based subsistence economy. Food, fuel (firewood, cowdung, crop wastes), fodder, fertilizer (organic manure, forest litter, leaf mulch), building materials (poles, thatch), herbs and clothing are all biomass products. Water is another crucial product for survival. Water is not biomass itself, but its availability is closely related to the level of biomass available in the surrounding environment. Once the forest disappears, the local pond silts up, the village well dries up, and the perennial stream gets reduced to a seasonal one. The water balance gets totally upset with the destruction of vegetation; in a monsoonal climate with highly uneven rainfall over the year it means greatly increased runoff and floods during the peak water season and greatly increased drought and water scarcity in the lean dry season.

The magnitude of India's dependence on biomass for meeting crucial household needs can be appreciated by looking at the energy situation. We as Indians love to point out that India has the world's tenth largest industrial output. But even then over fifty per cent of the fuel consumption in India is for such a fundamental activity for survival as cooking. In developed countries, cooking consumes less than one per cent of total national fuel consumption.

But even more important for India is the fact that over ninety per cent of the cooking fuel in India is biomass. Even urban households are heavily dependent on firewood as fuel.

Biomass resources not only meet crucial household needs but they also provide a range of raw materials for traditional occupations and crafts and are, hence, a major source of employment: firewood and cowdung are important sources of fuel for potters; bullock carts and catamarans are made from wood; bamboo is a vital raw material for basket weavers. Traditional crafts are not just being threatened by the introduction of modern products, but also by the acute shortage of biomass-based raw materials. A study from the Indian Institute of Science—the first in India on the changing market of bullock carts—reports that people in Ungra village in Karnataka can now no longer afford to buy new bullock carts with the traditional wooden wheel because wood has become extremely expensive. Similarly, traditional fisherfolk now find it very difficult to make new catamarans because the special wood they use is extremely scarce and expensive.

Several reports from all over India portray the extreme difficulty of hundreds of thousands of basket weavers in eking out a bare existence because of the acute shortage of bamboo. In Maharashtra, nearly 70,000 mat and basket weavers have been protesting against the discriminatory prices and small quota of bamboo given to them, whereas big paper mills have been leased out large bamboo forests.

In Karnataka bamboo was available to paper mills at Rs.15 a tonne; it was available to basket weavers and other small bamboo users in the market at Rs.1,200 per tonne.

Even biomass resources like thatch have become so scarce that maintenance and repair cycles of mud and thatch huts have increased considerably. A government report from Bastar, of all places, as it is still one of the heavily forested districts in India, points out a village where no new hut has been built over the last two decades because the entire area around the village has been deforested.

Despite this near-total reliance on biomass resources for bare survival, nature in India has steadily undergone a major transformation. There are two major pressures operating on the country's natural resources today. The first, generated by population growth and thus by increased household demand for biomass resources, has been widely talked about. The poor often get blamed for the destruction of the environment. But the second set of pressures, generated by modernization, industrialization, and the general penetration of the cash economy, is seldom talked about even in policy-making circles.

Modernization affects nature in two ways. First, it is extremely destructive of the environment in its search for cheap biomass-based raw materials and in its search for cheap opportunities for waste disposal. Unless there are strong laws which are equally strongly implemented, there is no attempt made to internalize environmental costs, both public and private industrialists prefer to pass them on to the society. Governments are happy to give away large tracts of forests for a pittance and throw water pollution control laws to the winds to get a few more factories. Second, modernization affects nature by steadily transforming its very character. In physical terms, the tendency is to reduce the diversity in nature and transform it into a nature that is full of high-yielding mono-cultures. The ecological role of original nature is also usually disregarded in this transformation.

In social terms, the transformation is generally away from a nature that has traditionally come to support household and community needs and towards a nature that is geared to meet urban and industrial needs, a nature that is essentially cash generating. Excellent examples of such transformations are the pine forests in place of the old oak forests in the Himalayas, the teak forests in place of the sal forests in the Chottanagpur Plateau, eucalyptus plantations in place of natural forests in the Western Ghats, and now the proposals to grow oil palms in place of the tropical forests in the Great Nicobar Islands. Both these phenomena—the destruction of the original nature and the creation of a new, commercially oriented nature—have been taking place simultaneously in the Indian environment and on a massive scale.

The effect of this massive environmental change has been disastrous for the people, especially when we realize that in a country like India, where on one hand we have an extremely high level of poverty and on the other hand a reasonably high level of population density, there is hardly any ecological space left in the physical environment which is not occupied by one human group or another for its sustenance. Now if, in the name of economic development, any human activity results in the destruction of an ecological space or in its transformation which benefits the more powerful groups in society, then inevitably those who were earlier dependent on that space will suffer. Development in this case leads to displacement and dispossession and will inevitably raise questions of social injustice and conflict. The experience shows clearly that it is rare to find a case in which environmental destruction does not go hand in hand with social injustice—two sides of the same coin.

The destruction of the environment clearly poses the biggest threat to marginal cultures and occupations like that of tribals, nomads and fisherfolk which have always been heavily dependent on their immediate environment for their survival. But the maximum impact of the destruction of biomass sources is on women. Women in all rural cultures are affected, especially women from poor landless, marginal and small farming families. Seen from the point of view of these women, it can even be argued that all development is ignorant of women's needs, at best, and anti-women, at the worst, literally designed to increase their work burden.

Given the culturally accepted division of labour within the family, the collection of household needs like fuel, fodder and water is left to women. As the environment degrades, and these become increasingly difficult to obtain, women have to spend an extraordinary amount of time in foraging for fuel, fodder and water in addition to household work, agricultural work and caring for animals. The available data on the existing work burden on women is downright shocking. In many parts of India, women work for fourteen to sixteen hours every day and it does not matter whether they are young, old or pregnant and whether it is a Sunday or any other holiday. Day after weary day the routine repeats itself and year after weary year fuel and fodder collection time periods increase. In many parts the women may have literally reached their 'carrying capacities'.

The worst situation is in the arid and semi-arid parts of the country and in the hill and mountain villages. In all these areas trees and forests have been steadily destroyed on account of a number of factors—soil and climatic conditions, small size of land holdings, lack of irrigation, etc. As a result, there is now an acute biomass famine in these areas. In all such areas women can spend as much as five to six hours every day, in some households even ten hours every day, just collecting fuel and fodder. On the contrary, in a state like Kerala, where eco-climatic conditions permit a rich green cover, the work burden on women is much smaller. Even the minimal land reforms in which landless families have been allotted one tenth of an acre, have meant access to a few dozen coconut trees, which help to provide at least half the fuel requirements.

The Chipko Movement has given us numerous examples of this dichotomy in male-female interests, and the role of the women in preventing deforestation has been paramount in the movement. Even the Chipko experience with afforestation confirms this dichotomy between men and women and stresses the role of women in ecological regeneration. Even though many crucial household needs could be met by rehabilitating the local village ecosystems —by planting fuel and fodder trees, for instance—the men do not show any interest in doing so. It is women who are doing all the afforestation work organized by the Chipko Movement.

The new culture created by the penetration of the cash economy has, slowly but steadily, psychologically alienated the men from their ecosystem. Employment for them means work which can bring cash in their hands. This employment can be found mainly in the city and hence means mass male migration. Even when the men are in a village a job is still something that must earn cash.

If these are the problems, then what do we do about them? First of all, there must be much more holistic thinking regarding the management of our land and water resources. And this will not be easy unless a determined effort is made. For all the talk about the need for a scientific temper, it must be recognized that the current methodology of scientific analysis carries within itself an extremely unscientific practice, that of reductionism. It is this reductionist approach that has today produced both natural and social scientists who know more and more about less and less: who know how to cure a disease but create another disease in the process. Ecology is the first scientific discipline that has actually forced people to integrate and not reduce.

Nothing could be more important for planners and politicians today than to rebuild nature. But this can only be done if we re-establish a healthy relationship between the people and their environment. Then only a nature that is useful to the millions, not for making millions can be re-established. Regardless of what happens in the West—its electronics revolution, its biotechnology inventions, its communications satellites, its efforts to mine the oceans and its efforts to build solar cells and windmills—and regardless of how much we may want to catch up with the West in the name of modernization, rebuilding nature and rebuilding its relationship with the people will remain the only way to solve the problem of poverty and possibly even employment. With some 100-150 million hectares of waste and near-waste lands and with the crying need to produce biomass, this country can never get a better opportunity to harness the power of its people to the power of its land, to strike at the roots of landlessness, poverty and unemployment, all at the same time.

If we were to construct a concept like Gross Nature Product, we would find that for the poor it is this indicator which is many times more important than the conventional Gross National Product. In fact, we can even say that those who do not get much from the conventional GNP—the poor—are the ones who are most critically dependent on the Gross Nature Product.

In other words, it is not enough to preserve biological diversity in just those areas of our country where the flora and fauna are genetically rich and diverse by setting up biosphere reserves, and national parks, but that biological diversity must be preserved or recreated in every village ecosystem. Concentrating on the production of a few commodities is totally inadequate in a society which is only partly monetized, and where the vast majority still have to depend on access to free biomass resources from the immediate environment. Every village has to become a biosphere reserve.

An indicator like Gross Nature Product would probably reflect far better the changing reality in a country like India. Unfortunately we do not know as yet how to construct such an indicator. But I am sure if we do, we will find that while the conventional GNP has gone up, the Gross Nature Product has steadily gone down, the former acting as a parasite on the latter.

May/June 1986

[From the Fifth Vikram Sarabhai Memorial Lecture given in New Delhi]

The Tribal Soul of India

JEREMY SEABROOK

TALASARI, 150 KILOMETRES NORTH OF BOMBAY, is close to the Gujarat border; a cluster of tribal villages built on outcrops of red rock, huts of coarse grass and bamboo, reinforced with mud and cowdung and surrounded by hedges of euphorbia and thorn. Wild morning glory and showers of cerise bougainvillaea spill over the thatch. In the compounds grow plantain, mangoes and tamarind, from the seeds of which a tangy juice is made to give savour to the staple, rice. Oval-shaped craters of paddy-fields cover the landscape like links in a long earthen chain.

The *adivasis*, or Tribals, were originally the owners of the land and forests. They lived outside the cash economy until dispossessed of their land by Hindu and Parsee landlords, a process legalized by the British. It wasn't long before they became bonded labourers. The *adivasis* were pushed back to the poorest land. They were compelled to do forced labour. Half their produce was given to the landlords. They still remember how people were mistreated by the rich: the man strung upside down over a fire of chillis for stealing a mango; women forced back to work within hours of giving birth; a man yoked to a plough harness with a bullock.

Here and there you can see traces of the former landowners' estates: in the middle of an empty field are concrete posts and a metal gate swinging on rusty hinges, once the ceremonial entrance to a great farm. In the 1940s the Communist Party of India led the *adivasis* in a series of revolts and uprisings, which culminated in the abolition of bonded labour. After Independence, under the Land Ceiling Act, the landlords had to sell off large holdings of land. Many found ways round it: there is no restriction on the land that can be used for orchards, and as a result there are vast plantations of papaya, chickoo or mango, with palatial houses in chickoo groves; others simply transferred land to their relatives; some maintained their power by becoming moneylenders.

The efforts of the CPI at that time were heroic. It duly benefited from the people's gratitude, and the area was a party stronghold. But in spite of ending the worst abuses, poverty and oppression remained. Most families have to find work in the dry season in neighbouring towns, or in the brickfields (the region is full of ugly red scars where farmers have sold their topsoil to the brick industry). When the monsoon comes they must work in their own fields, and they support themselves during this time by taking a loan until their own rice is harvested. In the rains, the streams become torrents which can't be crossed, so they need to buy two or three months' provisions—chillis, lentils, flour, and when there is sickness or a wedding the moneylender is the only recourse at very high rates of interest.

The CPI came to take the people's support for granted; big landowners themselves became prominent members—the powerful are not squeamish about the guise they assume in order to maintain their affluence. The party also shows the limitations of so many communist parties in its lack of understanding of the culture of the people it was eager to emancipate. Godavari Parulekar wrote a book about the struggles of the *adivasis*, in which she describes them as 'illiterate helpless creatures living in separate little huddles in hills and vales and jungles.' They were 'culturally backward', and it had taken the CPI to rouse them from the slumber of centuries.

During the slumber of the CPI in the early eighties, a few Jesuits gave the impulse to a new political grouping, the United Workers, articulating the contemporary grievances of the people after the fashion of liberation theologians in Latin America. There has been a Mission and school in Talasari since the 1930s, when some of the tribals were Christianized. The Communist Party, seeing its strength threatened, accused the Jesuits of trying to convert people. There were a number of attacks on Christian villages by angry party members. The United Workers, drawing no doubt on memories of the messianic fervour of the old CPI, had raised great hopes among the people, promising revolutionary change and the imminent overthrow of the oppressors of the people. There was a big *morcha*, violence against the moneylenders and shopkeepers. The leaders were arrested, and expelled by the Jesuits, so that the Mission could distance itself from their activities.

In this tense political context, the *Maharashtra Prabodhan Seva Mandal* (MPSM) works with the tribal people; a rural and educational development project, led by a former atomic physicist, which seeks to give the validity it deserves to the traditional culture of the *adivasis*, their respect for the environment, their sustainable economy, their vast knowledge of living and growing things. It is an enterprise that strikes not only against the values of conventional development economics, but also against the narrow economism of the Communists, as well as against the official State structures that are dedicated to the incorporation of the 'backward classes' into the mainstream of Indian life. Indeed, MPSM seeks to avoid all forms of colonizing people; not least because the culture of the *adivasis* offers an alternative to the attempts at development which litter and lay waste much of the countryside of Northern Maharashtra; ill-conceived dams which displaced more people than they helped, dairy schemes that depend upon imported breeds of cattle that are difficult and expensive to maintain, deforestation that for industrial timber has contributed to decrease rainfall as well as removing a source of food and medicine.

Vasudha is collecting 'unknown' information about *adivasis* culture for MPSM. She lives in a hut in one of the secluded hamlets; a cool mud house pervaded by the sweet smell of grass and cattle; cattle, being the people's most precious possession, live inside the huts. Vasudha, herself a Hindu, says 'Their culture is as dense and involuted as the foliage of the forest; as impenetrable too. We are always learning.' Vasudha was a teacher in Bombay until she went to work as interpreter for a friend who was researching into *adivasi* art. 'The motifs of their paintings reflect the richness of the culture.' We visit a hut where a marriage has just taken place: on the wall, a picture has been drawn, a representation of *Palghat*, the goddess of vegetation, a fertility symbol. Vasudha speaks with enthusiasm of the culture, when she tells of the '*kansari puja*, the song after harvest which is associated with the corn goddess. It is sung for three days, partly in the house and partly in the fields. It is not fixed in time, space or location, but is part of an ancient epic, the narrative of which is not linear. The *adivasis* call themselves "Kings of the jungle". Nobody quite knows their origins, whether they are autochthonous, even pre-Dravidian. They see themselves as a separate religious group; the process of Hinduization is also a form of colonialism, just as the Christian missionaries were, or the attentions of the Communist Party. The trouble is that the educational system makes them ashamed of their own culture, inferiorizes them, suppresses knowledge that is vital for their survival, and indeed could be vital for ours, if we really care about a sustainable future.'

Even the *adivasi* children know the names of hundreds of plants and trees and their uses, many of which have always supplemented a meagre diet of cereals and pulses. They know which shrubs are good for fuel, lighting, medicine. They can make a wicker fish-trap for when the streams are in flood; they catch shrimps in holes in the river bank by means of a powder made from tree-bark which acts as a narcotic. They can catch wild hare, quail and partridge, and they eat wild fruits and berries richer in vitamin c than any other. They know the use of *ak* or *rui* to ease fever, because its leaves are ten degrees centigrade cooler than the surrounding atmosphere; its lilac-coloured buds are used as hair ornaments. The fruits of the *bhindi* tree are good for jaundice; *neem* assuages sickness; *jamun* can be made into an inky paste to heal wounds and skin disease.

Winin Pereira is a member of MPSM and maintains a documentation centre from his house in Bombay. He says 'For the *adivasi* a tree is not simply a tree: it is also food, shelter, a meeting-place, a deity and a familiar landmark. It is fuel and fodder and a source of building material. An *adivasi* "reads" trees as a good reader reads words: in their entirety, at a glance. The botanist, on the other hand, reads trees as a neoliterate reads words—letter by letter.'

In the village of Savroli, the paddy fields are parched by the February sun. A girl of seventeen, working in nearby brick-fields, is collecting juice from the palm-trees: a thick milky drink which ferments lightly in an earthen pot and is mildly alcoholic. From a thatched hut set in a small bamboo plantation comes the sound of a woman keening. Her child died four days ago, and the neighbours are saying that she neglected the baby by leaving her with a child too young to look after it. The thatch on the house must be renewed before the rains, and the *bunds* built up around the paddy-fields.

Most of the huts have wide eaves, with wooden pillars forming a veranda. Inside they are cool and spacious. Nothing could be further from the image of backwardness associated in the Western mind with the idea of 'mud huts'. Anil Agarwal has said that 'of the various types of traditional building materials available, mud is the most widely used and will remain so long into the foreseeable future.' Available locally, it is cheap, climatically suitable, requires a minimum of labour and is aesthetically pleasing. A man whose parents had been bonded labourers shows us his house with pride. One corner is fenced off as a byre. The interior is uncluttered: storage vessels and palmyra mats; a stiff cape of strong grass used for working in the rain. The sun slants through a narrow aperture in the wall, illuminating the furls of sweet wood-smoke from the stove of three bricks. Three big vats of plaited straw and reinforced with dung contain rice: one for use this summer, one for sowing, the third in case the harvest fails. Pulses are tied in bags hanging from the roof, secure against rodents. A baby lies in a cotton sling oscillating in the shade of the veranda; a granddaughter is threshing *toor*, a kind of vetch which gives off a fragrant dust; the pods will be fed to the cattle.

The *adivasis* formerly lived by barter to supplement those things in which they were not self-reliant, and they still exchange rice for dried fish, bombils and sardines, with the vendors who come from Bombay. But the market economy thrusts more and more deeply into their lives; the little shops in Talasari sell Britannia biscuits, Vim, Lifebuoy and Lux soap, sweets, *bidis*, cigarettes, Vick and aspirin. Many people now sell the wild grass that grows in the monsoon which goes to feed the milk-producing buffaloes of Bombay. This means that their own cattle must graze as best they can.

Night in the village: a vast expanse of stars, the spectral white trunks of *Kahandol* trees. The crickets rasp, a silver moon sends long shadows into the rocky hollows. The children at night school are reciting *Marathi* after a day in the fields tending cattle or looking after younger children. Shanti, a widow of twenty-two who is working in Talasari for 150 Rupees a month, is slightly tipsy. A boy of eighteen tells how his family lost three cows last year; a seventeen-year-old talks of his ambition to join the army. A young man stumbles on the unlighted path. He stops when he sees us. Angrily he says 'Why have you come here? Why can't you leave us alone?' The village has been raided by the Communists, and many people fled in terror into the jungle. The defeat of the United Workers has dashed all the high expectations and left a legacy of great bitterness; the moneylenders, the employers of labour in the big orchards, the police and the officials are still in control.

In the school the youngest children are making a model of their village. The teacher is keen to insert into the curriculum—a tight schedule pinned to the wall, with a month by month breakdown of the work officially required of her—a programme that will validate and reflect positively the children's experience. Among the older children the demands of exams leave little space.

Winin Pereira points out that the school gardens are full of imported and exotic plants: African marigolds, geraniums, dahlias. Just beyond the compound, the fields are full of wild flowers, plants and shrubs. He asks, 'Why don't you grow what is familiar to the children in the gardens? Why don't you find out the fruits and berries and roots which they eat?' The teachers themselves do not always appreciate the indigenous, the homely and the locally grown; their teaching itself has its origins in the distant, the imported, knowledge that is produced elsewhere. Pereira has been analysing the text-books in use in the school; the life they evoke is overwhelmingly urban, industrial and Western.

He insists that rescuing traditional knowledge from the oblivion to which formal education would consign it is not an exercise in nostalgia, but a quiet search for practical alternatives to industrialized, monetized patterns of development, one that celebrates the local and sustainable, prizes human above material resources. That the European Greens should have 'discovered' that all living creatures are interdependent, and that they in turn depend upon the non-living parts of the universe, he regards with wry detachment: after all, the *adivasis* have always known this. 'Conscientization,' he says, 'is not only for the poor.'

July/August 1987

Life in Ladakh

HELENA NORBERG-HODGE

I WAS LIVING AND WORKING in Paris as a linguist when I was asked to go to Ladakh as part of a film team to do an anthropological documentary. Once there, I liked it so much that I decided to stay when the film was completed. As a linguist the Ladakhi language was tempting because it had not been written down or analysed in any way. Ladakhi is described as a Tibetan dialect, but in fact it is as distinct from Tibetan as Italian is from Spanish; it is related to Chinese, so it is not an Indo-European language. It has an extremely complex grammar and is very challenging. With a Ladakhi monk I compiled a dictionary, and spent a lot of time travelling by foot throughout the country collecting folk stories and folk songs while working on the grammar. The more I learned to speak Ladakhi, the more I became involved with the people. Speaking the language fluently gave me an opening into the life of the Ladakhis and an insight into their values and world view and I became deeply fascinated by their culture.

This was one of the very few places in the world that had really stayed outside of Western industrial influence and a place which demonstrated in a dramatic way that human beings could live at a surprisingly comfortable level without the technological gadgets that we have grown dependent on in Western societies. In spite of the fact that this was one of the most difficult environments anywhere in the world, the Ladakhis were managing to feed, clothe and house themselves, yet a lot of educated people including Ladakhis themselves thought the Ladakhis were backward.

I tried to convince the Ladakhis, tourists, and government officials that this was not the case, and that they should try to develop Ladakh a little differently and not allow the country to be totally overwhelmed and destroyed by outside influences and industrialism. Instead they should respect their gentle culture. A culture in harmony with the earth. A culture without violence. The people here are among the happiest people I have ever encountered anywhere. They are a deeply joyful and contented people. Initially I didn't believe it possible that they were so profoundly happy under the surface but now, after nine years, I can say it with conviction: the peace of mind and happiness of the Ladakhi people is for real.

The Ladakhis have enough and ask for no more. One of the key elements in all this is that they have kept the population relatively stable. Traditionally the Ladakhis have practised polyandry, which means that one woman has more than one husband, and thus you have a number of women who don't marry and bear children; they remain celibate. These women become nuns and have a certain respect within the community.

Once a Ladakhi friend of mine said to me: 'I don't think I am going to get married, I will become a nun.' She was a scholar. It suddenly occurred to me that she lived in a society where they had had a choice of marrying, or not marrying, for generations, whereas in our Western society if we didn't marry we were outcasts.

Most of the people of Ladakh are Buddhists. The basic teachings of the Buddha tell you that you will not gain your happiness from acquiring ever more material goods. So one could not call them materialistic. And yet everything that I am describing is changing. One of the most tragic changes has been a psychological one. I have watched young Ladakhis, who previously thought of themselves as having all the material goods they needed, suddenly think of themselves as poor and deprived. In 1975 I went with a friend named Norboo to his village. All the houses were unusually large and beautiful. I said to him, 'Show me the poorest house.' He thought for a while and then replied, 'We don't have any *poor* houses.' Last summer I overheard Norboo saying to a rich tourist, 'Oh, if you could only help us Ladakhis, we are *so poor*.' In comparison with what they perceive as the infinite wealth of the Western tourists coming to Ladakh, they are getting an inferiority complex and suddenly becoming more materialistic. They see acquiring *modern*, Western goods as a way of improving their own worth; blue jeans and sunglasses become means of maintaining self-respect.

My work over the past years is based on an understanding of these psychological changes, and trying to reverse this trend. I am hoping that by linking pre-industrial Ladakh with the post-industrial West, we will both benefit. Ladakh can be a very inspiring model for us. And we can help the young Ladakhis overcome their newly formed inferiority complex by letting them know that we view Ladakh as a model of sustainability.

In Ladakh the response has been very positive. I am quite amazed just how positive. Some years ago we started the Ladakh Ecological Development Group. And in the last year the membership has doubled. What this group is saying makes a lot of sense: respect your own culture. You can maintain your own dignity and self-respect and still be modern.

The West is coming full circle. The most modern thinking in the West is ecological thinking. In Ladakh they already have it. They have inherited a world view which we now in the West are coming closer and closer to again. The Buddhist world view in Ladakh has been passed on from generation to generation. Even simple farmers live according to the essence of Buddhism. Their attitude to everything is much more fluid than our own. They see themselves as part of a whole flow, and are much more connected to everything around them, to the earth, to other human beings. However, if you came out there you would see them as quite ordinary, quite earthy people, and that is what they are. You experience with them that the spiritual and the material are not separate.

In the last nine years there has probably been more change in Ladakh than in the previous thousand years, and it's been a change for the worse. The tourists coming from outside Ladakh bring alien influences. The Ladakhis have been living and farming for centuries and suddenly the tourists come in and spend £50 a day. It is something incredible and beyond most Ladakhis' comprehension. The tourists give the impression not only of infinite wealth, but that it comes easily. If you are a modern person you do not dirty your hands and work. You spend your life travelling around the world and taking pictures of other people. Ladakhi people get the impression that the work in the modern world is just pushing a few buttons. When the tourists come along and take photographs of them while they dig in their fields and harvest, they are made to feel very silly indeed for spending their time working and getting dirty when they don't have to; all they need to do is to get industrialized. The older and more mature Ladakhis are very disturbed by all this.

'Modern' people in the West, especially in America, spend $3,000 to buy composting lavatories; they spend twice as much on brown bread as they will on white. They will pay money to go walking on a holiday in Ladakh and don't like using a car. They prefer natural materials to artificial ones, homespun wool to polyester, stone to concrete, wood to plastic, even herbal medicines to synthetic ones. There is talk of voluntary simplicity, organic agriculture, renewable energy—'sustainable societies'. Our group is trying to point out that certain aspects of Ladakhi culture are the ideal of what you can rightly call the most modern thinking in the West. We have plenty of books and magazines, like *Resurgence*, to show them, and we have had real success with them.

The basic principles of traditional Ladakhi society are very much in tune with all the principles outlined in the West as being essential foundations for a sustainable society. Using renewable resources you work more closely with the earth, you have a more decentralized, smaller-scale structure, political and social, and a greater degree of self-reliance. The Ladakhis are as self-reliant as many people in the world, and we are showing them how the goal of many modern thinkers is exactly those basic principles.

Our work is to show that you can bring about changes in tune with ecological principles. We have also been able to demonstrate a tangible alternative to industrial development. Ladakh is very cold in winter. At the same time there is a lot of sunshine, and simple passive solar energy technology is ideally suited to the conditions. About five years ago we organized a project to demonstrate passive solar energy very successfully. We were able to show that the Trombe Wall makes a dramatic difference. In fact such a difference that you need no additional fuel even though temperatures fall to minus 40°. This is in contrast to the effect of conventional development which was to import coal and kerosene over the high passes of the Himalayas.

The president of our group is a Buddhist monk who has written some wonderful plays to introduce all these ideas. For example, one play is about a traditional family who saves everything they have to send their son away to a college in Kashmir. When he comes back he is a completely different person, despising everything about his own culture. He sets about installing a lavatory and refusing to eat the whole-wheat brown bread. He doesn't want to do anything the traditional way. When his grandfather is ill he insists on having a Western doctor rather than the traditional doctor.

This Western-trained doctor is a Ladakhi who lived for seven years in America while studying. So he starts telling the family that 'modern-thinking people in America are buying brown bread, giving birth to their babies at home, and breastfeeding them'; he says that 'all the time I was in America I was told how lucky I was to be a Ladakhi.'

July/August 1984

Hopi Art of Living

KATHLEEN RAINE

IN OUR WORK-RULED WORLD of jobs, careers, professions, even of vocations, there is something that is lacking—something I myself have forgotten, not only to name, but to know—life itself in its simplicity. To work we were sentenced when man and woman left Eden, but in that first world, for which we were made, which was made for us, life was something else, was for living. So we all remember it was once. Now as I write I see that the rain has stopped and the sun come out, and in my garden are roses and birds in their green world. I glimpse that world, I glimpse the sun and clouds, but I am not there, I cannot stop what I am doing, what is or what I conceive to be my task. Even if I were to stop, to go out into that garden, I would be thinking, planning.

Yet our weary civilization has a great longing, not for achievement, not for the high arts of the Renaissance, the wonders of the world, but for something simple and primordial that we have lost. But now it seems to me that all that is over; if I could—but I cannot—I would lay down that burden, that responsibility, and be with the leaves in the garden, the tree outside my window —an acacia, beautiful with its heavy white flowers—with the birds who always have time, with the clouds and the rain. In our terrible urban civilization, who has time for life itself? Some pray, some meditate. These may perhaps bring that moment, or they may be yet another distraction, like early morning physical exercise or switching on the news almost as soon as we wake. We do not listen, we do not see the real world very often.

I have memories of a brief visit to Old Oraibi, a Hopi village in Southern Arizona. Old Oraibi reminded me of my own childhood, of Bavington and its people, my old school companions, and our tasks interwoven with life itself—drawing water from a living spring; collecting the warm eggs from the hens' nests, gathering gooseberries from the bushes among the long wet grass in the garden.

I had been invited to a conference in Los Angeles, and had chosen to make the journey by train because I wanted to see the scope and scale of America. Day after day through the corn-belt, empty of life, few houses or farms, just anonymous silos for storing grain, and then on to desolate country with an occasional oil-rig speaking not of life at one with nature but of violation and conquest. But as we came to the West, nature soared in those great mountains still supreme in their wondrous skies. That was the America I longed to enter.

This I said to a group of those gathered for the conference on that first evening, little expecting that such a wish would be realized. But a doctor and his wife—I was meeting them for the first time—said they knew the Hopi, often visited them, would take me. This I took to be mere courtesy, but it proved otherwise. Next day Mrs Sanford came and said we would leave for Old Oraibi at the end of the conference; they had telephoned their Hopi friends and we were expected. Dr Sanford had lived as a doctor in that village and had received initiation into the religious rites of the Hopi.

And so I found myself driving on those great modern motorways that cut through the age-old Arizona desert with its ecology of cacti and lizard, its clarity of skies, its seeming inviolateness though our very presence there, the cars, the motorways, was a violation. Then after the cactus, the luminous rainbow-desert of arid earth whose hues were those of light and rock; and again on into such remoteness as I had never conceived, and a beauty that is like an absolution of light and of the unsullied mountains. At last we saw the *mesas*, those plateaux where the Hopi villages on the summit look like a broken line of the rocks on which they stand.

Arriving at Old Oraibi we found we were to be lent the schoolteacher's house, the teacher (not a Hopi) being at that time away. Quite a modern house, and close by some modern caravans in one of which two nuns had set up their mission. One came from England and the other was an American. Their little room had in it a number of books about the Hopi and their customs. Impervious as the white races ever are, these two nice women were setting about their task of destroying an indigenous culture in the full assurance that they were conferring the great benefit of an alien religion on this conquered ancient people. In one direction a signpost pointed to the Mennonite mission; the Presbyterian mission had been twice destroyed by lightning (Dr Sanford told me that the Hopi, with their knowledge of magic, claimed the credit for this event). Other missions were all around—I had the impression of a besieged fortress with guns trained on it from all directions.

There was also a store, with the usual products of the canning industry and the same trash as one would find anywhere in the world. Television was already the trojan horse within the houses of the people themselves who might call down lightning upon so obvious a target as the Presbyterian church but had opened their doors to a far worse enemy of their culture.

'Henry' S—for all Hopi are also given Western names at school—was to be our host; he was the friend of Dr and Mrs Sanford, and he took us that first evening to his garden to cut squash and corn for our evening meal.

I write from no diary or record but as I remember that visit to the *mesas* of some twenty years ago. I recall Henry driving us (they have cars on the *mesas*) to his garden, no more than a shallow depression in the sand, perhaps a little bigger than a tennis-court. Under a juniper tree a box and some garden-tools, and on the tree hung a *paho*, a feather charm, a sign that Henry's garden was under the invisible protection of the spirits of the land. In that sand no modern machinery designed to 'conquer' intractable nature would avail. The Hopi way is to take a long cane, drill it down into the sand, and then drop the seed deep into the earth where a little moisture is found. In due course the corn will sprout.

Henry in his garden was at ease, in his true place on this earth; he cut some cobs of corn, and some fine squashes, and we all feasted that evening. While the doctor and his wife exchanged news of the village and the people they knew, Henry spoke of things closer to his heart: of the eagles and how they protected their people. Every year a nestling is taken from an eyrie, and kept on the roof of one of the houses of the village. It is fed and tended and made much of; for it is important that the young eagle take back a good account of the Hopi people when it returns. For when the day comes the young eagle is sacrificed, so that its spirit may return to the eagles who protect the Hopi.

Henry's expression of deep reverence as he described how the eagle was killed in a painless and instantaneous manner; how they would never hurt or injure the eagle they love; made me understand that such sacrifice is performed not in hate or enmity towards the living creatures, but in an act of love. And the eagle-spirit returns to the wilderness to be the mediator and intercessor for humankind with the one life in all nature. For humankind, already strayed away, by however little, from the harmonious life of ever-living happy earth.

Henry told us of a man who had been a long way from the village, in a wild lonely place, and there he had heard voices conversing. They were discussing the affairs of the village; of how they could help the people living there. The man was surprised to hear such talk in such a place and he went to look for the speakers; but found no one.

Next day Henry drove us far into that same wilderness, ever more beautiful as its seemingly barren monotony revealed variety and beauty, flowers, a great lizard, a stack of rock where eagles circled and were nesting. A great natural mound of earth around the stack was scattered with shards of broken pottery, left by tribes who had migrated, Henry told us, breaking their vessels before they left.

He told us, as a king might, that we might take some pieces away with us. Whether remembered history or mythology I do not know, but Henry spoke of the ritual migrations of the tribes from this spot, the centre, to the four quarters of the land. They had gone, and they would return to that same centre.

Further on we came to a creek, in a gully of that beautiful striated rainbow earth, where Henry's grandchildren who had come with us melted away among the bushes. We sat on the steps of a house that had been his mother's, where all her belongings still remained; far from the village in the very living heart of the wilderness itself. She had lived in, not near, nature. There even Henry was returning home from the human world of exile.

This primordial unity with the earth was already under threat. The modern men were constructing a ski-slope on Mount San Francisco where the Hopi gods lived above the summit—what gods can prevail against the profit motive and the American cult of bodily fitness? There Henry told us the creation myth of this people who had ascended up the hollow stem of a willow (or was it a rush?) to reach this world.

There are five worlds, of which this is the third and lowest of the cycle. The fourth, he said, will already be a little better, as we pass the lowest point of descent and begin to rise again towards the higher worlds from which we have descended. Even now here and there on this earth the fourth world is beginning to appear. But before it comes, Henry said 'there will be bad times for my people, and for your people.' His mother had been a seer and she had known these things.

Twenty years ago. When we left Henry had ceremoniously told me that I, or my children, or my children's children, would be welcomed by himself or his children or his children's children. But already our insatiable greed has discovered some sought-after mineral wealth in a canyon close to the *mesas*, into which I had looked down as one does in dreams. The Hopi are under threat of eviction from their land, so close to the omphalos, the centre of the world from time immemorial. 'But,' said Henry, 'It is not what happens that matters, it is how we behave when it comes.' When we took our leave he was in tears. As I am when I return there in thoughts. Unshed tears. Those tears that there are in things *et mentem mortalia tangunt*. From time immemorial.

November/December 1987

Indian Resistance

RUSSELL MEANS

THE ONLY POSSIBLE OPENING for a statement of this kind is that I detest writing. The process itself epitomizes the European concept of 'legitimate' thinking; what is written has an importance that is denied the spoken. My culture, the Lakota culture, has an oral tradition, so I ordinarily reject writing. It is one of the white world's ways of destroying the cultures of non-European peoples, the imposing of an abstraction over the spoken relationship of a people.

So what you read here is not what I've written. It's what I've said and someone else has written down. I will allow this because it seems that the only way to communicate with the white world is through the dead, dry leaves of a book. I don't really care whether my words reach whites or not. They have already demonstrated through their history that they cannot hear, cannot see, they can only read (of course, there are exceptions, but the exceptions only prove the rule). I'm more concerned with American Indian people, students and others, who have begun to be absorbed into the white world through universities and other institutions. But even then it's a marginal sort of concern. It's very possible to grow into a red face with a white mind; and if that's a person's individual choice, so be it, but I have no use for them. This is part of the process of cultural genocide being waged by Europeans against American Indian peoples today. My concern is with those American Indians who choose to resist this genocide but who may be confused as to how to proceed.

You notice I use the term 'American Indian' rather than 'Native American' or 'Native indigenous people' or 'Amerindian' when referring to my people. There has been some controversy about such terms, and frankly, at this point, I find it absurd. Primarily it seems that 'American Indian' is being rejected as European in origin—which is true. But *all* the above terms are European in origin; the only non-European way is to speak of Lakota—or, more precisely, of Oglala, Brulé, Diné, Miccosukee and all the rest of the several hundred correct tribal names.

There is also some confusion about the word *Indian*, a mistaken belief that it refers somehow to the country, India. When Columbus washed up on the beach in the Caribbean, he was not looking for a country called India. Europeans were calling that country Hindustan in 1492. Look it up on the old maps. Columbus called the tribal people he met 'Indio', from the Italian *in dio*, meaning 'in God'.

It takes a strong effort on the part of each American Indian *not* to become Europeanized. The strength for this effort can only come from the traditional ways, the traditional values that our elders retain. It must come from the hoop, the four directions, the relations; it cannot come from the pages of a book or a thousand books. No European can ever teach a Lakota to be Lakota, a Hopi to be Hopi. A master's degree in 'Indian Studies' or in 'education' or in anything else cannot make a person into a human being or provide knowledge into the traditional ways. It can only make you into a mental European, an outsider.

I should be clear about something here, because there seems to be some confusion about it. When I speak of Europeans or mental Europeans, I'm not allowing for false distinctions. I'm not saying that on the one hand there are the by-products of a few thousand years of genocidal, reactionary, European intellectual development which is bad; and on the other hand there is some new revolutionary intellectual development which is good. I'm referring here to the so-called theories of Marxism and anarchism and 'leftism' in general. I don't believe these theories can be separated from the rest of the European intellectual tradition. It's really just the same old song.

The process began much earlier. Newton, for example, 'revolutionized' physics and the so-called natural sciences by reducing the physical universe to a linear mathematical equation. Descartes did the same thing with culture. John Locke did it with politics, and Adam Smith did it with economics. Each one of these 'thinkers' took a piece of the spirituality of human existence and converted it into a code, an abstraction. They picked up where Christianity ended; they 'secularized' Christian religion, as the 'scholars' like to say—and in doing so they made Europe more able and ready to act as an expansionist culture. Each of these intellectual revolutions served to abstract European mentality even further, to remove the wonderful complexity and spirituality from the universe and replace it with a logical sequence: one, two, three.

This is what has come to be termed 'efficiency' in the European mind. Whatever is mechanical is perfect; whatever seems to work at the moment—that is, proves the mechanical model to be the right one—is considered correct, even when it is clearly untrue. This is why 'truth' changes so fast in the European mind; the answers which result from such a process are only stop-gaps, only temporary, and must be continuously discarded in favour of new stop-gaps which support the mechanical models and keep them (the models) alive.

Hegel and Marx were heirs to the thinking of Newton, Descartes, Locke and Smith. Hegel finished the process of secularizing theology—and that is put in his own terms—he secularized the religious thinking through which Europe understood the universe. Then Marx put Hegel's philosophy in terms of 'materialism', which is to say that Marx despiritualized Hegel's work altogether. Again, this is in Marx's own terms. And this is now seen as the future revolutionary potential of Europe. Europeans may see this as revolutionary, but American Indians see it simply as still more of that same old European conflict between *being* and *gaining*. The intellectual roots of a new Marxist form of European imperialism lie in Marx's—and his followers'—links with the tradition of Newton, Hegel and the others.

Being is a spiritual proposition. *Gaining* is a material act. Traditionally, American Indians have always attempted to *be* the best people they could. Part of that spiritual process was and is to give away wealth, to discard wealth in order *not* to gain. Material gain is an indicator of false status among traditional people, while it is 'proof that the system works' to Europeans. Clearly, there are two completely opposing views at issue here, and Marxism is far over to the other side from the American Indian view. But let's look at a major implication of this; it is not merely an intellectual debate.

The European materialist tradition of despiritualizing the universe is very similar to the mental process which goes into dehumanizing another person. And who seems most expert at dehumanizing other people? And why? Soldiers who have seen a lot of combat learn to do this to the enemy before going back into combat. Murderers do it before going out to commit murder. Nazi ss guards did it to concentration camp inmates. Cops do it. Corporation leaders do it to the workers they send into uranium mines and steel mills. Politicians do it to everyone in sight. And what the process has in common for each group doing the dehumanizing is that it makes it all right to kill and otherwise destroy other people. One of the Christian commandments says, 'Thou shalt not kill,' at least not humans, so the trick is to mentally convert the victims into nonhumans. Then you can proclaim violation of your own commandment as a virtue.

In terms of the despiritualization of the universe, the mental process works so that it becomes virtuous to destroy the planet. Terms like 'progress' and 'development' are used, as cover words here, the way 'victory' and 'freedom' are used to justify butchery in the dehumanization process. For example, a real-estate speculator may refer to 'developing' a parcel of ground by opening a gravel quarry; 'development' here means total, permanent destruction, with the earth itself removed. But European logic has *gained* a few tons of gravel with which more land can be developed through the construction of road beds. Ultimately the whole universe is open—in the European view—to this sort of insanity.

Most important here, perhaps, is the fact that Europeans feel no sense of loss in all this. After all, their philosophers have despiritualized reality, so there is no satisfaction (for them) to be gained in simply observing the wonder of a mountain or a lake or a people *in being*. No, satisfaction is measured in terms of gaining material. So the mountain becomes gravel, and the lake becomes coolant for a factory, and the people are rounded up for processing through the indoctrination mills Europeans like to call schools.

But each new piece of that 'progress' ups the ante out in the real world. Take fuel for the industrial machine as an example. Little more than two centuries ago, nearly everyone used wood—a replenishable, natural item—as fuel for the very human needs of cooking and staying warm. Along came the Industrial Revolution and coal became the dominant fuel, as production became the social imperative for Europe. Pollution began to become a problem in the cities, and the earth was ripped open to provide coal whereas wood had always simply been gathered or harvested at no great expense to the environment. Later, oil became the major fuel, as the technology of production was perfected through a series of scientific 'revolutions'. Pollution increased dramatically, and nobody yet knows what the environmental costs of pumping all that oil out of the ground will really be in the long run. Now there's an 'energy crisis', and uranium is becoming the dominant fuel.

There's a rule of thumb which can be applied here. You cannot judge the real nature of a European revolutionary doctrine on the basis of the changes it proposes to make within the European power structure and society. You can only judge it by the effects it will have on non-European peoples. This is because every revolution in European history has served to reinforce Europe's tendencies and abilities to export destruction to other peoples, other cultures and the environment itself. I defy anyone to point out an example where this is not true.

So now we, as American Indian people, are asked to believe that a 'new' European revolutionary doctrine such as Marxism will reverse the negative effects of European history on us. European power relations are to be adjusted once again, and that's supposed to make things better for all of us. But what does this really mean?

Right now, today, we who live on the Pine Ridge Reservation are living in what white society has designated a 'National Sacrifice Area'. What this means is that we have a lot of uranium deposits here, and white culture (not us) needs this uranium as energy production material. The cheapest, most efficient way for industry to extract and deal with the processing of this uranium is to dump the waste by-products right here at the digging sites. Right here where we live. This waste is radioactive and will make the entire region uninhabitable forever. This is considered by industry, and by the white society that created this industry, to be an 'acceptable' price to pay for energy resource development. Along the way they also plan to drain the water table under this part of South Dakota as part of the industrial process, so the region becomes doubly uninhabitable. The same sort of thing is happening down in the land of the Navajo and Hopi, up in the land of the Northern Cheyenne and Crow, and elsewhere. Thirty per cent of the coal in the West and half of the uranium deposits in the US have been found to lie under reservation land, so there is no way this can be called a minor issue.

We are resisting being turned into a National Sacrifice Area. We are resisting being turned into a national sacrifice people. The costs of this industrial process are not acceptable to us. It is genocide to dig uranium here and drain the water table—no more, no less.

Now let's suppose that in our resistance to extermination we begin to seek allies (we have). Let's suppose further that we were to take revolutionary Marxism at its word: that it intends nothing less than the complete overthrow of the European capitalist order which has presented this threat to our very existence. This would seem to be a natural alliance for American Indian people to enter into. After all, as the Marxists say, it is the capitalists who set us up to be a national sacrifice. This is true as far as it goes.

But, as I've tried to point out, this 'truth' is very deceptive. Revolutionary Marxism is committed to even further perpetuation and perfection of the very industrial process which is destroying us all. It offers only to redistribute the results—the money, maybe—of this industrialization to a wider section of the population. It offers to take wealth from the capitalists and pass it around; but in order to do so, Marxism must maintain the industrial system. Once again, the power relations within European society will have to be altered, but once again the effects upon American Indian people here and non-Europeans elsewhere will remain the same. This is much the same as when power was redistributed from the church to private business during the so-called bourgeois revolution. European society changed a bit, at least superficially, but its conduct toward non-Europeans continued as before. You can see what the American Revolution of 1776 did for American Indians. It's the same old song.

Revolutionary Marxism, like industrial society in other forms, seeks to 'rationalize' all people in relation to industry—maximum industry, maximum production. It is a materialist doctrine that despises the American Indian spiritual tradition, our cultures, our lifeways. Marx himself called us precapitalists and 'primitive'. Precapitalist simply means that, in his view, we would eventually discover capitalism and become capitalist; we have always been economically retarded in Marxist terms. The only manner in which American Indian people could participate in a Marxist revolution would be to join the industrial system, to become factory workers, or 'proletarians' as Marx called them. The man was very clear about the fact that his revolution could occur only through the struggle of the proletariat, that the existence of a massive industrial system is a precondition of a successful Marxist society.

I think there's a problem with language here. Christians, capitalists, Marxists. All of them have been revolutionary in their own minds, but none of them really mean revolution. What they really mean is continuation. They do what they do in order that European culture can continue to exist and develop according to its needs.

I do not believe that capitalism itself is really responsible for the situation in which American Indians have been declared a national sacrifice. No, it is the European tradition; European culture itself is responsible. Marxism is just the latest continuation of this tradition, not a solution to it. To ally with Marxism is to ally with the very same forces that declare us an acceptable cost.

There is another way. There is the traditional Lakota way and the ways of the other American Indian peoples. It is the way that knows that humans do not have the right to degrade Mother Earth, that there are forces beyond anything the European mind has conceived, that humans must be in harmony with *all* relations or the relations will eventually eliminate the disharmony. A lopsided emphasis on humans by humans—the Europeans' arrogance of acting as though they were beyond the nature of all related things—can only result in a total disharmony and a readjustment which cuts arrogant humans down to size, gives them a taste of that reality beyond their grasp or control and restores the harmony. There is no need for a revolutionary theory to bring this about; it's beyond human control. The nature peoples of this planet know this and so they do not theorize about it. Theory is an abstract; our knowledge is real.

All European tradition, Marxism included, has conspired to defy the natural order of all things. Mother Earth has been abused, the powers have been abused, and this cannot go on forever. No theory can alter that simple fact. Mother Earth will retaliate, the whole environment will retaliate, and the abusers will be eliminated. Things come full circle, back to where they started. *That's* revolution.

~~~~~~~~~~~~~~~~~~~~~~~~~~~~

July/August 1981

[A speech given in South Dakota in 1980]

Women in the Desert

NOMI NASH

OUR FRIENDSHIP BEGAN one spring with our common interest in children and almost immediately grew into our common curiosity about each other. We have an ancient strong bond: we are enemies; that strong connection of the 'Other'. We have gentler bonds: we are both tough women with soft hearts living without our husbands in a fiercely family-oriented—even tribal-oriented—land and we both love laughter. Those bonds could find expression in the expansiveness of the desert where eternal boundlessness evaporates boundaries built by tactful tiptoeing words sometimes called for in conversations between enemy/friends.

Words are loaded with emotional reverberations and in this particular constellation even more so when she and I speak the names of places in this land. You see I am careful even here in writing to an unknown audience. I have written 'this land' rather than 'Israel' for convinced as I am that this is Israel, my friend, who in my imagination sits beside me as I write, is equally convinced that this is Palestine. I want to honour both of our convictions and this indeed takes some inner wrestling which goes deeper than mere tact.

And so we ride, side by side, Awatif and Nomi. She from the side of Ishmael and I from the side of Isaac, two brothers from the area of Hebron—through which city we now drive—with distinct destinies stemming from the antipathy of their mothers, Hagar and Sarah. These thousands of years later it is up to the mothers to embrace and thereby redeem the brothers from their antagonisms.

Bumping along the winding roads in my little round red car Awatif casts me a mischievous sidelong glance, 'Is it really me you want to be with in your tent in the desert?' I hear what she means and I grin back, 'As a matter of fact, I have had fantasies of a beautiful man; my lover under the desert stars . . .' and the laughter rises from our bellies. Two middle-aged women enjoying girlish giggles, sharing visions of romance, stories of marriage, stories of our children. Two women talking of the ordinary and extraordinary things women have always talked of. Love, laughter, tears, pain, joy. This was not sentimentality. I believe it's called Soul. With the presence of soul there is the hope of our being the bearers, as women have always borne, of the kind of love that may dissolve the antagonisms of hostile brothers.

The trick is in how one plays out the tension of opposites, and she and I are not always successful. We have misunderstood each other, but even with the misunderstandings we don't give up the path. Tenacity and patience to endure. That helps us. Enjoying the gracious hospitality of her home, her delicious meal and the laughter-filled stories the four children and I are making up, the conversation takes a turn and Awatif says, 'Why does everybody want to live

231

on this small piece of land?' and she gives me a pointed look. The point pierces right into my heart for I believe she means 'Why have all you Jews moved in on us?', and the point shoots quickly from heart to head making a very passionate connection that wants to come out with burning declarations of historical and political import, the true stories of agonies and hopes, of depths of suffering, heights of heroic bravery and breadths of generosity, of poetry and utopian humanism, of genuine messianic dreams.

I look carefully into her face, as she does into mine. In her beautiful black eyes I see all those same passions that surge through me. The stories may be different, but the passions are the same. In the depths of her eyes the timeless impassioned cry of 'Why?' burns, and it's a far greater question than the encapsulated words of her sentence or my unuttered answers can take care of. In a brief but intense moment the Soul has burst forth from both of us and in the face of that, all history melts. Melts but not disappears.

Passions that could have caused a battle of opposing sides, Muslim and Jew, instead recognized one another and with their heat kindled a connection that had more to do with Eros than with Mars. To remain true to our affection for each other as well as for our people, we let the fire soften the discussion by brewing it into a mixture of Islam, Christianity and Judaism; each religion, claiming in its own way, this small piece of land which has a unique intensity. Our conversation was summed up neatly by Awatif's saying, 'Some countries have natural disasters to threaten security: tidal waves, earthquakes, volcanoes. And what do we have here? Religions!'

I admire the dignity and truthfulness of Awatif's remarks to me which are never the over-used, over-idealized love and peace slogans. In the midst of our warmly searching for a 'way' she asks with her straightforward quietness, 'And if there is a war again don't you think we will fight each other?' I answer, 'Yes'. And we both nod out heads sadly. But is that the truth?

Our way that day was winding, as winding as the ancient serpentine paths of initiation. We drove though her country, through my country, but not through *our* country.

We both call the area through which we drove the West Bank. This odd bit of unity in our common phrase refers to the west bank of the Jordan River, which lies *east* of the country in which we live, and though our common phrase does not reflect a common point of view it does reflect, as rivers do, an image rather than an ideology. The Jordan River from above looks like a serpent in agitating coils, winding its way down the centre of a long valley.

Winding along the rounds of the roads each of us talkatively points out the beauty to the other: the rounded hills now gold and red with the autumn colours of the vineyards and orchards, the sun-bleached white stones of the terraces tracing the rounded and very gentle hills. 'These stone terraces have been here from Biblical times,' I add to our conversation. And then, silence. In her silence, I hear her rejection of my claim to those terraces being Jewish. What we say and what we don't say.

True to our sense of Truth neither of us claim absolute knowledge though we do cherish our traditions and that is as it should be. Awatif then points out to me her uncle's estate on a distant hill. 'The Israeli government has told him that he must use the land to make a hospital or a school or they will take it away from him.' Though I sympathize, even empathize, with her uncle's plight I understand the necessity behind my government's position. It is I this time who is silent, yet I know she hears my withheld argument. What we say and what we don't say. It's all taken down. It's a lump we not only swallow but it seems we make a meal of it.

That morning Awatif had driven in her little round red car, just like mine, to my home. We live in separate parts of Jerusalem, and we have our separate names for this beloved city, she calling it Jerusalem to me, and Al-Kuds when speaking to Arabs. This is not duplicity, it's civility.

Sitting on my terrace, made of the typical rough hewn gold-pink stone of Jerusalem, eating Arab cakes she's baked and Jewish cakes I've baked, 'Come! The rains have stopped and we won't get washed away in the flash floods of the desert.' The sun was shining through black billowing clouds. 'Come! Let's chance it!', and a very fast scramble with food, utensils, old clothes and tent, all loaded on to and into my car. I made a quick call to Gidon, a professor of anthropology living and working at the Desert Research Centre of Sde Boker in the Negev, to say we were coming his way. Gidon was pleased and promised to take us to the Bedouin with whom he worked, about a kilometre south. 'Come, have lunch in my home but be sure to come by noon so that there is time to have the necessary visit with your Bedouin hosts and to set up camp before sunset.'

We drove along the high route in hills that continue from hilly Jerusalem into Bethlehem then winding, through Hebron, small villages, graceful farms, graceless settlements, towns, finally the city of Beersheba and—at last—the vast desert of the Negev spotted here and there by army camps with their tents and Bedouin camps with their tents. Both groups of tents appear equally lazy and peaceful. This no longer surprises me, though it continues to puzzle me.

Awatif and I have come from Jerusalem to the desert, from ancient city to ancient land, from navel of the universe to its circumference. And I am aware of a sense of destiny.

Lions used to roam in these places. The tribe of Judah, of the city of Jerusalem, even to this day has the lion as its insignia. My great fondness for lions and the cat family is gratified by the pleasure of leopards, once again, seen roaming in the Negev. I take that as a good omen. I take my friend and I, roaming the desert in all our abundant leonine qualities as a good omen. Golden lion, just as Jerusalem is called the City of Gold, was (and probably is) the animal of the Great Goddess of this part of the world. Wilful and proud, bursting with nature's energy, the goddess is making her re-entry into human consciousness. How shall we play it this time around? The bonds of loving connection, as well as ecstasy, and the bonds that fetter. Such a delicate balance of all is needed. So many of us feel we need the space to roar and roll and play and glow. But we keep ourselves well aware of history's lesson of what the blond beast might do, if not properly played with.

One enters the desert suddenly and we are enveloped in an immediate sense of reaching outwards to never-ending horizons and gently rolling backwards and forwards into the millennia.

For some time we had been bumping slowly along the roadless hard-packed dusty sand which covered the car entirely making it look like an integral part of the desert. We travelled in spaces of nothing but waves of hilly sands of varying heights. Eventually we saw tents distantly spaced and nestled against those hills and clustered about them, shaggy-haired lambs with long soulful faces. In this part of the world lambs look like goats. This makes a great deal of sense to me for with my fascination of opposites I enjoy this unification of sweet and rambunctious, of goat-footed devil and sweet-souled saviour, as was the scapegoat sent into this desert in days of old, as well as the ram who ransomed Isaac.

I was musing on this when the tent of our hosts with its cluster of lambs of brown, black and sandy white came into view. Joined by Gidon as our guide in this place of no landmarks we had at last arrived. We unfolded ourselves out of the loaded car.

Before us was a long tent, the colour of the sands, and divided into two roomy sections. Everything seemed in a blend of soft sandy shades. Quietly, from out of the tent, the men appeared as if in a slow-motion roll. Such a big quietness. The introductions were quiet, slow-motion and formal, the language Arabic, the mood gentle.

We were finishing our greetings with the solemn faced men when, slowly, the women appeared. Wonderfully jewelled through nose and ears and covered in layers of rich embroidery, they held their veils across the lower part of their faces. Having waited until the introductions with the men were finished they had come out of their side of the tent, right hands extended gracefully in greeting. I was moved when instead of shaking my hand, as the men had done, some of the women kissed it. I didn't know what to do with this touching gesture, so I just nodded and smiled. The women nodded and black eyes, glowing from above the black veils, smiled back at me. How warming it was. After a short while veils were dropped and hung softly from head to waist, over the long embroidered dresses. Everything and everyone seemed to be floating.

Awatif and I were gestured into the men's section where a fire had been quickly kindled and where mattresses and cushions had been tossed, finding, as if on their own, their accustomed places around the fire. The women had vanished without my noticing it. In the darkening light and quiet formality, Awatif and I reclined on a single long mattress, head to head, leaning on the large cushion between us. She put her arm around me and laughed, 'It's funny that Nomi is my introduction to this desert and to the Bedouin.'

The head of the family took to pounding coffee beans in mortar and pestle, creating the most beautiful sound and rhythm that wanted to be danced to.

Every Bedouin family has its own intricate rhythm in pounding coffee and the sound extends far and wide in the desert as an invitation for anyone hearing to come and drink. I dutifully presented my gift of bags of sugar which Gidon explained was from Al-Kuds. The formality of the presentation and the origin of the gift as 'Al-Kuds' (meaning 'the holy') gave an aura to my plastic-bagged, supermarket sugar that was comically absurd.

It was dusk, the tent was dark except for the fire in the centre and despite the charm my western mentality gained the upper hand as I worried how we were ever going to pitch the tent in the darkness. I noted that my earlier distinction of feminine time and masculine time was now reversed. It wasn't Awatif and I who had the woman's sense of time as defined by its emotion, feeling intruded upon by clock-time; it was now the men who had this feminine sense. This was obviously the time for human relations, not practicalities, if in fact any distinction is made between the two. Coffee was drunk, then tea was drunk (with good herbs picked nearby) and then coffee again, and probably tea would come next. I was beginning to feel a bit giddy and something like *Alice in Wonderland*.

I was instantly brought back into the mood of the place by the presence of the youngest daughter peering in at the entrance of the tent. Very naturally, as if we'd always known one another, she and I engaged in wordless comical pantomiming over the heads of the others who seemed to be in some serious conversation.

The girl disappeared and reappeared suddenly, placing in my lap—O! How wonderful!—a new-born brown lamb with a white splashy star on its forehead. Still so soft and clean and delicate. I happily embraced this tiny creature who just as happily cuddled against my chest, bleated softly and fell asleep. The little girl beamed at me from the tent entrance. The men talked. Then Awatif spoke to me in the tone I always thought of as great sobriety but learned on this trip to contain the driest humour.

'The father wants you to keep this lamb as a gift.'

'Oh really?! Can I? Wouldn't that be too much to accept? How wonderful!'

She continued looking at me with a serious face.

'Maybe you would like to give it to me?'

Immediately I offered it saying how nice it would be for her children. The dry tone continued and I began to notice sparkle in the eyes of the straight face as she offered it back to me saying, 'And where will you keep it?' and other such practical questions as I continued with bubbling words tumbling out of my mouth in excitement over this wonderful gift. Then she, in earnest, 'Nomi. You must be bigger than this!'

Awatif speaks English but not fluently and I ask, 'You mean I should be more grown up?' I receive an emphatic, '*Yes.*'

The gift was made sincerely and it might be rude to refuse. I pondered over Awatif's commonsense, my joy, and her dry amusement at my being a little girl. I carried the lamb out of the tent and walked with it up a bluff to where all the other lambs gathered. The little girl who had presented it to me walked alongside and we were joined by her older sister. They looked confused and sad when they saw me placing the baby amongst the other lambs but they generously laughed with me as I helped the lamb, on its wobbly legs, try to find the mother but instead finding the father and trying to nurse from him! They told me in words I couldn't understand but gestures I could that I shouldn't worry, the mother was around the corner and would soon come when she heard the baby cry. They reassured me that it was all right that I couldn't keep it when I explained, with words they couldn't understand but gestures they could, that I really loved the lamb but I had no land around my home as they did.

We were still with all the lambs petting them, talking, playing, when Awatif came up to me.

'They want to slaughter a lamb for you.'

This time I saw she was trying not to laugh.

'Oh my Lord! Please find the nicest way to say no thank you.'

I was grateful to have my calm interpreter take care of this awkward situation for I knew they were honouring us by offering a feast held only on special occasions. I was walking slowly back with the daughters when Awatif returned to us, this time with an out and out grin.

'They want to slaughter a chicken for you.'

'Oh please. Tell them I'm a vegetarian, tell them anything.'

She walked back to the men to relay the message.

By the time I got back all of the men were in a jumbled effort, trying to erect my modern and elegant tent with its collapsible chrome rods meant to make this task easier. It didn't. After several attempts which I would have sworn were slapstick comedy were they not accompanied by truly tragic looks of helplessness, the tent was finally erected. It seems we are not very good at each other's customs.

Some of the men piled into a small truck to take Gidon to his home and, I thought, to go to their own. Only later did I discover they made a special trek to find a dinner I would not refuse. I waved goodbye and returned to sit inside the tent where a couple of the men and the wife were continuing the seemingly endless ritual of tea and coffee.

I didn't see Awatif but heard her voice call merrily.

'Come in here.'

'Where is here?'

'In the women's tent of course!'

I hadn't yet seen that part even though it was wide open in the front, like the men's. Was it my imagination or was it really hung with crimson and gold tapestries? It was so dark I couldn't be sure of anything but the surety of the atmosphere. What made it so very different from the men's section? It felt warmer both in mood and in temperature. Even the fire in the centre was prettier. I mentioned this to Awatif who cocked her head and smiled, 'Of course; it's the women's.'

The three girls were seated around the fire, the eldest making bread, the middle daughter tending the fire, while the youngest sat beside me enlisting me as playmate in a pat-a-cake type of game. I can't recall ever being in a busy situation of cooking and fire-building that had such an ease and restfulness about it. Meltingly so. An absent-minded efficiency. The sun had set but the sky still had some light in it and from my place inside the tent I gazed in rapture at the beautiful silhouetted profile of the Bedouin girl, the breeze slightly blowing her veil, standing in the tent entrance, silently looking out at the sky. 'I will always hold this beautiful view in my memory,' I promised myself.

Awatif and I watched the three daughters: their graceful movements like soft music, patting out the dough, placing it on the pan, delicately folding it as it baked (without burning fingers), moving the twigs of fire (without getting burnt), the quiet talk that fell like water, the good smell of the bread, large, round and flat.

On our first beautiful star-filled night we lit candles, got cosy in our sleeping bags, and told each other stories of our private lives and future hopes. A beautiful picture of peace and unity between two women on different sides of an on-going war. Just on that night an air base practised its manoeuvres and the sound was that of a full scale war at its height, screeching, exploding, bombs, bullets and missiles.

Oddly enough, since I had already fallen asleep in a state of desert-enchantment where I'm always convinced I can hear the stars' music, the war-sounds failed to make a frightening or even worrisome impression at the time, blending, as they did, into my dream state. But then, enchantment doesn't answer the problems of war, and dreams can become nightmares. We mentioned it in the morning, but said nothing more. There is too much to say, so we went about the day fulfilling the purpose for which we had come. We enjoyed ourselves.

The name Awatif means 'emotions' and 'Nomi' means 'my pleasant one'. Without our ever talking of a quest for wholeness Awatif says to me, 'Like our names you and I will complement each other and make a whole.' God (and us) willing, lovely lady.

Amazingly, in the unmarked maze, we found our way back to the road. We returned the way we came: winding roads as winding as the ancient serpentine paths of initiation with some small initiation having taken place. Do I dare to believe that one day we will drive through 'our' country?

May/June 1988

Green Politics

Save the Planet

BARBARA WARD

THE CONSERVING SOCIETY may seem in one sense a very strange subject to consider because, if there is one order of life we do not *have* today, it is certainly a conserving society. We are living at the end of a period during which more has been wasted, more has been thrown away, more has been violently disrupted than in the whole of human history. Nor is there any precedent for the scale of our interventions. Nitrogen oxides from—among other things—coal burning and nitrogen fertilizer use and our freon aerosols could damage the critical ozone layer in the planet's atmospheric shield. We look like depleting our billennial reserves of fossil fuels in no more than a couple of centuries. Half the grain in the world is grown on lands made precarious by the pressures of over-cultivation, soil erosion and uncertain water supplies. And, in the next twenty years, we may add two billion more human beings to increase these pressures—an especially sobering thought when we recall that, if we allow *homo sapiens* a span of 500,000 years on this planet, the first billion was reached only in the early nineteenth century.

Yet it may be that the sheer scale of these vast changes, brought about in large measure by a steadily intensified application of science and technology to every aspect of human existence, is beginning to bring with it as great an upheaval in the field of human thought and vision. We are now emerging from our gigantic efforts with the beginnings of a fundamental change of ideas comparable perhaps to the scale of new thinking unleashed by the Renaissance.

We are all beginning to be increasingly aware of a profound and deepening conflict on a world scale that has only begun to take clear shape in this last decade of the 70s. On the one hand, for the very first time in human history it has become an accepted dogma of most of the human race that there shall be equality between human beings, that colonialism is not a permissible political system, that imperialism belongs to the past and that what we are trying to create is a planetary society in which all may enjoy dignity, equality and freedom. This is a fantastic change from the past because, as we know from human history since near the beginning of settled urban society in Sumer and Akkad five thousand years ago, the 'law' of international life has been imperial struggle and power. From Sumeria, Assyria and the Hittites to the Persians, Greeks and Romans, through the great invasions from the Steppes and the civil war in China, the experience of mankind has been the violent, predatory competition of rival centres of power. The Buddha's picture of earthly existence as a 'melancholy wheel' calls to our minds blind cycles of violence, conquest, triumph, decay, collapse and renewed conquest. These phases of human triumph and human collapse seemed as inevitable as the revolving seasons or the movements of the planets. Nobody thought it wrong or peculiar that the Romans should succeed the Greeks and the Greeks did not think it odd that they should take over from the Persians. There was no feeling that something was going on that was politically unacceptable or morally wrong.

Now, in the twentieth century, the world is acquiring a new insight—that enslavement, colonialism and inequality are contrary to the nature of the universe, or as we would say, to the will of God. This is one of the great new beginnings in human history. Its moral roots lie, I believe, in the Greek tradition of citizenship and the Jewish tradition of moral responsibility. But it is in Christian Europe that elected assemblies, the limits of monarchical power, the issue of freedom of conscience and the rule of law were most strenuously debated, achieved, defeated and renewed—from Magna Carta to 1776.

But the level of debate and action was still city and state. Naked power ruled world relationships and, by a supreme paradox, the Europeans who were debating the great issues of freedom and equality at home were also providing yet another example of imperial conquest in the world at large.

In the last four hundred years, from Vladivostok to Valparaiso, they took over everything they could lay their hands on, settled stretches of country that were empty, made other bits empty that were not empty. They set up a colonial empire based on the economic subjugation of the dependent peoples. They opened up mines and plantations to serve their own economies. Trade was the chief spur to expansion.

Yet, by a paradox, these same colonialists, by virtue of their domestic debates on freedom, responsibility and equal rights, created the anti-colonial movement, the first human acceptance that the freedoms claimed *within* national societies apply to the planetary community as a whole. Just as trade, science, technology and communications were creating an interdependent world society, the ideal that it should be a society of equal partners grew in irresistible force. Politically that ideal has been all but realized. Economically and socially it is, as we well know, still so far from achievement that the world's division of wealth—eighty per cent and more for the quarter of the world who live in the ex-imperial countries—has not changed much in spite of fantastic increases in economic growth in the last two or three decades. In fact, the greatest international debate of our day—the debate on the New International Economic Order—has at its root the plea that the political acts of emancipation (which are not yet complete) should be followed by the full economic and social emancipation which can come only in a co-operative world order recognizing the same obligations, the same justice, opportunity and equity as domestic society.

In the middle of this passionate debate a wholly new set of problems confronts us, creations of our new knowledge and science and power. Our starting point is the revolutionary change I have already mentioned. With our new knowledge, new medicines and cures, we have so accelerated the rate of population growth that at the minimum there will be two billion more people, largely in the Third World, in the next two decades. Thus just when we are making fundamental claims of equity and opportunity for humanity, the numbers who have the right to make these claims are enormously increasing. So we come starkly up against a new, entirely unforeseen question. If people are to be fed, to be healthy, literate and employed, the resources involved are infinitely greater than in a world of uncaring poverty and domination. In fact are the needed physical resources going to be available?

Let us begin with the fundamental resource on which we have built our bonanza of a society and economy over the last twenty-five years—fossil fuels. Half the world's more accessible oil reserves have already been consumed in a century. Other fossil fuels will last longer but their ultimate exhaustion is not in doubt. No less basic than energy is the problem of expanding food supplies. In parts of Africa, in the mountainous areas of the Third World, even on land becoming steadily more urbanized everywhere, the signs of land shortage are appearing. As growing pressures of people press ineluctably on these exposed soils and search there both for food and fuel, forests are cut, soil erodes, flooding increases and thus the very basic means of meeting the demands of this enlarged humanity are being undermined by the sheer pressures upon them.

Thus at one and the same time we are on the one hand looking to the vision of a humanity which will share its resources, a humanity which will accept a measure of equality and justice and recognize itself as a responsible planetary society, while on the other we see emerging the deadlock that perhaps there will not be the physical resources to turn vision into reality.

This is a debate which did not exist fifteen years ago. This is a subject that was not discussed, say, at Uppsala quite simply because it had not yet emerged. But it is now the framework of the world's agenda of the late 70s and the 80s. Upon our ability to take this contradiction and resolve it in human and in moral terms depends, I believe, the survival of the planet, because it has within it the stuff of ferocious conflict.

There will be no stopping the demand for equality. There will be no check on the demand for human respect. There will be no quiet acceptance of resources so skewed that overeating and overdrinking are prime health problems in wealthy countries and such tragic starvations as the Sahel are repeated and repeated among the poor.

A vast debate has grown up round this conflict and, if I may be forgiven a very trivial description, I would say that it is between optimists and pessimists that we can see some of the main lines of the debate. The optimists on the whole fit well in to the mood and spirit of the last three hundred years. They are the children of Francis Bacon, who believed in the use of science for the improvement and betterment of man's estate and the accomplishing 'of all things possible'. They are the children of the Renaissance in their faith in rational solutions to human problems. They are still children of that great vision of progress which from the eighteenth century came to dominate the Western view of man's destiny, the vision of an ever greater scientific ability to command nature, of an ever greater ability to meet the fundamental physical needs of man—and conceivably some of his psychological ones as well—and to go forward to new triumphs of knowledge and will.

Let us look at one or two concrete examples of how 'the optimists' dismiss warnings about pressures and shortages and the need for a new sense of responsibility and sharing as simply 'a failure of nerve', a lack of confidence in the tremendous achievements of the recent centuries. I would put now in the very front rank of the optimists all those who believe that energy, the use of energy, is the solution to the provision of resources and that in the plutonium fuelled fast-breeder reactor and later, in fusion power, we have the certainty of almost unlimited energy. With this scale of energy there can be no long-term shortage because we shall have the power to make anything out of anything. Silicon is capable of an infinitude of uses and what, after all, is silicon but the second most common element, combined with oxygen in the sands of the ocean and the sands of the sea? Sand is not likely to run out very soon, especially if we throw in the Sahara. And what is true of sand can be true of granite and common rock. So long as the energy problem does not check us, the other problems of resources can be solved by extracting the needed minerals from the poorest ores or even from seawater—thanks to the enormous creativity of our steadily widening scientific command.

But for heaven's sake, say the pessimists, consider what your programmes entail. With the fast-breeder reactor you are proposing to base your energy systems on a lethal poison that can also be used to make nuclear bombs—plutonium—and although you argue that the reactors themselves will both produce and consume all this plutonium in the processes of electricity generation, and although you may invent all manner of new gadgets for keeping it from the terrorist, you are overlooking a fundamental fact. All round the world, the steadily growing number of establishments producing the needed fuels and equipment will be manned by some of the most intelligent and highly trained young people on the planet. And already we know from the Baader Meinhoff group that for some of them, this lethal cancer-causing element with its half life of 25,000 years (quite apart from other as lethal but more transient nuclear poisons) will be seen not as the fuel required for a world-wide bonanza in more energy but as an indispensable instrument in bringing the whole system to an end. Why? Because they regard modern society as infamous and its destruction the only solution for dedicated radicals.

It is because of this internal threat that so much of the reassurance we are being offered by nuclear scientists has such a hollow ring. Even if you can store nuclear wastes in undisturbable rock formations—or invent such safety areas —and go on piling up more and more of them, what is the guarantee if the very people who control the safety systems are those who are out to see they do not work? Here, say the pessimists, is the fundamental risk. You cannot trust the custodians. When a whole shipment of uranium was 'lost' in transit a few years ago, high officials in one of the international agencies were found to be involved.

The case for caution in our use of science is not, of course, confined to energy. I have taken energy as the key simply because energy is the basis of most other scientific breakthroughs and applications. But one would also have to say that in the whole of the evolutionary process the carbon-chlorine bond which plays a leading role in the modern chemical industry—it is, for instance, at the root of many plastics, pesticides and drugs—is barely known in nature. It is as though in the long process of evolution it had been abandoned as one which was not wholly advantageous to the continuance and improvement of organic life. We are using a vast number of chemicals with this bond—DDT, PVC, PCBs, Kepone and the dioxin released at Seveso all belong to this group. Nor is it an isolated case. In the United States and parts of Europe, researchers are drawing up 'cancer maps' in which particular forms of cancer are linked to chemicals in the air and the industries which are producing them. This is an entirely new fact, unknown ten years ago and it must be admitted that our knowledge and testing are still very imprecise. But there *is* evidence of widespread increases in different forms of cancer and there is growing evidence that the introduction of wholly new and inadequately tested chemicals may be at the root of this stealthy undermining of basic human health.

There is no less pessimism when we turn to the functioning of the world economy. The most fundamental are undoubtedly the still largely unchanged economic and social consequences of the long colonial years. Pessimists can point out that in spite of all the confidence in the 'trickle down' theory of wealth from richer to poorer or in the stages of growth through which nations in turn will pass—and indeed, some of the ex-colonial areas have achieved rates of expansion twice that of the nineteenth century—the fact remains that after twenty-five years of the largest spurt of economic growth that our planet has ever seen, the proportion in which this wealth is divided between the established, ex-imperial 'North' and the developing 'South' has hardly changed at all. Something like eighty per cent of the wealth is controlled by the peoples of the industrialized North; eighty to ninety per cent of the trade; ninety-three per cent of the industry; nearly one hundred per cent of research skills and institutions. The conclusion, they argue, is obvious. Peace is a dream and delusion. We shall soon be confronting an age of revolt, of revenge, an age in which the present orderly search for a new economic order by negotiation and compromise turns into an angry, destructive and terrorist chaos from which the final confrontation of nuclear war may all too easily emerge.

This is the pretty state of the world economy at this moment. It clearly prompts the corresponding political problem. Are we reaching in the relations between states and peoples, a genuine point of no return? Are the despairers right? Will our world, as the Bible foretold, go up in flames because, after all, the human race has been given no guarantee of foolproof survival if they behave like fools. On the contrary, for the greedy, the thoughtless, the arrogant, God's judgement has already gone forth: 'Thou fool, this night thy soul shall be required of thee.' So do we give our verdict for despair? Do we foresee the ending of this whole strange experiment? Will the great trinity of the last three hundred years—science, economy, nation—prove, after all, to offer us not progress, but extinction?

I do not want to deny the extremity of our crisis. Yet I profoundly believe that the final verdict does not lie with despair. Nor do I think the reasons for this belief to be simply a gritting of one's teeth, a tightening up of the emotional muscles in expectation of a fatal blow. There are, I am certain, rational grounds for modest hope and that the courage we need is not the stoical courage of facing the worst but the joyful courage bred of new possibilities, new visions and new hopes. To begin with the very simplest, the debate which I have tried to outline would simply have been inconceivable a mere two decades ago because no one, including us, would have known what we were talking about. The whole complacency of the fifties and sixties has vanished. We are beginning to see, for the first time, where our scientific and technological arrogance could be taking us. It was, after all, only in 1962 that Rachel Carson published her *Silent Spring*. When she wrote that epoch-making book it simply had not crossed the public imagination that if you took the most dangerous pesticides and herbicides and sloshed them on everything to kill off pests and weeds, you might be endangering some of the fundamental life cycles of natural beings and systems. This type of insight could not then be made for it was only beginning to be known.

Since the first great step in any effective course of curative action must be knowledge, I think we have to recognize that it is precisely the science which so many of the 'despairers' see as the villain of the piece—because it has given man too much power—is at the same time man's greatest servant because it is giving us a completely new vision of our vulnerability and our intense interdependence. It is using knowledge to defeat the possible arrogance of knowledge, and the picture it gives us of our cosmos, inconceivably vast and infinitely powerful though it may be, comes back again and again to the minuteness and fragility of the systems and organisms that actually sustain our life. No organic life began on earth at all until the oceans safeguarded minute bacteria from the searing radiation of the sun, then billennia passed while phytoplankton's minute and infinite efforts helped create an oxygen atmosphere within which plants and the animals could invade the naked rock with the sun as the source of life and energy, of forests and fields, of the extravagant variety of species contriving to survive in their niches and habitats—all in intimate dependence upon each other. At last after three billion years of life, it was ready to begin to be the home of man, the innovator, capable in greed and arrogance of cutting down forests, wasting soil and spreading deserts but equally able, working with an increasing grasp of natural things, to begin civilization itself with settled agriculture.

This picture of mingled power and delicacy little known until our own day will give a completely new background to our imagination, and it may well be that now, in these critical decades of the closing century, we may be witnessing science itself as witness not for power but for care and restraint, for matching in our economy and the interdependence which are basic facts of natural life and bringing a startling new witness—the witness of tested scientific fact—to the intimations of unity and interdependence that have harried the visions of sages, poets and prophets since the beginning of human time.

How can we deny our unity when our fossil fuel combustion and deforestation could cumulatively lead to a heating up of the world's climate by some two degrees Celsius which would mean so extensive a melting of polar ice that all the world's sea ports would be submerged? How can we cling to irresponsible unchecked sovereignty if, beyond a certain degree of use of nitrogen fertilizer, freon aerosols and coal combustion, the essential ozone in the atmospheric shield might be depleted, leaving our whole species open to new risks of skin cancer?

And we should notice one point. Those changes are not single vast cataclysms. They are cumulative—a little more coal or oil burnt each year, more aerosols in use, more thermal pollution from increasing numbers of power stations. Separately, they might cause no upheaval. But they add to each other —just as nuclear wastes would continuously and irreversibly grow—and then comes the point established by science in all its clarity and risk virtually in our own time—the point of the 'threshold', the degree of heat, waste, pollution and radio-activity or chemical transformation beyond which reversal is no longer possible because the species, the system, the habitat has been, by almost imperceptible steps, irretrievably destroyed.

To all our arrogance, to all our overwhelming confidence, to our human pride, science brings the quiet concept of the threshold—the one step too far beyond which there can be no more repair. And if *all* do not exercise restraint, the efforts of the few do not avail. This is the new vision of unity.

November/December 1978

Green Spirit

MAURICE ASH

WE HEAR ON EVERY SIDE —even, at last, in Britain—that all the parties are seeking the green vote. One may be forgiven for being the more on one's guard. The superficiality of it all—the mouthing by party leaders of slogans ('We do not inherit the earth: we borrow it from our children', etc.) that once had the ring of truth when spoken by those who minted them ten or twenty years ago —this is not so much what is distressing, as the threat to the spirit of the green movement. For, paradoxically, the green movement itself has lost, if not its way, certainly its momentum. The conditions for a hijack exist.

Were this just a question of the force of that movement passing into the mainstream of society, one would not have cause for complaint. Certainly, purism about 'greenness' should not enter into the question. But one remembers how, once, Christianity was suborned by Rome—how it was used by Constantine and his successors—and one is troubled.

Christianity, which marked a shift in the comprehension of an equally ravaged world, was hopelessly (and murderously) divided between the Athanasians and the Arians—between belief in the Trinity as the model of the reality, and the indivisibility of God: between the authority of the Church, and of inner truth—so that in its division it became the pawn of a rotten Empire. It did not save or change that Empire, but condoned its dying spasms. The analogy between that piece of history and our situation today is not so far-fetched. It is less the residual strength of a threatened civilization than the weakness of the alternative to it that accounts for how things now stand.

Now, when I speak of the 'green movement' I am talking of the political and social dimension of the new paradigm of thought. Its prophet was, above all, Schumacher—though there were others as important as he in forging the mould. This paradigm itself, of course, is profoundly influenced by the new physics of quantum mechanics—*pace* the 'non-observing self' long known to Buddhist thought—as also by the later philosophy (after his recantation) of Wittgenstein, by ecology, and so forth; and the green movement stands to it all in much the same relationship as Hobbes (and hence the nation state) once stood to Galileo and his laws of motion. But the division in the green movement is as persistent as that which has benighted each succeeding shift of pattern, from the time of Christianity itself onwards.

I am referring, in the first instance, to the strain of millenarianism strongly evident in the green movement. This idea of a new age, of a second coming, is perhaps endemic in the West. Our tradition, it almost seems, cannot do without divine intervention if harmony by the will of God is to be attained in life on earth. This notion, after all, is virtually inherent in that of God itself:

certainly of a divinized humanity. It could be said to be the motive force of Christian culture and hence that, however illusory it might be, we have no option but to embrace it. To do otherwise, after all, would be to wipe the slate clean, to deny our culture and its true riches: and that surely, we could not do. Yet this question will not leave us in peace, and if merely to vary the pattern were only to compound the problem—if, even in a hundred years' time, it were to make our last condition still worse than our first, and the disharmony of humankind in the midst of creation yet greater—then perhaps some other force than millenarianism must be found.

To put it differently, perhaps Toynbee was right in saying that the most important event of the twentieth century has been the coming of Buddhism to the West. I do not say this to proselytize (I would not know how to do so myself, though I would take issue with those Western liberals who seem to have put on the mantle of the missionaries in decrying any other culture than their own), but I say it only to underscore the scale of the problem. Nor would I be diverted by any talk of the essential unity of all faiths: for by their fruits they shall be known. I only want to avow that, scratch many a 'green', and you'll find a millenarian underneath: and that, not only is this off-putting to a sympathetic public, but—as the record of European green politics all too clearly shows— distasteful to many another 'green', not least those with a different notion of a green heaven. It also makes the green movement a somewhat prickly lot to handle.

To this main strain of apocalyptic green thought, of course, other facets could be added. There is, for instance, the school of Armageddon which, though it has enormously raised our consciousness of nuclear war, makes any calm discussion about international affairs impossible; and there are those hostile to new technologies, of themselves—although to them some credit is due for having counterbalanced the once general belief in the technological fix. However, the other side of the division in the green movement is represented just by all the fragments of which it is compounded. The isolation of these activities each from the other—though all attest to some important common ground, some change of climate—is as much a structural weakness as is millenarianism.

The weakness of this one-eyed, one-off approach to green issues—be it the protection of wildlife, or advocacy of open government, or opposition to Cruise missiles—is not just that it leaves untouched the heart of the matter, the roots of our present condition: but rather that, being itself precisely unecological, it even aggravates our general condition. Protectors of the countryside, for instance, care little for the cities, and understand them and their inhabitants less: whilst protagonists of open government by parliamentary decree leave unasked the abiding question of the centralizing forces in our society.

Categorically, this is not to imply that to all social questions there is one, and only one, green solution. The balance between wildlife and human satisfaction, for instance, will always be disputable. What matters is the balance itself, rather than Descartes' assertion that 'Man should become the Lord and Master of Nature.' The corruption, however, within the bud of any one-eyed green campaign is, as it was in classical times, with those 'forever seeking after some new thing': namely, in its appropriation by the sensationalizing 'media'. For the shallow knowledge that very word bespeaks conveys no communication of change: no change of pattern, that is, for that must come simultaneously at many related points. Inevitably, therefore, it must come out of our personal depths. It was, after all, the strength of Schumacher that he could see the whole —the technological, the social, the philosophical: all of a piece. Those greens who cannot see the whole are flawed.

Between millenarianism, then, and at best a sort of green pragmatism, what course is open? This question might helpfully be put another way. In our times we have virtually invented 'the environment'. However, does this signify for us a paradise lost, or is it merely necessary in order to provide the context for some meaning in our lives? I would opt for the latter: and I would do so because, for me, it is the replacement at the centre of our lives of meaning by knowledge that accounts for our presently untenable predicament ('alienation' is perhaps a more established mode of discourse for all this). The point is that by our knowledge we have but fragmented the world and, the trust we put in providence having long since faded, the task is to achieve coherence again. This implies neither the making of Utopia, nor mere practicality. It signifies, rather, the discovery of another way of life, one which would be implicate in our ordinary practice.

The politics of knowledge, let us be clear, is concerned with the distribution of the fruits of technology—all within a context which assures that the power of that technology rests with the state. In so doing, for instance, it determines what passes for 'education', for it is as fodder for the machine that this kind of politics treats of young people. And if the politics of knowledge generates (as it does) both irremediable dislocations of social structure—like unemployment and inflation—and concomitant personal irresponsibility towards the settings upon which we are dependent, well, this is only to be expected of a dualistic culture like ours, in which the very notion of knowledge derives from the fragmentation of matter. In what, then, might a converse politics of meaning consist?

Meaning lies in pattern. A politics of meaning, therefore, must lie in the search for patterns of life that bestow meaning. This speaks of the importance of connections: it says that it must be evident to all involved with such a politics how any one thing bears upon another. Thus, for example, in such a politics education would not be an abstraction imposed from outside, determined by 'subjects' into which life is most dubiously divided, but would stem from wheresoever it was practised. This is as much as to talk about community. Yet this must not be confused with 'community politics', as it is now practised, for that sort of politics takes the state as given and operates with whatever is left over from it: whereas a politics of meaning must precisely question the state itself—that is, the nation state, which is the given of our political life—as the creature, par excellence, of the politics of knowledge.

A politics of meaning, in other words, is essentially constitutional. It must be concerned with those structures most propitious for a green world. But this does not imply some once-for-all constitutional change; it does not imply that, within some newly achieved structures, the old politics of getting and spending can be resumed. Rather, it implies that the constitutional process itself must become the continuing stuff of politics.

Such a process is simply one of putting things in their right and proper order: it is therefore a politics of which an aesthetic sense is at the heart. This virtually proposes itself, then, as a politics of place. To comprehend the connections of things is the prerogative of place, of local life. In Britain it is one of our grander self-deceptions that we have local government. We have no such thing. We have rather, certain largely disconnected agencies of the state, subsumed under the titles of ancient earldoms revived about a hundred years ago for the purpose, once again, of serving the crown's administration. As the inherent contradictions of the nation state have mounted, however, so must that institution seek to keep control by using the one instrument that supplies its ultimate rationale: an instrument of measurement—namely, money. And so the hollowness at the heart of local life becomes more and more exposed. In the result, all Britain has to show the world is the inexcusable and brutal ugliness of its cities, empty even of self-sustaining life: cities in which people have been snared in pursuit of their appetites for gain, and which now can only be abandoned to dereliction.

Perhaps this seems like a counsel of despair? If so, I would first say that it is one of the greatest disservices we do ourselves to suppose—no doubt, out of the mechanistic cast of our minds—that all social problems are subject to solution. We are learning better in this respect, fortunately, but we still have a long way to go in simple realism. Secondly, and in all realism, more is likely to result from the crude collapse of the old way of life than from any painting of the new. Surely, we shall live to see the dissolution of the ministries!—for, by and large, they no longer believe in themselves. However, I can also see all manner of hope springing up around us: from the growth of local 'amenity' societies (often much to the displeasure of elected members of 'local government'—but, one wonders, do these ever pause to question the course of their own inadequacy?) to signs that the citizens even of Glasgow are beginning to take their city back from its commissars.

So what is all-important, I suggest, is that we keep our sense of direction: and the direction of green politics is local life—together, conversely, with the end of the nation state as we know it. Participation in the politics of the nation state should be not wantonly to disrupt it—for how could one excuse the compounding of misery?—but to take away its powers as they bear on local life. Above all, it should not be to patch up that state itself, for it is fundamentally flawed. So there is a role here for greens of all parties to engineer an abdication of the authority of the state as we know it, and so contrive another of those quiet English revolutions of which so much of our history has been composed.

All this may seem far from the environment—or from whales, or co-operative rather than competitive business, or other ostensibly green causes. If so, then I suggest this is symptomatic of how far dependent we have become upon 'them' at the centre of politics to do things for us. It is this dependence that is the source of our problems: of the loss of control—responsibility, indeed—that underlies environmental pollution, etc., and that bespeaks the extra-ordinary centralization of affairs in Britain. The 'environment', taken all in all, is nothing but the recovery of control over our own lives. What we do with that control, however, is the next question.

One is talking, in basic terms, of the replacement of the nation by the local state. This is not to propose the political restoration of a whole set of small nations. The nation state itself was largely a function of common language as that language became the vehicle of the power of 'knowledge'. The technology that accompanied this will not go away, and where its scale is commensurate with the difference between one nation state and another—that is, pre-eminently in the area of 'defence'—no doubt our present institutions must remain. But this technology and this power have dragged in their wake all manner of functions that belong to the small scale of life, and it is against this deprivation that the rebellion of the local state must occur.

However, this is to speak but of the skeleton of change. If the nation state is bound somehow to persist, it must do so, not so much in parallel with the local state—though confederate forms might become more common—but as an accepted anachronism to a different cast of our minds. It is the attempt of the green movement to live with the nation state that largely accounts for its inner confusions. The nation state is the political expression of a dualistic cast of mind, and all its disjunctions are inimical to ecology. The shibboleth of 'democracy', atomistic in concept as it is, is simply what makes the scale of the nation state tolerable. The cast of mind, then, concomitant with local political life is radically different from that which now dominates our existence. The passions governing the future will be quite other than those to which we now give precedence.

Whilst the dominant values of a dualistic culture are good and evil (for these predicate the distinctiveness of persons from the world), the predominant value of an ecological society is what is beautiful, seemly, 'of good report' (for this concerns belonging). This, in short, indicates the chasm to be crossed if our civilization is to continue. We shall have to learn to think qualitatively again, rather than quantitatively. Instead of 'growth' being the criterion of policy, appropriateness must be our concern.

As well as rationality we must admit intuition: inward knowledge (the gnostic) must balance external. The female principle must play as much part in our affairs as the male. The processes of an ecological society are necessarily non-dualistic; and this dictates a balance between the person and the world that only the structures of local life could accommodate. We must know and be known as now we cannot be.

The values of the old order have all but run their course. The structures built on them may end with a bang or a whimper—with a collapse of the credit structure of the Western world, or a slow disillusionment with materialism. Meantime, in this unreal kind of twilight, green politics, lacking the structures in which it could flower, may seem in eclipse. But underneath, in the privacy of people's minds, the readiness for change is growing. We must make sure that when it comes it is well founded.

September/October 1984

Green = Ecology?

JONATHON PORRITT

AT 12.45 ON SEPTEMBER 21ST 1985 the Ecology Party changed its name to the Green Party. For a party whose contribution to history has as yet been a little slim, this was undoubtedly an historic moment.

For those of us who have been pushing to change for the last four years or more, the relief was overwhelming. The simple fact is that 'ecology' is too much a mouthful on the doorstep: too scientific, too sterile, too middle-class. It allowed for none of the compassion, the hopefulness or the 'warm embrace' of green politics.

Moreover, it had long since become apparent that 'Green' could not (and should not) remain the exclusive preserve of the Ecology Party: the word is now in considerable demand, covering a multitude of different meanings. There is much to be gained from this, in that widespread use and increased familiarity enhances the credibility of green politics. But potentially there is far more to be lost, in that the 'poaching' by other parties may become so sophisticated that the difference between radical, holistic green politics and the reformist, if not reactionary environmentalism of the major parties could be entirely obscured. As Tony Jones, the Green Party's Press Secretary, put it: 'If we don't change our name, Green will mean what William Waldegrave and Bill Rogers want it to mean. We now have a classic opportunity to put all the other major parties on the run.'

Throughout the debate, many dissenting voices were raised—mainly by those who felt that so much had been achieved over the last ten years in the name of the Ecology Party, that a change would just confuse the voters and the media. And being a Party that tends to take its decentralist aspirations fairly seriously some questioned the right of *any* central body to dictate to local groups on an issue of such importance.

But one suspects that their real concern ran deeper than that. From its very inception, the Ecology/Green Party has always stated unequivocally that *all* its policies flow naturally from certain fundamental ecological principles concerning the way we live and our relationship with other life-forms on a strictly finite planet. Ecology may be a mouthful on the doorstep, but it provides much of the intellectual and scientific authority on which the Ecology/Green Party depends. Will the primacy of those principles now be lost in a welter of all-purpose, vote grabbing greenery?

I suspect not. And the reason why not is to be found in the chaos and confusion that currently exists within the German Green Party. The German Greens do *not* acknowledge the primacy of ecology, but see it rather as just one part of their politics, of equal importance to sustainable economics, grassroots democracy, human rights, peace etc. This mattered little in the early days when the business of establishing the 'broad church' of the German Greens kept fundamental differences in check; but now it is the differences that dominate, and there is little sense of a political, intellectual or spiritual centre to the German Greens today. It has taken some getting used to (for success and newsworthiness are compelling qualities) but most Greens in the UK now recognize that the German model is emphatically not for us.

So we are likely to continue with a Green Party that still stands four-square on its original ecological principles (and thus rejects the whole spectrum of conventional left/right politics), and that from now on will be even more determined to impose its definition of green and repudiate those of other parties. This is a wholly constructive and useful debate and it should be welcomed by greens of every persuasion. And developments in both the Labour Party and the Tory Party indicate that they too will not be averse to getting their oar in.

Just prior to their Conference, the Labour Party brought out its *Charter for the Environment*, a document full of huffing and puffing (the constant reference to 'sustainable growth', Labour's equivalent of the equally meaningless SDP's 'green growth', was particularly irksome), but a real breakthrough for all that. It is good to see one of the major parties at least acknowledge that caring for the environment is not a threat to employment prospects, but rather one of the best ways of generating good work left to us in a declining industrial economy. And a further significant advance was achieved when the Labour Party, inspired by the earlier example of the TGWU, voted overwhelmingly against nuclear power: all it needs now is a two-thirds majority next year for this to become official party policy.

It was no doubt these developments which encouraged Doug Hoyle to proclaim to all and sundry that the Labour Party was *the* Green Party—a claim which was systematically taken to pieces by no less a 'green' than Mr William Waldegrave, newly promoted Minister for the Environment, Countryside and Local Government, in a witty and powerful speech at the Tory Conference.

'One of the most enjoyable games for me,' he said, 'is to imagine who is the most incongruous politician who can be persuaded by his PR Department to put on his green wellington boots and say straight to camera that he is against pelting otters with acid rain. It is hardly possible to imagine a more absurd spectacle than Mr Hoyle standing up in Bournemouth and announcing that the Labour Party is the Green Party. If I were a member of the Green Party, I would be calling upon it to sue Mr Hoyle for defamation.'

Talk of the pot calling the kettle black—or, in this case, grey! For despite Mr Waldegrave's sturdy efforts to persuade Mrs Thatcher of the importance of green issues, the government's record remains little short of disastrous. There is just so much 'greenspeak' a politician can get away with before being taken to task, and there are many Tory MPs who are going to have to address themselves to this challenge before rather than after the next general election.

January/February 1986

Politics or Real Change?

CLIVE PONTING

THE WORLD IS FACING A CATASTROPHIC DISASTER brought about by a whole variety of causes: growing population, increasing exploitation of non-renewable resources, the use of advanced technology with its massive social consequences, the threat of nuclear power (let alone nuclear weapons), huge damage to the environment with incalculable long-term effects, the appalling maldistribution of power and resources between the First and the Third Worlds. The list is almost endless. All of these problems are regularly discussed in the media and at major world conferences yet the amount of effective action taken is minimal. There are two reasons for this. The first lies in the perception of the problem by the overwhelming majority of people. The second in the reality of the political system.

Many thoughtful people, who are not subscribers to the green approach, are well aware of the problems outlined above. But they do not see them as the inevitable result of a system that could not operate in any other way. Rather they see the problems as manifestations of the odd malfunctioning of an otherwise efficient system. The consequence is that they believe that ad hoc and partial solutions can be found that fall short of any radical restructuring. A particular habitat can be saved, more aid can be given to the Third World, the dumping of nuclear waste near their homes stopped. All of these actions have a beneficial effect but they are a mere drop in the ocean compared with the magnitude of the problem. The political system is prepared to concede these limited and partial demands simply because they do not involve fundamental alteration to the existing system.

The function of a political system in any country in the world is to regulate, but not to alter radically, the existing economic structure and its linked power relationships. The great illusion of politics is that politicians have the ability to make whatever changes they like. In practice they are constrained by a whole range of forces and institutions many of which are outside of their control. On the surface, politicians do make changes. Nobody could deny that Thatcherism has been an attack on many groups, for example the educational system. But the aim here is not to try and make it do something radically different. The aim of the Thatcherite 'reforms' is to force the educational system to be more responsive to the needs of the current economic system and to produce people who will fit into that system and not question it. Similarly the Labour Party's nationalization of the railways and coal mines might have seemed an attack on private economic power. In practice it was a matter of rescuing from the 'dustbin of capitalism' industries that the capitalist system had destroyed and which would have collapsed without state intervention. In other areas, such as the law, the armed forces and the police, politicians have little power to affect these largely unaccountable institutions.

On a larger canvas what real control do the politicians in any one country have over the operation of the international monetary system, the pattern of world trade with its built-in subordination of the Third World or the operation of multi-national companies? These institutions and the dominating mechanism that underlies them—the profit motive as the sole measure of success— are essentially out of control and operating on auto-pilot.

In a deep sense, therefore, the purpose of politics is to validate the existing system. The politics of the Soviet Union and other communist states makes this obvious with their one party, one candidate system in which the vote is used to demonstrate acceptance of the current organization. But is politics in the West really very different? Do the opposition parties offer a real choice or just a slightly different way of running the system which is usually not borne out in practice when they get into government?

All of this has profound implications for green politics and the question of whether the political system provides a route for the implementation of green policies. The first problem in Britain is that under the current electoral system the Greens stand virtually no chance of ever gaining power without proportional representation (PR). Neither the Conservatives nor Labour are prepared to introduce PR because the current electoral system works to their advantage and therefore they see no reason to change it. But what would happen if the Greens did get into parliament? The example of the German Greens is perhaps salutary. They are now badly split between the 'realists', who are prepared to compromise with the existing system in the hope of achieving some improvements, and the 'fundamentalists' who refuse to make any compromises.

This illustrates one of the laws of politics in Western societies. In order to gain power, groups have to become more respectable so as to pose less of a challenge to the system so that by the time they gain power they have effectively become neutered. The Labour Party provides a classic example of this process. Begun as a movement of genuinely radical thinkers who wanted to change the way society was organized, it rapidly altered. Although still, in theory, committed to fundamental change, such as total nationalization, it fought elections on a gradualist and limited programme until it was reduced to Herbert Morrison's dictum 'Socialism is what a Labour government does'. Now it offers little more than a slightly more egalitarian way of running existing institutions.

Once in power any green government would face an insuperable problem. The very system of government makes real solutions impossible. A vivid illustration at the moment is the inner cities. The problems here are complex and multi-faceted involving every form of social and economic institution from education to roads, planning, health care and housing policies, to unemployment and welfare problems. If ever a problem required a holistic solution this is it. But Whitehall can only work in terms of departmental responsibilities. The result is that a dozen departments, each with their own vested interests, are trying, with no great enthusiasm, to devise a coherent policy while protecting their own interests. Not surprisingly they will fail.

On a larger scale it is worth considering the problem of the destruction of the tropical forests in Brazil. Just how can we stop this assault which threatens the climate and eco-system throughout the world? In Brazil powerful interests, that have a major say in government, have a vested interest in continuing because they can make a quick profit. They do not have to bear any long-term costs for the damage they wreak. But more important there is no mechanism whereby the rest of the world could make Brazil act against its short-term interests for the benefit of the world as a whole.

The outlook therefore is, I believe, gloomy. There appears to be little way to stop an economic system that is out of control. In the not too distant future the inherent contradictions of the system—the destruction of the resources it needs in the long-term and the collapse of whole eco-systems (we are already seeing the first signs in sub-Saharan Africa)—will pose real questions about its ability to continue. The reaction of the political and economic system will, almost certainly, not be to change direction but to try ever harder to make the system go on working. This will inevitably mean greater pressure within society for people to adapt their lives to the needs of the system and even less tolerance of dissent. We will move towards a more authoritarian democracy, of which there are currently plenty of signs in Britain.

Is there therefore no hope at all? I cannot pretend to be optimistic about the future but if there is hope then it has to be at a much deeper level than politics. The real changes have to be made not in politics but in human values.

This is not to decry green politics, but rather to accept its limitations. For the foreseeable future it can be little more than a mechanism for publicizing green ideas, putting them in front of a wider audience and helping them gain acceptability. All of this is, of course, important. Neither does a need for new values prohibit action to try and improve the current situation even in small ways. Groups and organizations that are working in this field from Oxfam to Intermediate Technology and the organic movement in agriculture need support. Practical action is also possible by trying to start new enterprises from organic farms and smallholdings to co-operatives and many forms of community living; all attempting, in however small a way, to think and operate differently from the existing framework.

There can of course be no guarantee of ultimate success. These seeds, and they can be little more at this stage, may never grow into a new way of organizing society and the economy. The seeds may fall on very stony ground and the conditions for their survival may disappear under the pressure of a conformist, authoritarian society struggling for its existence under pressure from a collapsing economic and political system and ecological disaster. But one thing is certain. The seeds for a new and more hopeful future can come from nowhere else than the small groups that exist today.

But real, fundamental and permanent change can only come from a new set of values. This is where the contribution of E.F. Schumacher is so important. He was one of the few people to see that this provided the only secure road forward by emphasizing that politics and economics are not neutral but reflect moral values. The reason for our crisis is that the current system both reflects and helps to mould existing economic, social and political values. The majority of people are brought up today to believe that the current way of running affairs is the only possible one—that is why they so rarely question it. This is the reason why it is so difficult to use politics to change values. A Green Party in power could not change values except in a totalitarian system like the Soviet Union which consciously set out after the 1917 revolution to mould people into a new image. For a Green Party to do that would destroy the very values it enshrines.

The solution is therefore more difficult. Values must change first and then we have to hope that this can in some way be articulated into the political and economic system. Schumacher saw this clearly and this is why the concentration on him as an economist is unbalanced. He was a brilliant and original economist but just as much he was, in the widest sense, a religious thinker. Too much attention has been paid to his book *Small is Beautiful* and not enough to *Guide for the Perplexed*. The values which he saw as the most important for the new way of thinking and living: compassion, the ability to make connections and think holistically, the willingness to forego immediate gains for long-term benefits and the emphasis on real creative work and the inner nature of humankind are crucial to a new approach. They emphasize eternal questions rather than the immediate external world.

The answer to the current crisis is therefore both simple and difficult. We cannot expect existing institutions, values and ways of thinking to rescue us from the mess they have themselves created. We need instead a set of values that reflect a more humane and dignified approach to life. Without that change there will be no lasting solution to the problems that beset us, only short-term political change. These values are not new; they have existed for centuries in true religious thought but have only rarely been applied. These must be at the core of the fundamentally different green approach to life. It is not possible yet to say how this new approach can eventually be in a position to create a better world. Only the hope that it will can be there.

The green movement is therefore asking for the most difficult of all changes: a revolution that is both non-violent and which does not devour the very values it encapsulates. Perhaps that is not possible. Even if it does not succeed there is still hope. People living now will, through a programme of practical action and concentration on real and lasting values, have led happier, more useful and better balanced lives. That in itself would be no small achievement.

March/April 1988

Land Use

Perennial Agriculture

WES JACKSON

THE CONTAMINATION AND LOSS OF THE SOIL is the loss of ourselves as a people. In the USA we are now losing from two to four billion tons of soil each year, an amount equal to the loss of seven inches of soil from four million acres.

The story is as old as civilization. Two thousand years before Christ, the Tigris and Euphrates rivers of Mesopotamia watered an area so rich that early Biblical scholars believed that somewhere there was the Garden of Eden. An extensive irrigation system brought life to remarkable cities. The area today is a desert of shifting sand in and around the great buildings and monuments of Babylon.

The hillsides are bare now as they have been for centuries. The ditches which carried the lifeblood of the land are quiet and the harbours of their commerce filled in.

King Solomon, three thousand years ago, purchased so many cedars from the King of Tyre he had to marshal 80,000 lumberjacks to cut the trees and 70,000 men to skid the logs from Lebanon to build the temple. The cut area was placed under cultivation and in an historical instant, the soil began its search for a new home in the sea. Both to the east and west of this region the story is similar in all but minute details.

In the USA we suffer in part from a history of early abundance and in part from the legacy we brought from Europe, where rains are so light that soil runoff is scarcely a problem. When our ancestors landed on the virgin woodlands and prairies of our young continent, they encountered for the first time the thunderstorms and the associated quick drenchings and then went on to add such soil-exposing row crops as corn, cotton and tobacco. Fossil fuel has allowed erosion to accelerate at an ever faster pace. Huge tractors and their equipment can now completely wipe out the clear evidence of agricultural decay.

Civilization *has* brought its prophets, most of them eloquent, impassioned, knowledgeable but in a real sense, prophesy has failed. So have the organizations, including the US Soil Conservation Service. Saddest of all, perhaps, is the failure of stewardship. Mennonite farms in Kansas fare little if any better than those of their non-Mennonite neighbours. Amish farms in Pennsylvania are experiencing erosion, though not nearly so badly as their non-Amish neighbours. The most ecologically correct stewards have fields losing their soil.

This failure at agriculture is the primordial germ of the 'human condition' which philosophers and thinking people have long discussed. I believe it is the very essence of the human condition as outlined in Genesis.

As gatherers and hunters we could take our food without thought for the morrow. Early gardening changed all that but perhaps not very much at first. It is easy to imagine that in our hemisphere one group or another supplemented its diet with such annual crops as potatoes, beans, amaranth and corn, while in the old world, wheat, rice, barley, oats, etc., were featured. As the garden increased to become a field, a new global landscape was being born and with it the realization that we could no longer take without thought for the morrow. Perhaps up to seven days is all the gatherer and hunter had to actively plan for, but the serious planter had to think of an entire year, at a minimum. The biblical Joseph became famous as the first secretary of agriculture by planning on fourteen years: seven years of plenty to be followed by seven years of famine.

But with all our planning none of our cultural information was adequate to arrest the wasting away of the soil resource. Both Plato and the biblical Job knew the score, but it made little, if any, difference.

Agriculture will remain a tragedy so long as it is kept separate from the problem of the human condition. The recommendations of philosophers, economic theoreticians, social planners and anyone else worried about the human condition appear almost as random ideas of what to do next.

I don't believe that any solution which is more the product of civilization than the product of nature is trustable. We have to have both! We must study and understand what Wendell Berry calls the 'natural integrities' that *preceded* agriculture. We must find the connection between agriculture and wildness.

Henry David Thoreau, asked, 'Would it not be well to consult with Nature in the outset, for she is the most extensive and experienced planter of us all.' In his Journal of 1859 and again in his 'Huckleberries' lecture, Thoreau struck a compromise which he felt would satisfy the demands of civilization and natural order. He suggested that each town preserve 'a primitive forest' within its borders of 500 or 1,000 acres 'where a stick should never be cut for fuel, a common possession, for instruction and recreation.' This was for the purpose of people learning how *nature's economy* functions.

George Perkins Marsh, a contemporary of Thoreau, developed the rich insight that 'the equation of animal and vegetable life is too complicated a problem for human intelligence to solve, and we can never know how wide a circle of disturbance we produce in the harmonies of nature when we throw the smallest pebble in the ocean of organic life.'

With agriculture, we destroy some of the information of nature and substitute cultural information. But cultural information is incomplete, partly because the time frame of the human is never as long as the time considerations of patient nature.

I believe the Genesis version of the fall is substantially correct but I would expand it to explicitly state that the *root of our fall* is inherent in the *root of agriculture,* and the root of agriculture can be found in a garden. Small must have been beautiful in the earlier garden, but as the size of the patch increased to the size of a field the number of people engaged in the food-getting process diminished.

The cultural language necessary to keep the food coming even from the patch-type agriculture, was necessarily fine-grained. But as patches were aggregated into fields, the cultural language was inadequate to rejuvenate the area.

All the canals which had contributed to the greatness of Babylon and Canaan *did* silt up, and we can see a repeat of this history time and again down to our own time as we observe the soils which are becoming salted in southern California or in the lower stretches of the Colorado which supports great wealth and numbers.

We can get away with destroying a certain amount of nature's information and maintain high-yielding *patches* without resorting to a slave economy. Patch-type agriculture is within the limits of ecosystem redemption. Perhaps as important is that we can work the patch and not get too bored by such work and have it enhance rather than reduce our aesthetic dimension. At the patch level, both humans and nature can accommodate the products and makers of civilization in high-yielding annual crops such as rice, corn, wheat and soybeans, or carrots, spinach, broccoli, potatoes, sweet corn, green beans and the like. But when we move to the field level with any of these crops we will want, if not need, slaves as we always have. They can be human slaves, fossil or uranium energy slaves, draught animal slaves, or fields themselves as slaves, for they would be the source of alcohol energy for tractor slaves or for the draught animal. Human slavery is out. Fossil or uranium energy will soon be going out, leaving the field as the energy source and the draught animal to help us. At the field level, on sloping ground, in most cases, there is still no information system complete or compelling enough to prevent the rush of useful atoms toward the sea with each rain or insistent wind.

Our current agricultural system is nearly opposite to the original prairie or forest which features mixtures of perennials. If we could build domestic prairies we might one day have high-yielding fields which are planted once every twenty years or so.

Lately agriculture has been coasting on the sunlight trapped by floras long extinct. We pump it, process it, transport it over the countryside as chemicals, and inject it into our wasting fields as chemotherapy. Then we watch the fields respond with an unsurpassed vigour, and we feel informed on the subject of agronomics. That we can feed billions is less a sign of nature's renewable bounty and our knowledge and more a sign of her forgiveness and our discount of the future. For how opposite could the annual condition in monoculture be from what nature prefers? Roots and above-ground parts alike die every year so through much of the calendar year the mechanical grip on the soil must rely on death rather than life. Mechanical disturbance may make weed control effective, but the farm far from weatherproof. In the course of it all, soil compacts, crumb structure declines, soil porosity decreases and the loss of a wick effect for pulling moisture down diminishes. Monoculture means a decline in the range of invertebrate and microbial forms. Microbial specialists with narrow enzyme systems make such specific demands that just any old crop won't do.

We do manage some diversity through crop rotation, but from the point of view of various microbes it is probably a poor substitute for the greater diversity which was always there on the prairie or in the forest. Monoculture means that botanical and hence chemical diversity above ground is also absent, which invites epidemics of pathogens or epidemic grazing by insect populations which can spend most of their respiratory energy reproducing, eating and growing. Insects are better controlled if they are forced to spend a good portion of their energy budget buzzing around hunting, among many species in a mixture, for the plants they evolved to eat.

I think it is possible to return to a system that is at once self-renewing like the prairie or forest and yet capable of supporting the current human population.

Because of advances in biology over the last half-century, I think we have the opportunity to develop a truly sustainable agriculture based on the mixtures of perennials. This would be an agriculture in which soil erosion is so small that it is detectable only by the most sophisticated equipment, an agriculture that is chemical-free or nearly so, and certainly an agriculture that is scarcely demanding of fossil fuel. This is exactly what we are working on at our research centre, The Land. We are developing mixed perennial grain crops.

We were not surprised to read that annual crops fail to stop wind erosion approximately sixty per cent of the time. We were pleasantly surprised to learn that *perennial* grasses grown anywhere, but particularly in semi-arid climates, are the most efficient producers of granular soil structure and that when it comes to forming soil aggregates, the roots are the most active part of the grass crop, and that it is more effective than simply adding grass clippings or hay to the soil. A legume and a grass together do a better job than each growing alone.

The soil loss problem is another matter; one which ultimately boils down to how a living community is going to deal with the bombs, miniature bombs as Professor Beasley at Iowa State calls them. These rain-drop bombs measure 1.12 inch each on the average and fall at a velocity of twenty-five feet per second. On a bare field they shatter soil granules and clods, compacting the area below, reducing infiltration, creating craters and eventually carrying the detached particles seaward.

We have learned from the literature that one acre of bluestem, above ground, can hold over fifty tons of water from such bombs. This is significant, for it is not unusual out our way to have a two-inch rainstorm in thirty minutes, yielding a weight of 226 tons of water.

As we anticipate our breeding programme involving perennials, we have learned that the barriers to yield improvement through crossing of perennials are significantly fewer than the barriers which affect annuals. Wild plants, with only a moderate degree of assistance by us, respond with an overall vigour which is much higher than that demonstrated by their relatives struggling in nature. We have nine foot tall perennial sunflowers, wild senna is over five feet tall, Maximillian sunflower is loaded with blossoms far beyond what I have observed in nature.

We plan most of our experiments with two important biological questions in mind. First of all, are perennialism and high yield mutually exclusive, and secondly, can a polyculture or mixture of perennials outyield the same perennials in a monoculture? This has led us into numerous other questions. For example, there is the very important, yet so far as I can find, not asked question, 'What is a perennial?'

Another consideration important in our thinking, and probably the most radical, is the idea of introducing succession to agriculture. In annual monoculture we have successfully denied our fields the opportunity to go beyond the first stage or two of succession. Agriculture has depended upon successfully fighting what nature wants to do. But if we are serious in our enquiry of what nature will require of us, then we must be prepared to reject an agriculture based on the near complete denial of succession, except at the patch level.

Succession is an ecosystem's way of obeying a fundamental of biology. We know that for all levels of biological organization there is a juvenile stage, a mature stage, and the inevitable senescence and death. It happens to cells. It happens to tissues, organs, organ systems, and to the individual. It also happens to species, which evolve, often with a flourish, settle down and then become extinct, changing into something else or dying out. It seems to be a property of life, part of the great round. When it happens to plant and animal communities we call it succession. I think that revolutionary agriculturists will have to have it central in all considerations.

I began to think seriously about ecological succession in agriculture as we considered putting together mixtures of species which would simulate the tall, mid, and short grass prairies. All plants in the mix need not be seed producers but may be there for other purposes such as nitrogen-fixation or to serve as a host for a critical mass of certain insects which stand ready to nip a potential epidemic of other insects. We looked over our inventory of plants in the herbary and picked some for an experiment. We noted, however, that the aggressive types, such early stage invaders as Illinois bundle flower or Maximillian sunflower, had few weeds in the plot material. On the other hand, the plots of the climax species, purple prairie clover, which were not weeded were mostly taken over by cheat and other weeds.

These two conditions represent extreme ends of succession on the prairie and thinking of this observation, what about the intermediate species which represent other stages between the invaders and the climax? The question now became, can *we* be participants in succession? Thinking ahead a century, perhaps some of our descendants will plant their bare fields with high-yielding luxuriant perennial mixes—aggressive species which outgrow the weeds. They would then closely follow with other species, plants with less total potential energy but with more elaborate information systems and perhaps a more efficient use of energy overall. After twenty years they would perhaps have accelerated their domestic prairie to the climax stage with a relatively high yield along the way. The presumption here is that the information system of the prairie has evolved to accept succession as a reality as much as gravity.

The problem is, where do we begin? What do *we* build on? I think that a long time ago nature gave us two important ecological concepts which became religious philosophy. These concepts centre around the idea of redemption and transcendence. On the first, nature has shown us that we can damage an area and that it will eventually redeem itself, perhaps not completely, perhaps not for a long time, but eventually and to some degree.

The idea of transcendence is one that even the most ardent zealot of reductionist science can't ignore. There is nothing about the properties of hydrogen and oxygen which gives a clue about the properties of water. The properties of both are completely transcended by what water can do. We can move up the hierarchy of the sciences and see that at every step of the way, more *is* different. As we approach the cultural level, we have a clear example in the power of transcendence in the Amish compared to the conventional farmer of today. Wendell Berry has written of the fifty-six acre Amish farm in Indiana which grossed $43,000 and netted $22,000 in one year. As Wendell sees it, the reason a conventional farmer could not do that is that as the circles widen and move away from the farm much of the harmony of the organic world is left behind, incorporating more of the non-harmonious industrial world. Useful information, much of which we are unaware of or cannot comprehend is lost. The Amish simply believe that the highest calling of God is to be stewards of the land and that this is tightly tied to an aesthetic ideal. Because economics is not foremost in their thinking, they are *able* to make sound economic decisions. By being obedient to a higher calling 'all these other things are added' unto them. This is a practical kind of transcendence that *all* can experience.

July/August 1983

[A shortened version of a talk given to the Schumacher Society of the USA]

A Man of Decorum

JOHN LANE VISITS WENDELL BERRY

WENDELL BERRY? The name was unfamiliar. In point of fact it was unknown to me when first I came across his work, almost by chance, inadvertently. The contact was a little green-covered pamphlet, some thirty pages in length, which had fallen into my hands. *The Agricultural Crisis: A Crisis in Culture*, like so many other well-intentioned texts, did not immediately strike me down. Yet within a few pages I knew, with that rush of joy with which we recognize the exceptional, that I was reading a masterpiece. I had, it seemed, stumbled across an author of undoubted substance, saying things which had to be said and saying them with a natural genius as pure and whole as Thoreau, or, to sharpen the resemblance, H. J. Massingham. The last time I had experienced this recognition was in 1973 when I read a book by an unknown German economist, E. F. Schumacher. *The Agricultural Crisis* produced a similar shock.

Who, then, was its author? He was, the pamphlet informed me, an American, a farmer, living in Port Royal who taught at the University of Kentucky. He had written three novels, four volumes of poetry and several collections of essays, in addition to *The Unsettling of America*—the book, I learned, from which the pamphlet had been extracted. This was interesting but not enough. I wanted to know more. Utterly unforeseen the chance to do so soon came my way.

I had, as it happened, already arranged to visit the States so (with a cheek which still brings blood to my face) I wrote to Mr Berry to ask if I might call to see him while I was in his country. Time was short so, in addition, I decided to 'phone the University of Kentucky to see if I could contact him direct. 'Yes,' the receptionist drawled in her strangely unfamiliar accent, Mr Berry had taught at the University but was 'one of those ecological types who do not believe in 'phones'. At this point I began to experience real doubts about the propriety of my visit. Then things happened fast. I heard from Wendell Berry courteously inviting me to stay and, on the eve of departure, the book he had mentioned in his letter, and sent by separate post, arrived at home. I opened it, a most handsome volume; *The Unsettling of America: Culture & Agriculture*, was in my hands. I read it on the flight to San Francisco; all 233 pages of it.

It is difficult to convey the qualities of a book which Gary Snyder is quoted as saying is 'about culture in the deep, ripe, sense: a nurturing habitat'. For awareness that farming cannot be considered as an issue apart from the larger culture, that agriculture is as much a spiritual discipline as a means of growing food, gives *Unsettling* (as it is affectionately called in the Berry household) its rare authority and comprehensiveness. The subject is pursued in its wholeness. The way we grow our food, treating land, resources, and ultimately people as infinitely expendable; the neglect of agriculture, the rape of the soil, which had driven millions of families from their land and 'unsettled' whole communities, the importance of memory and tradition, household and place, are the themes the book develops with an undoubted authority. For this book is not just another criticism of modern orthodox thought and practice, another worthy enquiry into the sickness of our time; *Unsettling* is written with a passion of love and hate: a love of all that is comely, convivial and fully human and a desperate and savage anger against all that is rapacious, mean and abstract in our contemporary life. It is a deeply personal and moving testament of one man's vision of the responsibilities of being alive. So that by the time I landed in Louiseville I knew my journey was worth while.

I was met by Tanya Berry, Wendell's wife. It was late on a Friday night at the wet end of March. Yet the long journey from the airport along the featureless freeway, the silent, empty, country roads, provided as perfect an introduction to what I was about to experience as I could have wished. For as the car's headlights picked out one by one the landmarks of their world —his parents' home, his brother's farm—I began to appreciate at first hand one of *Unsettling*'s most radical themes: the importance of settlement, of place, of roots; the association of tradition and experience, the enactment of connections. 'Oh love,' he has written in one of the poems I had not then read, 'Oh love, open, show me the country. Take me home.'

Home, in fact, is the small village of Port Royal four or five miles from the Berry's farm, Lanes Landing, which stands isolated on its own land. Five generations of Berrys have lived in or about this place and all but one of them, his Irish great grandfather, a cobbler and undertaker, have farmed their own land. Wendell's brother still farms in the neighbourhood, his parents live there, his seventeen year old son, Den, attends the local school and helps on the home farm. On the maternal side, the Perrys have lived there even longer, for six generations, the first Perry settling in Port Royal soon after the Revolution. Stanley Spencer's affection for Cookham was no more intense than Wendell's for Port Royal.

As we travelled Tanya told me something about their own holding where they had lived since 1964. It was, she said, seventy-five acres in size, but since much of it was both steep and wooded much of it was uncultivatable. None the less they worked a cow, a Jersey, which provided all their dairy needs, and also had eleven Cheviot sheep, four beef cows, three calves and a colony of bees. Draught horses had been used since 1973 and they slaughtered their own meat. There was no time to discuss why they stocked no poultry as I noticed we had stopped in front of their smallish wooden-paled house. Stepping out of the car, the spell of hastening, secret water went over my mind. And then, improbable, haunting, from far and wide, as if to greet me a chorus of frogs gurgling the immense activity of resurgent life. I had arrived.

I met Wendell in the morning, Sunday morning. He was much taller than I had expected, almost gangly, with inimitable strides; the gestures few, the frame vigorous, the old farming clothes appropriate for a man who worked the land. His face, too, was memorable, long and rather narrow; his eyes, bright and clear, zestful with courage. It was, I thought, the face of an intensely practical man yet intellectually serious and refined—and amused. Laughter plays a large part in their family life; laughter punctuating every seriousness.

Breakfast over, Wendell drove us, Den and I, along the road in front of their house bordering the broad Kentucky River. We were on our way to his brother's farm, a beautiful, wintry, wooden house amongst trees. His brother was a Senator absent on State business for a few days. Once in the yard father and son worked as one, quietly calling the two Belgian mares, Peggy and Nell, from their grazing to the shafts; harnessing them, buckling their leather harness, driving them into the field amongst the other standing beasts. Den drove the wagon, Wendell cut the sisal, spreading the tightly packed bales of hay in a wide arc. It was my first experience of the use of horses but not, I hope, my last.

> It's the immemorial feelings
> I like the best: hunger, thirst,
> their satisfaction; work-weariness,
> earned rest; the falling again
> from solitude into love;
> the green growth the mind takes
> from the pastures in March;
> the gaiety in the stride
> of a good team of Belgian mares
> that seem to shudder from me
> through all my ancestry.

As we were leaving the field on the journey back Wendell pointed out a distant place where a skirmish of earth at a field-entrance marked heavy use. It was not, perhaps, something I would have noticed myself. Yet Wendell's grief at this destruction, this impairment of the structure of the soil, reminded me in its sorrow of the letter written to the President by Chief Seathl of the Dwamish tribe: 'Every part of the earth is sacred to my people,' he wrote in 1855, 'Every shining pine needle, every sandy shore, every mist in the dark woods, every clearing and humming insect is holy in the memory and experience of my people. We know that the white man does not understand our ways . . . The earth is not his brother, but his enemy, and when he has conquered it, he moves on. He does not care.' Like every other thinking white man Wendell has learned the prophetic wisdom of those words and his caring was highly concerned, as Blake, another prophet, would have it, with the minute particulars: the stewardship of a farmer for his own fields, the love of a husband for his wife, the concern of a father for his son. For Wendell charity begins at home. 'We must begin in our own lives,' he writes, 'the private solutions that can only in turn become public solutions.'

Returning, we sat in the kitchen talking of many things; Den in his bedroom listening to rock, Tanya busy with the lunch, occasionally joining in. The kitchen is a small, clean room modestly furnished with everything except books which line the walls of both the downstairs rooms in considerable abundance. In point of fact throughout the day we were to talk a lot about our favourite reading. Had I read Andrew Marvell's poem *Appleton House* he asked. Did I know Kathleen Raine's *Blake and Tradition* which he had been reading this winter. He was concerned, he said, that her enthusiasm for neo-Platonic thought had devalued the importance of matter. Was C. S. Lewis still read in Britain? Was I familiar with the novels of Edward Abbey or the work of John McPhee? And so it went on.

Because I wanted to know something about their lives, we soon passed from literature to biography. Wendell told me that in the early years of their marriage (and he is now forty-six), in a period of exploration before the deepest roots were struck, the two of them had travelled widely both in Europe and the States. At that time Wendell was still teaching at the University and Lanes Landing was unfarmed; they used it, they needed it, he said, as others need a 'country retreat', as a place of refreshment and refuge. But farming won, it was in the blood. As a boy he said he had learned a good deal about animals from his father so that it was a small step and a natural one to take up farming for himself—to develop his own relationship with the land, to live in place, to combine the craft of nurturer of both earth and words. For words too had their way of winning and Wendell has never ceased to write, dividing his time between writing (in a hide-out, high up overlooking the flowing river) and his work on the farm and in the house where everything, the writing as well, is regarded as something of a joint project between himself and Tanya. To date, alas, in addition to *Unsettling* I have read only two collections of Wendell's verse but three novels and five other books of poetry have been written together with those books of essays—*The Long-Legged House* (1969), *The Hidden Wound* (1970), *The Unforeseen Wilderness* (1971) and *A Continuous Harmony* (1972)—which if *Unsettling* is anything to go by must be amongst the finest written this century. He is, I believe, a prose stylist of great power and one who urgently needs to be better known. In a more practical vein Wendell also writes for a bi-monthly organic farming magazine, *The New Farm*, which is published by the Rodale Press. The latter work provides him with a small income and welcome opportunities to travel.

From writing and agriculture ('What breed of pig do you find in North Devon?') we drifted to the problems of the planet, the broken pattern. His grief at this breakdown was palpable and, at times, painful. Protest, of course, was inevitable—and Wendell obviously enjoys a fight—but by itself it was not enough. 'We must criticize from solid ground,' he told me, 'from a position of sanity, from doing something positive ourselves; a constructive alternative.' But the Powers of Darkness were no abstraction: for Wendell 'an infinitely greedy sovereign is afoot in the universe, staking his claims.' 'Right now,' he continued, 'with the threat from nuclear power the rural areas, where you and I both live, are in the front line.' Had I seen the strip-mining in the Appalachians? 'Yes, yes,' he said, 'It is Armageddon—the Beast.'

We ate in the kitchen. Then after luncheon, a projected visit to a neighbouring farm cancelled because of the rain, we returned to one of Wendell's favourite themes: the breakdown of decorum in the modern world. 'I'm trying to argue,' he continued, 'that there's a relationship between art and place and that the name of this relationship is decorum, which has an ethical dimension.' We had moved from the kitchen into the living space, another simply furnished, book-lined room. As a practical intellectual, an integrated man for whom body and soul, marriage and community, community and the earth are naturally and harmoniously joined, it is hardly surprising that the old sense of universal order and its destruction should hold a special place for him. 'We find these ideas in Dante, in Milton's *Paradise Lost* and Shakespeare,' he told me, 'even in Blake, who believed that whenever we attempt to become more than a human being we become much less than one. Macbeth's cry, how does it go, "I dare do all that may become a man, who dares do more is none"—he speaks it before he moves over to his wife's side, before he murders Duncan and breaks the chain of being —isn't this the perfect metaphor for our own behaviour which has placed the human will in charge of itself and the Universe?' And then the words which I shall always remember: 'There is an urgent need for us to rediscover our proper place in Creation by living within our limits, by being human—not by trying to be gods. By restraints we make ourselves whole.'

The rain had eased. I followed Wendell into the barn, wooden, white-painted, chaste as the house itself which is only a stone's throw from where it stands. Inside, as in so many barns, it is mysterious with the hum of an animal life that has its life in us. It was like an elegy to see him in it, too. For to be with Wendell in that barn, to be with him on home ground—as he milks the cow, attends to the lambs, feeds the calves—is to understand his spirit in its purest form: its sanity, its erotic bond with the earth, its love of the ordinariness of the material world where spiritual qualities can become earthly events. 'These are the works of God', he writes in *Unsettling*, 'and it is therefore the work of virtue to make or restore harmony amongst them.' Milking the cow may seem a long way from such high-sounding sentiments but for Wendell it is, I think, very close; 'a sacrament by which we enact and understand our oneness with the Creation, the conviviality of one body with all bodies.'

Tanya returned me to the airport the next morning past the living scenes and places which were so familiar to them both, past the Kentucky river with its wintry fringe of sycamores and water maples, past his brother's farm with its grazing mares, his parents' home, the local garage, the school in Newcastle where Den is bussed each day (nearer Louiseville she pointed out the gleaming headquarters of the Colonel Sanders Fried Chicken empire, a centre of considerable local employment).

By contrast with these natural scenes New York, on the eve of a major transport strike, was like a being crazed. But as I rushed amongst the crowded streets (the agitation an infection, the rain now very wet), I thought back to the quiet homestead I had left and the care of a man for the earth, the foundation of life and hope. For to have been alone with Wendell on that snug, wet, Sunday afternoon, talking as we were talking in the dusk, was a touchstone of everything exploitative and artificial, a touchstone of everything sane and natural in the world in which we lived. In his whole attitude, in his very intonation, there was a sense, a foreboding, a prophecy of doom: doom for all independent masters, doom for all true workmanship, doom for the end of a civilization that had doomed men and women to mechanical life. But I was hearing something more than an epitaph for an immemorial way of life. I was listening to the voice of a lover; a celebrant of the materiality of the world; a man of hope; a practical man whose head, whose hands and heart, were even now engaged in the creation of an Ark, 'potent with healing and with health'. A cell of good living, as Eric Gill would have called it, in the chaos of our world.

July/August 1980

Feeding People Should Be Easy

COLIN TUDGE

IT REALLY ISN'T DIFFICULT to feed human beings. We are able to eat almost anything, and the food to which we are best adapted—seeds—is one of the most widespread in the world, and one of the easiest to grow. In addition, though the world is very crowded in places and we have no cause to be complacent about the rising population, there is as yet, in theory, plenty of leeway. For every man, woman and child on Earth there is about a third of a hectare of arable land, mainly devoted to the kind of crops that humans need; and there's another three hectares of permanent pasture for every person, producing a wide variety of meats.

Yet, as all the world knows, somewhere between a tenth and a fifth of the world's people—400 million to a billion—are positively underfed. At the other end of the scale, a few hundred million contrive to be rather grotesquely overfed, and die prematurely from 'diseases of affluence', ranging from diabetes through coronary heart disease to a variety of cancers that are considered to be diet-related. In theory, there should be a fairly broad band in the middle—at least fifty per cent of the world's population—who are neither undernourished nor overfed. In practice, however, the ones who at present are properly fed have a strong tendency either to slip downwards, into malnourishment, or to race headlong into the diseases of affluence.

But if it is easy in theory to feed people, why do we make such a poor job of it? The reasons, in detail, are many and complex, but we can make one simple, overwhelming, and stunning observation. It is that there is no agriculture on earth that is expressly designed to feed people.

If you were setting out expressly to feed people, whether you were in England, Ecuador, or Ethiopia, then you would not do the things that are generally done in those countries. You would do the following.

First, you would ask what it is that human beings need to eat. There has been tremendous controversy on this in the decades since World War II, but the glimmerings of a consensus are emerging. Human beings are very variable but they are all the same species. Almost all of them need somewhere between 1,500 and 3,000 kilocalories of energy per day, of which about five to fifteen per cent should be in the form of protein, around ten to twenty per cent should preferably be in the form of fat, and the rest, ideally, would be 'unrefined carbohydrate'—that is, plant food with the fibre left in. They also need some 'essential fats' (which in practice are polyunsaturated fats) plus a short catalogue of minerals and vitamins.

If you fall below this band of requirement then there are various kinds of trouble. On less than 2,000 kilocalories a day it is difficult to suckle a child. If the diet contains less than ten per cent fat then it can be difficult to attain 2,000 kcals, because unrefined carbohydrate is bulky and if there are no concentrated forms of energy—such as fat—it can be difficult to eat enough even if the food is available. If you go significantly above the narrow band of acceptability then you run into other difficulties. With an intake above 3,000 kcals per day it is difficult to avoid obesity, especially if you also eat a lot of protein. If forty per cent of those calories are in the form of fat—as is the case in rich Western countries—then you are at high risk of coronary heart disease and other diet-related diseases.

The second question, then, is how the right amount of essentials can be supplied in the right proportions. What is immediately obvious to the agriculturalist is that most of what humans need—and in the right proportions—can be supplied simply by growing grain. Grow enough wheat, rice, maize, oats, rye, barley, sorghum or millet and you supply all the energy and virtually all the protein that people need, plus some fat (especially in the case of maize and oats) and a fair proportion of vitamins. Such shortcomings as there are in the grain seeds can largely be made good by growing pulses—chickpeas, pigeon peas, broad beans, kidney beans, ground nuts and soya being the main ones. There are very few areas in the world where cereals and pulses cannot be grown —from sorghum and groundnuts in the Sahel, to maize and kidney beans in central America, to wheat and broad beans in the Middle East. In the wet tropics cassava or some similar tuber can take over from grain to some extent; and in temperate lands wheat, oats, barley and rye are abetted by potatoes.

With these basics taken care of, the rest should be plain sailing. There are no countries south of the Arctic Circle that cannot grow fruit and vegetables. Small amounts supply missing vitamins (notably A and C) plus minerals.

There is nothing startling in this. It is simply a description of what most people imagine traditional agriculture to be, everywhere in the world. The products of such agriculture manifest in practice as bowls of rice with a garnish of cabbage (as in much of China) or bread and hummus and fragments of goat's or sheep's cheese (Greece) or vegetables, bread and potatoes with a few ounces of meat (wartime Britain). People simply do not need animal products in large amounts. A sprinkling will do, just to add flavour, underwrite the quality of the plant protein, and supply some minerals, vitamins and essential fats.

But this simple straightforward pattern of doing things is not achieved everywhere and, where it is, there are many signs that people are changing to something else, either by choice or because they are being forced to change. So why aren't simple and correct things done, and why do people change when they are doing the right thing?

There are many reasons for failing to reach the ideal: poverty, exploitation— the list goes on. But we come back to design. It is possible to produce adequate crops of sorghum even in bad years in the Sahel, and to do so furthermore with very little modification of traditional methods: scientists at the International Crops Research Institute for the Semi-Arid Tropics (ICRISAT) have done this.

But the country is not geared to produce such crops consistently. ICRISAT's research is new, not widely known, and not widely applied. Even if it were, the farmers of the Sahel, as in most of the Third World, lack the kind of supports that Western farmers now take for granted and which are essential; supports such as timely advice (on the state of the weather and pests); grants; easily repaid loans; and a measure of security.

Much of Ethiopia could be irrigated, but it is not. Ethiopia relies heavily upon its cattle up in the hills, and quite reasonably, because it has excellent grasslands. But the grasslands need management if they are to go on producing. They are so little understood that scientists from Addis Ababa, Norway, and Britain are only now putting together a complete description of what kinds of grasses there actually are.

In short, neither the Sahel nor Ethiopia are innate disaster areas, but the world in general has stood around and not done the conceptually simple thing that needs to be done, which is to upgrade, in a hundred different ways, the local agriculture. Much more commonly, indigenous agricultures have either been neglected totally or swept aside to make way on the one hand for cash crops (which include cotton in the Sahel), and on the other for some facsimile or pastiche of western agriculture. In short, much of the agriculture of the world is not designed to feed people because it has simply been left to hazard or obliterated.

But the agriculture of the West, which has so often been imposed on people, and which some countries have voluntarily adopted, is not designed primarily to feed people either. It is designed, primarily, to make money. Yields are heavy, inputs are high, labour is saved, and value is added; the easiest way to 'add value' is to take the grain that could support people and feed it to animals.

But there are four shortcomings to this approach, all of which are observable. First, farmers often cannot afford the necessary inputs, so the advent of the new high-input high-output methods paradoxically causes more people to starve. Second, though total output is higher, more is diverted to livestock, so the total number of people that can be supported is reduced. Third, many countries have discovered to their cost that the high-input high-output methods of the West do not always work in their own countries, at least without radical modification, which often is not forthcoming. Fourth, the diet that such agriculture supplies, assuming it works, is of the high-fat, low-fibre variety that in the long term is pernicious.

However, there are two very powerful reasons why the 'rational' and traditional styles of agriculture, based on high intakes of cereals and on modest intakes of meat—intake geared to what is easiest to grow—give way so easily to the more concentrated Western style. For one thing, the Western approach generates more wealth (value added, less labour) and it concentrates that wealth in fewer hands (landowner plus labourers, rather than peasant farmers). We live in a world where enterprises that generate and concentrate wealth inevitably come to dominate those that do not.

Secondly, the Western-style diet, based on Western-style agriculture, is designed to be seductive, because seductive food sells in greater amounts. Meat is nice: human beings like it. The more that's produced, the more people will eat. Fat slips down easily, especially in combination with carbohydrate. Let the meat be fatty then, and let the oilseed plantations spread. And it does not take much to convert a traditional, nutritionally desirable, low-fat high-fibre diet into a modern, western, high-fat one. Add a spoonful of oil to a bowl of rice and you have doubled the calories and turned a very low fat meal into one in which fifty per cent of the calories are from fat. If people are undernourished, then the introduction even of modest amounts of fat is a boon. But if people are already eating the kind of diet that is theoretically ideal then the addition of yet more fat is deeply pernicious, both economically and nutritionally.

There are signs of improvement. The notion that countries afflicted by famine should simply be given 'aid' is giving way to the notion that what counts in the end is long-term self-reliance, and that the key to self-reliance is not to mimic the agricultures of the West but to build upon local crops, traditions, and skills. Western countries themselves are turning away from the ultra-high protein-and-fat diets of the 1960s, such as the steak-and-six-egg breakfasts that were once commonplace in the United States. But for every example of benign enlightened intervention in poor countries you see other examples of what seems very like perversity. I find it hard to believe, for example, that Malaysia really needs to build up an Australian-style dairy industry, which it was bent on doing when I was there in 1980. And wherever you look in the world these days you see the hamburger—based not on the crops that grow locally, but on meat, which generally means beef, and on wheat (for the bun) and potatoes.

In short, we are perfectly capable of feeding ourselves both well and indefinitely. There are signs of enlightenment. But the most powerful forces in the world, and in particular the force that requires the making of money, are reducing the likelihood that we can all feed well, and are tending to ensure that the haves grow fatter and the have-nots remain in the cold.

May/June 1986

A Good Going On

LAWRENCE D. HILLS

WHEN I BEGAN the Henry Doubleday Research Association on an acre of leased land, my old landlady, Mrs Amy Hobbes of Southery, the Norfolk village where I first grew Comfrey, wrote to me and said, 'I am so glad you got a good going on.' For that which is good goes on, like good land and good people in villages everywhere. Happiness may be fleeting, and enjoyed by only two people, but good goes on for others also, not only for those who are part of our lives but for the far future. Good has duration as well as existence.

The old fairy tale ending, 'They lived happily ever after', is far more than one of the rootless phrases of an age that cannot tell clichés from epigrams. It held up an achievement and an ideal to be cherished and rejoiced in by every couple throughout their lives together. The good that goes on can make them princes and princesses if they are fortunate to care enough for each other. Many of us are clearly not capable, for one reason or another, of creating the mutual and lasting happiness that is good and goes on, for there are so many broken marriages and loves that grow cold, just as there are ruined farms and devastated continents.

We are all married to our world, sharing its atmosphere and its seven polluted seas, for better for worse, for energy richer, for resource poorer, in nuclear war or population explosion, till the death of our sun shall us part. With every baby's birth a new love affair begins. So we should cherish our world and all the family of living beings we share it with, so that good may go on. Ours is a good world, with the right moisture, temperature range and atmosphere for our kind of life to enjoy. It is ours to love and to cherish through the sunlit centuries.

It is this attitude of mind that unites what can be called 'the organic movement' which, like everything which is alive, has grown and changed through the decades. Those who believe that only money, possessions or personal power over others matter think short, and pursue their immediate satisfaction in whatever way they can find it fastest. But ecologists, conservationists, vegetarians, self-sufficiency seekers, health cranks, anti-nuclear demonstrators, organic farmers and gardeners are all united by their respect for the future. We have only learnt this respect relatively recently, when we came of age and grew up to agriculture, which gave us the responsibility to think ahead.

When we became farmers and gardeners, raising and rearing our crops and stock, we stayed in one place long enough to learn to love a garden and a home, to put our roots down so deeply that today we build a landscape into our minds between the ages of three and fourteen which we shall remember all our lives.

Behind us we have more than three hundred generations of farmers who loved their land and strove to leave it more fertile than they found it, for all good farmers farm as though they would live for ever and hope that those who come after them will farm as well. Even though the only land that is left in our lives is a suburban garden, we who think ahead to next spring's sowings with our January seed order, or to this autumn's fruit tree planting, are reaching back to our neolithic past.

This is not so very far back if we think of time in terms of space, for if we see our long history as hunters and gatherers as one page of a book, our three hundred generations as farmers and gardeners is just the height of the top line of print.

As far as we can know, hunting bands numbered twelve to fourteen, killing large game by co-operation, and bringing it back to their families, sharing it out as Eskimos do, so that no widow or child was left unfed. This gave us not only man the hunter, but woman, the playgroup organizer, the peace maker and settler of disputes and the leader of a second group that not only cared for the children but defended them. There were places for aunties, grannies and grandfathers whose long memories were the equivalent to books, in a system rather like a successful modern commune.

This system was not forced on woman by primitive male chauvinism, but by the fact that human beings are the only species that can have a family composed of a baby, a toddler and a swiftly wandering four-year-old, when fawns and foals can follow the herd after a few weeks. This is why our marriages are made to last, so that we can in an emergency gather up the children and leave a band which we dislike and choose one we prefer.

Our friendships are also lasting, not so much from the mutual trust of comrades in a common task against danger and death, like the unity of the crew of a B29 or a Wellington, as from the deeper friendships of women sharing an extended family. All toddlers clutch at a woman's heart with small trusting hands, even the children of strangers, and the real pleasure from peeping into a pram at someone else's baby is simply the 'cavewoman' rising in us. The male equivalent of the dark passions from the past is when the captain of a sinking ship orders 'women and children first'.

Sharing the care of the children, so mothers could take time off in turn, dashing across a forest glade to stop a three-year-old picking up a snake, caring for the injured hunter who had to stay in camp, are all inherited from thousands rather than hundreds of generations. We are not morose and solitary beasts, but cheerful gossips, building our minds by the telling of tales as children do when they clamour to be told a story.

Women were the first conservationists, because they must think ahead for their children's future. We can grow away from the past, but always by building on its foundations, for though it is possible to change human nature through the generations, we cannot change the elements that build it without an explosion. Courage, self-sacrifice, tolerance for others and above all, respect for the future are all qualities we have inherited from our fore-bears.

This is the fundamental difference between organic and inorganic thinking. Those who think organically think ahead to the fossil fertilizers and the fossil fuels running out; to the persistent pesticides, PCBs, CFCs and still newer pollutants adding up to danger in the soil, the sea, the atmosphere and the body fats of every living creature; to the toxic metals that industry pours into the environment, and the lead from petrol that gathers in the brains of our children because both sellers and users prefer to risk their mental health for better engine performance and slightly lower prices.

The inorganic say cheerfully, 'I have no time for all this gloom and doom, what has the future done for me? It may be true in the long run, but in the long run we are all dead.' To a businessman ten years is the foreseeable future; a politician sees as far as the next election, and a trade union leader to just beyond the next round of wage increases. Far too few people have the courage to think ahead twenty years to when North Sea oil runs out, or the thirty-five until world population will have doubled.

The phrase 'a good going on' expresses what all countrymen and country-women desire for the land they love and the village that is home—the stability of life enjoyed for its own sake as a gift from God and the continuity of the generations. Just as without memory there can be no music, just disconnected sounds, without a future for our hopes and our children we are incomplete. Today, even apart from the threat of nuclear war, the future we are building out of short-sighted greed and indifference gives us the urgent duty to shape it into one that is worthy of the past.

Millions of people today are 'presentists', living only in the present for immediate satisfactions, especially drug taking, alcohol and whatever diversions are fashionable—from football team following to jet-setting between ever more identical airports, hotels and beaches. Still more are 'visualists' who look on the world as a TV programme. They choose the channels provided for them and watch bombs exploding, people falling, buildings blazing, and rusty freighters full of boat people reluctantly rescued from a crueller sea, taking the privilege of the wealthy, which is to enjoy disaster for others from comfortable seats. When they tire of death and hunger they can switch channels more cheerfully to show business, for to them the world is without reality, just a shadow show to amuse the grown up children of an age of technology.

In the microprocessed future that has been planned for us our place will be in front of our TV screens, for there will be no need for travel. TV teams will bring the whole world in colour to be watched for our amusement, and everything from visits to the doctor to high-level conferences will be made through this tyrant. Our post, our newspapers and our books will be transmitted to our rooms by silicon chip controlled apparatus, and for every possible purpose we can be connected to a computer, so we can press numbered buttons that will measure our opinions and measure them statistically.

The cheerful band of gossips round the campfire, and the children exploring the small world of a forest glade under the watchful eyes of mothers, aunties and neighbours, with all its possibilities of growth and development, will have gone for ever, because of our laziness and indifference that are crippling the mental development of our children.

Two out of three school age children in Britain watch TV for twenty-one to thirty-five hours a week and though there are no figures for our pre-school toddlers, in the USA they average fifty-four hours a week in front of the electronic babysitter. In the Victorian age, a few children of working mothers were given opium to pacify them, now almost all our children are robbed of real childhood by commercial pressure and the force of fashion that persuade us to gamble their minds and the future of our race.

Children learn to walk, speak and awake to thinking as they move from being babies to toddlers, learning more in the first three years of their lives than in any later period. Through play they develop their knowledge of things, their relationships with other children, their physical control, their five senses and their imaginations.

Playing is the important 'work' that children do. They learn through imitating other children and the adults who tell them stories, talk to them and provide illustrations of every day activities. Talking to children and being 'helped' by them is perhaps the most important work that we, the *adults*, may do in our lives, for all that we make or do in our working week-days may well be scrap metal or scrap paper in ten years, but our sons and daughters are the future of the world. The evil that men and women do is often buried with them, the good they do in encouraging the imaginations and sensory development of their children will live on when their own failures are forgotten.

Children learn to speak by talking with real people who communicate the meaning of words, but television only reproduces the sounds. We are blunting our children's senses, stultifying their imaginations and putting them into a passive state that leaves them unemployed rather than doing their real work which is play. A naked infant in the dust of a Third World country, pretending that a row of date stones is a camel caravan, is mentally safer than one which sits staring hour after hour at a colour TV screen.

Nowhere in the world is there a man or woman in their fifties who has spent an entire infancy in front of a TV set. We know the TV children who demand everything advertised and more from their parents, but these are a phenomenon of the last fifteen or twenty years, and limited to the countries that have the incomes to buy not only the sets but the goods advertised on the programmes. We cannot know yet how the TV children will grow up, because all over-forties have so far had normal childhoods.

Those who are concerned with any advanced technology have a driving urge to develop it to its ultimate limits. The theology of science fiction makes it easy for the greedy sciences of space and communication, where it is more profitable to travel expensively than to arrive, and which starves research on recycling, pollution control and the environmental effects of ozone holes and the greenhouse effect.

We in the organic movement think of the world as a whole, and we cannot allow technology to take us into a future of converging collision courses. Simply because something can be done there is no reason why we should go on doing it until it distorts our society. The decision of what we should or should not do must go before the jury—the ordinary people who will have to suffer the consequences of the technology, not only immediately, but in to the far future.

When we became farmers and gardeners, we took on the responsibility of thinking ahead because we had the power to change the environment for all the rest of the lives on Earth. Now we have acquired more power—fossil fuel power, electrical power, nuclear power. The greater the power we can harness the greater the responsibility. Therefore we have to recognize certain limits to what we should do, and to draw clear lines between what will endanger the future of our race and its neighbours on this our one world, which we should be able to enjoy together till the sun grows cold.

May/June 1989

Suffering of Salmon

JILL SMITH

THE LIFE CYCLE OF THE WILD SALMON is extraordinary. It begins in some high fresh-water spawning ground, lives and grows a while in the fresh water river, then makes a journey down river, often incredible distances, reaches the sea and a salt water environment, then travels seas and oceans thousands of miles from the place of its birth. The Atlantic salmon reaches as far as the Arctic circle. Its life is one of response to turning cycles, solar, lunar, patterns in the magnetic field of the Earth.

When the salmon has lived in the oceans some years, it begins to experience the vast primal urge to return to its place of birth in order to spawn. The journey is almost unimaginable to us; the navigational knowledge unerring and the drive to reach the goal undeniable. Across the oceans they come, finding the mouth to their own river, waiting for the spate of fresh water, then up river against its flow they go, swimming, leaping, overcoming almost all obstacles, no longer eating, prey to disease and predators and finally, almost exhausted, reaching the place where they themselves were hatched, to spawn as their last magnificent act. A few survive, mostly females, known now as kelts, to return to the sea again.

I came to live on the Isle of Lewis with little knowledge of salmon, only tales half remembered told of seas of silver fish.

I became increasingly aware of salmon farming as I watched it grow almost daily. I passed the hatchery tanks every time I went on the bus. I saw loch after loch filled with square cages. More and more I wondered at the life these magnificent beasts were forced to lead and the pain of those in the cages, seemingly as tortured as any battery hen or pig. Learning of how the wild salmon lived, I could only feel that to deprive these animals of their freedom and prevent them from following their primal urges was a grave act of cruelty.

The day a helicopter flew back and forth over my house, carrying tanks of salmon smolts, young fish, from hatchery to cage, I determined to find out as much as I could about salmon farming. I was told that to move the smolts by boats would take two weeks, cost as much as the helicopter, and cause most of them to die of the trauma.

Instead of the vast urge to reach the spawning grounds being fulfilled, the fish are 'milked' of eggs and milt. The fertilized eggs hatch and the small fish grow in hatchery tanks on land, tanks with heavy lids shutting out all contact with the environment. The small fish are dependent on being fed by farm workers (as indeed are the larger fish in the cages). Recently, near me, there were large losses of fish when someone went on holiday, failing to clean the tanks properly.

The small fish are transferred to the cages in which they spend the rest of their lives. I have been told that a cage of nine square metres may hold five tonnes of fish. Fifty such cages may hold between them a quarter of a million fish, which are then grown to three kilograms each. To cage these magnificent creatures in such small spaces should not be acceptable in a civilized society.

The power of the urge to return 'home' was totally affirmed for me the day I stood watching a river which was almost dry. Most of the fish were waiting in the loch at the bottom for the spate, but still a persistent few forced themselves up the bare few inches, splashing along, not even covered, wriggling over the rocks.

I have stood on a huge bridge over still, dark waters where fish once swam in their thousands, following and influenced by energies of earth and moon, and watched the pathetic leaps of fish in cages that now fill this beautiful place, leaps of despair and confusion. An old man nearby told me they used to watch the shoals of wild salmon pass by following the sprats, 'and now we see never a one'. I saw only thousands of jelly-fish, and sensed abandonment. The wild salmon have now rejected the changed energy of this place, keeping away from the cages in horror, taking another route.

Near Shetland a particular kind of jelly-fish can sometimes sting whole cages full of salmon to death. The fish have no way to escape predators, sitting there as prime targets, unable to flee or hide. Predators are many: seals, otters and birds. There are regulations for farming fish, but many are ignored. Cages are supposed to have predator nets around them, but this is often not done and the nets are not totally effective anyway.

The ecological dangers from fish farming are many. Lochs are being severely polluted and ecosystems changed and destroyed. Cages are often not sited where there is a strong flowing current out to sea, so effluent, faeces, chemicals and waste food fall to the bottom, changing the loch environment. There are 'dead' areas and areas where one species over-flourishes, choking and destroying the life of everything else. Sometimes gases bubbling up can reduce oxygen levels and endanger the fish in the cages. Plant and shell-fish life is being changed and destroyed.

The wild salmon themselves are in severe danger of becoming extinct. Should any salmon escape from the cages and somehow manage to breed with the wild salmon, they lack the homing imprint for a particular place, so the offspring will have a much weaker imprint and the number returning to spawn will be considerably reduced.

It is considered fine to restock a river that has lost its wild salmon with those from elsewhere or from farms, but it doesn't work—the fish has the genetic imprint of its original river or, in the case of the farmed ones, of none.

As with other intensively farmed animals, the salmon are fed prepared meal and medication to ward off disease. The effects of these are passed on to other creatures round the farms and are also in the salmon flesh which is eaten by the unsuspecting public.

The wild salmon acquires its pink colour from a form of shrimp which is part of its natural diet. The fish meal fed to farmed salmon contains an artificial colourant, canthaxanthin, which is known to be carcinogenic and is banned as a food colourant in the US. This colourant is affecting other fish in the lochs who eat waste meal. Many people catch small fish known as 'cuddies'; those now found near farms are bright red and bitter in taste. Shell-fish are also affected. These were once an important part of the local people's diet.

Salmon are very prone to lice, and to eradicate this in the farms they are dosed with a chemical called Nuvan. This is sold for use as a pesticide in hen houses and labelled 'Dangerous to fish, do not contaminate ponds, water-ways or ditches with chemical or used container.' It is supposed to be administered in carefully measured amounts with a tarpaulin around the cage, the tarpaulin being later towed out to sea and the chemical released into fast-flowing out-tide currents. The chemical is toxic if allowed to come into contact with skin or inhaled or swallowed, and operatives administering it should wear protective clothing. In fact, bucketsful of the stuff are often just poured into cages with no tarpaulins, in a slack tide, by young lads or lasses who wear no protection and have little knowledge as to what they are handling.

At the 'appropriate' time the fish are 'harvested'. They are starved, sometimes for four weeks before, in order to reduce the artificial colour of the flesh to an acceptable pink and 'improve' the texture. In some cases they are hit over the head with a metal pipe and thrown into a tank, but more often they are just gashed and left to bleed to death, floundering about in blood. Apparently this is preferred by the processors.

At first I was loath to criticize what is one of the few fast growing industries in the Highlands and Islands, bringing money and employment to the community, but I find a majority of the farms are owned by multinationals and most of the better paid jobs go to outsiders. Most farmed salmon is sold abroad or to the affluent parts of Britain: it is certainly not feeding the local people. In 1987, 12,700 tonnes of salmon were produced from Scottish fish farms and the total catch of wild salmon was 1,271 tonnes.

Many local fishermen who fish round the sea lochs and coasts are losing their livelihoods. The fish are disappearing and often access to the boats is obstructed by cages.

My major concern, though, is for the plight of the salmon itself. The suffering of these magnificent creatures, deprived of their whole natural life cycle, should not be denied.

September/October 1989

Small Holdings

JOHN SEYMOUR

TWO DANGEROUS MISCONCEPTIONS have done enormous damage to the land of England and that of other Western countries in the last century. They are the failure to distinguish between food-output-per-acre and profit-per-acre, and the failure to consider the input/output ratio of agriculture.

These two errors in thinking, inevitable when city minds try to apply themselves to rural matters (and after all our rulers are city people—this is inevitable in democracies which have a preponderance of urban voters) have led to several developments. The most important of these are the enlargement of agricultural holdings by consolidation; the replacement of men and women on the land by machines and chemicals; and monoculture.

The city economist has been given the wrong brief. He has been told: 'make farming pay even though the price of food is kept low.' Well the easiest way he could do this (the only way in fact) was to enlarge the size of holdings. If a man can earn a bare living on a hundred acres he can certainly earn a good living off a thousand. It didn't require any great genius to see that. And so 'agricultural economists' (who are not great geniuses as it happens) have consistently said: 'enlarge the size of holdings,' and holdings have been enlarged. The effects of this have been to drive people off the land into the towns (where they have still got to eat of course), to increase the output-per-unit-of-labour of land, to *decrease* the yield of food per acre, to increase the money profit (in other words to make the few remaining owners of the land richer), to impose a pattern of monoculture on the land (just take a drive through East Anglia to see what I mean), to divorce animals from land, and, most damaging of all perhaps, to alter drastically the input/output ratio of land.

By the input/output ratio I mean the ratio between input of such things as fuel, fertilizer and pesticides on the one hand and the output of consumable food for humans on the other. With a purely peasant husbandry you may get a fairly low output of food per acre but then you will probably have a negligible or even perhaps non-existent input of fuel, fertilizer and pesticide. In fact in some parts of the world purely peasant agriculture is enormously productive with little or no input. But our vast mechanized farms have become completely hooked on a vast input of power, chemicals and fertilizers. It so happens that power, fertilizers and pesticides and herbicides used on the land all come from oil, and if oil really *did* become scarce the output from large mechanized farms would drop to nil.

But oil has been so cheap as to be in effect free, and farmers, governments and economists have all gone all-out for a high-input agriculture. Animals are no longer kept to tread the straw and create farmyard manure. After all, sulphate of ammonia can be created out of the very *air*—why hump about vast tonnages of farmyard manure? Ah, but to fix nitrogen from the air takes *power*—in huge quantities. It takes ten tons of coal-equivalent to fix a ton of nitrogen. But the land has been farmed for decades now with no stock (the stock are all shut up in Belsen-houses remote from the land on which their food is grown, or back to which their dung should go), with perfect or almost-perfect monoculture (weeds are dealt with by spraying with chemical herbicides—no longer by sound rotational husbandry), with the application of greater and greater quantities of imported or artificially-created chemical fertilizer, and with the input of vast amounts of imported fuel oil and the use of quantities of massive and highly sophisticated machinery.

All these developments have come about for one reason—to save labour. In the era of almost-free-fuel labour was by far the biggest cost, and every big farmer has always had one overriding consideration: 'how can I save another wage?'

The 'heart' of the land has suffered enormously from mechanical/chemical farming. Every honest farmer realizes this but he has hitherto always been able to say: 'It doesn't matter—I can keep shoving on greater and greater quantities of artificial fertilizer.' Now the price of nitrogen has shot up to the sky and farmers are beginning to think again, but for many of them it is too late. They are hooked. If any of the white-straw-crop monoculturists in England tried to farm now with no artificial fertilizer they would be bankrupt in two years. The soil would produce next door to nothing. The situation is extremely dangerous.

How can we repair the damage that has been done? By one way and one way only: getting people back on to the land. The 'high farming' of the eighteenth and nineteenth centuries in England, good peasant farming in those parts of the world where there is good peasant farming, was accomplished by *men and women*. The folding of sheep on light arable land (the 'golden hoof'), the yarding of cattle and carting out of the resulting farmyard manure, fuel-free horse cultivation, row-crop cultivation to clean the land (i.e. kill weeds without chemical herbicides): all these things took *labour*. The only way nowadays that we are going to get men and women to labour on the land is to *give* them land, or allow them to buy it. Either in co-operative groups or as individuals the owner-cultivator must come back into his and her own. 'Make a man the owner of an acre of desert and he will turn it into a garden—make a man tenant of an acre of garden and he will turn it into a desert,' said Arthur Young, and never was a truer thing said.

If we are to avoid catastrophe we must cut the land up into far far smaller holdings. The Danes did it in the 1890s, with the result that the average Danish holding is now under fifty acres and the Danes can knock the British farmer (with all his subsidies—the Danes are completely unsubsidized) out of the market with any product they like to send across here. Maybe Danish farmers don't drive Jaguars. So what?

My own solution would be a graduated tax on land. A man who owns more than his fair share of his own country should pay a tax for this privilege. A man owning grossly more than his share should have to pay a colossal tax on every acre, so as to force him to drop some of his land on the market like a hot potato. If every land owner had to pay a tax on his land he would have to farm it intensively and efficiently, and sell off what he could not farm intensively to somebody who could. Piss or get off the pot in fact.

Then the planning laws would have to be altered so as to allow the thousands of new husbandmen to build houses on their holdings. Our country would become fruitful and fertile again: a country dressed and tilled by the hands of men and women and not one simply gouged and raped by insensitive machines and chemicals. This country could produce every bit of the food it needed (three quarters of an acre of cultivable land per man, woman, child and baby —with plenty of rough grazing beside), and we could cock a snook at Arab oil sheiks and prairie farmers alike.

Further, we could sleep more soundly in our beds a'nights.

September/October 1974

Do Not Discard the Cities

ELAINE MORGAN

MANY SOCIAL AND POLITICAL INITIATIVES in their early stages attract an assortment of different kinds of people whose aims have not yet been integrated one with another and this seems to be true of the movement represented here today—so that *Resurgence* for example has not yet been able to find a single adjective capable of describing its aims in the way that *Tribune* can call itself a Socialist magazine or *The Universe* a Catholic newspaper.

In some cases this is not much of a problem because the movement may be firmly held together by the potent political binding force of hatred—hatred of another clan, race, party or nation. I don't think many *Resurgence* readers would make very good haters and I am thankful for that. But perhaps it is all the more important then to try to be clear about what we have in common so that although we may be working in small groups, and far away from one another, at least we can be sure we are working in the same direction and not getting in one another's way.

Some people imagine that our ideas are powered chiefly by a kind of nebulous and windy idealism and some starry-eyed illusions about human nature. On the contrary, I think the one thing all of us have in common is the capacity to face and accept a single very hard fact and the consequences that flow from it— the fact that the material and biological resources of this planet are finite, while the rate at which the human race is squandering them continues to escalate as if they were inexhaustible.

Even ten years ago this idea was regarded as new and bizarre nonsense: sometime between now and then it has got itself lodged in the public consciousness. Perhaps it happened when the oil crisis predicted by E.F. Schumacher arrived bang on time and sent the first shudder through the world economy. Nowadays, very few people dispute the general thesis. They simply assert, like Micawber, that something is bound to turn up to enable the growth curves to go on zooming, and if they aren't zooming too well at the moment it's probably because of the monetary system or some other little spanner which they hope to take out of the works quite soon now. They admit that for our grandchildren or great grandchildren the crunch might really come, but we needn't worry yet. They have adopted a madly optimistic motto which reads: 'It is earlier than you think.'

We, on the other hand, believe with Schumacher that 'the party is over', with Barbara Ward that the energy jag is beginning to run out of steam now, in our lifetime. So we and they have a different idea of what constitutes 'progress'. When we speak of adapting to a situation where cheap and limitless supplies of fossil fuel are not available, they say we are moving backwards. To us it feels like forwards, because we have good reason to believe that this kind of world lies ahead of us in the twenty-first century as well as behind us in the eighteenth. They believe that progress consists of moving even faster in the same direction because it has paid off in the past: we feel constrained to point out that however much you are enjoying your trip, if you find your car is heading for the edge of a cliff it is not a reactionary move to slow down.

The interesting question is what determines the dividing line between them and us? Because this division does not run along any previously established lines —not along lines of class, nor ideology, nor race nor sex, nor generation. Nor even IQ, though I have a feeling that our side includes a higher percentage who not only have the native ability to think, but have kept up the habit of doing it.

Let us be painfully honest about this. I think the facts are on our side. I think what we believe is true. But our reasons for accepting it are no more objective than their reasons for shutting their eyes to it. They cannot bear to think that the phase of material affluence and gigantism and speed and centralization may be coming to an end, because they love it: we can bear to think of it ending because for one reason or another we love it less. That is why our message appeals to such a wide assortment of people.

It appeals to people in the Third World and in rural areas who have always been at the losing end of the centralizing process; to non-competitive people who don't fancy clawing their way up in the rat-race; to non-acquisitive people who don't get their kicks out of owning things; to poets, artists and craftsmen and aesthetic types because many of the results of modern technology are so ugly and the things it destroys often are beautiful; to mystics because an overcentralized society puts a disproportionately high premium on logic and devalues other modes of perception. I believe it is also beginning to appeal to certain urban areas which already sense that they are moving into a post-industrial phase—communities which the growth machine has used up and spat out and left to rot.

Now I'll put my own cards on the table. I'm not much into aesthetics: I can't reliably tell a good building from a bad one. I'm not at all into mysticism, though I know some very nice people who are. I only lived a really isolated rural life for two years and could never get my compost to behave the way it should. True I've got very little interest in acquiring material objects—but I presently earn my living in, or by, television, which is not only a highly competitive field but one that Dr Schumacher would like to annihilate.

And yet in a way that is what brings me here because what I write is drama, it is about the way people relate to one another, and that is what interests me most of all. And one of the most horrible things about a society hooked on GNP and centralization is the way it tends to deform and trivialize and fragment and debase human relationships. So, like the rest of you, when I'm told the party is over I can bear to believe it. There were some things about it that weren't so hot anyway, and we must find a way to something better balanced and more durable. But how?

Some measures we're all agreed on. Things like recycling, conservation, decentralization, reducing the demand for energy and developing new natural sources of it, reducing dependence on large scale chemical-intensive international agribusiness. Some people, finding city life intolerable, have chosen to go back to the land and that is one good move to make. You're healthier, less parasitic, more self-sufficient, you bring new life and energy into the places you move to, and you learn a lot which you can share and pass on.

But with the best will in the world, not everybody in a country like Britain can do this. Apart from the fact that most of them would view the prospect with horror we cannot, as good conservationists even *wish* to see it happen unless by careful and easy stages. We can't on the one hand worry about a Schweppes pop-bottle being discarded when it could be re-used, and on the other hand ignore the fact that our cities and industrial towns contain millions and millions of houses—as well as all the shops, factories and so on—which are worth very much more than pop bottles and which we certainly can't afford to discard. The cost would be literally prohibitive. It can't be done.

I believe we can and should and must search for ways of preventing any further concentration of numbers in the big cities. I also think this is going to be easier than it once looked because some of the forces that caused them to grow are going into reverse. But there cannot be a mass exodus unless in extreme crisis. For the immediately foreseeable future these places are going to be there.

It is also a fact that some urban communities in favourable conditions have succeeded in creating, or preserving, a good confident mutually supportive kind of society. Where this has developed, I believe it is even more precious and more worth preserving than the bricks and mortar. It happened in South Wales where I live. For a long time now people have been leaving, especially the young and ambitious, but that feeling is still not dead. It is one reason why I like it there and have no intention of moving out to a more pastoral area if I can help it. And there are people even in badly hit central city areas who feel the same way.

I know these problems are not being neglected by this movement. The Intermediate Technology Development Group and other voluntary bodies are encouraging little groups and initiatives in the centres of places like London and Manchester and Liverpool. The object is to create jobs in places from which industry has moved out; to start it on a shoe string in tiny units so that the unit can be self supporting; to concentrate on craft type labour-intensive jobs so that a lot of labour can be expended on a small amount of material; sometimes to offer work and self respect and a hope of integration to some of the rootless disoriented people who drift to city centres. All these are excellent aims.

And yet all it shows is that every place is different. I don't think this is the technique I am looking for personally. Some of us in the valleys are determined to do something to combat unemployment there. After a period of relative prosperity it is well above average again and looks like rising.

Our problem is a large scale one. For example if a steelworks shuts down in Ebbw Vale or a factory closes in the Neath Valley because the regional employment subsidy has been cut back, it can throw thousands of people out of work at the same time. They are not isolated drifters and unemployables; they are skilled people used to earning high wages and with a powerful sense of solidarity.

Now I know it is better to light one candle than to curse the darkness, but I do not think I would have the courage to go up to a shop steward on the day after such a shut down and say: well, two or three of you could get together in a little shed and learn leather work and make belts, and we could find a shop in Cardiff that would offer them for sale.

It might indeed be done; I suppose it would be better than nothing, and I do fervently believe that small is beautiful, but a transition of scale of that degree of abruptness would somehow seem like a horrible joke. It would be too much too fast. And yet if nothing is done to replace those jobs most people will start looking for jobs down in the coastal conurbation. And the saddest part of that is, as a recent survey established, that most of the people who move out would much prefer to stay.

We shall soon need to do some solid thinking on the question of how small is small for a country like Britain? It is ecologically sound to move away from the car and back to the bicycle, and not for Birmingham to make all of them either. And when we have fixed on an appropriate sized production unit for any given product—it might be a workshop with perhaps twenty-five people —from which end are we going to approach that scale?

Are we really going to have to work towards our appropriate technology by starting right back at square one? Confine ourselves to recolonizing the really dormant, derelict places putting in two workers and a pile of spare parts and a spanner, and hoping they'll build up to a thriving two dozen? Or could it be possible to work from the other end?

Let us take an example from my own area. Every morning about 10,000 people living in the valleys get up early and get into cars or wait for buses and proceed down the valleys through Pontypridd and on down to Treforest Trading Estate. They do a day's work in a factory and then make the same laborious journey home. In winter they'll be making both journeys in the dark.

For some, working on large complex machines, it may be inevitable, but for many it is economic lunacy. They may be engaged in—to take a simple example —operating sewing machines in a dress factory, each woman sitting behind one of a whole long row of sewing machines. In a meeting recently I proposed that it might be more sensible to take the machines to the people instead of the people to the machines. I was immediately accused of advocating cottage industry and sweated home labour.

I honestly don't see it. If instead of twenty-five machines in one Treforest factory you had five groups of five, one in the Rhondda valley, one in Merthyr and so on, the journey to work could take ten minutes each way instead of an hour each way, the working atmosphere would be more relaxed and informal, the workers could put their bus fare or petrol money into their pockets, and the country would have to import less oil.

It seems obvious that given the choice of working locally and saving the cost of transport most of the women would be very glad to do it even if their wages were cut by £1 a week—they would still be better off financially and certainly a lot less exhausted by Friday night. And if the firms were allowed to pay them £1 a week less on that condition, they would have a powerful incentive to begin decentralizing some of the large factories and moving some of the processes out to where the workers actually live and where floorspace costs less in rates and rent.

The reason why this cannot even be advocated at present is that most trade unions begin calculating the rate for the job only after the worker has crossed the factory threshold. They don't charge for travelling time or the cost of getting there. There would be difficulties in the way of introducing such an idea: there would have to be some kind of pooling system so that workers at a distance wouldn't be handicapped in applying for jobs. But there might well be pressure to introduce such a concept as the cost of commuting goes on increasing. If it were introduced, some of the large plants would begin splitting up and converting to the small is beautiful principle overnight, and the real quality of life for everybody would be enhanced.

What we really need is a lot of diversified manufacturing units on a small to medium scale scattered through the valleys, where possible producing things their own population uses and presently imports—there are 800,000 plus people living there and that's not a market to be sneezed at; and where possible using local raw material—coal is running out but the Forestry Commission has blanketed the mountains with timber.

The local authorities have laid down infrastructure and built factories and waited for them to be occupied—but too many are empty and some that were occupied for a time are now empty again. The government money previously offered to lure them is now being poured into the city centres instead—if only because the fear of violence and disaffection is greater there than anything they can fear from us.

So if the manufacturers won't come in and invest their money, whatever can we do? Where is the capital going to come from? Here we are up against the powerful myth that the go-ahead centralized growth areas are full of enterprising people who deserve to be prosperous and successful because they have saved up their money to invest instead of squandering it on riotous living: the prosperity is therefore the remit of thrift.

In fact it is precisely in some of the economically so called backward areas that the collective overdraft is lowest and the percentage of personal saving is highest. They do practise thrift—if only because they have never felt quite secure—and what happens to the money they save? It goes into a building society to help them buy a second-hand house and is reinvested in new housing elsewhere. The redundancy payment from the steelworks goes into the bank and the bank lends it to build office blocks and commercial precincts down south because banks are always readier to lend half a million pounds than to lend £15: part of the weekly wage may go into a trade union pension fund, and the unions invest it in multinationals because it is easier and simplifies the accounts. The more thrift they display the faster it trickles away to subsidize the forces of centralization and that makes me rather angry sometimes.

We are looking for ways of by-passing these bottlenecks and making people aware of the leaks and finding ways of stopping them up so that places like ours will not repeatedly have their economic lifeblood drained away and their communities broken up because the jobs have moved away and left them stranded.

They originally came from the farms and quickly learned how to be miners. In the war they soon learned how to make shells and parts of aeroplanes. It is certainly not beyond their capacity to learn how to channel their redundancy money into workers' co-operatives and move into some of the empty factories and lure some body to do the market research and accountancy. It can be done. We are trying to do it.

From a beautiful place like Felindre Farchog maybe all this discussion of factories and miners and money and production seems far less idyllic than talking about crops and livestock and the countryside. But for a long time yet we shall need an industrial sector in some shape or form as urgently as we need you. The forces we are fighting against are precisely the same as the forces that destroy the country villages, and if we can win a few skirmishes next year that will make it a little easier for you to win a few the year after.

Some people are trying to drop out of the over-centralized society altogether and replace it by starting in the simplest and most primary terms from the bottom; we are working from inside it and from further up the technological scale, but the aim is the same—to get the scale reduced. I am sure our aims converge, and with any luck working from different starting points we may some day meet in the middle.

July/August 1977

[From a talk given at a Resurgence *conference in Newport, Wales]*

Women's Issues

Women's Toil

VALENTINA BORREMANS

I WAS BORN somewhere on the Congo, upstream from Kinshasa. My Belgian father died when I was three, my black Nounou knew no Flemish and my mother, who reared me, was French. I lived for several years in London and New York before going to Mexico, where I have been for the past twenty-three years.

For more than a decade, I have lived in a village on the south slope of the Sierra Madre. And I have made about a dozen slow trips through South America. These were the outgrowth of my work with CIDOC, the Centro Intercultural de Documentación, which I directed from its opening in 1966 to its closing in 1976.

When we founded CIDOC, development was still two-thirds utopia; today it is a mess which can be studied empirically. My perspective is that of woman and I want to examine not the *promise* of development to women, but its actual *impact* on women. To do this I propose criteria for research on the effect which certain tools have on women. These are the tools which purportedly lighten women's toil, toil which extends to death.

By toil I mean the burden imposed on women through those things they must do because they are women. These include economic activities for which, more often than not, they are not paid, and subsistence-oriented activities, which economists cannot adequately measure. I am interested in the impact of new tools on the hardship, strain and drudgery with which women are burdened. I do not speak about lightening the toil of some individual women. Rather, I am looking for criteria which assess the toil of women as a group.

Research on women and tools has multiplied during the seventies, but is of two profoundly different kinds. One looks at tools which lighten women's total lifelong toil. This research is done mostly by women who are themselves helped by the new techniques which they adopt. This inventive vernacular adoption of new techniques by women is rarely called 'research'; indeed, it is generally overlooked. Few reporters recognize the genius who makes an oven out of a gearbox as a researcher.

The other kind of research is that *for* women. Its primary purpose tends to be the increase of women's productivity. It measures the 'improvement' of women's well-being as viewed by the expert.

The two types of research are at odds with one another. Research by women tends to keep them outside the market, and to limit the community's productivity in monetary terms. But it also generally lightens the total burden carried by women.

The second type of research drafts women into development. It is carried out by experts, sometimes in consultation with clients and, as I shall show, increases both women's burden and sexist discrimination.

Both high and low technology can be appropriated by women themselves for their own purpose. I want to focus primarily on simple techniques that are locally available, cheap, non-compulsory in their use. This technology that is ecologically 'soft', socially 'decentralizing', mechanically often 'intermediary' can become the subject of both research *by* and *for* women. Organic agriculture, gobar gas, passive solar heating, but also arguably microprocessor-equipped knitting machines can be made subservient to either subsistence or to growth. Horticulture can be used by women to keep the household largely outside the cash-nexus and the market. On the other hand, it can also serve to multiply cash ties within the community, to increase everyone's commodity dependence and to increase the cash flow.

Under the label of 'women's research on appropriate technology' (henceforth AT), research *by* and research *for* women have been hopelessly confused. I want to disentangle them because they are in fact separate, albeit complementary. Only when the complementarity between research by and for women is recognized can we find a democratic balance between those technical and legal priorities which help women to lighten their own burdens, and those other priorities which make women somewhat less unequal competitors for money.

As an example, let me cite a certain village where women reassert their control over the hoe and garden. Such a reconquest is quite likely at the end of a decade during which households headed by women have increased everywhere; doubled in nations such as Brazil, tripled in others such as Morocco. Thanks to the new alchemy of organic agriculture *cum* AT, the recovery of the hoe by women is in no sense a romantic regression. Formerly undreamed of results can now be obtained with comparative ease. The new technical potential, however, does mean conflict with men as well as among women themselves.

The claim to the hoe cannot but challenge the interests of males. The reconquest of the garden as *women's* domain reduced female 'manpower' for weeding on the cropland where men drive tractors, cuts into the acreage and water supply now controlled by men, and removes women from men's control at work. And the recovery of the hoe strengthens women against men, no matter if the hoe is used for subsistence or for a cash income. But these two ways of using a woman's garden are in conflict with one another.

In Chile, a given plot can easily grow the thirty-five species of vegetables, the fowl and fish to keep two women and five children in good health. But the same plot can be farmed as a truck garden which supplies a farmer's market with quality produce. Income thus generated can enable the seven people to survive on junk food. In the first case the hoe becomes the symbol of a new subsistence; in the second, of self-enslavement, 'participation' and economically measurable growth. The two AT gardens represent opposite visions of the good life, opposite expressions of woman's view of woman.

Economic development has been tried for thirty years and has now become a subject for the social historian. For a large part of the men and women whom development has affected, it has meant the *modernization of their poverty* which must be distinguished from the *feminization of poverty* which has been empirically associated with it. I shall first mention three traits of gender-less, modernized poverty, and then list three further traits that aggravate it for women.

Everywhere subsistence activities have been degraded in the process of industrial growth. It has become more difficult to walk, to work, to build one's own house, to feed one's family, to learn a trade without buying into school. Everywhere kinship, neighbourhood, village square and dozens of other support networks have been reduced to the cash-nexus. Gifts of all kinds are dissolved into money. Everywhere professional norms have replaced vernacular values. Not someone from the village, but an outsider is believed to know how best to say something, treat a disease, get a job done.

These sad social side effects of development are increasingly recognized. And they are as unavoidable as the much better publicized ecological side effects. Like pollution, the modernization of poverty affects both men and women. But there is another class of side effects which have been little noted, but which specifically affect women and contribute to what I have called the 'feminization of poverty'.

Inevitably, development deprives women of their *gender*-specific tasks. It turns them into a *mixed* labour force; it makes them the second sex. Everywhere development forces women into something formerly unknown: individual competition with men. Through development women are 'liberated' to enlist in a struggle with men for the same job, a struggle they are doomed to lose. Up to now, the crucial importance of sexism as a side effect of growth has been overlooked.

We easily forget that 'work' which can be done indiscriminately by either men or women simply did not exist in pre-industrial societies. If examples appeared, they were confined to slaves, untouchables and outcasts. No farm implement, no household utensil, no domestic animal in a pre-industrial society is handled indistinctly or used in the same way by men and women. Genderless tools are an invention of the nineteenth century, the tools used in what is now called work.

The facts that I mention are widely documented and I have seen nothing to contradict my statements. Yet I find no evidence that any of the many agencies engaged in 'technology transfer' have ever seriously questioned what they do. For the last thirty years technical assistance has meant the export of a genderless work ethic, genderless tools and the destruction of gendered subsistence. But the elimination of gender-defined tasks and the creation of a mixed work force, within which men and women compete, has always hurt women. This process gives a chance to a few women, degrades many and brings these two groups into conflict with one another.

Let me say more about the destruction of gender. In every pre-industrial society, two distinct halves make up the local tool kit. Each community has its unique way of dividing the burden of existence, the grasp on reality, the use of time and space. Weaving, milking, potting are done either by her or by him. The same task in the same culture is never done by both. Under the rule of gender, women could not, individually, compete with men; they were locked into their own domain. Not individuals, but gender domains were opposed to each other.

In the majority of cultures women's domain was never considered of equal dignity. Under the rule of patriarchy women were excluded from public power. Women's tasks and tools were openly downgraded. Every woman was in this way united with every other woman in a multiple common inferiority. But under the rule of gender women could not become individual losers. And development has changed this. Now, each woman is forced into competition in a man's world. True, development has somewhat weakened patriarchy. But this is greatly offset by the effect of compounding older patriarchal dominance with new sexist discrimination. Development individualizes woman's inferiority making it into something previously unknown, something personally degrading.

Industrialization, however, has no monopoly on the spread of sexism. AT can do equally well or better. For this reason I strongly recommend research on the dangers of genderless AT but I do so not because I am opposed to genderless AT. I welcome tools that fit the hands of women as well as those of men. But I call for research on the sexist effects of genderless AT because, even more effectively than industrial machines, AT can transform proud women into handicapped humans of the second sex. Sometimes this cannot be avoided. But I see no reason for blindly promoting it. Only research *by* women in each village and neighbourhood can ensure that the new wrenches and pliers, the new gauges and glues, the new fish tanks and hand mills, or a new breed of goats, above all empower the hands of women. Such research just cannot be done *for* a village by experts.

A second gender-specific effect of development must also be kept in mind. The economically measurable benefits of growth have accrued disproportionately to men, and have been produced disproportionately by women's unpaid work. This fact has been hidden by a simple device. Modern housework, the unpaid upgrading of commodities into use-values, has been denied recognition as an economic contribution to growth.

Recently this has changed. Ten years ago, Esther Boserup and Barbara Ward launched research on the economic impact of development on women. Since then, dozens of studies have confirmed and expanded their suspicions.

It has been shown that economic growth has always added more to the working hours of women than to men.

It has been shown that with the expansion of the cash-nexus, women's control over cash always declines. By 1975 women, considered throughout the world, provided two-thirds of all working hours and received ten per cent of all paid income.

It has been shown that paid labour does not decrease women's unpaid shadow work. It forces women to be deprived of leisure, mutual help and social control by gossip. The gum-chewing housewives in the laundromat are no political match for a group of women in conversation at the river.

It has been shown that, contrary to popular myth, stress on women grows when households are connected to gas, water, electricity and sewage. This is now an established conclusion reached by the historians of housework. When a faucet is installed in the home, water usage increases twenty-five to fifty times. Each drawn bucket requires little effort, but moving the toilet indoors, new standards of cleanliness of body, clothes, linen and fixtures increase the total toil connected with water.

And it has been shown that these trends appear in all political systems. Everywhere women pay the bill of economic growth by toiling in more shadow work and less desirable wage labour. In Minneapolis the housewife is turned into an unpaid taxi driver to shuttle kids from school to scouts to dancing lesson, while being forced to hold a job to pay for the second car. In Kiev she queues at the butcher shop and the apartment exchange office, while seeking employment in order to buy goods on the black market.

Again, I do not mention these inevitable effects of economic growth because, in principle, I oppose all growth. Without selling some herbs from the garden, women who have reappropriated the hoe will not have the money to buy salt for the goat or a pump for the windmill. I mention the replacement of patriarchal subordination by sexist victimization because this exchange is consistently associated with growth, is rarely considered in development policy and is decisive for anyone who wants to assess the impact of AT on women.

We must learn to ask questions such as 'Up to what point does gobar gas reduce the total effort of women? When does it *increase* this total effort, even if it reduces the particular toil traditionally involved in the procurement of kitchen fuel?' For answers to these questions, only research *by* people, *by* women can be trusted. Expert advice *for* people must be mistrusted, even if it comes from the new, soft, conscience-massaging establishment, possibly represented by a woman.

Development also has a third, equally inevitable gender-specific side effect. It deprives women of the traditional initiative which has enabled them to initiate cultural change. Of the three untoward effects of development which hurt women, this loss of initiative has been the least noticed but may be the most important to remedy, to recover.

To understand what women's initiative meant, we must review how vernacular cultures change. They do so by acquiring new traits. For our purposes here, tools are the decisive new traits. As I pointed out earlier tools have never been genderless. They never fitted 'human' hands, only those of either men or women. If a new tool was brought into a vernacular universe, this incorporation was done by either men or women. And any new object, method, vegetable, breed or skill which was recognized and accepted as the culture's tool, was immediately associated with either men's or women's domain. Tools were adopted by being locally gendered. Tool-making meant the gendering of reality.

And women were as powerful to gender reality as men. Both participated in cultural initiative. And neither could enlarge their own domain without, in some way, affecting the opposite one. When the women in Jura adopted a new carrying net to gather the high mountain grass, the men had to adapt the shape of the old hay sled to receive the new load. Three dozen operations, each gender-specific, followed one another like the steps of a dance until the barn was filled. At each stage, both men and women could make an innovation in their technique, challenging the partner to follow the new step. In contrast, today's gender-neutral tools tend to be under man's control.

Again, I do not mention this evidence because I want to go back. I know that in the Jura *he* led the horses, a prestigious task, while *she* carried the luncheon basket and the rake. Nor do I cite gendered innovation because I want to return to a split set of tools. For me, convivial tools mean a *balance* between networks of subsistence and relations of production. I do not know if the former *must* be gendered. But I strongly believe that attention to gender is particularly important for those who explore the ways in which AT can spread. Throughout history, such diffusion has always been gendered, and had little need for missionaries or educators.

The loss of gender, the destruction of subsistence and the impotence 'to gender' new tools have consistently hurt women in an exquisite way by wedding the inferiority of their gender to individual sexual discrimination. What industrial development began in the sixties, fashionable AT could now consummate and perfect. The new tools are cheaper; therefore, they can spread more equally. They are less violent; therefore, more seductive. They allow each one who uses them to fancy him or herself a 'worker', a creator of wealth. In retrospect, economic growth, with its three sexist side effects, seems to have been waiting for AT to wipe out subsistence completely.

July/August 1983

Historical Concepts of the Body

BARBARA DUDEN

FOR SEVERAL YEARS I have tried to understand how German women in the eighteenth century experienced their bodies, and how a physician in Eisenach interpreted their complaints. As I studied these women, my own feelings about my body began to change. At first I felt condescending towards these women; it seemed to me that they did not know their bodies and were unable to recognize their real needs. However, the more I came to understand and believe those women, the less I took my own body for granted. My own body ceased to be for me a non-historical, natural fact.

I had always taken for granted that I *have* a body. None of the women I studied referred to herself by using a possessive pronoun. I have organs and know where they are, but none of those women visualized her own innards. Whatever lay beneath their skin was for them enveloped in darkness. When I go to a physician I want to get rid of a disease or a pain, or prevent a future breakdown. None of those women went to the doctor to get something fixed; they went to his practice to find comfort in their suffering. Nothing like my categories of health or life, sexuality or reproduction appear in their discourse.

My body and theirs belong to two kinds of space, generated from different axioms. My body cannot be used as a map of theirs. If I want to understand what those women have to say, I have to detach myself from the certainty that the body that I perceive as mine is a natural fact.

One of the needs that we have come to take for granted is the pursuit of health. This need has been only recently coined, and body history can show when, how and why. I can find no expression of such a need in any historical source before the late eighteenth century. Neither the women nor the physician I study can conceive of health as a goal. They cannot think of 'health' as something which is attainable, and therefore will not pursue it as something desirable. Medicine then was not hooked to the pursuit of health; the intrinsic linkage between health and medicine began to emerge only two generations later.

I will first share with you some observations on more than seventeen hundred women from the small town of Eisenach, who have served as a foil against which I can contrast the modern body. Then I will pick out three recent themes that we tend to take for obvious epistemological axioms, and point out what kind of perceptions the acceptance of these axioms excludes.

My women appear in the diary kept by Doctor Johannes Storch from 1719 to 1742. He published his records in seven voluminous volumes. Many of the women he saw appear as only one entry; most of these are peasants or town poor. On the other side there are some five hundred women whose records appear three or more times over the years. These are mostly the wives of artisans or ladies from the small court. Occasionally some of the rich women saw the doctor more than once in a day. Thirdly there are patients whom the doctor prescribes to but never sees: he knows them only through messages they send.

Dr Storch's entries in his diary vary in length from a few lines to several pages. He first mentions his impression of the woman's appearance, the humoral character that he attributes to her at first sight, and her husband's social status. The next entry into each record relates the woman's own story which is followed by the physician's reflection on what she has said. He concludes with his prescription of drugs or bleeding, his dietary advice and his opinion about the result. There is little evidence of any physical examination; on the rare occasion when a woman allows Storch to peep under her lifted skirt or to palpate her swollen breast, he mentions this with a mixture of embarrassment, consternation and pride.

The meaty parts for me are the stories the women have to tell. No doubt the male doctor must have sometimes misunderstood, misquoted or edited a story. However, the accent and stress, the word-order and metaphors make them sound distinctly different from the language the doctor uses to reflect on these complaints. The women speak about hot flashes in their face and fire that rages through their marrow. They accuse cramps, contortions and stabs in their bellies; needles cross their skull; they have the white or the red flux and feel their flesh opening or closing or tightening up.

They have a rich, precise and vivid language that gives them the power to describe the misery they are in. They feel that their blood curdles or clots or is thinning out. Their skin becomes moist, fluffy, dry, puffy or red. They speak about their acceptance of irremediable discomforts that I have great difficulty to imagine.

They have wounds that continue to fester, sores that stay raw for years, rashes and itches that seem to be constitutive parts of their existence. Without any prodding from the physician they volunteer these details, but they do not present them as symptoms of a disease. What they present to the physician is the verbal embodiment of their constant, habitual reality. Their metaphors express their experience of daily suffering of discomfort, toil and often of pain.

They do not come to a physician to be diagnosed or to get rid of a disease. Especially when they are poor, they come to the physician as a last resort. They come when, without him, they do not want to continue their suffering. From their outpouring they expect that their burden be made bearable again. The visit to the medical practice gives them the occasion to make a formal, almost public confession of what they feel like. They want the doctor to accept their self-revelation, and from this they expect consolation and renewed strength to carry on.

In fact, the physician does not respond to their symptoms but to their stories, to their character and to their station in life. If occasionally he takes the initiative and proceeds to an examination, this is nothing but an inquisition into more details out of his patient's past, usually her menses. When occasionally a woman comes to the doctor with a question, it is probably of the same kind. Could her present amenorrhoea be the result of her anger in an argument with her godmother at the baptism of her child? Could a fright that she experienced in puberty and that then constricted her breast be the cause of her menses' recent irregularity?

Dr Storch's consultation-room can no more be reduced to a clinic than it can be reduced to a witchdoctor's church. Medical historians have studied what medical men have said to each other. They have followed through the ages how medical discourse on the body has evolved. But what patients said has been less documented, and how their complaints have shaped the mental guidelines of their physician's practice has been left almost unexplored. Storch's performance cannot be deciphered unless we explore the opposition in him between the learned doctor and the practical man.

Dr Storch is a social upstart. He studied in Jena, read widely and over the years acquired a broad medical education. He translated parts of the work of Georg-Ernst Stahl from Latin into German and in his theory kept close to the teachings of Stahl. As a learned doctor he seeks respectability and the approval of his peers. Storch began to publish a century after William Harvey had published on the movements of the heart, and he acknowledges Harvey's discovery, in England, of the circulation of blood. But he cannot disengage himself from his patients' imagination. His patients' verbal embodiment of their bloody suffering eclipses Harvey for Storch.

Much of Storch's prescribing and bloodletting has the stated purpose to entreat the blood of those suffering women to flow and ebb at the rhythm that befits each patient. The body of his theories does not fully match that of his practice, and on the latter physician and patients largely agree. And yet he views this body of female experience as a man. There are certain matters on which he prescribes against the desire of his patients, and then complains because they consistently disobey his advice. The women, like the doctor, fear that their blood could become too thick and lumpy. But unlike the doctor the women want to heat up their body, bring themselves to a paroxysm, expel their juices, push out the curdled blood. In contrast to them the practitioner wants to control the internal movements of their blood, lead the blood into its appropriate path, entice it to move in the right direction, and finally pull it out. The man and women have dissymmetric views about the same flesh and blood. Several kinds of body are contemporary in Storch's diary.

In Storch's practice the cobbler's wife embodies a different kind of experience than the lady at court. Storch responds to this difference, which is not mere kowtowing in order to keep his rich patient. He responds to a kind of body that is unlike our standardized three-dimensional body-map. The body of tradition is the embodied response to the challenge that is given by one's story and *status* at a precise time and place.

Medical history tells me that in the early eighteenth century medical science had made major advances, but the effectiveness of medical care had not improved. Neither of these two observations are relevant to what I read in Storch's practice. For instance, he has studied the embryology of his time. As a young man he has dissected some bodies. And yet the women he treats—and not only in the perspective of the women, but also in his—have no localized uterus; they have rampaging wombs. Their 'mother' is anxious, and when it hurts it is perceived as roaming through the blood. Dr Storch accepts such statements and builds his prescriptions on them: he advises strong bloodletting at the left ankle to bring the mother to rest.

His view on pregnancy fits into the same picture. Pregnancy is not perceived as a clearly identifiable state. A bloated belly might result in a haemorrhage, in the expulsion of a mole, a monster, a miscarriage, or a happy birth. As long as I held to my modern concept of an abortion I could not but ask what was 'really' happening in such cases. Were these women hedging and performing secret abortions? Were they victims of an illusion? Was the doctor just looking the other way? I had to unlearn to colonize the past with my verities or to use my own body as a bridge into the past.

In comparison with Dr Storch's patients I am out of touch with historical time and space. My body can fit anywhere because it belongs nowhere. I have lost the old art of embodying a keen sense of reality, and I feel anaesthetized because the categories I was educated to describe myself cannot be felt. The modern body is the result of a self-description in which we use professionally defined concepts and notions. We constantly visualize our anatomy, which literally means our dismemberment. From gradeschool on we mirror our innards in charts that illustrate our skeleton and blood flow, our muscles, glands and nerves as separate systems.

I did not grow into the art of suffering the macrocosmos of Eisenach or of any other place. As a result of this, I am not embodied in a microcosmos shaped by me in accordance with the aesthetic rules of my culture. The body I visualize is an anaesthetic cluster of non-historical facts. For example, I had to identify with woman as a fact. When I tried to find out more about this one, I entrusted myself to the guidance of other women, and once more I was given further pictures and maps, albeit from a different perspective. I gained so-called self-knowledge by constructing a body image that could now be compared to a layer-cake of texts. From this body of description and measurements and norms I can pull out any number of sheets that all fit together, although each sheet is inscribed by a different profession and each sheet defines for me a different set of needs. My needy body has become the rationale for a prolific service profession: the transmogrification of the body befits that of society, and the radical newness of modern society will be understood only when we perceive how the image of the body has been transformed.

The needy body and the productive society fit each other; they are spun out of the same yarn. To illustrate their consistency I will reflect on three themes that are common to them: reproduction, sexuality and health.

The term 'reproduction' does not occur in Storch—nor any term that covers a similar field. There is no eighteenth century concept that comprises all and only those things in which today gynaecology deals. Storch kept a separate diary on the women who came to his general practice, as he kept one on children and on soldiers. But this does in no way make him into a gynaecologist: he deals with the woman's whole vita (*biòs*), not with the woman as an agent who reproduces life (*zoé*). As a result of this lack he also has no concept like our sexuality, which we can oppose to reproduction.

Sexuality has now become something which people are prone to attribute to themselves, but not so reproduction. We might refer to our reproductive organs, but I still have met no women who would say 'I have already reproduced three times.' Reproduction was meaningless to Storch's patients; they still thought in terms of generation. Children were then born from women; the womb had not yet been integrated into a reproductive apparatus. Women were still delivered by other women; not babies by professionals. Women were said to give life to their children; medicine was still far from assuming the mandate to protect human life within their womb. The very concept of a 'life' that can be publicly entrusted to medical care does not appear before 1770 and then in the writings of the 'medical police'.

There simply was no grab-bag like our 'reproduction' in which insemination, pregnancy, childbirth and even lactation would fit. Reproduction has been derived from 'production', when this concept around 1850 became important for the understanding of political economy. By that time everyday wants were rapidly being translated into needs for commodities, and as a result all goods came to be perceived as the result of a culturally disembedded process which was called production. Capital and labour were called the productive factors, while the womb and housework came to be understood as the factors through which the labour force itself is reproduced.

Homo economicus was outfitted with a biological body that reflects this economic division of tasks. 'Reproduction' was ascribed to the woman as her specific destiny, and thereby the body attributed to her became a living proof for the natural origin of economic concepts. The endowment of women with a reproductive apparatus resulted in a cultural disembodiment of the process of generation in analogy with the disembedding of a productive economy that signalled the end of cultural self-sufficiency and subsistence.

The emergence of 'sexuality' reflects in terms of the body a new view about the physical universe, and does so parallel to the way in which reproduction reflects a new view of society that is economic. Unlike sexuality, that is absent in Storch's practice, lust is present, but it occupies a minor place. For Storch, as for most of Galen's pupils, lust itself was not a medical issue. Lust attracts the doctor's attention only when it becomes too hot. Only intemperate lust is then classified into the medical category of the 'excess', together with the abuse of wine and beer, overeating and all kinds of self-indulgence.

Our 'sexuality' begins to take shape only after de Sade. With and after de Sade 'sexuality' becomes visible like a photographic plate that slowly develops. Juliette willingly, Justine unwillingly are mere screens on to which club-members project their view about sexuality. Only at this point does the history of attributes towards lust approach what Michel Foucault has called an epistemological fault-line beyond which sexuality is one of those multiple texts that together constitute the anatomized body.

When, much later, Freud describes libido as psychic energy, he does so by lifting entire sentences from an article by Helmholtz. He ties human nature to the new mythology that sweeps the academy in the wake of discoveries in physics. As 'reproduction' has tied the body of women into the context of the labour force, so sexuality roots us in physics. Through many centuries and until the mid eighteen-forties, the cosmos was perceived as the result of a dissymmetric complementarity between body and movement, force and matter. 'Energy' as the one ultimate reality, as the last stuff of existence, becomes the dominant theme only around eighteen-seventy. The age-old *mater*, 'materia' shrivels into the 'principle of energy conservation', a kind of cosmic housewife. Energy and sexuality are but two expressions of one theme: the genderless monism of the ultimate stuff. Sexuality reinterprets lust as thoroughly as reproduction has reinterpreted generation. The older words, namely lust and generation, are still in use, but their old embodiment has vanished. History is no quarry. The better the historian remembers the past, the deeper he knows that nothing from it can be recovered.

Finally, our pursuit of health has extinguished the art of regeneration. Suffering regeneration has been replaced by the ideal of anaesthetic maintenance and repair. The mentality of the body-engineer and the body-accountant can be more prominent in the promoters of self-help than among doctors.

Regeneration, not the pursuit of health as a goal or a norm, was the central concern of old medical traditions. Overcoming my incredulity about women's statements opened my eyes to what is central to other texts of past times that I formerly misread. The women relieve themselves by telling their life-story (their biology) and they ask for purges. The doctor stimulates their outpourings of words and of blood. Both pursue the regeneration of the patient: they try to enhance the women's ability to suffer, to carry on the embodiment of the world as it happens to be, as it is. From our perspective this scene is gory and absurd.

I cannot help imagining that in the perspective of those women our pursuit of health looks equally revolting and nonsensical. This is so because in 1740 their world is still constituted under the *Ancien Régime*. It does not yet incorporate the pursuit of happiness as an inalienable right. It does not place science and technology at the service of a social pursuit of anaesthetic health.

September/October 1985

Woman's Home Rule

ROSEMARY RUETHER

WESTERN WOMEN'S LIBERATION has become associated with the right to work. This has produced a home-work dichotomy and splits male and female to opposite sides of the economic spectrum: men have become associated with production, and women the managers of a consumer support system. Women, even in the professions, have found it difficult to compete with men. They are still regarded as managers of the domestic support system, and women's work there is seen as invisible and unpaid. Women, therefore, have not been able to take advantage of their theoretical rights. Women have not had wives.

This split of home and work, the separation of women away from exchange value labour, is characteristic of industrial society. It is not primordial. An African woman still manages a large part of the economy of the entire society at home, as the home is the economic structure. She participates in handicrafts, agriculture, commands the transformatory processes, turning the raw into the cooked, herbs into medicines, raw materials into clothes, baskets and pots, and is also involved in marketing. The African man protects the village, carries on warfare, clears and fences the fields and makes weapons. Grown men are therefore freed by women and youth to engage in political discourse.

These roles did not disappear in the industrial revolution, although the roles became less egalitarian. Women ran the family not only in the peasant class but also among the gentry.

The transition from rural to urban life originally affected only a small section of society. It created a new elite of males whose power was no longer based on personal prowess, such as the hunter and warrior, but on the inherited monopoly of economic power, land and knowledge. The political sphere was monopolized to define women and the lower classes into a relationship inferior with themselves. Women were gradually excluded from power, except as place holders for male heirs. They were also excluded from cultural roles: priests and scribes. No biological differences were necessary for this changeover; large muscles were not necessary to swing incense upon an altar or to push pieces of paper around a desk. The religious laws and ideologies of these times established patriarchal doctrines which were written into the Canon Laws and the Bible.

Industrialization is the second major turning point in the socio-economic evolution of women. It added a new economic dependency of women to the legal dependency already established in classical patriarchy. It was already the case with upper class women, although the lower class women could still take part in the economy provided it was family-centred. Industrialization removed these self-supporting functions from the home. In a traditional society, if you stayed at home you'd survive. Today you'd starve. The family becomes dependent on an economic sphere outside and beyond its control. Women are transformed from an active economic labourer to a manager of consumption, an ornament to her husband's economic prowess.

These new frustrations explain why women's liberation became a mass movement only in the nineteenth century. Many poor women were forced out of the home into the severe oppression of the factory. There was a strong conflict between the liberal doctrines of equality, an equality which excluded women—liberty, and *fraternity*, and with women who took up their fight through liberalism and with the new ideologies of bourgeois romanticism which expressed women's biological differences from men and their need to stay in the home. This was the clash between liberalism, romanticism and feminism which still exists to some degree today.

Childhood also became a doctrine for the masses, whereas until now it had only been the case in bourgeois commercial society. The home became privatized into a space for private life and nurture in comparison with the open centre of business and commerce of earlier peasant and aristocratic culture. Now childhood was prolonged to keep children out of the economic market. The child was seen as an innocent being to be shaped into a fit social being.

Women's new role was defined by this and the new ideology of true womanhood. It was a compensatory role in the new industrial society. The bourgeoisie had taken over the aristocratic class and, as a reaction to secularization, social revolution and industrial society, they had become reactionary and conservative. 'Home' and 'womanhood' were capitalized whereas the natural rights of birth were challenged. In the home, emotions and intimacy could hold sway in a world dominated by technological rationalism. The subliminal spirituality could compensate for the fierce materialism outside. It could give peace to the bourgeoisie from the ugly world they were creating outside the factories. It was a home realm of nostalgic religiosity to which men could retire under threat. Women became the priestesses of the home.

This idealization of the home removed women completely from the realm of public affairs. Women, who in the eyes of the Church were seen as evil and the devil incarnate and therefore unfitted to take any part in the world outside, were now too noble and pure to descend into the base world of men and politics. This became the jargon of the conservative churchmen and politicians.

This split creates a dualism in modern public rhetoric. The private self is defined apart from the public world. Religion becomes private and is shaped by this split. It partially reverses the images of masculine and feminine. Classical Christianity saw women as less spiritual than men. The nineteenth century saw them as more so, but also as more stupid.

But the ideology of 'womanhood' is a myth. The leisured middle class woman could display the wealth of the industrial masters, yet there was intense sexual and social oppression and a proliferation of the houses of prostitution. The distinction between the lady and the working woman, between the pure asexual mariolatry of the 'lady' and the carnal working woman was exaggerated. The contrast was exploited between Mary and Eve, between the white lady and the black woman, between the middle class and the working class woman.

This split entered the women's struggle in nineteenth century politics. Middle class feminism either did not speak to the cause of the working class woman, or was patronizing to her. The working class woman wanted better wages and better economic conditions, but had little help either from her brothers or her sisters. So despite the large numbers of women at work, neither the ideology of womanhood, or the planned relation between home and work was adjusted in Western society. Women's day was subservient to the men's work day, men *with* wives.

In the 1830s and 1840s criticism of the family and private property included criticism of the exploitation of women. Marx and Engels analysed the relation between socialism and women and saw the conflicts in the contrast between factory labour and the notion of feminism. They saw socialism as the basis for women's emancipation and the restoration of women to the realm of productive labour.

The Marxist solution is limited, however. Social values do not reply to the split between male and female values. In the USSR women are still stereotyped in home and work roles, and only make the lower echelons of the political and power world. The male pattern of alienated work becomes the exclusive pattern for living and human values. The Marxist solution is a *total integration of women into alienated labour*, by drastically reducing the amount of work in the home and by collectivizing the public sector. It is the emancipation of women through the collectivization of alienation. The family loses social determination and becomes a fleeting interaction of personal relations. A totalitarian society is created and the self loses its autonomous base. In the USSR people become absorbed into their private lives and ignore the public world.

Socialism seems at present to depend on the obliteration of the female sphere into the masculine, so that if people become equal it is *women* who are abolished. The alienation of self-determination into macro-collectivization happens instead. The local bureaucracy controls your life. The values created in the home are replaced by conflict, work and warfare.

For the creation of freedom and equal roles, for justice and humanization, can we not instead envisage a process of socialization that works the other way round, which *abolishes the male sphere into the female sphere*. Why not resocialize the home by bringing power to it, bringing access to work and political decision making in an integral relationship between the autonomous self-determining community?

Some aspects of this pattern have been seen in China and in Cuba, where the local base of the commune is seen as the basis of the larger networks of society. People have a sense of gaining control over their own lives. This also happens to a degree in the Kibbutz. It brings back to people the control over the means of production. Giving people control over the means of production does not necessarily mean giving it over to the state. It means working, living and childbearing on a local basis.

A humanized society must be one that is reintegrated into those values that have been cultivated *powerlessly* in the female sphere: co-operation, mutual support, celebration, the exploitation of feelings and personal relations. Work should be seen as self-expression, mutual help and fulfilment of being, and not as alienated labour. We do not live to be able to work, but work in order to be. It is not minimal survival but fulfilment of being, where work is reunified with creative self-expression and takes place in a community of mutual affirmation.

The recovery of the world of work for women is a struggle to de-alienate work and to rediscover community.

March/April 1978

Traditional Ways

The Patron Saint of Ecology

STRATFORD CALDECOTT

FOUR YEARS AGO, Pope John Paul II declared Francis of Assisi the patron saint of ecology. Francis was the 'raving lunatic' (Voltaire) whose linen drawers caught fire one night as he was sitting by the hearth, and who was so reluctant to harm 'Brother Fire' that the blaze had to be extinguished against his will. When he washed his hands, he used to choose a place where the water would not have to be trampled under foot. He would move worms, too, off the road in case people trod on them, and put honey and the best wine out for the bees in the depths of winter. He instructed the friars not to cut down the whole tree when they went for firewood, so it could have hope of sprouting again.

So far so good. But then we read that this same Francis scourged himself and rolled naked in snow or brambles to cure himself of lust, and fasted so much that his body finally gave out under the strain. He once addressed the devils who were keeping him awake in the following terms: 'Devils! I command you on behalf of God almighty, use all the power given you by the Lord Jesus Christ to make my body suffer. I am ready to endure everything, for I have no greater enemy than my body; in this way you will avenge me on this adversary and enemy.'

Does this not confirm an accusation often levelled against Christianity: the accusation that at its heart flourishes a sinister dualism, a masochistic hatred of everything that binds us to the earth? Even a saint who loved animals as Francis did, it seems, could not resist this sickness of Christianity, and was forced by his conditioning into despising his own flesh—the flesh which he nevertheless shared with the animals he loved. Francis, to this way of thinking, was a man divided, a living symbol of the ultimate failure of Christianity to acknowledge the unity of all Creation.

What follows is a rather different interpretation.

In each of us there are two selves: the real and the illusory, the true and the false. One of these has to prevail at any given moment. The victory of the true self is what some religions call enlightenment or liberation, others 'salvation'. They tell us that the true self—the Self with a capital 'S'—exists always, but is consciously realized only in the few. This Self is not other than God. And that person whose 'self has become the self of all beings, having renounced the fruit of action, attains perfect peace,' as the *Bhagavad Gita* tells us.

The various religions put this truth in different ways. Maurice Blondel has expressed the Catholic version quite concisely: 'The true will of man is the divine will.' It follows that we have no will that is truly our own. Indeed, the misguided attempt to create one lies at the root of the false self. As St Francis comments on the *Book of Genesis*: 'A man eats of the tree that brings knowledge of good when he claims that his good will comes from himself alone and prides himself on the good that God says and does in him. And so the fruit becomes for him the fruit that brings knowledge of evil.'

To become enlightened, we must therefore renounce the 'fruit of action', the mysterious fruit that was forbidden to Adam and Eve, and instead let God act through us. Our artificial self must die, so that 'I live, and yet no longer I but Christ lives in me.'

Now, obviously Francis had no horror of physical substance as such. Indeed, his path to sainthood could be said to have begun when he faced and overcame his disgust at leprosy, forcing himself to kiss a leper in friendship. By so doing, he confronted biology at its most terrible, and was able to find God there in the midst of it. 'What had previously nauseated me became a source of spiritual and physical consolation.' The act of doing something his false self shrank away from was one of his first 'mortifications', the practice of which he kept up all his life. Another typical example was during a time of freezing wind: Francis became aware that he was afraid of the cold blowing through his thin habit, so he rushed to the top of the nearest hill and stripped naked, standing there until he had overcome his fear.

Francis's whole method involved discovering whatever the false self desired, and doing the exact opposite. It was this false self that was his 'adversary and enemy', the self that is accreted together by thieving things that do not belong to it. Francis's hatred was directed, not at the cells and sinews of sensations of his body, but at the false will that misused them, and the sense of being separate from God. No wonder that those devils in fact left Francis to sleep in peace, after being ordered to attack his body. They could not obey: they were told to attack their own Master, Francis's false self.

As for the apparent contradiction involved in all mortification—that of trying to destroy our will by exerting it, of acting in order to renounce action —this dissolves when it is looked at more closely. Francis was not aiming to *save himself* by penance: only to signify his willingness to be saved. Like all 'religious actions' this was a ritual performance, a kind of gesture made in acknowledgement of the invisible world, an invitation to God to act.

Truth comes when it chooses; but it would not be fitting for it to arrive without having been asked. So first of all it inspires us to ask. In something of the same spirit, a Zen monk who believes in instantaneous *satori* will sit for hours at a time in *zazen*, refusing to fall asleep or fidget. The Sufis have a saying, 'The truth is not found by seeking; but only those who seek will find it.'

Francis grew up in relative luxury. His father was one of the rich, rising merchant class of Assisi, and named him after France, the country where he did much of his trade. So the boy learnt all the popular songs of the troubadours, and as he got older could afford to lead the wild youth of the town in the latest fashions, and spend his father's money on the pleasures of the body. Along with many of his friends, he fought against Perugia in a vicious local war, and he was imprisoned for a time. After that, he set his sights on leaving the merchant class behind. He wanted to become a knight, a nobleman, to win some fair lady by might and daring. He did not get very far. Riding off towards Apulia, dressed as richly as could be, a generous impulse made him give most of his finery to a destitute knight he met on the road. And before long he was turned back by a dream to Assisi.

After a long period of self-questioning, a crucifix spoke to him in a ruined chapel. It told him to repair the Church. Taking this rather literally, Francis rushed off and sold some of his father's fabrics without permission, bringing the money back to the local priest to help him keep the place up. When his father, raging mad, came looking for him, Francis was hiding in a hole in the ground. He stayed there a solid month, afraid to come out. On going home he was beaten severely and locked up in disgrace. It was his mother who finally let him out—his mother who had wanted to name him John, after John the Baptist.

Then came the dramatic gesture by which he ended his old life once and for all. In front of the whole town, which by this time had been thoroughly scandalized, and in front of the Bishop, to whom his father had appealed for justice in the matter of the stolen money, Francis tore off his clothes, renouncing everything he had from his human father. From that day on Peter Bernadone would curse his son whenever he saw him pass by. A servant of the Bishop gave Francis a cast-off tunic, and he marched off into the woods, determined to repair old churches with his bare hands. He was singing as he went.

That gesture of renunciation has also been called the moment of his 'marriage'. For he had not given up his desire to win a great lady. Some time before, he had started to think of poverty as a person. He called her 'the most beautiful woman in the world'. From that time on, he wanted only to be found completely faithful to her. He would consistently refuse to touch money or property, and took the gospel so literally that he would not even store up food for tomorrow. With those who followed him into his new way of life, he elevated begging for alms into a sacred ritual, a symbol of total dependence on the God who is charity. It is only in the context of this love affair with Lady Poverty that his enthusiasm for every kind of mortification can be understood.

Undoubtedly Francis derived joy from his penances. There was nothing gloomy about them. G. K. Chesterton wrote, 'He devoured fasting as a man devours food.' Of course, in his enthusiasm he tended to overdo it: he would often fall ill, and only then start to be more gentle on himself. Brother Stephen was once rebuked for cooking the friars too good a meal, so the next day he served only crusts of bread, to be met with Francis's wry remark, 'Dear son, discretion is a noble virtue, nor shouldst thou always fulfil all that thy superior biddest thee, especially when he is troubled by any passion.'

On his companions, Francis practised his 'discretion' more consistently than he did on himself. He threw away their hair shirts and the painful metal hoops some of them had started to wear. If he noticed any of them going around with long, hungry faces he would advise them to eat a proper meal—and to pray for their joy to be restored. Awareness of the presence of God always drives out depression. They should be happy, not 'gloomy and depressed like hypocrites'. He told them once: 'If, in the matter of eating and drinking we are obliged to deny ourselves those superfluous things which are harmful to the body and the soul (notice that it was never his intention actually to damage the body), we must forgo even more so excessive mortification, for God desires loving kindness and not sacrifice.'

Perhaps the greatest temptation Francis had to face came from his very devotion to Lady Poverty. In 1210 he obtained papal approval for his way of life, and permission to preach without being a priest. His followers became an 'Order' within the Church—and this is where the subtle Serpent raised his head. Francis for a long time tended to fall into the feeling that this was 'his' Order. After all, he had started it, and he was at the centre of it. Only after a long struggle could he renounce all desire to lead except by example, give up the exercise of power completely, and hand the movement back to the Holy Spirit, the 'true Minister General of the Order'. It was at that time that he had several prophetic visions, and knew that the days of strict poverty were coming to an end. He knew he could not impose his Lady on those who would come after.

As he lay dying, his words showed that he was at last at peace with himself. 'I have done what was mine to do: may Christ teach you what you are to do.'

Meister Eckhart calls detachment the 'greatest and best virtue', by which we can 'by grace become what God is by nature'. It seems to start with the realization that any desire to *know who I am* is just another ploy of the false self. Any 'self' that I am capable of 'knowing'—of turning into an object of my consciousness—cannot possibly be my own. *That* Self, the true one, can be known only by and in God. Our role is not to *know* but to *be* ourselves. We must be content to say, with Francis, 'What a man is before God, that he is and nothing more.'

Detachment in this sense is the inner dimension or Franciscanism. Whatever compromises have taken place under the pressure of history and society, and with the end of begging from door to door, the relationship with Lady Poverty will always remain secure for those who are not attached to any image of themselves. Anyone who is fully detached in this way automatically becomes what the gospels call a 'peacemaker'. He or she no longer participates in the polarization of self and other, friend and enemy, which is necessary for those who have something to defend.

In this way, by detaching him from all things, Lady Poverty freed Francis to look for the good in everything and everyone he met. Without any 'self' to worry about, he could not be concerned about possible personal advantages and disadvantages. Consequently he was able to respond to things as they really were. Through 'Brother Sun' he saw the Light of Life; through 'Sister Water' he saw the baptism of rebirth; through a lamb on its way to market he saw the Lamb of God; through wood the Tree of the Cross. The Book of Nature reflected the Book of Scripture, and in both he could read only a single Word, the divine *Logos*.

The ability to make any lasting peace depends on the ability to see and address the good in both sides. Against the advice of the townsfolk of Gubbio, Francis went to speak to a wolf that was preying on them and their flocks. He told it that if it would stop doing this the people would no longer hunt it, and that because he recognized its need to eat he himself would persuade the townsfolk to lay out food on a regular basis. The wolf shook hands on the bargain, and for the rest of its natural life came and went freely in the town without incident. Eventually the people buried it affectionately under their church.

In Trevi, where Francis was trying to preach, a noisy ass got loose in the square and no one could catch it. Francis said to it, 'Brother Ass, please be quiet and allow me to preach to the people.' When it did so, immediately standing perfectly silent, everyone was amazed and, 'fearing that the people might take too much notice of this astonishing miracle', Francis 'began saying funny things to make them laugh.'

In both cases, what made a miracle possible was the fact that the saint cut through the ordinary way of looking at the world and, instead of treating the animal as a dumb beast, addressed it as it existed in the presence of God. He was involved not with some fragment of the world outside himself, but with a particular aspect of the wholeness in his own heart. He spoke as though the animal could understand him, because he was really speaking to God, through one of the innumerable types or Forms of beauty and goodness that subsist in the Supreme Identity.

All things are equally intelligent in God: flocks of birds and crowds of people listened to Francis's sermons with the same attentiveness, responding not to the words as much as to the intention or spirit which animated them. Of course, it did not always come off. People tend to be entrenched in their own habits, and unprepared to give them up. And there is at least one story of Francis turning aside to preach to a flock of birds, who flew off when they saw him approaching. 'Then he came back and began to accuse himself most bitterly, saying "What effrontery you have, you impudent son of Peter Bernadone" —and this because he had expected irrational creatures to obey him as if he, and not God, were their Creator.' For a moment, he had become attached to the image of himself that others saw—that of 'the saint who could speak to animals'. But birds are hard to fool. Only God can hold their attention: never the false self, the thief of Eden.

Francis rapidly became the most universally popular of Christian saints— canonized only two years after his death. He is the patron saint of Italy as well as of ecology. There are three main Franciscan Orders in the Church—one for men, one for women and one for men and women remaining 'in the world'. Taken together, these Orders form the largest such family in the Church. The Third Order, for example, numbers several million.

People sometimes quote that notorious text in Genesis, where God gives humanity 'dominion' over 'every living thing that moves upon the earth', as one of the supports for speciesism and industrialization. But nowhere in the

Bible is 'dominion' any excuse for oppression and exploitation: on the contrary, it is a sacred duty that imposes on the ruler a full and terrible responsibility. Humanity will be answerable before God if we do not mediate properly the goodness of God to the rest of Creation.

Ecological disasters are but one example of the 'retribution' we bring upon ourselves, a case of Creation joining with God 'to fight against the madmen'. Floods, plagues, lawlessness among men—the Bible links them all together as the natural consequence of injustice. It is perfectly legitimate to interpret this 'injustice' to include our mistreatment of nature: if not a violation of nature's rights, then those of nature's Creator.

That, at least, is how the Franciscans have interpreted it. 'Open your eyes, alert the ears of your spirit, open your lips and *apply your heart* so that in all creatures you may see, hear, praise, love and worship, glorify and honour your God lest the whole world rise against you,' St Bonaventura has written.

The Christian experience of the world is sacramental. Through being united with Mary in the Person of Christ, God was united to all human, animal, vegetable and mineral nature from the beginning to the end of time. God is present in one way as the essence of personality, in each of our neighbours. The same God is present in each of the seven sacraments of the Cosmic Roman Church, the Church made up of all those who truly love. And there is an eighth sacrament: de Caussade's 'sacrament of the present moment', by which Christianity links up definitively with the wisdom of Taoism. But above all, God contains the entire universe in its most real (that is, its uncreated) form, and is present in all things as their sustaining cause.

The world is both created by God from nothing, and also emanates from God like light from the sun. The world is not made from anything other than God (for there *is* nothing else): yet God is supremely simple, and therefore cannot be divided up, or in any way modified by creation. God therefore resembles the number One, which is contained within every other number—but which itself contains them if you look at them as fractions of a whole. In either case, One itself remains inviolate: if it did not, all the other numbers would cease to exist.

The sacredness of the world means that there is nothing at all which is merely a thing, nothing which we may treat as mechanism, as lacking 'resident divinity'. By this, our entire way of life since the Renaissance stands condemned. The seventeenth-century 'enlightenment' was really a falling into darkness, and the scientific revolution was an attempt to find reality by systematically looking in the wrong place—by trying to 'stand over' what should have been 'under-stood'.

This may look like an excessively negative conclusion. But we will never get anywhere if we do not admit our mistakes. Having admitted this one, there would be nothing to stop the modern world from re-integrating the knowledge it has stolen. Facts are true, even if they have been torn from the body of nature (as Bacon advocated) by torture, and *no* truth should be rejected. The point is that any truth which is appropriated by the false self becomes a shirt of Nessus. It becomes the means of our corruption—and probably the means, eventually, of our purification. In our own day, the nuclear bomb has become the symbol of that robbery, and of that corruption.

We are living in a time when all moral compromises are being reduced to absurdity. Sometimes total war can seem so inevitable that we are tempted to despair. But despair is called a 'sin' because it is always a mistake. Only the hopes of the false self can be dashed in this way. Furthermore, every religious tradition suggests that politicians have less power to destroy us than they imagine. I have heard it said that the world is being kept in existence partly because a small number still remember to 'walk in a sacred manner on the earth'.

The archetypal feminine presence in the Bible—and in the Jewish/Catholic tradition which gave us the Bible—is named Sancta Sophia, Holy Wisdom. She is the beautiful one who 'reaches mightily from one end of the earth to the other', who 'orders all things well', against whom 'evil cannot prevail'. Solomon 'preferred her to sceptres and thrones', and 'accounted wealth as nothing in comparison with her'. It would be wrong to assume such statements to be merely allegorical. The Bible is one long love story, relating the tale of Sophia's separation from her lover, and her eventual return. The separation and consequent tension between these two lovers is the 'space' in which creation takes place. As long as the separation lasts, God—who as Absolute and Infinite is naturally neither 'he' nor 'she'—has to be represented as primarily masculine, to balance the femininity of Sophia.

Holy Wisdom, the 'Soul of the World', the 'Woman Clothed with the Sun', is supremely real, not an allegorical invention. She is the beggar maid St Francis saw in a vision, and to whom he gave the name Lady Poverty.

Unless, like him, we unite ourselves with her we will never be able to make our peace with the Earth.

May/June 1984

A Defence of Sacred Measures

JOHN MICHELL

IT IS NECESSARY TO OPPOSE with the utmost vehemence the proposal to abandon our traditional standards of weight and measure in favour of the metric units invented at the French Revolution.

The fundamental reason for emphasizing the importance of this issue is that it clearly epitomizes the conflict between two contrasting philosophic or cosmological points of view. The first is expressed in the ancient belief, orthodox for many thousands of years and only recently denied, that eternal and human values (the two being inseparable) should govern the social order and institutions. According to this view, human nature, though always varying, remains essentially the same in all times. There is one philosophy, one religion, one science, though for each of these there are infinite expressions. Humanity and cosmos are alike in this, that both are constant and made in the same image. Both are therefore measured by the same standards, and for this purpose the ancient units of metrology were designed. Against this view is the newly received idea that the universe and its inhabitants are ever subject to purposeless change mechanically operated; that eternal values are a delusion, human values incidental; that the only true religion is idolatry, the worship of the chance material products of the time; and that the interests of the state idol are more important than those of the human individual and should be consulted above all else. By this reckoning the body of the idol provides a more appropriate source and standard of measures than the human frame, and this is the origin of the metric system.

The point at issue is whether an enlightened, humane and scientific civilization should adopt as its standards of measure units such as those still in use in England, which were formerly, and for good reason, regarded as sacred, having the advantages of tradition, inherent meaning and natural application, or whether the metric system, which has none of these qualities nor any of its own to replace them, is the more appropriate.

According to the first of the philosophies contrasted in the preceding paragraph the adoption of sacred standards of measure, together with an appreciation of their significance and value, is essential in order to achieve and maintain true civilization.

Sacred measures are those units which relate to natural constants on more than one scale and demonstrate the unity between the macrocosmic body of the universe and the human microcosm. The present British units, the foot, mile, acre and the rest, are by this definition sacred; the metric units are not. The origins of the two systems and the implications in their use are contrasted in the following paragraphs.

The foot and the other linear and land measuring units that relate to it are of indefinable antiquity. They were known to the Sumerians, Chaldeans and the ancient Egyptians and appear once to have been universal, for they survive in different parts of the world, wherever the interests of the people are still given precedence over those of modern technology and commerce. Their advantages for all human purposes are obvious. A carpenter gauges an inch by the width of the thumb and its tenth part using a practised eye; a builder estimates the length of a wall by the two yard span of the outstretched arms, and a surveyor paces by the yard. Cloth is sold by the cubit, the distance from elbow to finger tip, and other such units as the span and handbreadth were formerly used which have now generally become obsolete. Ancient societies regarded their standards of measure as their most sacred possessions and they have been preserved with extreme accuracy from the earliest times. A craftsman soon learns to what extent the parts of his own body deviate from the conventional standard and adjusts accordingly.

Sacred units of measure apply not only to the human scale but also to the astronomical. For this reason they were said, at a time when such language was more generally understood, to have been 'revealed' to us, not invented by us. The purpose of ancient science was to maintain and invigorate an esoteric tradition, the primeval heritage, rather than to pursue innovations not, as evolutionists have supposed, because of any deficiencies in the positive intellect of early people, but because education was formally directed on Platonic principles towards the development of the inherent sense of proportion by means of musical and mathematical studies, with the result that cosmology, the science of discerning and codifying reality, was respected above all.

According to Plato in *The Laws*, the stability of ancient civilization was maintained by the application of a canonized law of proportion, a code of musical harmonies, to which artists and musicians were obliged to refer in all compositions. The canon was essentially numerical, capable of being interpreted in the appropriate terms for use in the various arts and sciences, as music, architecture and astronomy, and extending to such matters as theology and the art of government. Its corresponding geometrical expression was the figure, conceived as the synthesis of all geometrical types, which St John described as the ground-plan of the New Jerusalem and Plato as the mystical city of *The Republic* and *The Laws*. This figure was the symbol of the cosmos, and its dimensions, measured by the sacred units, the most important being the English foot and mile, reproduced the principal dimensions of the solar system, revealing accurate knowledge in some remote age of the measurements of earth, sun and moon.

It is thus claimed on behalf of units of measurements such as the foot, furlong and mile, whose preservation has hitherto been the honourable charge of the British nation, that they have a profounder significance than as mere arbitrary standards of length; that they are integral in the human view of the universe and can not therefore be excluded from any social scheme founded on human rather than idolatrous principles. The philosophy, which provides the justification for their use, recognizes the existence of a natural law, reigning within both human nature and the universal soul, some knowledge of which is essential to the orderly conduct of human affairs. The word 'human' is here emphasized, because the interests of the true science and of the people are not naturally opposed but complementary, and when the principles of this science are again established, as they inevitably must if the re-enactment of the destruction of Babylon on a more grandiose scale is to be averted, the conduct of affairs will be directed towards the benefit of the people as a whole rather than of one class, the financiers and industrialists. In this event, the advantage of adopting sacred units of measurement, those which are inherent in the natural order and not simply the reflection of a transient, atheistic political philosophy, will again become apparent.

The history of the metric system, by which it is proposed to replace our traditional system of metrology, is indicative of its character. At the time of the French Revolution, when the Goddess of Reason was ceremonially installed in Notre Dame, a number of people, many of whom were by all other standards apparently sane, were struck by the remarkable notion that the facts of nature, even the cycles of the sun and moon as manifest in the weeks and months of the calendar, might be varied by government decree. The revolutionary calendar, with its ten month year and twenty hour day, the most spectacular feat of idolatry since the Tower of Babel, collapsed at once, but its companion, the metric system, was successfully imposed on the French people.

According to Napoleon, who lightened the penal sanctions by which its use was enforced, 'it violently broke up the customs and habits of the people as might have been done by some Greek or Tartar tyrant.' Despite popular rejection and following a number of bloody riots in which opposition to the compulsory use of the metre was suppressed, the metric system survived in France and was extended in the interest of uniformity to other European nations, always with the active assistance of the police or military.

The metre was originally intended, following ancient precedent, to be a geodetic or earth-measuring unit, one ten-millionth part of a quadrant of the meridian measured through Paris. Its length was finally established in 1798, as accurately as the scientific methods of the time allowed, as equal to 39.37 inches. A particular reason why this length so commended itself to its inventors was that it corresponded to no existing or traditional unit. In other words, it was purposely designed to be unlike any unit which had ever been found convenient in actual use. The old sacred measures, properly understood, promote harmony, stability and knowledge. The new atheistic system, conceived in ignorance and arrogance and nurtured on the blood of the people, is the fitting servant of the forces of greed and materialism that are currently favouring its adoption in England.

This defence of the foot against the metre is based on two qualities that distinguish the foot from its rival. First, the foot is the established measure of the British people and has been so from the earliest times, at least since the building of Stonehenge. It is universally known and is used in many countries including America, where on account of the republican common sense and practicality of the people it is to be retained. To abandon it to enforce the use of an alien system can in no possible way benefit the public interest. The compulsory introduction of the metre, which in the improbable event of popular opinion being consulted, certainly would be rejected by the great majority, is thus clearly defined as an act of tyranny.

The second argument in favour of the foot may to some appear excessively mystical. It is however the more essential of the two, and is here included for the consideration of those who are sufficiently experienced to understand its implications, and with an appeal for the indulgence of those who are not. The foot, stated above, is a sacred unit of ancient cosmology, designed to illustrate the hermetic philosophy of 'man as the measure of all things' and to promote harmony on earth by assisting the influences of true proportion to become active in human affairs. The way of thought that attends the use of the foot locates the centre of the world within each individual, and encourages us to arrange our kingdom after the best possible model, the cosmic order. The ancient method of acquiring this model was not astronomy but initiation, for those who presented themselves, suitably prepared, to the priests of Hermes were admitted to the study of the sacred canon, which demonstrated the link between the created, visible world and the creative world of archetypal notions, and provided the criterion for the discernment of truth and illusion. Those insufficiently curious to seek initiation could rest assured on the word of initiates, such as that given by Plato, that 'things are far better looked after than we can possibly conceive.'

That the inch, foot, furlong, mile and acre are of very ancient and sacred origin has been demonstrated elsewhere. The fact may not appear of any great interest at the present time, but sacred means preordained and eternal, and to these epithets neither the metric system nor the theories behind its promotion have any claim. Naturally, each generation has the right to select whatever system of measurements it finds most appropriate, but it must then be content to be judged by its choice. It is therefore the right and duty of those concerned, before the final decision is made between the foot and the metre, to consider carefully the origin, history and meaning of the two systems in order to see which one is most in accordance with their ideals and interests and best designed to promote civilized human values.

In Jung's phrase, the balance of the primordial world is upset. The art of government, as practised from the earliest times, is to discern and weigh the various interests within the community, preserving dynamic stability by application of the mystical law of proportion. The decline of this esoteric science and the fragmentation of the canonical society prepared the way for the development of the new philosophy of civilization, which attaches more importance to external form than to essential reality. In consequence, the respect formerly given to the concept of a sacred order based on eternal values was transferred to the nineteenth century doctrine of 'the survival of the fittest', a pernicious phrase favoured by dictators, millionaires and other modern aberrations, and advanced by them in justification for all excesses.

The proposal to introduce the metric system into England is another episode in a lengthy historical process by which the natural rights of the individual, including that of participation in decisions affecting his own immediate interests, have been eroded, often by measures ostensibly designed to protect them. The destruction of local independence that followed from the Reformation; the confiscation of church and common lands on behalf of the state and its monopolists; the extinction of the labourer's small-holding, compensated for by the benefits of the poor law and workhouse; by such events the process is illustrated. Throughout the eighteenth century central government increased its power over the people whose interests it was shortly to betray by the following proceeding. Soon after the Napoleonic War the government adopted a remarkable theory of economics, which held that the country's wealth could be increased by the simple expedient of printing more money. This new paper money was issued through bankers and jobbers, to whom it mostly adhered, thus generating a new dominant class whose wealth and influence soon exceeded all others. This class is strictly parasitic, because it neither creates nor produces anything of human value, nor does it profess to rule for the benefit of the people as a whole. Its growing influence has led naturally to a corresponding decrease in the fortunes of everyone else. Its values have become universally accepted and embodied in theories of government, the natural function of rulers to balance the various interests within the community being disregarded. Finally, the native parasites have now been swallowed up by others larger and more anonymous, so that it has become no longer possible for the individual to identify the source of the authority by which he is governed.

The religion that has been engendered by this process is idolatry and the idol is that very 'image of the beast' described by St John in Revelation 13, whose ritual is the worship of material form. The appropriate unit by which this idol is measured is the metric system: and so it is proposed. Yet, vast and inflated though it is, the idol is but a created thing with no claims to immortality. After the nature of such monsters its appetite ever increases, and each year ever greater sacrifices are demanded of the people, until the time comes for its destruction, and of this there is no lack of portents. In contrast, the foot belongs to a tradition of which it has always been said that, even though it may be suppressed and vanish for centuries, it will always recur for its spores are deeply embedded in human nature, and the truth to which it refers is constant and unique. The submergence of this tradition coincides with the dark periods of history; with its cyclical rebirth the light of civilization is restored. To institutionalize the dark ages by giving authority to the metric system would be an act of folly inconceivable in any other age but our own.

November/December 1978

So He Settled in a Village

TRISTRAM BERESFORD

IN HIS YOUTH, Manibhai Desai was a blower of bridges. This was the accepted thing in those days for young men of his means, standing and education. He was not an anarchist, but like others of his age-group he was a patriot and burning for Purna Swaraj (total independence of India). So he opted out of university without telling his parents (who as Gujerati Brahmins would surely have objected), and after Gandhi's arrest in August 1942 he went underground. The slogan was 'Do or Die'. The question, naturally, was what to do. To students, like the group he led, sabotage was an obvious answer; this was the view of the local branch of the Congress Socialist Party to which he belonged. He was twenty-two years old.

On 10th February 1943, under arrest in the Aga Khan's Palace in Poona, Gandhi began a three weeks' fast. He was an old man, and ailing, but he wished to remind his followers that *satyagraha*—as he conceived it—does not seize power, does not even seek power, but that power accrues to it. Underground workers felt that he did not approve of their activities and Desai was one of the many who decided to come out into the open and practise resistance to the Raj by peaceful means. Within months he was arrested for civil disobedience, tried, convicted and sent to prison.

In jail he found a number of other Congress Party prisoners. He read Karl Marx and Nehru, and studied the theory of *satyagraha*. His first contact with Gandhi was through the mind. But here were others in Sabarmati Jail who knew Gandhi, and who formed a favourable impression of the young man's aptitude and ardour. They persuaded him to let his emotions cool and complete his B.Sc. He graduated in April 1945 in physics and mathematics. The same month, in Bombay, he had his first interview with Gandhi, who was so weak after two years in prison, and because of the burden of those times, that they conversed by exchanging words on a pad. Gandhi was seventy-five; Desai fifty years his junior. As a consequence of this first meeting he trained for six months at the Sevagram at Segaon near Wardha. From there he went to Uruli Kanchan in the spring of 1946.

Uruli is a village in the Deccan. Although there are five rivers in the area—headwaters of the Bhima that flows into the Krishna below Kurnoul—there was little irrigation in those days, and it was the centre of a dry tract: black cotton soils over lavas, good for monsoon crops (if the rains came) such as millet, sorghum and groundnut; in the hot weather producing nothing but a mindless coma in a shimmering landscape of gneiss and schists.

Uruli had a number of other things to recommend it from Gandhi's point of view. It satisfied just about all the negative criteria he looked for in a place that was in need of community development. It was dirty, poor, shiftless and vicious. It lacked leadership, cohesion, public spirit and nearly every social amenity. It suffered from seasonal unemployment. But it was a village. Gandhi found peace among its disorders. He had set up a Nature Cure Centre in Poona, twenty miles away. He moved it to Uruli, and established an Ashram there. He spent eight days in the village in the spring of 1946, until summoned to Delhi by Wavell, who sent a special train. Desai remained.

It was not a beginning so much as an introduction. The apprentice could see for himself what might be done in the area given time, but he had not committed himself yet. He had family ties in Gujerat; he had a good degree; he had ambitions; India was not yet free. There was the bond of his caste; he was a stranger there, and was being side-tracked into a backwater to do social work from an Ashram in a poverty-stricken Marathi village.

He spent a year weighing up the situation; went north, found Gandhi, gave him his diagnosis of the problems at Uruli Kanchan, and volunteered his services for twelve years without pay. Gandhi shook his head. 'Not enough time. You must leave your bones there.' A few days later, travelling together to Patna, Desai saw Gandhi a second time. Alone with him, in his compartment, before daybreak, he pledged his whole life. Gandhi touched him on the shoulder and gave him a signed chit for one lakh of rupees to the Sevagram at Wardha. From that moment, Desai was on his own. They never met again. It was 13th April 1947—Jalianwalla Baug day. He returned to Uruli Kanchan with £7,500 from Campaign Funds.

One of the first acts was to bring in qualified doctors to run the clinic. In 1948, on the farm belonging to the Ashram, he founded the Gir herd, which later became famous, and is still there today—about 300 strong.

I said this was the story of one man, but that is not how Desai would wish it to be told. My object has been to show how, in this instance, one man drew confidence from another; not only conviction, but identity of purpose. From the outset Desai sought to act as Gandhi (at his most effective) acted; using the same code, requiring the same code from his helpers; believing in the force and simplicity of truth; believing cowardice to be worse even than violence, but renouncing violence to the point of refusing to seek the moral coercion of an opponent; and, as the *satyagrahi* should, remaining open to conversion to the opinion of others.

In men of action I have known there has been an element of bravura in their decisiveness; in Desai there is an acute sensibility, as if he sees in the dark. He moves with assurance, knows the way exactly; and yet it seems not to be a matter of *having* his way, because his own will is not engaged. Like Gandhi, he is a *brahmachari* (celibate) and a vegetarian; he lives simply, without personal possessions, without pay. Like Gandhi, he is a good tactician, though what exactly that means I am not sure—if to be adept in anticipation and response, then the Zen Master is a tactician also. So too was Nicholas Ferrar —like Manibhai Desai, 'a merry pragmatical fellow'—to whom it was a fact of experience that he who has attained to the well-timing of things has found a way to accomplish great designs with ease.

No, Desai would not approve of this. He would prefer that I tell the story as a collective experiment to which power has been accruing, now, for a quarter of a century. I shall do it his way. There are several chapters. The first, and quite the longest, was preparing the ground.

When you introduce a new idea into a hidebound environment, however receptive some people may be to it and however ripe for change you judge the time to be, in the opening moves of a campaign the better part of valour is discretion. It is positively a virtue to hide your light under a bushel. Ostensibly, visibly, you have little to show above ground; below ground, you are digging the foundations.

After Gandhi's assassination on 30th January 1948, it was necessary to canalize passions locally by providing as many outlets for surplus energy as possible. There was one thing that most people wanted: a proper school. For this, government finance was available. A start was made on a piece of land that became vacant when two local businessmen fell out over a plan to build a pulse mill. Desai was made headmaster, with thirty pupils. He was active not only as a teacher but as a producer of plays—assisted by the young men of the village, organizing excursions for them, and every kind of diversionary activity. He had differences of opinion with gamblers, drunkards, and others euphemistically described as 'shabby night-time entertainers'.

He heard that the Pathan money-lender was out for his blood, and one fine morning he received a note that he was to be cut to pieces. Desai called on him next day and confronted him publicly. Let him say when and where he was to be killed, and he would be there punctually. The man left the district. There were differences too with the more orthodox members of the Ashram, who disapproved of stage shows, even though they were historical pageants, and considered it unfitting for a headmaster to dress up as Sivaji, or Man Singh, or Balbheema, and other heroes of that kidney. Nor was it fitting for a Brahmin to advocate bloodmeal as a fertilizer for the grape garden. Desai's ruse was to act, whenever possible, not in his personal capacity, but as agent of the Sarvodaya Sangh, the Community Development Association that existed for the prosperity of all. In this way it was often possible to disarm criticism.

But the biggest problems of all were the 'socio-economic diseases'—the apathy and venality arising from idleness and under-employment—and these could not be tackled until he had put heart into those in the village who wanted things to be better. Until they found their voice, and spoke up for what they wanted, there was little he could do. He needed their self-confidence, before he could begin to build in earnest.

Until 1960, most of the agricultural development was on land owned by the Ashram. With the dairy herd and arable crops, the eighty-five-acre farm paid its way, although the Ashram itself was sometimes short of money, and dependent on charity. As water became available, a start was made with grapes—a valuable crop in this part of Maharashtra. Experiments were done on wheat and millet: three quintals an acre/year without water—twenty-two quintals under irrigation, a gross margin of £60 an acre. By this time, Desai had given up school-teaching, and was finding practical ways of working among his ex-pupils. The school had grown, and so had their horizons. They did not leave the district. There were prospects where they were. The first farming co-operative to be launched was at Bhavarapur, nearby, with twenty-five families working on eighty acres of pooled land under lift irrigation. For this, and all subsequent irrigation projects, there were government loans; staff-work, supervision, advice and accountancy were provided by the Sarvodaya Sangh. The Bhavarapur venture was the first of many. Other outlying communities had noted what water could do for them, and were in the queue for services the Centre had to offer. Pipes, not electric power, were the limiting factor, so a factory was started by Desai's growing team of specialists to make spun concrete irrigation pipes; later a metal shop was added, turning out roof-trusses and other components for a developing community.

In 1967 a new institution, the Bharatya Agro-Industries Foundation, was organized and registered under the Public Charitable Trust Act. 'The purposes of the Foundation,' I quote, 'are to develop agriculture, horticulture, animal husbandry and other allied activities; to increase food production along modern lines; and to help the village farmer to improve his socio-economic status.' 'During the past twenty-two years'—says the Foundation's *First Report* —'the life of the village of Uruli Kanchan has been revolutionized through community development work. The Central Council of Gosamvardhana, New Delhi, has recognized the success of the Ashram Goshala (Dairy) with the Saurashtrian Gir breed, in production and management, by conferring on it the Gopal Ratna Award.

'The vineyards of the Ashram, which did pioneer work in this line, have produced record yields, with the result that the acreage of grapes is increasing under the guidance of the Foundation. Expansion of vegetable crop production is continuing, along with fodder crops, such as alfalfa, berseem, oats, barley and hybrid Napier grass, and are taking their place in intensive cropping programmes under irrigation. Experience in these fields, and the success achieved, demonstrate that the most effective instrument to fight hunger is *voluntary non-government organization of devoted persons* [their italics] who accept a united approach, concentrate on practical problems, work on a non-profit basis, and are always mindful of the needs of the farmer. Accordingly, the Bharatya Agro-Industries Foundation was registered as a Public Trust on 22nd August 1967.'

In the last ten years, especially in the last five, the work and influence of the Centre at Uruli have grown very rapidly indeed. There is nothing similar to it in this country—unless it be Dartington Hall. It is a combination of Cultural and Community Centre, Retreat, Hospital and Clinic, School, Advisory Centre, Crops and Livestock Research Institute, Experimental Husbandry Farm, Cattle Breeding Establishment, Artificial Insemination Centre, Frozen

Semen Bank, Engineering Institute, Rural Crafts Complex, and Planning and Development Agency whose work now extends into many areas in the north of the State of Maharashtra. It is a Research Farm—one of three in India—for Dr Kurien's Indian Dairy Corporation, and covers the four south-western states from Gujerat to Kerala. The State government has recently offered 150 acres to the agricultural nucleus for a Foot and Mouth Biochemical Project, which will eventually turn out annually 3.4 million doses of Quadrivalent vaccine under Government of India licence. Aid in cash and in kind has been received from Australia, Denmark, New Zealand and the United Kingdom.

The Foundation's own farms make large profits from the sale of milk and crops, especially grapes—Thompson Seedless, yielding fifteen to sixteen tons an acre, which would be considered a lot, even in California. The Trust is a charity, so all income is ploughed back into new schemes, There are now forty-one lift-irrigation co-operatives in operation, under the guidance of the Foundation; they cover 18,000 acres of land, involve thirty-six villages and 1,700 families. Cash crops include 4,000 acres of sugar-cane, for which a factory— capacity 200,000 tons a year—was built in 1969. This crop alone represents new income of £1½ million a year for the growers. The school at Uruli, enlarged by donations and government grants, with teachers (since 1966) paid by the State, has three main streams, academic, agricultural and technical, and 1,500 pupils, mostly farmers' children. The BAIF team under Desai is now 100 strong—twenty veterinarians, eight research workers with PhDs, twelve agricultural graduates and sixty other employees. It is good to know that there are agricultural economists on the staff, and that the accountancy unit is being strengthened this year as a service department to the executive committee.

From the agricultural angle, the achievement to date is impressive, both at the centre and in the co-operatives. It is unusual to see so many resources con- centrated under an acceptable guiding authority. They have new rust-resistant wheats from Pusa, like Niphad and Kalyan Sona; stiff-strawed paddies for catch-cropping in sugar-cane; Sudan-grass hybrids and lucernes for fodder; improved millets, insecticides, herbicides, and fertilizers—and visiting pro- fessors, too—but all of them would be of little use without two other things: water and electricity. With these, holdings of a few acres become glass-houses without glass, growing three to four crops a year, depending on water supply.

On the margin between the desert and the sown is sugar cane, ten feet high, waving in the sun. With river management, gully plugging and erosion control, the potential is growing. The electrical pumping load is doubling every four years, and the product of an irrigated acre may be worth £300 a year, or £2,000 in the case of grapes. Here is economic growth taking place under one's eyes, in patches, as so often happens, transforming a countryside. According to the recent census, it is lowering the birth-rate too.

Among developments I have seen or know of in India, Pakistan and else- where, the project in Uruli Kanchan is the most impressive, and in scope and scale the most promising. So many others, after too short a gestative period, having started with a plan rather than an idea, lacking the afflatus that has wafted Desai along from the beginning, have failed to achieve a self-sustaining basis, or to enlist the essential spirit of service to others. Some schemes, despite an opening fanfare, have never taken off at all; such virtue as they had, and all the cash, have drained away into the ground. BAIF is one of those which has come through.

The founding impulse was ideological. It has not so far been dissipated by success, and the original code survives not only in the person of Manibhai Desai but in his very able staff. Naturally, the problem of succession is much in his mind. As a guru, he has his chela; but there are always difficulties in handing on to a successor a movement you have largely built yourself. Desai combines the asset of purity—as Louis Dumont defines it—with a fund of worldly wisdom. He is wise in his generation and a child of light as well. Now purity is a gift, a talent, and in India, where the priestly caste normally takes precedence in popular esteem, purity is a more effective way to power than wealth or force or politics. But worldly wisdom is acquired through action; it is not an endowment, and no teacher can equip his successor with it.

November/December 1978

[From the Journal of Agricultural Economics, *Volume XXIV, Number One]*

The Cathars

IAN MEADOWS

AT THE END OF THE TENTH CENTURY a powerful spiritual force was apparent throughout Southern France. It came to be called Catharism. By the beginning of the thirteenth century it was such a threat to the authority of Rome that in the midst of the already disastrous crusades against Islam an entire crusade, the Albigensian, was mobilized to crush the so-called heretics of Languedoc. The sudden diversion into Languedoc, the fifty years duration of the Albigensian Crusade, the one million casualties and the utter devastation eloquently illustrate the tremendous importance of the peaceful Cathar movement which came so close to changing not only Europe, the Mediterranean and Moslem worlds but the course of history as well.

In the context of this crucial two hundred year period it is essential to start by chronicling the emergence of a radically changed Richard Lion Heart, after his battles and contacts with Saladin and Islam. Richard spoke better French than English, was a Troubadour initiate and thoroughly familiar with the brilliant culture of Southern France and Spain. He had early contact with Saladin and, soon, a little-known side of his nature began to peep through— that of a man who saw the senselessness of the never-ending combat and who had the foresight to realize the immensity of what might be achieved through peace and unity in the Mediterranean.

Thus Richard left the Levant on a secret mission. To convince certain powers in Europe that a treaty of friendship and co-operation with Islam could herald a splendid future for the region. Richard not only persuaded his captors to release him but convinced them of the plan. Alas, whilst history tells us that he died in a totally untypical siege of a tiny castle we now have information that he was assassinated before he could return to the Eastern Mediterranean and translate the alliance into more tangible form.

Richard's removal was the first counterstroke by the opposition. The second was the onslaught against the Cathars and the last, total obliteration of the Knights Templar, who had died in defence of Christianity but whose resources both human and material (their ability to finance the building of thirteen new cathedrals in France in readiness for the new era is an example) placed them in direct conflict with Rome.

With the Cathars finally dispersed after the fall of heroic Montsegur castle in 1244, the French crown held undisputed routes to the Mediterranean. Plunder and confiscations handsomely rewarded the northern barons and the Inquisition reigned supreme with torture and repression authorized on a massive scale. If the Crusade was supposed to have restored order and sanctity, the wars and massacres of the succeeding decades, including the persecution of the Piedmontese Waldenses by Rome, prove just the contrary.

It seemed then that the chance to bring about a new spiritual order had gone for ever, but the spirit which the Grail symbolized did not die and, true to an ancient prediction, was to appear again in an age called Aquarius when the forces of good and evil stand poised for battle; when the need for a new way of life becomes imperative if something is to survive the holocaust that is so clearly gathering force.

What happened seven hundred years ago is important because so much of what took place at that time is happening again. And, as then, we still have the chance to avert a tragedy that could mean the end of the world as we know it. It requires only a slight nudge of the imagination to see how the present world situation could bring us to the brink of disaster within a decade. The continued artificial pressure on urban communities, the headlong rush at the bidding of invisible, unscrupulous capitalism, the phoney oil crisis, the never ending thoughtless jostle.

I suspect that a Cathar elder of yore, invited to attend a 1973 symposium, would have found it ironic that half the world quite heedlessly and needlessly, was prepared to die for the American automobile industry. The roles may have changed in this century but the implications, and dangers have not.

Now if some readers think I am sneakily advocating a 'Cathar' approach as a remedy for current ills I am not. The Cathars rarely if ever fought themselves or struck a blow in anger, their very philosophy made this unthinkable. They did not seek protectors, yet the shrewd lords, landowners and fighters of Languedoc fought readily and long in defence of *les bonshommes* (the good men) of their communities.

Some will argue that, knowing the size of the storm threatening them they had no alternative. This is nonsense; they could have negotiated favourably and let the Roman legates work their will. Toulouse was as strong as its northern opposites. Instead they chose to fight on behalf of those Cathar men and women who preached a simple pure apostolic creed, shared their skills in the common good and whose deceptively simple creed beginning 'From this point on I promise to give myself to God, to never lie, nor swear, to kill no animal, nor to eat meat, egg or milk produce,' was in fact an undertaking of which few were capable. It also showed they had perfect comprehension of the only vaguely understood politics of meat commerce and its power. But they did eat fish, and the reason why has eluded many scholars. In brief these frugally living people commanded the respect, love and backing of an entire population. And the way they died in myriads, with only one major case of recorded abjuration shows the inner strength of their belief and inspiration.

The Cathars were the repositories of a long, human tradition going back to the very fountain head of human knowledge. The generally propounded theory is that preachers who still carried the verbal tradition and teachings handed straight down from Christ slowly made their way towards western

Europe via Bulgaria and Italy. The ideas found in the *Sistis Sophia*, the Book of Enoch, are apparent in their beliefs and known preaching. But it is equally clear that they had access to almost every major source of human knowledge and achievement. It is part of their tragedy that so much of their literature was burned or destroyed by the Inquisition. Up to now most of what we read in history books is merely a reflection of what Rome and its allies released in their one-sided version of Catharism. So, it is perfectly understandable that one of the first tasks undertaken by today's Societé du Souvenir et des Etudes Cathares was to seek out some of the lost documents, analyse research and then, after careful study and appraisal, begin publication of their findings.

Current Cathar thinking is perhaps best expressed in the articles of the Societé: 'The Societé will combine studies of the past together with the influence of Cathar doctrines on philosophy, science and art right up to the present day; will bring such research to successful conclusion. The Societé will honour the memory of the Cathars and follow the example of their sense of freedom of thought and perfect purity of manner. Its aim will be the realization of universal brotherhood based on each individual's personal spirituality. All dogmatism and denominational or political sectarianism will be avoided.'

Long ago it was asked 'what would the Cathars have done had they come to power?' The answer is that they never sought power, it had no meaning for them, and a similar reply would still hold good today. The solution to our present ills lies in recognizing them right down to their roots; then with clear consciousness thereof, and with wisdom, to do something about it. For that happy state to be reached, of course, a complete re-education is necessary. A seemingly hopeless task but not impossible given the time and the will to *begin*.

The ancestors of the Cathars had few illusions about earthly, material success whatsoever be its form. Basically they believed that a life lived well here on earth was preparation for the new city of God, a city inhabited by people once again made purer, freed from fear, and the clutch of evil. Their concept of the seventh seal and the final destruction in an eighth period of time may sound odd, but strangely enough the predictions made several thousand years ago have held up remarkably well.

March/April 1974

Three Ways for India

JOHN SEYMOUR

'NOT BY ABSTENTION FROM WORKS', said the Lord Krishna, 'does a man obtain freedom from evil. Not by mere renunciation does he attain perfection.' The god was making one of Hinduism's recurrent attempts to counter excessive other-worldliness.

I had the luck to attend (as an honorary, unofficial, supernumerary student) the first school organized by the Government of India to train officers to run the new Community Projects Scheme. The words of Krishna, as recorded in the *Bhagavad Gita*, were constantly quoted to us by people who came to exhort the future Project Officers to greater efforts. 'The renunciation of works,' said the Lord Krishna, '*and* their unselfish performance, can both lead to the soul's salvation. But of the two the unselfish performance of works is better than their renunciation.'

The secretary of our school evidently did not think so. He did not subscribe to the Lord Krishna's view. He was a typical young, Western-educated Indian, who performed his work with great efficiency. But at the end of the term he made us a farewell speech in which he informed us that this secretaryship was the last job that he would ever take. He intended to go into an *ashram* and take the robe. He would become a contemplative. He did not believe any more in action. No good could come of action; only evil. He wished the Community Projects every success—but he would not take any part in them.

Not less remarkable than this young man's statement was the way in which it was received by my fellow students. No one showed any surprise, and certainly no amusement. One imagines the ribald comment which might greet such a disclosure in an equivalent group in the West. The man who got up to reply said that we all fully appreciated the secretary's sentiments; indeed, that every true Indian had the desire eventually to retire from the world, and to lead a life of contemplation.

Apart from this world-renouncing secretary, everyone at the school showed considerable fervour to do good by works—under, of course, that weary facade of cynicism that the contemporary Westerner finds it necessary to maintain. The secretary was in a minority of one. But it was among the rest of us—among the people who agreed with Sri Krishna—that I found the most interesting division of opinion. And this was a fundamental difference of opinion as to what sort of action to take. There were among us some people whom I heard described, perhaps unkindly, as the 'wild men.' They were men dressed in *khadi*, or homespun, *dhotis* and *gibas*, many of them with shaven heads, others wearing Congress caps, and they had the light of fanaticism in their eyes. Mostly they were followers of the late Mahatma Gandhi. These people were as much in favour of doing good by works as anybody else in the school—but they differed from the rest of the student body in the manner in which they wished to do it. Their point of view was very well put to us in the last of the speeches in which the *Bhagavad Gita* was quoted.

This peroration was made by an old man—an old associate of Mahatma Gandhi. He was wandering about the roads and villages of India, preaching the Gandhian code, and he just happened to be passing by Nikokherri at the time. He was asked in—on the spur of the moment—to speak to us. He was incredibly worn and thin, dressed as Gandhi used to dress, and he spoke more movingly and affectingly to us than any of the other speakers, politicians and others who had come to exhort us. He told us how the Gita describes the choice that Lord Krishna gave to the hero Arjuna during the great battle described in the *Mahabharata*. 'Either,' said Krishna, 'you can have my own help in this battle, or you can have that of my army. But if you choose my personal help my army will have to go and help the enemy to fight against you, for that is fair. And if you choose to have my help, and not that of my army, I will not carry arms nor take any action in the battle. Except that I will drive your chariot and give you advice.' Arjuna, who did not know then that his friend Krishna was God, unhesitatingly chose to have Krishna—unarmed—to help him, even though he knew that this meant that Krishna's well-equipped army would go over and help the enemy.

After telling us this story the old man said: 'Now do not let India make the mistake that Arjuna avoided. Do not let us take the material help—the foreign money, the machines, the chemicals, the weapons—and neglect the spirit and the essence of Mother India. For we cannot have both.'

The old man's speech could hardly have been expected to please the American Agricultural Extension Officers who were with us, nor did it altogether appeal to the majority of my fellow-students. The latter were not a representative sample of Indian manhood: they were mostly drawn from the old British-trained Civil Services, and they were highly Westernized. Most of them felt that India should take all the material help that she could get from the West, and that Indians must develop a more materialistic attitude to life before they can do much good to their country. But the 'wild men' liked the speech.

There seem to me to be here three separate and conflicting points of view. First, that of our secretary, who wished that nobody should take any action at all. Second, that of the majority of the students, who wished to see India develop, in a modified way, along the lines of the Industrial Revolution. And, third, that of the followers of Mahatma Gandhi, who wished certainly to take action but who wished to take it in an Indian way, and to avoid at all costs Western materialism.

The secretary represented a tendency which Hinduism has always shown to move towards abstention from action. The interpolation of *Bhagavad Gita* into the far older epic of the *Mahabharata* was one of many attempts to counteract this tendency from within Hinduism. The founding of the Arya Samaj within recent years was another. At the present time India is not in a world-renouncing mood, and our secretary does not represent an important or a powerful faction. Our 'wild men', our American advisers, our Westernized civil servants, our old follower of Gandhiji, were all agreed that action must be taken. But they were divided on what sort of action to take, and more important, they were divided on what to take action for. Some of them said: 'Follow the West. Learn what we can from America and Europe.' The others said: 'Do not adopt the materialism of the West.' And it is this latter difference of opinion which constitutes the great debate in India today: the debate which seems of far greater importance to Indians than the dispute between the capitalists and the communists of the West.

As I travelled about India I constantly received the impression that the great issue in India is not the issue between capitalism and communism but the issue between capitalism and communism on the one hand, and the ancient Indian non-materialistic philosophy on the other. The first aim of both capitalism and communism is said by their adherents to be to end poverty. This can be done, it is thought, by creating more material wealth, or by distributing more fairly the material wealth which already exists. But the other kind of Indian—it would not be an over-simplification to call him the follower of Mahatma Gandhi—is not interested in ending poverty—at least, what we in the West are apt to call poverty. He wants everyone to have enough to eat of course, enough and no more, but saving that he does not see anything wrong in what we in the West call poverty. In fact, he believes that poverty is desirable. He agrees with that other Asian who told us about a rich man and a laden camel.

I am convinced that the foreigner who goes to India is prone greatly to underestimate the importance and prevalence of this peculiarly Indian way of thinking. The average visitor to the country lives with Westernized Indian friends, reads only the English-language press, and comes to look upon the Gandhian type of Indian either as a picturesque crank or as a nuisance and a bar to the country's progress. This blinkered view does not achieve any conception of the strength of this anti-materialistic philosophy, and tends greatly to overestimate the importance of the struggle between capitalism and communism in India, not realizing that these two ways of life seem very much the same to the majority of Indians—and both equally repugnant.

The difference of aim between the followers of Gandhi and those who look to the West stems from an entirely different conception of what is the Good Life. The Indian who looks towards Moscow or Washington wishes above all to mechanize agriculture, so as to displace a proportion of the cultivators from the land and thus bring about the classic Industrial Revolution. When this has happened India will be a land of material plenty—as the United States indubitably already is—and every Indian will drive a car, eat frozen food, and sit in an air-conditioned room watching a television set.

The follower of Mahatma Gandhi, however, does not want any of these things to happen. He does not wish to mechanize agriculture. He points out that an acre of land ploughed by oxen, provided it is ploughed deeply enough, does not produce less food than an acre ploughed by a tractor—slightly more, in fact, because of the dung of the oxen. He freely admits that the acre can be ploughed in fewer man-hours if ploughed by a tractor, but, he says, what about all the hidden man-hours behind the tractor? The man-hours that were needed to make the tractor, and which are needed to maintain it, and to maintain the fantastic urban structure that makes tractors possible? Also, he does not see any advantages in saving man-hours in the village if all the result is that nine-tenths of the ploughmen are to be forced away from their homes, to go into the towns and, presumably, spend their lives producing more tractors.

And he is obsessed with the old idea in Hinduism, the idea reiterated again and again and again in the *Bhagavad Gita*, that the ends never justify the means. If, for the laudable end of relieving hunger, it is necessary for even one man to spend a part of his life at a factory bench, or down a mine, and if these are not good ways for a man to spend part of his life, then there is no more to be said about the matter. One must endure hunger. Or better, of course, if it is possible, find some other way of relieving it. That the ends *never* justify the means is the law of Karma yoga, or the way of salvation through works. Action must be performed as a sacrament, with no attachment to its results.

And, of course, your Gandhian does want to abolish hunger. It is his first aim, but he thinks that this can be done by improving farming and village life in other ways than by mechanization. A man can walk all day behind a plough and a pair of oxen and, if he is not in debt or in trouble, his mind will be at peace. If he wishes to do so he can think and meditate. But no man can stand at a conveyor belt in a factory and meditate. Nor can he enjoy real peace of mind when he gets home. Then, the follower of Gandhi insists that whatever he uses shall have been made by a craftsman who enjoyed making it: not by somebody who made it in boredom, simply for commercial gain. 'Civilized simplicity' is an expression one constantly hears in India. The essential Indian does not look upon mechanical and electrical contrivances as manifestations of a high civilization. He looks upon them as barbarous: signs of the West's immaturity and lack of true culture as compared with the East.

The first thing which surprised me when I really began to move about in India was the prevalence of the Gandhian way of thinking. And my first reaction to it was one of resistance. I thought it foolish for a man to squat on the floor for hours every day, twiddling a *charkha* or spinning-wheel in order to spin just enough yarn to clothe himself, when a machine in a mill could do it in a few minutes. But then I went over a few big cotton mills, and did not like them very much either. But I felt that it was important for India to end her food problems, and at first I thought that she could do this only by mechanization. Also, I have always disliked colour-prejudice, and I felt that for a coloured nation to enter world politics as a Great Power might do a lot to break this down. And to become a Great Power India must mechanize and industrialize. Then, as I wandered further and thought more, I remembered the behaviour of the existing Great Powers, and I began to realize that India could best assert her superiority by not becoming a Great Power.

I began to remember what was happening to my own country under the impact of modern commercialism and industrialism. I remembered watching the process of turning my green and pleasant land into one enormous and, to me, perfectly revolting garden suburb. I compared in my mind the old type of English countryman, with his dignity and integrity, his salty speech and earthy wisdom, with the new countryman—the shoddy, flashy suit, the smarmed hair, the detribalized, characterless language, the snatches of foreign song. I remembered the culture in which music is something which dribbles out of a loudspeaker when you turn on a tap, and in which art is an advertisement for hair-cream; where work means standing and watching a machine, and leisure sitting watching somebody else play football. 'Work is prayer,' say the followers of Gandhi.

I argued with my Indian friends about it, always at first taking the Western point of view. I valued literature, and how, I asked, can you have literature if there are not any books? Books are made from paper, which is produced in a paper-mill, with big machines. True, I was shown a paper-mill in which the only motive-power was a bull which walked round in a circle, but I was not altogether convinced by this. I was more impressed by the man who pointed out that in my own country far better literature was produced before the introduction of the giant paper-mill and the high-speed press than has been written since. I contended that the gramophone and the wireless helped to extend the appreciation of music. An Indian said to me: 'When was the best Western music written, before the invention of these machines, or after? How did Mozart get along without a gramophone?' I pointed out that in Mozart's day music was for the few. Now, thanks to the wireless, it is available for the many. 'What do the "many" actually listen to?' he asked. 'What will you hear coming from wireless sets as you walk along the streets of any city in the world?' What indeed?

The 'many' at least, had a living folk music before. Now they have commercialized canned drivel. Good music, the music of Mozart for example, is available over the wireless for all, but only the 'few' listen to it: the same 'few' who listened to it before, only then they played it themselves, or listened to their friends playing it. And a live dog is better than a dead lion any day. The living music of India, I discovered, is music that people make themselves, or listen to their friends making. It is not something that comes out of a machine when you turn on a tap. That is dead music. Of course I heard plenty of Bombay cinema music too. In India, as in England, live art has to fight a rearguard action against dead art—commercial art. But in India I felt that the living has more hope of success. I saw live drama, based on the village: a drama which, if it is not killed by the cinema, might conceivably one day become great drama. Because it has its roots, as all real art must have, in the soil of a great culture. India taught me that art is not a thing that you can feed into one end of a machine and expect it to come out the other end alive.

In short, the impact which India made on me, against my strong resistance, was to make me lose confidence in what we call progress in the West—even in our best sort of progress. I now find myself constantly asking, as I heard so many Indians ask, 'Progress—to what?' And of our famous efficiency, 'Efficiency—for what?' Industrial efficiency produces more goods per man-hour. I have no doubt of it. But what do we want with all these 'goods'? What do we do with them when we have them? Are they really good? The Gandhian idea lacks novelty, of this I am perfectly aware, but it does not lessen its importance. It is an old idea which has become blunted over the centuries. As a sharp, living idea it can only be found nowadays in India.

The question that one constantly hears in India is: 'Does such or such a thing get you any nearer God?' The Indians believe in God. I am an agnostic, but I know what Indians mean. They mean: 'Does something—progress, efficiency, productivity, television, whatever it may be—does it get you any nearer to fulfilling yourself; to achieving a keener awareness of reality, or a better communion with the rest of humanity, or with the Infinite; to justifying in any way your being here?'

And when I ask myself this question about so many of our Western ploys and institutions and apparatus I have to answer in the negative. They do not get you any nearer to God. And I believe that nine-tenths of the product of our Western industry is not only useless but is harmful. It simply serves to distract our minds. It were better had it not been made. Made, it were better if it were destroyed. Further, I believe that if our civilization goes on developing along the road of commercialism and industrialism it will destroy itself, not by war, but by destroying our minds. The impact of India on me has been to make me lose confidence in the present trend of my own civilization.

May/June 1977

Steady State

Person-Planet Connection

THEODORE ROSZAK

SUPPOSE THE EARTH IS A SENTIENT BEING, capable, in her own mysterious way, of intelligent adaptation and skilful manoeuvre for the sake of defending her life-giving mission in the universe.

If you wish, take the supposition to be no more than a convenient hypothesis and formulate it as objectively as possible—as in the 'Gaia hypothesis' of Lovelock, Epton and Margulis which proposes that we conceive of the Earth's 'living matter, the air, the oceans, the land surface as parts of a giant system, able to control temperature, the composition of the air and sea, the pH of the soil and so on, so as to be optimum for the survival of the biosphere. The system seems to exhibit the behaviour of a single organism, even a living creature.'

But if the hypothesis is convenient, why not yield to its poetry as well? For the Earth is in no way more beautifully known to us than in the ancient imagery of goddess and mother. Then recall what James Watson said of the double helix. In science, there can be ideas that are too beautiful *not* to be true.

Further: suppose that we, in body, mind, and spirit, are subtly crafted into the fabric of the planet's sentience as her risky experiment in self-conscious intellect. Which would seem to be no more than the evolutionary continuities of sound science require: that the whole of our being find its place in the natural continuum, our star-gazing wonder as well as our toiling chemistry.

Finally, suppose that the experiment we represent has become so dangerously infatuated with its monkey cunning, its remarkable power to subjugate and reshape, that it now jeopardizes the integrity of the global biosphere. That should be the easiest, if the most troubling assumption of all, since its validity is the justification of the environmental movement.

What, then, does the Earth do with her mischievous human children to change their lethal ways?

We might regard the sudden prominence of professional ecology as one recourse she tries. At the eleventh hour, she brings a small contingent of biologists around to the most comprehensive science of all, the systematic study of the planetary whole as the arena where culture and nature interact.

But ecology, while an indispensable expedient and one that has rallied a significant public concern, cannot rescue us on its own. It is too highly technical, too much of a specialist's approach. If our only hope were that a global political consensus might form out of the ecologist's facts and figures, we would surely have a long wait ahead of us. Even then, would the motivation for change that emerged from the warnings of experts be anything more positive and reliable than a grudging surrender to necessity?

The countless local pollutions that assail us each day may be irritating or ugly enough to force piecemeal adjustments here and there, now and then. But the big issues, the questions of species-wide survival and of planetary life and death that require us to rethink our culture from the ground up —the health of the atmosphere and all the seas, the vitality of the soil, the warming of the polar ice caps, the stability of the ozone, the future of the world food supply—these are vast imponderables for ordinary people to take in. Regarding such bewildering matters, the specialists might go on arguing for decades, some arguing honestly, some arguing as the hirelings of official and corporate interests. And we may not have decades.

So—let us imagine—the Earth, in the urgency of her need, hits upon another strategy of survival, a course of wise indirection that does not at first glance look even remotely 'ecological'. *She transforms our moral identity,* working from within us to find the one motivation that is most capable of changing our bad environmental habits. *She awakens our sense of personhood and makes common cause with it.*

Again, if the formulation seems too fanciful, phrase the idea as non-anthropomorphically as you wish. Say that, beyond a certain threshold of advanced economic development, an ecopsychic feedback mechanism is triggered that alters the human values schedule in ways that function synergistically to restrain the growth rate and to stabilize the emotional anxieties of industrial populations—or jargon to that effect. But bear with me if I use a more traditional diction and speak of the Earth as an intentional agency, a mother striving to preserve and nurture her living variety, if only to emphasize that any hint of environmental self-regulation which enters our ecological thought (and how can ecologists do without the notion?) ties us to the oldest natural philosophy of our species: the worship of the Great Goddess.

However we choose to phrase the matter, the strategy of survival under discussion is grounded in one simple fact of social life. Both the person and the planet are threatened by the same enemy: *the bigness of things.* The bigness of industrial structures, world markets, financial networks, mass political organization, military establishments, cities, public and private bureaucracies.

A 'simple' fact. Possibly I have made it sound too simple. We might, of course, complicate the analysis without limit; but in doing so we must be careful not to obscure one utterly novel and vitally important insight into human affairs. Namely, that the scale of things is *an independent factor of social reality,* a force and influence in its own right over and above ownership, control, and ideological commitment. It has taken our peculiar modern experience with urban-industrial systems to learn this lesson. We now see that, whatever our goal (progress, economic abundance, justice, revolution), vastness of scale can defeat our noblest intentions. The bigness of economic and political structures, *whether under private or socialized auspices,* estranges person from person, private conscience from public responsibility. It dulls our moral sensitivities, forcing us toward impersonal, hierarchical, domineering conduct. Only in this age of

Frankensteinian science and technology have we come to see that human beings can create systems that do not understand human beings, and which will not serve their purposes.

Here is a dilemma that calls into question both the individualist and collectivist traditions of political thought, for both these have been converted into ideologies of industrial bigness: big profit, big power, big systems. Capitalist individualism, for all its libertarian rhetoric, matures into a superscale corporate economy where there are no longer free markets or free people; it becomes the world of multi-national giants, of organization people and the lonely crowd. Socialist collectivism rebels heroically against the grinding inhumanity of capitalism, yet it remains tied to big industrial values, to the myth of progress and the mystique of science. Accordingly, power gravitates toward managerial elites, and the rest of the society becomes crusading cadres submerged in a single officially enforced identity: the people, the proletariat, the masses. Collectivism alters the ownership of the means of production, but (at least in its dominant Marxist-Leninist-Maoist versions) not the scale of social organization. So, inevitably, it preserves the mass and class rigidities on which all industrial systems depend for their workforce, their war machine, their market.

We need a third choice, a political ethic which is not bound to the alienated identities of individualism or collectivism. And this, I believe, is the sense of identity that the Earth brings us now as an ecological corrective: the sense of ourselves as persons, each unique, radically original, possessed of an unpredictable destiny. It is the self as Whitman sang of it in his great song:

> Each of us inevitable
> Each of us limitless
> Each of us here as divinely as any is here . . .
> I sing the songs of the glory of none, not God, sooner than I sing
> the songs of the glory of you.
> Whoever you are! Claim your own at any hazard!

No one can say in any detail what kind of world comes of such a shameless celebration of the self. I suppose the prescription is for a Taoist anarchy, an organic commonwealth of all peoples, beings, entities and existences. But we have no blueprints for such a future, no grand designs. Only of this much am I certain: we are at a juncture in history where personal psychology and planetary ecology—the world of nature out there and the universe of consciousness in here—join forces to subvert the urban-industrial dominance.

The person and the planet. Here is a connection—a political connection—which is a distinctly contemporary discovery, one that could only become apparent after our economic institutions had reached a certain critical size and complexity, a certain dizzy level of dynamism and unfeeling efficiency. Only now do we happen upon a contradiction in the social system that may be far more potent than the class contradictions to which Marx pinned his revolutionary hopes. We are undergoing the subtle interaction which the Earth uses to protect herself from our ecocidal pressure. As the scale of industrial activity mounts, so also (at least along one important line of contemporary dissent in Western society) do our expectations of personal freedom and fulfilment. This, in turn, becomes an obstacle to the further expansion and integration of the system. So the system begins to *dis*-integrate, a fitful process that gets registered in the news of the day as truancy in the schools, the soaring divorce rate, declining morale and rising turnover in the workforce, the demise of military conscription, a growing reluctance to compete and conform, a general distrust of leaders, experts, official ideals, public institutions—in brief, the spreading ethos of cynicism and recalcitrance that social theorists refer to as 'the twilight of authority', 'the crisis of legitimation'. But this disintegration is essentially creative, for, in our rising sense of personhood, we find a peculiarly postindustrial quality of life that is wholly incompatible with the mass processing of superscale systems. So we are moved instinctively to assert the human scale that will give us attention, respect, tender loving care. In asserting the human scale, we subvert the regime of bigness. In subverting bigness, we save the planet.

Because our social thought is still torn between individualistic and collectivistic alternatives, many commentators overlook the originality and promise of such personalistic values. Think for a moment of the humanistic and human potential therapies, and of the New Age religions that have flowered so prominently in our society over the last generation. There are critics who can see nothing in these forms of deep introspection and self-discovery but a disgraceful lack of social responsibility; they are therefore quick to put these exercises down as 'narcissistic', 'self-indulgent', 'escapist'. Of course, there are vices of this kind to be found if we look for them, along with a deal of commercial opportunism. Like everything else that becomes widespread and popular in our society, the search for personhood can become tainted with the selfishness and acquisitiveness of bourgeois individualism. It can be vulgarized into a commodity, an entertainment, an opiate. All this is too obvious for words.

What such quick, negative criticism ignores is the fact that, where these forms of self-discovery achieve their highest purpose (as they often do), they awaken in people a vivid awareness of their incommensurable uniqueness and provide ingenious means for shaping a free identity: 'doing one's own thing' in a sense that I think Socrates would have recognized as a commendable attempt at self-knowledge. If the full power of self-discovery takes hold, it weans people from alienated role-playing; it demystifies all competitive, other-directed standards of self-evaluation, until, at last, people grow fiercely restive with the massification on which industrial institutions are based. Moreover, especially in the case of New Age religions, the process of self-discovery often leads toward an ecologically healthy style of life; toward small communities devoted to 'simple living and high thinking'.

Perhaps the most impressive personalist manifestation of our day can be found in the many 'liberation' movements that have emerged over the last decade in all the industrial societies: women's lib, kids' lib, gay lib, gray lib, mad lib, fat lib, handicapped lib. We have no sociological category for such groups with their highly selective, psychologically sophisticated forms of consciousness raising. They do not aspire to become mass movements or political parties; they are not 'workers of the world' uniting into a disciplined rank and file. On the contrary, they insist on being small autonomous, intensely intimate. For want of a better name, I have called them *situational networks*: loose associations of our society's many victims held together by the bonds of shared suffering.

Surely no society in history has ever identified such a varied spectrum of victimization: displaced homemakers, homosexual Native Americans, battered wives, impotent men, inorgasmic women, disabled transvestites, unwed fathers, hookers, lesbian mothers, former cancer patients, the terminally ill—the list goes on and on. Is there anybody who isn't a victim these days? What about young, white, well-educated, upwardly mobile, affluent, urban males? Wasn't our world specifically created to serve their interest? But then think of the work of a popular satirist like Woody Allen. What do we laugh at in his comedy? Images of self-selected élites as victims, perhaps the most pathetic of all. Yes, the world serves their interest—*provided* they subordinate 'their' interest to an assigned, socially productive identity. Which means they are victimized by the system in exactly the same way (though more subtly by far) as all the excluded and oppressed: by the violation of their personhood. That is why we laugh at Allen's sad-faced, Valium-devouring clown because we recognize the irony of success in a world of depersonalized personnel.

What is it people find in situational groupings? Yes, they find mutual aid and consolation, perhaps a means of self-defence. But most immediately they find confessional freedom, self-revelation, the healing affirmation of fellow victims. The situational group may be the one sanctuary in our big, busy, bullying world where people can come together to tell their tale, sing their song, and so find full personal recognition for all that they are *as* victims and (most importantly) for all that they are *besides* victims. In the situational networks, troubled and stigmatized souls help one another toward the self-knowledge that lies beyond shame, fear, failure, and the suffocating stereotypes of the world. The networks are a means of casting off assigned identities—'old', 'gay', 'female', disabled', 'addict', 'ex-con'—and of asserting oneself as a surprising and delightful event in the universe.

How different all this is from the class consciousness and political agitation in which left-wing ideologies of the past specialized. Yes, here too we have an assertion of solidarity among the oppressed. But how much more refined are the varieties of suffering; how much greater the indictment of urban-industrial wrongs! Moreover, the victimized identities we deal with here are clearly seen as barriers to self-discovery that must be 'worked through', redeemed, finally transcended. So the project of the group (as in all the humanistic group therapies) is to grow beyond the false identities imposed by society at large, perhaps even by society's radical and revolutionary forces.

Recall how the women's movement was born out of the victimization which women experienced within male dominated New Left organizations whose monolithic class categories totally obscured the nitty-gritty, everyday, everynight reality of sexual exploitation within the movement itself.

'Class', we are coming to see, has never been a positive and fulfilling identity; it is, at best, a means of collective resistance, an instrument of power. But where self-discovery is concerned, power is the path, not the destination, and so cannot become an end in itself. That is why, whatever the seeming cost in immediate political effectiveness, the networks remain small, decentralized, locally autonomous, for this is the only context in which personhood can be expressed and respected.

From the viewpoint of conventional politics, situational networks are a hopeless obstacle to efficient organization; they do not produce serviceable cadres. But I think these profoundly personalistic groupings are part of a larger, unprecedented political task. Through their defiant celebration of diversity, a powerful new ethical principle enters our lives: *that all people are born to be persons, and that persons come first* before all collective factions, even those of revolutionary movements. And is this not exactly what the planet herself now requires of us? An identity that resists massification, a politics that draws us joyfully toward variety and decentralism?

It is tempting at this point to translate the person/planet connection into the familiar slogan 'small is beautiful', since smallness clearly plays a central role in this transformation. But *unless small means personal, unless it embraces the ethos of self-discovery,* it will be no solution to our problem. This is why the search for humanly scaled institutions cannot be construed as 'turning back the clock'. In the past things may have been smaller, but they were rarely personal. Rather, the institutions that governed life were stubbornly grounded in enforced identities of class, sex, age, race, caste. We do well to remember that, small as they were, the city states of the ancient world were slave societies and fierce bastions of male, military supremacy. So too, the sweat shops of early industrialism may have featured small scale, 'appropriate' technology, but they were instruments of brutal exploitation. For that matter, no institution is smaller than the marriage of one man and one woman, but if that marriage is built upon assigned sexual identities it is apt to become an ugly, oppressive relationship. Wherever personhood is not respected, Sartre's dictum holds true: 'Hell is other people'—even in a tiny room and among a few companions.

This is the missing dimension of E. F. Schumacher's economics, the main reason why he never worked out a calculus of 'right size'. He shrewdly perceived that small is necessary, but seemed reluctant to admit that it may not be sufficient. Something more needs to be added if we are to make proper use of the humanizing opportunity that small scale operations afford us, something borrowed from beyond the realm of economic analysis. We need to infuse small, decentralized patterns of life with the distinctly contemporary insights of humanistic psychology (the work of Maslow, Laing, Rogers, Perls, May) and personalist philosophy (Mounier, Mumford, Buber, Merton), with what we have learned from the most original art and vision of the modern world. Schumacher's economics is best seen as the ethical middle term between the world ecological emergency (which he understood more vividly than any economist of his generation) and a crisis of the human personality he only began to touch upon in his later writings. I think he would eventually have seen that his economics reaches out toward a new, non-material criterion of growth which can only be found in the cultivation of the person. 'Appropriate' scale is not ultimately a quantitative question; its true measure is the experience of authenticity.

After our long, strenuous industrial adventure we are being summoned back along new paths to a vital reciprocity with the Earth who mothered us into our strange human vocation. In a sense that blends myth and science, fact and feeling, the Great Goddess is indeed returning. But she returns to us by way of the deep self, out of the underworld of the troubled psyche. And her name this time is *our* name—yours, mine, his, hers, all our names, and for each of us the one name we have freely chosen for ourselves.

January/February 1979

The Management of Collapse

JAMES ROBERTSON

THERE IS A QUESTION that seems to crop up all the time. I have met it frequently in the last year or two in discussions with many different kinds of people—sixth formers, conservationists, industrial chaplains, government officials, architectural students, businesspeople, humanists, futurists, and even economists and bankers. The question is which must come first, changes in society or changes in the individual? Must political, social and economic reform come first, to create the kind of society in which people will be able to live good lives? Or must changes in the hearts and minds and way of life of people come first, so that they become the kind of people who can create a good society?

Many of us, I believe, now see that this question presents a false choice. Posing the question may help you individually to decide on your own course of action. Can you make your best contribution as a reformer—an agent of change in the institutions of organized society? Do your talents and inclinations fit you better for the role of teacher or priest? Or, by simply living your own life well, can you best help others to see more clearly how a new and better way of life would be possible also for them? But even for the individual person the choice cannot be exclusive. If we apply our question to society and people in general, we have to answer simply and unequivocally, 'Yes: society must change first and so must people, including me; so let's get on with it.'

But let us pursue the point a little further. What happens if we accept that industrial society is actually beginning to collapse and the post-industrial revolution is actually beginning to take place? What happens if we agree that the inhabitants of Britain are well-placed to play a leading part in this post-industrial revolution, just as our great-great grandfathers pioneered the industrial revolution two hundred years ago? What happens once we realize that a lot is already happening and many new growth points are already appearing which will provide the foundations for a new kind of society in the future?

One thing certainly follows. If the post-industrial revolution is actually beginning to take place and industrial society is actually beginning to collapse, one of our foremost aims must be to make the revolution happen peacefully and smoothly, fairly and justly, so that—in contrast to almost all the economic, social and political revolutions of the past—large numbers of people do not get badly hurt. In other words, we have to think now about how the society prevailing today can evolve step by step into the society of the future. We have to think now about how to cope with the breakdown of the old system at the same time as we build the foundations for the new, so that the collapse of the old and the emergence of the new become a single process of transformation.

Where, then, shall we start?

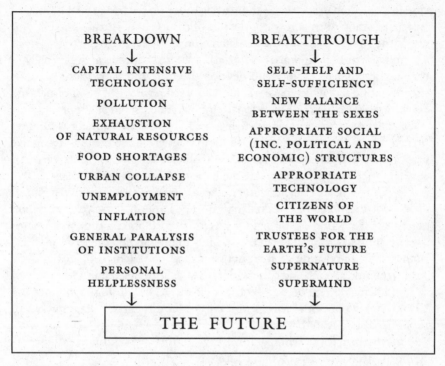

BREAKDOWN	BREAKTHROUGH
↓	↓
CAPITAL INTENSIVE TECHNOLOGY	SELF-HELP AND SELF-SUFFICIENCY
POLLUTION	NEW BALANCE BETWEEN THE SEXES
EXHAUSTION OF NATURAL RESOURCES	APPROPRIATE SOCIAL (INC. POLITICAL AND ECONOMIC) STRUCTURES
FOOD SHORTAGES	APPROPRIATE TECHNOLOGY
URBAN COLLAPSE	
UNEMPLOYMENT	CITIZENS OF THE WORLD
INFLATION	
GENERAL PARALYSIS OF INSTITUTIONS	TRUSTEES FOR THE EARTH'S FUTURE
PERSONAL HELPLESSNESS	SUPERNATURE SUPERMIND
↓	↓

THE FUTURE

The above diagram provides some ideas. It suggests that two opposing sets of trends are at work, one converging towards breakdown, the other converging towards breakthrough. The diagram is no more than a starting point for discussion. Different people might want to draw it differently in certain respects, omitting some of the trends it shows and substituting others they think are more important. But it does at least begin to suggest the shape of the present crisis in human history and the nature of the challenge we now face.

Most obviously, it suggests that a top priority is to intensify our efforts and speed up the progress already being made in each of the various approaches on the right hand side of the diagram that could help us to break through to a new kind of future: more self-help in housing, health and education; greater self-sufficiency in people-intensive agricultural communities working the land; more appropriate technologies for transportation, for generating energy, for building and construction work, for agriculture, for manufacturing, and for communication—technologies which will be small enough and flexible enough to be used by individual people and households and small communities, radical reform of political, economic and social institutions, and their deliberate redesign to serve the needs of people; greater efforts to establish recognition of the fact that every member of the human race is a citizen of the world community, and that every citizen of the world community—including especially those who live in the poorer countries—should be respected and treated as such; redoubled efforts to create in the heart and mind of every man and woman the sense that the human species, as the leading shoot on the tree of evolution, is in a special position of trust towards the rest of nature; much greater readiness to discuss the whole range of ways in which human society might be transformed by a fundamental re-appraisal of sex roles and relationships; and, finally, a sustained attempt to explore and develop those psychic capacities of human perception and will which have traditionally been regarded as paranormal, and therefore beyond the scope of rational people to understand and train.

Secondly, the diagram suggests that those of us who are working as thinkers and activists at different points on this new frontier should begin to recognize that we share a common cause and a common ideology. With vision, we could see our efforts converging to create the breakthrough to a new and sustainable future. With faith, we could commit ourselves to cultivate that convergence.

I do not mean that we should try to impose upon ourselves a common frame-work of action or thought by setting up umbrella organizations or by publishing joint manifestos. We should simply provide ourselves and one another with opportunities for discussion and communication, which will enable common ground and common goals to emerge, and allow us to see how we could help and reinforce each other's efforts. The 'Turning Point' meeting at Conway Hall on 29th November seems to have triggered a fair amount of cross-linked activity in that way.

So much, then, for the comparatively straightforward side of the task, covering the more positive aspects of the future.

When we turn to the negative aspects on the left hand side of the diagram, the outlook is more complicated. High inflation, high unemployment, the falling value of the pound in relation to other currencies, abysmally poor industrial performance, the energy crisis and other symptoms of disorder have left the governing elites in Britain with a sense of impending disaster. Top civil servants in Whitehall; the 'soft centre' majority of Westminster politicians from the moderate wing of the Labour Party, the Liberal Party, and the progressive wing of the Conservative Party; the big business barons of the CBI; the bankers and financiers of the City who have found they can no longer run for safe cover to the Governor of the Bank of England when the going gets rough; many of the trade union bosses who seemed all powerful only a year ago; and the Keynesian economic mandarins who took for granted until very recently that they had all the answers if only other top people would listen: in each and every one of these sectors of the establishment there is now a pervasive feeling that in some fundamental way the country is running out of control. The old mould seems to have crumbled. To quote John Donne's words about the break-up of the Middle Ages four hundred years ago, 'Tis all in pieces, all cohesion gone'; or W. B. Yeats more recently: 'Things fall apart; the centre cannot hold; / Mere anarchy is loosed upon the world . . .'

In spite of this slump in morale, unfortunately, the establishment is still imprisoned in the assumption that the top priority is to restore high levels of industrial investment, industrial profitability and industrial productivity to create the so-called 'wealth' that is thought to be needed to support the services and amenities that people want. So long as this assumption continues to prevail, none of them will put their minds seriously to the management of collapse.

The first need here, then, is to destroy the credibility of that assumption once and for all, and liberate from it all who are still its prisoners.

At first sight two simple facts should be enough to accomplish this act of liberation. They are already becoming fairly widely understood. First, from now on economic policies based on the orthodox Keynesian assumptions are bound to prove socially divisive and politically unacceptable before they have time to succeed, and are therefore doomed to failure on their own terms. Second, even if these economic policies did prove to be socially and politically feasible for a few years, their very success would only make the problem all the worse and the collapse all the greater when it comes; institutionalized materialism carries within itself the cancer that leads to inevitable self-destruction.

These two simple facts must be hammered home again and again and again. But in practice, of course, that alone will not be enough. To escape from the treadmill of institutionalized materialism, the people who now work in the institutions will need an alternative vision of what is possible. At one level they will need to become aware that 'quality of life' does not have to be identified with standards of material consumption; that 'health' need not be defined as something provided by institutionalized medical services, 'welfare' as something provided by institutionalised social services, nor 'learning' as something provided by institutionalized education; that 'politics' and 'government' have not always been consumer services provided by politicians and bureaucrats; and that 'work' need not necessarily be seen as another kind of consumer good, provided for job-consumers by employing organizations backed up by an ever-growing 'employment services industry' with an evergrowing range of products like redundancy provisions, unemployment benefits and industrial training courses. The people who now work in the institutions will have to be brought to see that all these things—wealth, quality of life, health, learning, power, government and work—are equally well if not better regarded as things that arise from, and are determined and shaped by, individual people from within themselves.

At another, more practical, level the managers of collapse will need to be shown feasible scenarios for various possible futures.

This way of exploring possible paths into the future turns on its head the kind of model-building used by the Club of Rome. It will enable the managers of collapse to see that the transformation of society that is now in prospect need not necessarily be fraught with inconceivable disaster all the way through, especially when concepts such as quality of life, health and work can be alternatively perceived. It is time we began to get down to this work of constructing alternative scenarios.

So let us apply ourselves with intelligence and compassion to the breakdown of the old as well as to the breakthrough to the new. As we proceed with enthusiasm, I believe that two things will happen. First, we shall find bridges being built at many points between those who are creating the society of the future and those who are helping the society of the past to collapse in good order; we shall find the breakdown of the old and the emergence of the new gradually coalescing into a single process of transformation. Second, more and more people will gradually become aware of a new sense of direction and purpose.

More and more of us will come to see the kind of future it makes sense to try to create. More and more of us will look at it, and ask ourselves if we like it and if we are prepared to work for it. And more and more of us will find that the answer is 'Yes'.

January/February 1976

We are Going to be Compelled to Live in Communities or Perish

J. G. BENNETT

THIS WORLD CANNOT LAST AS IT IS. Governments, great industrial and financial institutions, churches and international bodies have gradually come to dominate the life of the earth and collected more and more power into their hands. What is the future of these great institutions? Some have grown very large indeed—what we call superpowers, some have grown into great international corporations. That there are very large institutions on this earth there is no doubt. They are rather like the dinosaurs that dominated the earth a hundred and eighty million years ago and disappeared from the earth because they couldn't adapt themselves to the change of climate, partly because they had no mechanism for maintaining their body temperature and partly because they had very small brains.

One thing that anyone can see on looking at the great institutions of the world at the present time is that they have very small brains. I remember many years ago Ouspensky saying: 'If you want to understand the behaviour of nations you mustn't study animals, you must study the amoeba. The amoeba knows only one thing—to swallow or be swallowed. It has only one thing, a system that does everything for it; digestion, defecation or perception is all the same thing, it just opens itself to swallow what it can swallow.' That is what nations are like. I think that is probably a little bit hard, they have a little more intelligence than that and perhaps we can promote them to the dinosaur level.

We may regard this as a tragedy. Are these beauties to become extinct? Are only their skeletons to be found in a hundred million years? Some people may say 'It's about time!' What happened when the great reptiles found they were not able to survive was that a new, very humble insignificant form of life appeared—the mammals. They started very small, about the size of mice, but they had one property that the reptiles did not have of being able to regulate their own internal conditions. It was Claude Bernard who said 'to have a stable inner state is the condition of a free life.' Because the mammals could maintain a stable inner state they were able to survive the great climatic changes that killed off the dinosaurs. It seems that this analogy is very good for prediction and prophecy. Something like the mammals must be among us now which will, though now maybe very small and insignificant, perhaps be destined to inherit the earth. The question is—what is the change of climate that would kill off the big institutions and make their survival impossible? Which are the mammals of the future?

This human world of ours has for a very long time lived on the principle of growth and expansion. This has been particularly noticeable in the last two or three thousand years, but in earlier stages was not so. It has remained not so for some isolated and, from our point of view, insignificant groups. Until very recently nomads, nomadic shepherds and herdsmen in Central Asia and other places had no urge to grow. They were quite prepared to remain of one size, and for thousands of years to live in much the same way, moving from place to place. They were not able to be larger because of the limitations of pasturage. And they were superseded. They were even rejected and condemned by the settled people, and very soon after settlement came the doctrine of growth began to be established in the world. The first really great city in the world was Babylon, where the doctrine of growth was sanctified. It was the first city to have more than a million inhabitants.

It is an unforgettable thing to visit the ruins of Babylon stretching thirty or forty miles down the Euphrates, to see the vast size of this ancient city. Compared with this—and I've visited many many ancient cities—nothing makes the impression of Babylon. Babylon was the first city to live by the doctrine of expansion and growth and, strangely enough, this doctrine was picked up by the Israelites when they were in captivity in Babylon. They even put it into their own sacred books, into Genesis, and into the mouth of God so that it is said that He commanded man to increase and multiply and inherit the earth. It is not a truly Hebrew notion; it is much more a Babylonian notion. But it has spread throughout the world, and up to our time, two or three thousand years later, growth, expansion, increase, size, quantity, have been the real tests of success, even of virtue and merit.

This is the thing that is going to kill the great institutions, because they cannot live without expansion. No occult knowledge is needed to see that as soon as expansion stops, these great bodies get into trouble. Even when expansion is suicide, they have to expand because they know no other way to live. All of us have been so indoctrinated with the belief that more is better, that the more possessions one has the better one is, that the more one knows the better one is, the more that one can travel the better one is. We are so filled with this that any other way of thinking is very hard to adapt ourselves to. We are told, and no doubt it is true, that human knowledge is now doubling every ten years, and that this rate of doubling is increasing. This is regarded as wonderful, as is the fact that we are consuming more of the resources of the earth within twenty years than in the whole previous history of the world.

How can we turn from this doctrine of more to a real doctrine of better, from quantity to quality? There is now an established doctrine—I think it was Julian Huxley who promulgated it—of being the right size. We should learn from nature that if you want to survive, you must be the right size. Human beings twenty feet high could not survive, because their surface to volume ratio would be impossible and they couldn't support themselves. But this doctrine, this simple doctrine of being the right size, which is beautifully adhered to by mammals, was lost; it went out of gear with the great reptiles, the saurians. This has also happened with organizations. Nowadays, no institution thinks of what it means to be the right size. It always wants to be bigger. How are we to look to something else?

If we say that large institutions are going to fail, it might seem that the only thing to do is to return to the individual level and save ourselves in the midst of the chaos. But it is no more true to say that you can go from the great institutions to the individual than to say you can go in search of safety and survival straight from the dinosaur to the amoeba. After all, we as individuals are no more than cells in the life of this world. There has to be something more articulate, more organic, than that.

My guess is that people are searching for communities. There are now between one and two million people in America living in small communities, and there are something like ten thousand communities in different parts of the world, ranging from ten to a few thousand people.

So the search for communities is already in progress. People are experimenting in many ways with a new kind of society in the form of small settlements or communities. But how are they to survive? It is one thing to survive as parasites upon another culture, as the early mammals fed on the carcasses of dinosaurs. But that kind of thing only lasts for a time.

Communities cannot continue to be parasites upon the great institutions of the world, because these institutions themselves are going to rot away. If we are coming to a time when there will be the forced collapse of growth—and these times are scarcely to be avoided—then those that have power will certainly then seize and hold what they can. It is hardly to be imagined that this world will not in the next fifteen or twenty years go through very severe crises. But how to acquire the kind of self discipline that I think does belong to the future, how to give up the other part of the doctrine of more, and give up the doctrine of power, the wish to dominate? How can one community accept another community without wishing to dominate it?

Up to now the world has been as much coloured by the doctrine of power as it has by the doctrine of more. If we say that the things that characterize the true society of the future are the rejection of power and the rejection of more, these are easily said and everyone is saying them. But now we are coming to the time when talking about them and wanting them is no longer going to be enough. *We are going to be compelled to live this way, or perish, because this is the only way of life that is going to be possible on this earth.*

The only hope is a total acceptance of a higher aim than our own survival, a total acceptance of our need to be related to a higher power than ourselves.

We must also accept that human nature is not capable of doing this unaided. We must be free from the illusion that the individual alone can overcome the disruptive forces in his or her own nature. No community ever survives beyond the influence of the pressures that compel it to accept co-operation: as soon as pressure is relieved, disruption begins.

People will never accept one another unless they are under some external pressure or threat. It is only when they set their sights beyond humanity altogether, when they accept that the very purpose of their own existence and of the community which they are trying to create, and in which they are trying to live, is not mere survival. This is what the evolution of this earth demands, and because it is demanded the great intelligences that are directing the evolution of the earth will help communities that accept this task. This is why it is right that every community that wishes to survive should look about it and see what it can do for its environment.

But it should also look beyond that and try to understand—and never be satisfied with what it already understands, but always try to understand more and more—the purpose and meaning of life on the earth, because it is only by serving that purpose that inner stability can be found which sustains a community that is really capable of surviving.

We must learn that we can only put our trust in a power higher than ourselves. If we can do that, then these little creatures, these little communities capable of living in the new way, will in the course of time creep out of their burrows and begin to appear on the surface of the earth. People will see that a new form of life is possible. It will be very different from what we know at present. There will be new perceptions, new ways of touching one another, a new sensitivity towards one another, a new awareness of what life is and what it requires of us. These are the characteristics of the new race, but they are also characteristics that are inside us, because the new race will come from us, from our children, our children's children. It will not be an ad hoc creation. It will come from those who are capable of bearing children that have these qualities, and it will come from us if we set ourselves with real determination to serve the future and to open in ourselves the possibility of doing so.

November/December 1976

[From a talk given at Beshara, Swyre Farm, 1975]

Perils of Genetic Engineering

JEREMY RIFKIN

MANY PEOPLE THINK that genetic engineering is just a group of products or a set of technologies. The only thing comparable in historical terms to this technological revolution is the harnessing of fire. We are a Promethean creature, and we have been using fire technology for thousands of years. We have been burning, soldering, forging, and melting together inert materials from the earth's crust, transforming them into all kinds of combinations, such as steel, glass, and synthetics, that do not exist in nature. In fact, the final culmination of the fire technology revolution is the nuclear bomb. We've been trying to harness fire power for thousands of years and we've finally managed to harness so much fire power in one product that all we need do is drop that product and we can recast the earth as the fire ball that it was at the beginning of the cosmic story.

In the 1970s, two scientists did something in the world of living material that is comparable in importance to fire technology. They took slices of genetic material from two totally unrelated species and combined them, getting a new form of life on a molecular level that does not exist in nature. Recombinant DNA is a technology that now allows scientists to cross all species boundaries. In metaphorical terms, we can now heat, solder, melt, forge together living materials across all walls, creating new combinations in shapes and forms that never existed in nature.

Three years ago, Dr Thomas Wagner at Ohio University took rabbit genes that help produce haemoglobin and he placed those rabbit genes in mice embryos. Some of the mice grew up and passed the rabbit genes to their offspring through the germ line. So you now have a strain of mice with rabbit material permanently incorporated in their hereditary blueprint.

Genetic technology allows you to cross all species boundaries. You can't mix parts of a rabbit with a mouse in nature.

A few years after this experiment scientists at the University of Pennsylvania Veterinarian School under Ralph Linster did a similar experiment and it was quite impressive. They took rat hormone genes and placed them in mice embryos. The mice were born and they expressed rat genes. They grew up to twice the size of normal mice and passed that rat gene into their offspring. Then the scientists effected an even more impressive feat. A year later, they took human growth hormone genes and placed them into the mice embryos. The mice were born with human genetic material expressing itself. These mice grew twice as big as normal mice and passed the human genes into their offspring.

This is what I call 'algeny'.

An algenist is someone who wants to reduce all living organisms to the information coded in their DNA and nucleic acid. From that base information, the algenist then redesigns, edits and programmes new combinations of living things in an effort to find the perfect organism.

When you and I see a mouse, we treat it as a unique recognizable entity. If our children's children's children grow up in an algenic world they will likely see a mouse as merely the thousands of genetic instructions that make it up. They'll be able to programme traits in and out of the mouse at will, or take any genetic trait from that mouse and combine it with material from any other organism. We can already do that now. This is not science fiction.

The whole idea of the sacredness of a creature becomes archaic once you can eliminate species boundaries at will. We now can do that with recombinant DNA. The sacred unit used to be the organism, the species. Now the sacred unit is the gene. In fact, the sacred unit is no longer even the gene. With computer synthesizing techniques, the sacred unit is now the unit of information coded within the gene. So we are witnessing a new form of 'desacralization' of life with this newest technology.

To decide in advance how the genetic make-up of living things ought to be planned and executed is to raise the spectre of eugenics, the inseparable philosophical wing of genetic technology. Eugenics is the philosophy of using genetic manipulation to create a better organism or a better race or even a master race.

When we think of eugenics, we normally think of Nazi Germany, although I'd hasten to add that the United States supported a massive eugenics movement from 1900 to the Depression. Many American opinion makers and politicians embraced eugenics. States passed sterilization laws, and 70,000 Americans were sterilized because they were deemed biologically unfit.

When we engineer changes in a plant, an animal, a micro-organism or a human, there is at every step of the way a conscious decision that has to be made as to what are the good genes that should be bred into the species and what are the bad genes that should be eliminated. What are the criteria we establish for determining good and bad genes—efficiency, health, profit, utility, national security? These are very thorny social and political questions.

My concern is not with the re-emergence of social eugenics but with the new commercial eugenics. There is no evil party here. It's not that the corporations are evil, nor the scientists, nor the capitalists nor the socialists. The fact is we human beings want perfect babies. We want perfect plants, perfect animals, predictability and organization in our lives. We want to maintain some control over our future. There's one last reservoir of spontaneous, erratic, unpredictable activity on this planet, and it's living systems.

The academic movement known as social biology is just a more sophisticated up-date of a traditional eugenics doctrine. They will not go so far as to say you are your genes, but they do say that the more impressive determinant of behaviour is your genes, and the lesser determinant is the environment. In fact,

if you read the last part of E. O. Wilson's book, *On Nature*, for which he won
the Pulitzer Prize, he says the following: 'In time, much knowledge concerning
the genetic foundation of social behaviour will accumulate and techniques may
become available for altering gene complexes by molecular engineering and
rapid selection through cloning. The human species can change its own nature.
What will it choose? Will it remain the same, teetering on a jerry-built foundation of partly obsolete, ice-age adaptations? Or will it press on towards still
higher intelligence and creativity accompanied by a greater or lesser capacity
for emotional response? New patterns of sociality could be installed in bits
and pieces. It might be possible to imitate genetically the more nearly perfect
nuclear family of the white-handed gibbon or the harmonious sisterhoods of
the honey-bee.'

I find that incredible.

I think it will be years, if ever, before we can actually redesign and tinker
with complex mood and behaviour traits. But the question is not whether they
can do it, but whether society believes that the genes contain the instructions
for specific emotional behaviours. Once society begins to believe in nature
over nurture and becomes convinced that you are your genes, then we're
in big trouble.

Scientists are now increasingly able to identify certain genetic traits that cause
diseases such as Alzheimer's or Huntington's disease. Do you tell the person or
not? Think about what this means, not only to the individual and his family,
but to the employer. Will an employer want to hire somebody if that person's
medical chart shows when he or she is going to come down with certain
diseases, and possibly even when they're going to die? How will the insurance
companies deal with this? How will the government?

As we learn more about these genetic traits, who will make the decision
as to what genes should be bred into and what genes should be eliminated
from the germ line, the hereditary blueprint of the human species? Should we
entrust this authority to a Presidential Commission, as has been suggested and
passed in one house of Congress already? Should Congress be the agency to
determine what are the good and bad genes for the human species? Or the
National Institutes of Health? Or General Electric, Dupont, Monsanto, or the
economic market-place? Or the individual patient? Remember, when we deal
with genetic changes at the germ line level, we affect all future generations.
Are we wise enough and smart enough to design the blueprint for future
generations, who might have to survive in environments radically different
from the ones we're involved with now?

Increasingly, public policy is likely to reflect the idea that personality and
social behaviour can only be changed from the inside out, and that if we are
to effect changes in society then we better spend less attention on changing the
environment or the institutions and spend more attention changing the internal
blueprint of the individual species. That's a dramatic shift in social policy. I
dread such a shift. I hope it doesn't happen, but all the signs suggest that it will.

The way we relate to other living things comes to reflect the way we relate to human beings, and if we see plants and animals simply as matter for manipulation, information to be coded for utilitarian or productive ends, then there's no doubt in my mind that we will bring that same conditioning to our activities with human genetic engineering.

Let me give you an example. The first embryo transfer baby was recently born in Los Angeles. A donor sperm was used to inseminate a woman, and then after the embryo had divided for four or five days it was removed from her uterus and placed into a surrogate. The surrogate gave birth to the baby. It's interesting to note that the company that perfected the process learned much of the technique from their previous work in cattle breeding. The point is that there is no magic line to be drawn between humans and other forms of life.

Every species has an inherent right to have its own gene pool remain inviolate from contamination. The most cruel form of behaviour towards animals and plants is to attempt to change their nature by superimposing genetic traits of unrelated species into the hereditary make-up. From an ethical point of view I think it's impermissible. From an ecological point of view it's potentially devastating.

If we begin taking genetic traits and crossing species borders for short term, utilitarian gain, we're likely to undermine the delicate relationships between species in the ecosystem. The process could be irreversible and catastrophic in the long term. Earlier this year, in England, they took a sheep cell and a goat cell and created a mature sheep-goat. Those are totally unrelated species in nature. This is truly algeny, isn't it? Do we have a right to unravel the identity of a species and change it for whatever our interests happen to be? I don't think we have that right.

In Washington, the Republican administration is very intent on not imposing any serious regulations on this industry. They want America to be the first bio-technical civilization in the twenty-first century. They're anxious that the Japanese and Europeans don't get ahead of us in this, and so they're taking every step possible to ensure that investment capital in new products finds no impediment in terms of regulations that guarantee the health and safety of the environment and human beings.

How do we organize the age of biology? The most appropriate approach is to become a partner with the rest of the ecosystem. To balance our budgets with nature, to learn how to consume only as fast as nature reproduces. To place our social and economic production needs within the context of the rhythm and cycles of the natural systems that we rely on for existence.

The ecological approach to the age of biology is based on the assumption that we are all part of a large organism, Gaia, and that our economic needs and desires must be restrained within the context of the ecological realities in which we live. The ecological approach to the age of biology would place concern on a more equitable redistribution of the resources of the planet, on decentralized living patterns and simpler lifestyles, on using technologies that are congenial with rather than exploitive of the natural systems.

The other approach, the genetic engineering approach, is completely contrary to the ecological approach. The genetic engineering approach is based on the idea that renewable resources are fine, but they're too slow. If you let solar production dictate social consumption, we're not going to be able to have an ever-expanding growth curve. Therefore we have to find a way to engineer living resources to make them more efficient and more productive.

However, speeding up the production of living materials way out of proportion to the way solar production would do means that we are also moving out of proportion to the way nature can recycle. Because if we speed up the production of living materials it will result in the faster depletion of soil nutrients, making it more difficult to sustain life in the future.

This will be the political and cultural battle of the twenty-first century. Will we side with the ecological or genetic engineering approach to the age of biotechnology? Many people probably think we can have both. We can't, because in the final analysis they're so contrary in basic philosophical premise. Either we work with nature with its own rate of production and recycling, or we work against nature and try to create our own pace and tempo of organization.

On one side you have the forces of industry, the university science complexes and big government. On the other side, however, you have emerging constituencies championing the resacralization of life. You have the ecology constituency, the feminist constituency, the stewardship Christian constituency and many others.

I'm hoping that these various movements can create a new context. But to do so will require a very careful critique of the Enlightenment world view that has given rise to the present crisis. The world view of Bacon and Descartes, of Newton, Locke, and Adam Smith, Darwin and Karl Marx. It's a world view that seemed to make sense for a couple of hundred years, but it doesn't make any sense any more. If we can question some of the underlying principles of that world view and replace them with a new context based on the formula of empathy with our environment, then these movements will have a vision, a philosophy, a context in which to have our joint aspirations.

Many futurists say we're moving into the post-industrial information society. I think that's a misreading of the future. The computer is not a resource base. It's only a form of communication. In the palaeolithic era we had oral language, but did we have an oral economy? The computer is being grafted to industrial processes as a temporary management mode, but that's not the real role of computers. The computer is the management mode for the bio-technical revolution. It is the language of communication for the bio-technical revolution.

Futurists say there are two great high-technology futures: computers on one side, genetics on the other. The information sciences and the life sciences. But they're really only a single mode of production. The computer will be used to organize the life sciences. Because the products of the next age of history will be biological. They'll be made of living things, just like most of the products in the last few hundred years have been made of fossil fuels. The computer is the way to organize genetic engineering products because genetic structures are so complex and have so many characteristics that they require sophisticated computer management to programme them.

What is sacred about life if it's reduced to information flows? If life is only a matter of programmes that can be edited, changed, deleted, added at will? When I was growing up, to give a compliment to a person one would say that person is very knowledgeable. Today we're likely to say that person is very well informed. That's a revolution in how we see ourselves. To be knowledgeable assumes that there are certain truths that have some immutability to them. To be well informed is merely to be constantly updated and to be able to change as conditions change, but without any reference point, value orientation, or underlying principle behind it. What happens if a whole society starts to see itself merely as well informed? Where is the reference point for judging what is important and what is sacred?

Instead of the question, 'How can technology be used for good rather than bad?' we need to ask the new question, 'How much power is appropriate?' If all technology in history represents increasing influence and power over nature, is there ever a point where more power is simply inappropriate, because it either undermines the concept of life or the survivability of life? Is there a point where power is so out of scale, so uncongenial with our relationship to the rest of the planet and the universe, that it's simply wrong to exercise it?

Certain technologies, by their inherent nature, are inappropriate regardless of whether they're controlled by the people or not. Genetic technology is inappropriate philosophically to our definition of what life is all about. It should not be used.

March/April 1985

[From an interview by Mark Mayall, first published in East West Journal, *1984]*

The Message of Chernobyl

MORRIS BERMAN

I WAS HAVING DINNER with a German friend in Zürich in late June of 1986 when the subject of Chernobyl inevitably came up. Almost immediately the election in Neidersachsen (northern Germany) that had taken place two weeks before that became the focus of our attention. Only three weeks or so after the meltdown at Chernobyl, with the north of Germany saturated with radioactivity that had blown in from Russia, the voters of Neidersachsen had gone to the polls and, essentially, voted for either the Socialists or the Christian Democrats. The Greens received basically the same (very small) percentage of the vote that they had always received.

'I guess what puzzles me,' I said to Angela, 'is what it would take to get people to vote to protect their environment, and even their own lives. Apparently, they can knowingly eat a radioactive dinner and then go to the polls the next morning and vote for candidates who can be counted on to do nothing to alter the situation. I just wonder what it is that has to happen for real changes to occur.'

'Voting for the Greens is a very complex issue psychologically,' Angela replied. 'It requires a fundamental change of values. It's a depressing thought, but the election in Neidersachsen suggests that people would actually rather die than change their values.'

I thought about Angela's remarks in the weeks that followed; her words kept coming up in my mind over and over again. We tend to want to deal with events like Chernobyl or Three Mile Island in terms of direct political action, and that is of course necessary; but when you get right down to it, isn't it really, as Angela said, a question of values, and of changes of values? And if that is true, a further question suggests itself: What are the values involved here that are, somehow, regarded as being more important than life itself?

The image that comes to mind when I reflect on these questions is that of a circle, intersected by a plane, such that most of the circle lies below the plane, and only a small arc, or 'short circuit', lies above it. This can stand for a lot of things symbolically, I suppose; one of the most obvious might be that of the relationship between the conscious and the unconscious mind that is characteristic of mental process. Yet despite nearly a century of depth psychology and psychoanalysis, the one value that remains central to the Western industrial nations—among which the Soviet Union can be included—is the belief that the 'good life' is one run on the basis of conscious will and deliberate intention. If the larger arc, for example, can be seen to stand for our dream life, a larger wisdom guiding our lives, it is also the case that not very many people pay attention to it, or think there is much value in it. Our *values* are those of the conscious mind; we have very little faith in larger processes, and certainly not in invisible ones.

The ability to trust the self-correcting (healing) properties of your own organism, to stop manipulating the events of your life and simply decide that 'you' (little arc) are not in control of much of what happens to you, constitutes a radical change in values. This habit of 'intuitive surrender' (it is most definitely not the same thing as resignation) takes a lot of practice; in the beginning, especially, it can be quite terrifying. Since the little arc cannot see the larger arc that lies below the plane, it equates surrender—the decision to stop manipulating everything—with death. But from the viewpoint of the entire circuit, it is precisely the attempt of the little arc to run the whole show that is bringing the system down. What appears to be life is often therefore death, and vice versa.

This ignorance of the nature of circuitry is exactly what has led to the construction of nuclear power plants, to an event such as the Chernobyl meltdown, and to the ability of people to believe that nothing needs to be changed, despite all evidence to the contrary (*Keine Panik auf der Titanic* was a graffito I saw on a wall in Zürich shortly after my dinner with Angela). The ecological analogue of 'short circuitry' in individual psychology is the assumption that conscious manipulation of the environment will have no negative effects; even stronger, that conscious manipulation of this sort—of our lives, our bodies, the people around us, the earth—is the key to power. And finally, when the last layer is peeled off, the value system revealed is that power is equal to happiness; perhaps, even, to some kind of salvation.

Another image comes to mind at this point, and for me it is one of both horror and fascination—*unheimlich* (creepy, uncanny) as Freud said of certain phenomena. It is of a scene at the end of Stanley Kubrick's movie, *Dr Strangelove*, in which the American actor, Slim Pickens, dressed in cowboy boots and hat, is riding The Bomb, which has just been dropped, down to earth, as one would a bronco at a rodeo show, and shouting 'Yahoo' as he waves his hat in the air. This film, made in the early Sixties, was a kind of grotesque prediction of attitudes that are by now quite common. Dropping the bomb is the ultimate power; it represents total control, total technological mastery. Hence, in the movie, the act is portrayed as an ecstatic one, a celebration of victory, but a victory over life. Yet this victory over life does not make the cowboy unhappy; quite the opposite. The victory mentality is a 'happy' one, and is truly that of the short circuit.

It is tempting to dismiss this as an extreme case, but is it really? Do not it, and Chernobyl, lie on the same continuum? In the late fifties and early sixties we were regaled with stories of the 'peaceful atom', which was supposedly going to provide unlimited energy and thereby, by implication, unlimited comfort. This form of nuclear energy was part of the 'liberal package' of those times, and was sharply contrasted, by its proponents, with Hiroshima and the wartime uses of atomic energy. It seems difficult, nearly thirty years later, to buy the liberal package, or to believe that the contrast between peacetime and wartime uses of atomic energy is so stark.

Chernobyl and Three Mile Island are not the only nuclear disasters that have occurred; they are, rather, the only ones that couldn't be covered up. The 'peacetime uses of atomic energy' turn out to be wartime uses as well, but we can fail to see this because the 'bomb' here is being unleashed gradually, in a kind of time-release form, and the enemy is somehow invisible: not this nation or that nation, but literally the entire planet. And in both cases, the value system is identical: power is happiness, and that can't possibly be wrong, no matter what the evidence is to the contrary. Whether it is the voters in Neidersachsen or the French government officials who ordered the destruction of the *Rainbow Warrior*, we—all of us—are living in a delusion, that conscious control is all that matters, that one can never have too much of it, and that it is equivalent to happiness. In less dramatic ways, we are all like Slim Pickens, waving and cheering as we 'control' ourselves into the grave.

The heart of the matter, finally, is the question of alternatives. Angela was right: people would rather die than change their values, but this is only because they think their values are the same thing as their lives. Switching values is only possible for people who have another set of values to go to, or for those who have come to the conclusion that life is its own value; that the object of life, is life itself. This is equivalent to becoming aware of the part of the circle that lies below the plane; to understand that the key to happiness is not conscious control, but the absence of a control mentality altogether.

This is a difficult place to get to; it is a kind of *satori*, a thing hard to see and even more difficult to put into practice. Yet it really is at the centre of the whole thing today, the whole conundrum of Western technological madness. Demonstrations, civil disobedience, letters to the editor, public education regarding nuclear issues and dangers—all of this is important, even crucial; we cannot hope to change things without them. But the heart of the matter is nothing less than a psychic, or perhaps I should say spiritual, transformation: that if some control is a good thing, total control is pathology; and that a way of life based on trust is a happier one than one based on manipulation.

Such a quantum leap in consciousness is not as impossible as it sounds. On an individual basis, many people today have come to these conclusions and are struggling to turn things around in their own lives, to alter their own daily attitudes and habits. It is much of what the sixties and seventies were about. Whether this can influence the culture as a whole, and whether it can do so fast enough, is another matter; but it may also be the case that there is no other choice. In the last analysis, Chernobyl is about values, and it is to that question that we are being forced, relentlessly, to address ourselves as the year 2000 approaches.

November/December 1986

Trees of Life

HERBERT GIRARDET

THE DECLINE AND DEATH OF FORESTS in Germany and other European countries has had widespread publicity in recent months. West German government officials are now saying that according to latest surveys *half* the country's forests are affected or severely damaged by the forest disease. Many people had a chance, this summer on holiday visits to the Bayrische Wald or the Scheerzwald, to see for themselves just how bad the situation is. There is now hardly a healthy fir tree to be seen anywhere, and spruce trees too are dropping their needles and going dry.

When the tree sickness was first noticed in the 1970s it was mostly fir trees in upland regions on west facing slopes that showed severe symptoms of decline. Most foresters weren't too worried as initially it was mostly the older trees that were affected and it was generally thought that they were succumbing to old age. In 1980 and '81 spruce trees were also beginning to show signs of decline, again, at first, mostly older trees in the uplands. Their needles —particularly closest to the trunk—were going yellow and falling off; their crowns were thinning out; and some of them started to flatten off at the top, a symptom which was observed in quite a number of locations and was described as the 'stork's nest syndrome'. In 1982 there was a dramatic worsening of the condition of conifers. Pine trees were now also looking sick. In 1983 it was found that broad leaf trees were suffering from a wasting disease and it became apparent that virtually all species of trees were affected. The same symptoms that were observed in Germany were found in Austria, Switzerland, France and, to a lesser degree, Britain. Czechoslovakia, Poland and East Germany were even more severely hit than Western European countries with whole hillsides near industrial areas totally denuded of trees. In Scandinavia, and particularly Southern Sweden and Norway, growing concern was expressed about the decline of trees which was linked to acid rain and long distance air pollution from the industrial centres in Britain and West Germany.

Now, in 1984, the decline of forests in Western Europe is advancing with ferocious speed. In the Black Forest whole hillsides can be found to be denuded of trees—victims, it is thought, of acid fog that envelops them for many months of the year. The Deutsche Alpenverein (German Alpine Association) has recently published a report which envisages major landslides that may engulf mountain resorts in the Alps—the protective function of mountain forests includes the capacity of the trees' roots to hold the soil and loose rocks in place. As the trees die landslides and rock falls are likely to occur with growing intensity. It is also thought that the death of mountain forests will lead to flash floods in the valleys because the sponge effect they have will be lessened.

The decline of trees is not confined to the upland areas. The worsening condition of all kinds of trees can be observed in lowland areas. Nearly everywhere along motorways one can see trees with transparent crowns, trees growing brown and drying up, trees that have produced fresh spring green going yellow and brown in a matter of weeks. I have seen larches, beeches and oak trees in this condition in much of Western Europe. It is a depressing, a frightening sight. What is the cause of all this?

There are many theories about the forest disease that is upon us. Acid rain was the first catch phrase which tried to explain what was happening. Sulphur dioxide from power stations, factories, refineries and household chimneys is known to dissolve into rain to form sulphuric acid. It was suggested that this lowered the pH of the forest soil, affecting the roots of trees. It dissolved beneficial metals such as magnesium from the soil whilst exposing the roots to toxic aluminium. Research has shown that this can certainly be a contributory cause. It was also found that trees that grow in alkaline soil such as the lime-rich Dolomite mountains of Northern Italy were similarly affected. The theory was then that acid rain affected needles and leaves of trees first and foremost, causing a sort of paralysis in the living organism. Weakened trees then found it that much harder to defend themselves against fungus and insect attack.

It is now thought that not only sulphur dioxide but nitrogen oxides which are emitted from high temperature power stations and from car exhausts are also a major contributory cause. During hot sunny spells in the summer nitrogen oxides are known to react to sunlight, causing ozone (O_3) to form from oxygen (O_2) in the atmosphere. Ozone is toxic to plants and to trees in particular. Trees that grow near motorways seem to be particularly affected by nitrogen oxide and ozone poisoning. Forest campaigners in Germany are now saying that the introduction of a speed limit for cars here must be considered an essential pre-condition for improving things.

Fungi are also being discussed as a possible aspect of the problem, but there is not one single fungus that could affect the great variety of trees that are now suffering. Insects, and particularly spruce bark beetles, are clearly on the increase. Spruce plantations that are weakened by air pollution seem to succumb to insect attacks much more easily than healthy ones. There also seems to be a decline in the population of forest ants, the main natural enemies and predators of spruce bark beetles. A lot of money is now being spent to find the true causes of the forest disease. There is no doubt that we are dealing with a complex problem and that there are many factors involved.

The forest disease is now being taken quite seriously by governments throughout Europe. Sizeable reductions in the emission of sulphur dioxide and nitrogen oxides are now under discussion at the highest political level, but effective action to reduce air pollution now will probably not help most of the diseased trees and forests.

In the Black Forest one forester described the way his job has changed in recent years. He said: 'The way we used to work in the forest is now out of the question. Our job has changed from forester to undertaker. All we do now all day every day is to cut down sick and dying trees while their timber is still worth anything and to prevent the further spread of the bark beetles. We have tried to replant in areas where the forest cover is already gone. But the young trees—fir and spruce—usually die before they are two years old. Our traditional work was to plant, to thin out and fell trees. Now we have to cut down sick trees, without plan; we simply respond to the situation as we find it.'

November/December 1984

Tree Man

JEAN GIONO

FORTY YEARS AGO I was on a long hike, over uplands totally unknown to tourists, in that ancient Alpine region which stretches down into Provence. It includes the whole northern part of the department of the Alpes-de-Haute-Provence, the southern part of the Drome and a small enclave of the Vaucluse.

I saw nothing in that empty land but the bare and monotonous moors rising to about three or four thousand feet. Nothing grew there but wild lavender. After three days walking I found myself in the most desolate place imaginable. I made camp next to the ruins of an abandoned village, and had to find some water. Although they were falling down, the old houses huddled together made me think that in the past there must have been a spring or a well. And there was a spring but it was dry. The half-dozen cottages, their roofs fallen in and their walls worn away by wind and rain, and the little church with its crumbling belfry, were clustered together like the houses and church of a living village, but all life had gone from that place.

It was a fine day in June, and the sun was shining, but over these high moors, open to the sky the wind swept harsh and cold. It moaned in the shells of the deserted houses like a wild beast disturbed at its prey.

I had to move on. After five hours I had still found no water, and there seemed to be no hope of finding any. I was still surrounded by the same coarse dry vegetation. In the distance I glimpsed a small, black, upright silhouette. I thought it was the trunk of a lone tree, and without definite purpose walked towards it. It was a shepherd. About thirty sheep were resting in the parched grass around him.

He gave me a drink from his gourd, and then took me to his home, nestled in a hollow of the plateau. He drew his water—and delicious it was—from a deep natural well, over which he had set up a rough-and-ready winch.

He spoke little, as is the way of solitary people, but he was obviously self-reliant and confident. It was strange to find him in this bare and denuded landscape. His home was not a hut but a stone cottage, and I could see quite clearly where he had patched up the ruin which he had found when he arrived. The roof was solid and proof against the rain; the wind on the tiles sounded like waves on the beach.

His home was tidy, the dishes washed, the floor swept, his rifle oiled; his supper was simmering on the stove. I also noticed that he was freshly shaved, that his clothes were mended with such great care that the repairs were almost invisible, and not a button was loose or missing.

He shared his supper with me, and when I offered him my tobacco after the meal he told me that he did not smoke. His dog, as quiet as his master, was good-tempered without fawning.

It had been agreed that I would spend the night under his roof; the next village was still more than a day and a half's walk away.

Late that evening the shepherd fetched a little bag and emptied on to the table a heap of acorns. He carefully examined them one by one, separating the sound from the damaged. I smoked my pipe, and offered to help him, but he said it was his job. That was the sum of our conversation. When he had collected a fairly large pile of sound acorns, he counted them out into heaps of ten. In doing so he further eliminated the very small ones and those which were slightly cracked, for he continued to examine them very closely. When he had collected together a hundred perfect acorns, he stopped and we went to bed.

The company of this man was very peaceful. The next morning I asked him if I might rest at his home for the day. He found this quite natural, or rather he gave me the impression that nothing could disturb him. I did not really need the rest, but he intrigued me and I wanted to find out more about him. He brought out his flock and led them off to graze. Before leaving he dipped a little bag holding the acorns which he had so carefully selected and counted into a bucket of water.

I noticed that for a stick he was carrying an iron rod as thick as a man's thumb and about four feet long. I acted the man who takes a relaxing stroll and followed a route parallel to his. His sheep were grazing along the floor of a coomb and he left his dog watching them and climbed the hillside to where I was standing. I was afraid he was going to reproach me for my curiosity, but not at all: that was the way he was going and he invited me to accompany him if I had nothing better to do. He went another two hundred yards, to the top of the rise.

Having reached his destination he drove his iron rod into the ground, making a hole in which he placed an acorn, then closed the hole again. He was planting oak trees. I asked if the land belonged to him. No, he said. Did he know who was the owner? No, he didn't. He was not concerned about who the owners were. He just went on planting his hundred acorns with the greatest care.

After his midday lunch, he again sorted through his acorns. I must have been rather pressing my questions, but he answered fully and willingly. For three years he had been planting trees in this lonely area. He had planted one hundred thousand. Of these, twenty thousand had taken root. Of these twenty thousand he expected to lose about half, to rodents or to some other thing that might happen in the unforeseeable designs of providence. There remained ten thousand oak trees which were going to grow where none grew before.

It was then that I wondered how old the shepherd was. Fifty-five, he said. He was called Elzeard Bouffier. He had owned a farm on the plain, had spent most of his life there. He had lost his only son, then his wife. He had withdrawn to a lonely existence, and was happy to live quietly with his sheep and his dog. He had felt that the countryside was dying for lack of trees and as he had nothing very demanding to busy himself with, he had decided to do something about this state of affairs.

I said that in thirty years' time these ten thousand oaks would be magnificent. He replied with simplicity that, if God spared him, in thirty years he would have planted so many more that these ten thousand would be but a drop in the ocean.

He was also learning how to grow beeches and near his cottage he had planted a nursery from beech-mast. The seedlings, which he had fenced off from his sheep, grew sturdy and graceful. He was also considering birch for the floors of the coombs, where, he told me, there was water in the soil only a few feet below ground-level.

I left him the next day. The following year was the beginning of the fourteen-eighteen war, in which I served for five years. A soldier hardly had the time to think of trees. In fact, the incident had not made any great impression on me. I regarded it as a foible, a harmless hobby, and thought no more about it. After the war I found myself with a tiny de-mobilization payment, and a great urge to breathe pure air again. With no other idea in my head, I made my way back to those lonely uplands. They had not changed. However, beyond the deserted village I could see in the distance a sort of grey mist drawn like a veil over the higher land. Since the previous day my thoughts had turned again to the shepherd who planted trees. Ten thousand oak trees, I thought, really take up a great deal of space.

In five years I had seen so many people die that it was not hard to imagine that Elzeard Bouffier might also have died, especially as young folk of twenty think of men of fifty as old, with nothing left but to die. He was not dead. Indeed, he was very hale. He had changed his occupation. He had only four sheep, but now he had a hundred bee-hives. He had got rid of the sheep as they were a threat to his tree-plantings. He told me, and I could see, that he had not taken the slightest notice of the war. He had continued his planting, quite unperturbed.

The oak trees he had planted in 1910 were then ten years old and were taller than we were. It was a striking sight. I was at a loss for words; as he barely said a word either we spent a silent day walking through his forest. In three sections, it was eleven kilometres wide at its broadest point. When I reflected that it all came from his hands and the mind of one man without the aid of modern techniques, I understood that human beings could be as effective as God in matters besides destruction.

He had pursued his idea: the shoulder high beeches growing as far as the eye could see were witness. The oak trees were growing thick and strong, and were no longer at the mercy of rodents. As for the designs of providence, nothing short of a cyclone could now destroy the work created. He showed me healthy clumps of birch dating back five years to 1915, when I was fighting at Verdun.

With them he had carpeted the coomb floors where, as he had rightly thought, the water table was almost at surface level. They combined the tenderness and vigour of adolescence.

His creation seemed to be having a chain effect. It did not concern him: he stubbornly continued his straightforward task. But as I retraced my steps through the village I saw brooks running which had been dry for as long as anyone could remember.

The wind also scattered seeds. As the streams reappeared, so did willows and reeds, meadows, gardens and flowers and a certain way of life. But the change happened so slowly that people were not surprised and adjusted easily. The huntsmen who went up into the empty hills after hare or wild boar noticed the rich growth of new saplings, but put it down to the quirks of nature, so nobody meddled with the man's work. If it had been thought that he had anything to do with it he would have been stopped. But there was no reason to suspect him. Who, either in the villages or in officialdom, could have dreamt of such unwavering devotion?

From 1920 onwards I never let a year go by without paying a visit to Elzeard Bouffier. I never once saw him hesitate in his labours or show any doubt, yet God knows what trials he had. I kept no count of his setbacks; but it can be imagined that for such success he must have had to overcome adversity; that to ensure a venture so near to his heart should be victoriously accomplished he had to battle with despair. During one year he had planted more than ten thousand maples. They all died. The following year he turned from maples to beech trees, which succeeded better than the oaks.

To gain a clearer idea of this exceptional character, it should be remembered that he worked in utter solitude—to the extent, indeed, that towards the end of his life he lost the habit of speech. Or perhaps he thought there was no need? In 1933 he was visited by an astonished forest warden. This representative of authority warned him not to light a fire out of doors for fear of imperilling the growth of the 'natural' forest. It was the first time, said this worthy, that a forest had ever been known to grow by itself. At that time Bouffier was planting beech-nuts twelve kilometres from his cottage. To save himself the return trip —he was then seventy-five—he was planning to build a stone hut at the site of his plantings. He did this the following year.

In 1935, a veritable administration delegation came to visit the 'natural forest'. There was a Very Important Person from the Eaux et Forêts, a member of parliament and several technical experts. Speeches were made, without much point. It was decided that something must be done. Fortunately nothing was done, except the useful step of placing the forest under state protection and prohibiting charcoal burning. For it was impossible not to be captivated by the charm of these healthy young trees. No one was insensible to them.

One of the foresty experts was a friend of mine, and I explained the mystery to him. One day a week later we went together in search of Elzeard Bouffier.

We found him hard at work, twenty kilometres from where the inspection visit had taken place.

This forestry official was not a friend of mine for nothing. He understood the value of things; he knew when to hold his tongue. I gave Bouffier the half dozen eggs I had brought as a present. The three of us shared our picnic, and we spent several silent hours gazing at the landscape.

On the stretch of land we had covered grew a forest of trees eighteen to twenty feet high. I thought back to how it had looked in 1913, an empty moor. Calm and unremitting labour, the bracing air of the uplands, frugal living and above all peace of mind had given the old man almost unchallengeable good health. He had God-given vigour. I wondered how many more acres of woodland he was going to create.

Before we left him, my friend made a brief suggestion about certain species which would probably do well on that soil. He did not press the point—'For that very good reason,' he said, 'that he knows more than I do.' After an hour's walk, as the idea took root in his mind, he added, 'He knows more about it than anyone. He's found a wonderful way of being happy.'

It was thanks to this friend of mine that both the new woodland and Bouffier's happiness were protected. Three forest wardens were appointed, and my friend gave them such forceful instructions that they ignored the bribes and blandishments of charcoal burners.

The enterprise was threatened only during the Second World War. Vehicles were then running on gasolene and wood was in short supply. Felling started among the oaks planted in 1910, but they were so far from any road that the operation was unprofitable and it was abandoned. The shepherd knew nothing about it. He was thirty kilometres away, calmly continuing his work and paying no more attention to the second world war than he had to the first.

I saw him for the last time in June 1945. He was then eighty-seven years old. I returned to what had been a bare wilderness; but now, despite the scars left by the war, there was a bus which ran from the valley of the Durance up into the hills. I assumed that it was because I was travelling rather faster than I used to that I did not recognize the area through which I used to travel on foot; and I had the impression that the bus was taking me by a different route. It took the name of a village to convince me that I was indeed in the same area, once desolate and in ruins. I left the bus at Vergnons. In 1913, this hamlet of a dozen dwellings had three inhabitants. Nettles grew over the deserted houses around them. They were without hope. They could only wait to die—a state which is hardly conducive to living. Now everything had changed. Even the air: the dry, gusting wind had given way to a sweet, scent-laden breeze. A murmur like the sea came from the hillsides; it was the wind in the trees. And then, even more surprising, I heard the splashing of real water: there was a new fountain, no mean trickle but spouting generously, and—to me the most moving thing— a linden tree had been planted nearby. It showed already about four years of sturdy growth, an undeniable symbol of rebirth.

The village of Vergnons was the scene, too, of new efforts which could not have been launched unless there was a climate of hope. Hope had therefore been reborn. Ruins had been cleared, crumbling walls removed, and there were five new cottages, freshly plastered: each had gardens, where, in mingled but orderly profusion, grew flowers and vegetables, roses and cabbages, snapdragons and leeks, anemones and celery. It was now a place that was pleasant to live in.

From there, I continued on foot. The war which had only just ended had prevented the full flowering of new life, but its burgeoning was everywhere. On the lower slopes there were plots of barley and rye, still green, and in the narrow valleys fresh green pastures.

Now, only eight years later, the whole region is prosperous and flourishing. Where there were ruins there are now well-kept farms, witness to lives of contented comfort. The old springs, fed by rains and by snow stored by the trees are running again, and the streams have been channelled to good use. Beside each farmhouse, in a maple copse, a fountain runs over into a carpet of fresh mint. The villages have been gradually rebuilt. People from the plain, where land is expensive, have settled in the area, bringing a spirit of youth, activity and adventure. In the lanes you will meet well-nourished men and women, and boys and girls with cheerful faces who have rediscovered the delights of country feast days. Counting both the earlier inhabitants, changed beyond recognition now that life has become so much easier, and the newcomers, more than ten thousand people owe their happiness to Elzeard Bouffier.

When I think that one man alone, relying only on his own physical and spiritual resources, has been able to make the wilderness flower into a land of peace and plenty, I find human nature is to be admired. But when I consider the unremittingly generous spirit, the devoted selflessness, needed to bring about this achievement, I am filled with respect for this unlettered elderly countryman who successfully carried out a work worthy of God.

Elzeard Bouffier died peacefully in 1947, at a Home in Banon.

January/February 1979

[A shortened version of the author's book, The Man Who Planted Trees*]*

Notes on Contributors

MAURICE ASH co-founded Green Alliance and was its Chairman for many years. He has established a community on his estate which incorporates spiritual practice with manual labour.

ANIL AGARWAL is the Director of the Centre for Science and the Environment, New Delhi.

J. G. BENNETT was a mathematician, linguist and practical philosopher who studied under Gurdjieff and Ouspensky. He was Principal of the International Academy for Continuing Education at Sherborne House.

TRISTRAM BERESFORD farmed with a group of friends in Wales. He became deeply interested in agriculture and development in the Third World.

MORRIS BERMAN has taught and lectured widely in Europe and North America, and is the author of *The Re-enchantment of the World*, a highly regarded study of the holistic world view, and *Coming to Our Senses*.

VINOBA BHAVE was an Indian sage and non-violent revolutionary. He was founder of the Landgift movement whereby four million acres of land were given by landowners to be distributed freely among the poor.

ROBERT BLY is a poet, editor and translator of poetry from several languages. His many books include *Light Around the Body*, *Sleepers Joining Hands* and *News of the Universe*.

VALENTINA BORREMANS worked for many years with Ivan Illich in Mexico, where she has established a documentation centre and a library specializing in radical ecological and political books.

ROSALIND BRACKENBURY is a novelist and poet. She teaches creative writing in Edinburgh.

JOHN BUTTON, editor of this anthology, is a writer and lecturer on Green issues. He is the author of *How to be Green* and *Green Pages*.

STRATFORD CALDECOTT is an editor for Collins and Harper in London.

FRITJOF CAPRA is the author of *The Tao of Physics* and *The Turning Point*. He is also the founder of the Elmwood Institute in California.

KEITH CRITCHLOW is an architect concerned with sacred geometry, and is a regular contributor to *Temenos*. He teaches at the Royal College of Arts.

BARBARA DUDEN is an American writer specializing in concepts of the body.

ROGER FRANKLIN is a peace activist and was one of the founders of *Resurgence*.

JEAN GIONO was a French novelist with rich insights into rural France.

HERBERT GIRARDET is a writer and film-maker with a particular interest in the culture of South American Indians living in the rainforests.

ANDY GOLDSWORTHY is an artist. The leaves are his colours, the twigs are his brushes, the land is his canvas. He lives and works in Scotland.

HAZEL HENDERSON is an independent futurist. She is the author of *Creating Alternative Futures* and *The Politics of the Solar Age*.

ANNE HERBERT is a writer, journalist and activist. She worked on *The Whole Earth Catalogue* and *CoEvolution Quarterly*.

ROGER HILL has been practising acupuncture for many years. He is co-director of the Centre for Complementary Medicine, University of Exeter.

LAWRENCE D. HILLS was the founder and President of the Henry Doubleday Research Association, the largest organization working in the organic movement in Britain. He is the author of *Fighting Like The Flowers* and *Organic Gardening*.

IVAN ILLICH is a radical thinker, philosopher and historian. His books include *De-schooling Society*, *Medical Nemesis* and *Celebration of Awareness*.

WES JACKSON is co-founder of the Land Institute in Kansas and author of *Altars of Unhewn Stone* and *New Roots for Agriculture*.

PETRA KELLY is a recipient of the Right Livelihood Award (popularly known as the Alternative Nobel Prize). She is one of the founders of the Green Party in Germany.

ROGER KIRK is a Deputy Head Teacher in Devon.

LEOPOLD KOHR is the author of *Breakdown of Nations* and an original exponent of 'Small is Beautiful' principles.

SATISH KUMAR is the Director of Schumacher College and editor of *Resurgence*.

JOHN LANE is a painter and founder of Beaford Arts Centre. He is a trustee of Dartington Hall Trust, and author of *The Living Tree*.

IAN LEE was for many years a medical journalist. More recently he has been actively involved in the Cruisewatch movement. He lives in West Wales.

IAN MEADOWS is an author and historian. He lives in Cyprus.

RUSSELL MEANS is a major figure in the American Indian Movement.

YEHUDI MENUHIN is a violinist and world-renowned musician.

JOHN MICHELL is a cosmologist. He is the author of several books including *The New View Over Atlantis*.

JOHN MOAT is a poet and novelist. His books include *The Missing Moon* and *Mai's Wedding*.

ELSA MORANTE is a poet, novelist and political thinker. She has been widely acclaimed as one of the greatest Italian novelists of her generation.

ELAINE MORGAN is the author of *Ascent of Woman* and lives in Wales.

NOMI NASH is a Jungian therapist and is actively involved in the Peace Movement in Israel. She lives in Jerusalem.

HELENA NORBERG-HODGE is the founder of the Ladakh project. She has received the Right Livelihood Award.

DR MICHEL ODENT is known through TV programmes about childbirth in Pithiviers, France. He is the author of *Birth Reborn*.

JOHN-FRANCIS PHIPPS is the author of *Time and the Bomb* and *The New Diplomats* and is associated with Philosophers for Peace.

CLIVE PONTING formerly worked as a civil servant for the Ministry of Defence. He is now an author and lecturer and runs an organic smallholding in West Wales.

JONATHON PORRITT was until recently Director of Friends of the Earth. He is the author of *Seeing Green*.

KATHLEEN RAINE is a poet, Blake scholar and editor of *Temenos*. Her latest books are *India Seen Afar* and *Golgonooza: City of the Imagination*.

JEREMY RIFKIN is an American author and activist.

JAMES ROBERTSON is a futurist and author of *The Sane Alternative* and *Future Work*.

THEODORE ROSZAK is a cultural historian and author of *Person Planet*, *Where the Wasteland Ends* and *Making of a Counter Culture*. He teaches at the University of California.

ROSEMARY RUETHER is an American theologian with special interest in ecology and holistic philosophy.

E. F. SCHUMACHER was Economic Adviser to the National Coal Board. His book *Small is Beautiful* is recognized as one of the most influential of our time.

JEREMY SEABROOK is a writer and journalist living in London. He is the author of *The Myth of the Market* amongst other books, and editor of *Greening the Planet* magazine.

JOHN SEYMOUR is the author of many books including *The Complete Book of Self-Sufficiency*. He lives on a smallholding in Ireland.

PETER SINGER is Senior Lecturer in Philosophy at La Trobe University in Melbourne. His article 'Animal Liberation' in *The New York Review* attracted national attention and inspired the book of the same title.

JILL SMITH is a poet and artist living in the Outer Hebrides.

KEN SPRAGUE is a painter, a designer and a film maker. He teaches at North Devon College, Barnstaple.

E. P. THOMPSON, a distinguished historian and peace activist, is the author of *The Making of the British Working Class*. He founded END (European Nuclear Disarmament).

WILLIAM IRWIN THOMPSON is a cultural historian and founder of the Lindisfarne Association. His books include *Gaia: A Way of Knowing*.

COLIN TUDGE, author of *The Famine Business* and *Futurecook*, has written widely on food policy and nutrition. He used to be Features Editor of the *New Scientist* before joining the BBC as a presenter of science programmes.

JEAN VANIER is a servant of the poor and handicapped. He founded L'Arche Community in France.

CAROLINE WALKER worked in village development in South India for eight years. She now teaches at The Small School, Hartland.

BARBARA WARD was the founder of the International Institute for Environment and Development and is the author of *Only One Earth*.

Resurgence is published bi-monthly.

For subscription details, write to

Resurgence Subscriptions
Ford House
Hartland
Bideford
Devon EX39 6EE